MILT HARRADENCE

The Western Flair

C.D. EVANS

MILT HARRADENCE: *The Western Flair*

Mr. Evans has practiced criminal law for more than thirty-five years and is a Fellow of the American College of Trial Lawyers. He was the first Alberta lawyer to be appointed to the Milvain Chair of Advocacy at the University of Calgary Faculty of Law. He has appeared regularly as counsel at all levels of Court in Alberta and the Northwest Territories as well as occasional appearances in the Supreme Court of Canada, the Federal Court of Canada and in other provincial jurisdictions. Mr. Evans was a Bencher of the Law Society of Alberta for eight years and was appointed Queen's Counsel in 1978.

MILT HARRADENCE

The Western Flair

A MEMOIR BY

C.D. EVANS

DURANCE VILE PUBLICATIONS

Calgary, 2001

Durance Vile Publications Ltd.
Suite 612, The Grain Exchange Building
815 First Street S.W.
Calgary, Alberta T2P 1N3
www.durancevile.com

NATIONAL LIBRARY OF CANADA CATALOGUING IN PUBLICATIONS DATA

Evans, C.D. (Christopher Dudley) 1943 -
Milt Harradence: The Western Flair: A Memoir

Includes bibliographical references
ISBN 0-9689754-0-2

1. Harradence, A.M. 2. Evans, C.D. (Christopher Dudley) 1943 -
3. Lawyers — Alberta — Calgary —Biography I. Title.

KE416.H37E93 2001 340'.092 C2001-904289-2

Front cover photograph by Gold Photography, Calgary
Back cover photograph by William Bailey, Calgary

Book and cover design by Lori Shyba, Sundial Media Ltd., Calgary
Printed in Canada by Highwood Printing Inc., High River

Second printing, December 2001

"Cliff, this is a case for the Western Flare."

"The *what,* Senior?"

"The Western Flare, m'boy.
You take a shotgun, fill it full of red herrings,
fire it in the air and hope like hell one of
them lands on the head of a dumb juror."

TABLE OF CONTENTS

Acknowledgements

The publication of this memoir would not have been possible without the generosity of the following former partners, associates, juniors, students, friends and colleagues of Mr. Justice Harradence, several of whom choose not to be associated with some of Mr. Evans's more outrageous or controversial comments.

MAJOR SPONSORS

Gordon Arnell, Q.C.
Donald J. Chernichen, Q.C.
The Honourable Carole M. Conrad
Willie deWit
Alain Hepner, Q.C.
The Honourable Mary M. Hetherington
The Honourable John C. Major
J. Joseph Markey
The Honourable Peter W.L. Martin
The Honourable John W. McClung
Bradley G. Nemetz
Noel C. O'Brien, Q.C.
James J. Ogle, Q.C.
Larry L. Ross, Q.C.
Terence C. Semenuk, Q.C.
The Honourable Brian C. Stevenson
Earl C. Wilson, Q.C.

CONTRIBUTORS

John D. Bascom, Q.C.; Beresh Depoe Cunningham; Judy N. Boyes, Q.C.; Richard A. Cairns, Q.C.; Dennis Edney; Fix and Smith; Keith F. Groves; Robert J. Hall; Webster MacDonald Jr., Q.C.; Dr. Sheilah Martin, Q.C.; Ross G. Mitchell; M. Naeem Rauf; Stephen Reinhold; A. Clayton Rice; Lorne Scott, Q.C.; Peter F. Tarrant; John Zang.

FOREWORD

The Honourable J.C. Major

Puisne Judge of the

Supreme Court of Canada

THE AUTHOR, C.D. EVANS, Q.C., has ascribed to me the desire to write this foreword. To borrow an expression from the subject of the author's efforts, that is true, I had no choice.

The author makes it clear that this is not a biography of the Honourable A.M. Harradence but a memoir. I describe it as a glimpse, a glimpse into one aspect of this multi-talented barrister and jurist. A glimpse of a rare talent that in Alberta and western Canada had to paint on a canvas too small for that talent.

C.D. Evans declares his bias early. Milt is his friend, his mentor, his hero. This does not stop him from portraying a single-minded defence counsel standing alone against the system armed only with an enviable skill, energy, and sufficient paranoia to remain relentless in legal combat.

The reader will follow Harradence and his acolyte from Calgary and Costa Rica to places in between and through episodes that defy rationality except for the results they achieved.

I earlier said this book was only a glimpse of the man, but it is a glimpse that identifies enough of the Honourable A.M. Harradence that when the reader finishes he or she will understand that lawyer's obsession with the full defence of his client but within the highest tradition of the Bar and the rule of law. The reader will know that to Milt Harradence, the barrister, a case was never just a case, it was a cause.

I was one to learn that what I had dismissed as paranoia turned into reality. How else can I explain that almost a half century ago, Defence Counsel Harradence railed against the mounting dangers of the invasion of privacy but to see proof of it arrive in time to silence the scoffing.

This memoir is an informal look at the subject. There is much more that could be formally written about the Honourable A. Milton Harradence, Q.C., LLD. He was an elected but failed politician, as he describes himself. He was a distinguished and outstanding member of the Alberta Court of Appeal for almost a quarter of a century and was a member of the armed forces. He was all that and more, much more.

But the reader will conclude that while this is only a glimpse of Milt Harradence, it is enough to explain why his admirers, of whom I am one, aspired to emulate him, and to a person we failed.

The Honourable John C. Major
Ottawa, Ontario
2001

Photo of The Honourable J.C. Major: Philippe Landreville Inc.

INTRODUCTION

C.D. Evans, Q.C.

THIS WORK is dedicated to Dr. the Honourable A. Milton Harradence, Q.C., D.U.C, retired Justice of Appeal, my honoured and worthy friend, in recognition—as Swinburne of Captain Burton—*"of a friendship which I must always count among the highest honours of my life."*

This is my story of Milt. It is certainly not a biography, and was never intended as such. It is one view of a remarkable barrister through the eyes of a colleague who, over a period of more than thirty years, encountered him personally as well as professionally. These were weird and wonderful events in my life and the lives of many others, sometimes approaching the bizarre. This is essentially a memoir. Gore Vidal, in his *Palimpsest,* said:

> A memoir is how one remembers one's own life, while an autobiography is history, requiring research, dates, facts double-checked. I've taken the memoir route on the ground that even an idling memory is apt to get right what matters most.

But a memoir is to a great extent autobiography, of which H.L. Mencken observed:

> Every man writes most willingly and hence most entertainingly when writing about himself. It is the one subject that engrosses him unflaggingly, day in and day out. To be sure, he almost invari-

> ably lies when he undertakes it, but his lying is of a species that is not hard to penetrate... he can never quite fool a really smart reader. But his false pretenses, when detected, do not spoil the interest of his story; on the contrary, they add to that interest. Every autobiography thus becomes an absorbing work of fiction, with something of the charm of a cryptogram.

This memoir is not uncritical of its subject. Said Alfred Lord Tennyson:

> The worth of a biography depends on whether it is done by one who wholly loves the man whose life he writes, yet loves him with a discriminating love.

Mr. Justice Oliver Wendell Holmes agrees:

> But one may criticize even what one reveres.

If this is not a biography, it is a portrait. In what is now a famous cliché, Oliver Cromwell required his portrait to be painted "warts and all." And this is how my friend is portrayed in this portrait by me. Frequently, in this selective history, Milt presents as madly eccentric. But as Mr. Justice Major noted, correctly, "*without that eccentricity, Milt could not have been the person he was.*"

Of course, there are contradictory passages. Milt was/is a walking mass of contradictions, sometimes transparent, at other times enigmatic. This should come as no surprise whatever to those who took the trouble to know the lawyer and the man.

These anecdotes and escapades, moreover, are essentially true but not exhaustive. There are Milt stories galore. No attempt has been made to discover all of them. I am not Milt's Boswell, nor he my Dr. Johnson, although I did on occasion play Sancho Panza, *dubitante*, to Milt's *Quixote*. As word of this project spread abroad in the legal community, I was approached by colleagues with their "great" Harradence stories. Everybody, it seemed, had a funny story about Milt Harradence. In order to reproduce the story, it required that the informant's name be prominently featured as well. But this is *my* story about Milt, and it is a story about me and about the leaders of the Criminal Bar of his day. I therefore politely ignored most of those anxious volunteers and to them I say, write your own book.

Some readers may find this tribute wanting in at least two other areas: one, there is sparse discussion of individual cases defended by the great barrister; and two, there are few observations of the personal friends and the social life of Milt and his family. Dealing with the first, I can think of nothing more tedious to lawyers or laymen than a textbook analysis of ancient criminal causes; the cases I do refer to are settings for events significant or hilarious. Professor Russel Barsh, in his review of the *Memoirs* of the late Mr. Justice Morrow in the June, 1996 edition of the *Literary Review of Canada* said:

> Courtroom war stories rarely make thrilling reading. Most of the cut-and-thrust that takes place in a real courtroom is mere babble to the uninitiated ear, and most real law practice is about as thrilling as the instructions for next year's income tax.

As to Milt's private, social, and family life, I know very little: our relationship was that of close professional colleagues who shared a reverence for the law, common cause in defence of various scoundrels, and a commitment to professional excellence and ethical principles that today are seldom observed. To that must be added a love of adventure and constant wonder at the caprice and fecklessness of individuals and the mob. We did not "socialize." Social relationships are invariably shallow.

I have elected, most of the time, to call my protagonist "Milt" or "AMH." This has not, to quote Gary Schmidgall, Oscar Wilde's latest biographer (1994), "*been weighed lightly. Authors who assume first name familiarity with their subjects have always irked me, and yet I have obviously chosen to do so myself. This is in part because he is* the *Oscar; history's quintessential and only Oscar*...," as was Milt *the* Milt, history's quintessential and only Milt.

Throughout, I have received enthusiastic support from a number of persons whose opinions I value. I would not have finished this undertaking without the loving encouragement, diplomatic but firm criticism, and judicious editing of my beloved soulmate, Bernice Loraine Evans. The manuscript was read by the Honourable Mr. Justice Jack Major, the Honourable Mr. Justice John W. McClung, and the Honourable Mr. Justice A.M. Harradence, all of whom made helpful and constructive suggestions, many of which I incorporated in the book and some of which I ignored. I have the warmest affection for the ever-gracious Mrs. Catherine Harradence who contemplated my manuscript with that same serenity and good humour that characterizes her years of marriage to the mercurial Milt. The informed participation of Graham Price, Q.C., Kirsten Olson, and John Armstrong, Q.C. of the *Legal Archives Society of Alberta* and the very generous donations of the listed Sponsors and Contributors to finance this project made it all happen. To all, I am grateful beyond words.

C.D. Evans
Calgary, Alberta
2001

Chapter One

The Code of the Samurai

"THIS IS BIG!"

Those words have just been uttered with intensity at 3:00 *a.m.* into an ear whose equanimity has been sundered by the unwelcome jangle of the telephone.

"Uhhh?"

"Can you talk?"

"Uhhh, ahhh, (cough) I guess so ..."

"Who's there?"

Pause. "My wife."

Pause. "I'll call you tomorrow."

Click.

The next day, I encounter a fierce-looking Asa Milton Harradence, Q.C., at the Police Magistrates' Court. "What were you calling me about last night?"

This has not been an infrequent occurrence, inviting one of two possible responses by the great barrister:

One: "I called you?" or

Two: "Some day, m'boy, I may be able to tell you."

End of conversation. In either event, Milt looks mysterious and grim.

IT IS THE DUTY of counsel to undertake the defence of the meanest and basest of the realm, to conduct his or her cause with diligence, with ability, with dignity, with courtesy, and above all to conduct it with courage.

That duty is the great business of the barrister; all private considerations must give way to it, no matter how important they are.

In the history of the Alberta Bar, it was and is A. Milton ("Milt") Harradence, Q.C., who epitomizes the dignity, independence, and integrity of the Bar, who gave all there was to give in service and sacrifice in advancing a client's cause, and who never succumbed to the demands upon an advocate, be they ever so heavy and relentless. If one were making an ideal barrister, one would use Milt Harradence as a blueprint. Today, he is called a "role model." When he led the Criminal Bar over decades, not mere years, he was universally regarded by his peers, by the press, by the Bench, and by the public as simply the best in the business.

Because Milt Harradence is quintessentially a modest man, it would not occur to him to quote a comment attributed to a world-famous concert pianist, but I will quote it here: when a member of the fourth estate cross-examined the maestro upon the excellent pianists who were coming up in the concert world, he responded, agreeably, "Yes, there are many fine young technicians, some really brilliant young musicians." He paused, then added, "But next to me, they're all a bunch of soda jerks." And thus it was and is with Milt: when he practised, he was the Einstein of barristers, and the rest of us mere Neanderthal men.

Not that Harradence, Q.C., was obliged or minded to suffer slights with equanimity. In the late sixties, there burst upon the defence scene one Michael N. Starr, an intense, able, dedicated, and ambitious barrister. Milt Harradence was the acknowledged leader of the Defence Bar of the day. He had gone neck and neck and sometimes toe to toe with E.J. McCormick, Q.C., for several years; but about the time that Starr got into the ring, Mr. McCormick was devoting much of his professional time as the senior hired gun to the Federal Minister of Justice in the prosecution of narcotics offenders and otherwise applying himself assiduously to perfecting the techniques of a Rolls-Royce mechanic and the finer points of butterfly stitching an open wound (which was one of Mr. McCormick's sub-specialties, together with demonstrating the correct way of tying shoelaces, and how to properly carry and secure a briefcase). Anyway, Milt has always had a heart as big as a washing machine (I borrow from Saul Bellow) and quickly extended a welcoming hand to the rising Starr. One palpable gesture was to offer Michael a ride back uptown after a court appearance. Milt had few weaknesses or conceits, but he did have *inter alia* an attraction to vulgarmobiles, in this case a block-long Dodge convertible with double twizzlers and a sonic boom. Milt's reputation as a hot pilot was also well known. As they were backing out of the parking space, it appeared that the hand brake had been left partially engaged. Noticing the illuminated red light on the dash, Starr commented: "I hope you don't fly your plane this way." Diplomatic relations between the two were thereupon suspended.

One must be quick to comment that Harradence always enjoyed a jest, even if it was turned upon him. He was called to the Court of Appeal in 1979; he had practised for twenty-eight years before that, and prior to that had seen active service in the Armed Forces where he was a fighting man both fearsome and proud. I had occasion to comment upon his experience and his great age during my prosecution of a homicide, Harradence, Q.C., defending. The alleged murder weapon was a .303 Lee Enfield of some vintage, if not lineage. When presenting this firearm through the detective on the witness stand, I said, "Indicating a weapon of Crimean War vintage; my learned friend will be quite familiar with this weapon as he deployed a similar implement with telling effect at the battle of Balaclava." His Worship Magistrate Read, "Exhibit Three, a weapon of Crimean War vintage." Harradence (*soto voce*): "You little bastard." From that day forward, as they say, we remained the very closest of friends.

The calling of the courtroom advocate is the calling of the warrior. Some people were simply born to fight. It is a solitary, lonely occupation. Few do it well, most do not. Booker Prize winner, the late Paul Scott, said that those few bore "the mark of the warrior." It is no accident that Milt Harradence was an RCAF pilot at the age of twenty, a champion boxer, a tennis singles champion, a legendary stunt pilot—it is of note that his private planes were single-seater fighters: The P51, the Vampire jet fighter, the F86 jet fighter. One of his perfervid affiliations was that of Colonel of a group of middle-aged flying bikers called the Confederate Air Force, a wild bunch of dangerously deranged former fighter pilots who zoomed around North America stunt flying and piloting vintage aircraft upside down at low altitudes and lunatic velocities. Latterly, as Honourable Colonel of the 416 Tactical Fighter Squadron at Cold Lake, Alberta, Mr. Justice Harradence is also the oldest pilot in Canada, in November 1994, to have slow-rolled an F18 jet fighter. One hastens to add that this manoeuvre took place in the air, at Mach 3 Plus, and that the pilot, Mr. Justice Harradence, and the plane all survived.

During Milt's lonely incumbency as leader of the Alberta Conservative Party at a time when its fortunes were at the lowest ebb and it had fielded not one MLA in the Legislature, an unkind journalist remarked that the only thing that Milt got off the ground during the election campaign was his Mustang aircraft. That remark may also be attributed to the then Premier of Alberta, the Honourable Ernest Manning, who said:

> Well, I thought it was appropriate. Harradence and that Mustang have much in common: they're both noisy, expensive and obsolete.

The July 1975 edition of *Canadian Magazine* featured Milt Harradence as one of Canada's ten best courtroom lawyers, beginning: "When he strides into a courtroom, Calgary's Milt Harradence goes to war."

That *Canadian Magazine* article of July 19th, 1975, is appended. The following letter was received by Milt from the Honourable S. Bruce Smith, the retired Chief Justice of Alberta:

> Dear Milt,
>
> I am enclosing for your records another copy of the *Canadian Magazine* of July 19th, 1975. I congratulate you upon the great complimentary article about you.
>
> I must say that I thought you were much more entitled to be

> classed amongst the top ten Canadian lawyers than some of the people described in the article.
>
> My best wishes.

It was Harradence—my leader, my mentor, my benefactor, my friend—who taught me from the outset that there is only one approach in an adversarial system: Combat. A trial is a war featuring a series of battles, and (as Marjoribanks observed of the great Edward Marshall Hall, K.C.) one had to train for courtroom combat as vigorously as for war. Milt trained me in the rites and in the weapons—*and* in the courtesies—of traditional courtroom Samurai combat, just as the warrior trained his novice: in sword, with lance, dagger, and, for the exquisite evisceration of the opponent, the rapier. His array of armaments did not include a bludgeon: Milt was the master of the surgical strike.

Of course, the opponent might be said to be one's learned friend, far too often not so learned and not so friendly. But Milt was rather more personal in his approach, and I have inherited it: it is the witnesses for the other side, particularly the star witnesses, who are the opponents and are fair game. Over some ten years or so, when he was my leader, he led the charge, and I fought at his back for that time. And fight we did: no quarter was asked, and none given.

In an address to the Canadian Bar Association on January 31st, 1992, Mr. Justice Milt Harradence proclaimed his philosophy of combat:

> Once the courtroom doors are closed, war is declared. The philosophy of two prominent Americans then prevails. I refer to the remarks of General George Patton, the architect of the American version of the Blitzkrieg in World War II, who said:
>
> > *"No son-of-a-bitch ever won a war dying for his country; it was making the other son-of-a-bitch die for his."*
>
> And those comments of the famous coach of the Green Bay Packers, Vince Lombardy, who said:
>
> > *"Winning isn't the only thing— it's everything."*
>
> But winning in the courtroom must be accomplished by a strict

> adherence to the ethics of our great profession and the traditions espoused by Chief Justice McGillivray:
>
> *'And do as adversaries do in law—strive mightily, but eat and drink as friends.' (Shakespeare, Taming of the Shrew, 1.1)*

The techniques were practised and honed, and nothing was left to chance; if we were defending together on a trial, of course each had to protect his own client's back first, but there was always the common enemy, that sanctimonious whiner of a prosecutor and that lying scumbag, the star Crown witness. There was always a plan of attack and a deployment of the troops.

Examples are abundant, but my best recollection of the efficacy of the technique that we worked out over years was the cross-examination of the Crown's star witness in a celebrated fraud prosecution. Milt defended the head of a corporation alleged to have misdirected certain allegedly earmarked funds; I defended his wife, formerly the corporate secretary. The couple in jeopardy in the prisoner's dock had contracted lawful matrimony and had begat a putative progeny; indeed, Mrs. Accused was prominently pregnant at the time of the trial. As for the President, repeated applications of carrot juice had not arrested his failing eyesight, and by the time the trial came around Milt had him negotiating the courtroom with a white cane and all the accoutrements generally associated with the oppressive blindness of Milton (the poet, not the barrister). Fortuitously, on the day that we attended for an expected routine election for a preliminary inquiry, the Perfect Trial Judge came out of the chute. The prosecutor was caught by surprise as Milt elected trial by Magistrate, entered a plea of not guilty, then immediately moved the court to order the exclusion of witnesses, thus seizing the Judge with the trial. Then the defence amiably agreed to an adjournment so that the flustered prosecutor could try and get his act together, although little time was now available for the Crown witnesses to learn their lines. I learned then from Milt another strategy: frequently, the Crown is not prepared in a complicated document case alleging white collar villainy when they go into a trial without the benefit of a preliminary inquiry, which proceeding often helps the Crown more than it does the defence.

Thus it was in this case. The star witness was an accountant by training, and a successful entrepreneur by trade. He was also a bit full of himself. However, he had been doubtless warned by Crown counsel and the cops that Harradence was a formidable cross-examiner, and thus was psychologically prepared for the apprehended onslaught in cross. Milt and I therefore worked out a scenario that worked so well that we employed it on subsequent similar occasions, with devastating effect. When the Crown completed the examination-in-chief and advised the witness "please answer my learned friends," the star expected an immediate attack from Harradence, who was much my senior and naturally led for the defence. In the old Magistrates Court in those days there was a brass rail at about waist height that encircled the witness box. Most witnesses usually rested their hands on this rail while testifying. In this case, when the Crown turned the witness over to the tender mercies of the defence, one noted the witness's hands tighten on the rail, although an outward equanimity was maintained. The witness presented as youthful but porcine, "not in shape," as Milton had discerned, whispering loudly to me during the in-chief. Milt rose, fixing the witness with a piercing and venomous look that the witness knew would accompany his descent to hell on his demise. The hands clutched sporadically at the rail. The witness quailed. Whereupon, Milt smiled the smile of the tiger, saying, "I defer to Mr. Evans." I then rose to cross-examine, and the witness visibly relaxed. The technique was for me to lull the witness by using the "can you help me with this, Mr. Arbuthnot" approach with a reasonable voice and manner, and then put a series of questions to which Milt and I knew the answers. These were important questions, because the answers were necessary as admissions in favour of the defence. They were, however, non-controversial, and you could see the witness gaining confidence as the questioning progressed. When I finished, I thanked the witness for his help and sat down. He, in turn, much relieved, prepared to leave the witness box. At this dramatic point, Harradence, Q.C., rose like the avenging angel of death: "One moment." The witness paused, the hands clutched the rail, his eyes widened in abject horror and terror. Whereupon, Milt administered two body blows and a left hook to the head, and down went the witness and down went his testimony to the mat and for the count. In the result, the Crown was non-suited on the lady and a reserved decision acquitted the gentleman.

From the early days, therefore, Milt and I agreed that the best definition of justice ever articulated was that of Damon Runyon: "Justice is a blind dame weighing a fish."

Journalist Suzanne Zwarun, writing in the *Calgary Herald* newspaper on the occasion of the appointment and elevation of Harradence, Q.C., to the Bench in 1979, said:

> Harradence has been one of the country's most fascinating lawyers...Harradence had style. Even his enemies have had to admit that his performances were riveting and, often, successful...Harradence's genius in the courtroom, observers claim, was his talent for cross-examination, he played a witness like a violin. One court watcher figures it was his voice that carried the show. Harradence would often start out as though the witness was his cherished friend; he'd coax him along, sympathize, have a cosy little chat with him. Then came the zinger, the machine gun delivery that prodded the witness into the very admission Harradence was trying to pry out. There were times, I swear, that the witness never did figure out what hit him.

The objective was always the same: to utterly destroy the credibility of the witness. That is what the cross-examiner must set out to do and must endeavour to accomplish. In cross, anything goes, as long as it is within the bounds of professional ethics and the traditions of the Bar. Beating up on Bambi is nothing personal. That's what criminal lawyers are paid for. Of course, if the witness has some impudence and enterprise, it's more fun.

As the classic example of the destruction of a witness, the cross-examination by Harradence, Q.C., of an Assistant Commissioner of the Royal Canadian Mounted Police is instructive. The entire text of the famous cross is set out in the appendices to this tome; at this point, one can do no better than the *Alberta Report*, which reported the entire episode in its June 1977 edition, replete with a photograph of Harradence side by side with that of the shark, "Jaws," and the headline, "The Gruesome Grin that Calls a Kill! You Mean Jaws? No, Just Milt."

The article commences:

> "When Harradence starts a cross-examination with that smile" said a woman news reporter at the Law Courts building last week, "then you know that what is about to follow will be too horrible to watch." For a long time, she said, the smile had seemed sinisterly familiar— the head bent forward, the eyes peering upward toward the hapless witness, the broad, toothy grin. Then one day she placed it. The shark in the movie Jaws. That was Milt Harradence alright, just as he was moving in for the kill. It was therefore altogether foreboding last Thursday when Calgary lawyer Asa Milton Harradence, Q.C., ranked by a national magazine as one of Canada's ten best criminal lawyers and appearing before the Laycraft Commission on behalf of three Edmonton police officers, rose to address himself to a particularly savoury morsel. Here was no green constable or nerve-wracked detective on the stand before him. Here indeed was nothing less than an Assistant Commissioner of the Royal Canadian Mounted Police, the Chief of the Mounties in Manitoba.

The cross-examination is then set out over four pages, and the article concluded:

> A radio reporter observed that the Assistant Commissioner was visibly trembling when he left the box. He departed immediately for Winnipeg.

Sometime later, Milt encountered a Chief Superintendent of the RCMP who advised him that his cross-examination of the Assistant Commissioner was used as an example throughout the Force of what happens to the police officer who does not take notes.

The great ability of Harradence was with the trying-to-be-clever or lying or evasive witness: he, more than anyone I have ever known, has an unerring nose for weakness and an uncannily accurate instinct for the jugular. One is reminded of an observation by John LeCarré in the book *Smiley's People*, writing of Smiley's ability to sense that there was an important answer to a question that would help him, and he must find a way of putting that question so that the answer would be elicited:

> Some questions are hazard, some are instinct, some—like this one—are based on a premature understanding that is more than instinct, but less than knowledge.

Canadian Magazine, referring to Milt's "tall, handsome, commanding presence... who can often win a case simply on the force of his overpowering personality...the furrowed brow, the accusing finger, the roiling phrases," observed that "he's got an instinctive feel for the right move... criminal law is, as someone once said, five percent law and ninety five percent psychology. Harradence has the psychology." The magazine called him "a superb cross-examiner... like the Shadow, he can cloud men's minds so that they know not what is truth, and tend to throw the whole thing out of court."

Milt Harradence as a barrister was a natural psychologist, and a natural combatant, and he did have the smile of the tiger; and he had that great ability to get a witness into what Le Carré calls "the loser's corner, because (the witness) did not know—he could only guess—how much or how little Smiley knew already."

The Edmonton Journal newspaper, during the Laycraft Inquiry, described Harradence in action thus:

> The prime shuffler and adjuster is the well-known Calgary lawyer Milt Harradence whose hands are constantly in motion, drumming on the table, rubbing his face and covering his eyes. He wrinkles his already deeply furrowed brow, swivels around and shoots unbelieving glances back at the audience and press corps.
> The main knocker-downer ... the brilliant cross-examiner and former Alberta Conservative Leader starts his questions slowly and deceptively. Spectators have to strain forward to hear. But the voice gets louder, the questions more persistent and faster, a slash here, a slash there. He takes the witness' words and throws them back at them—with a twist. He seizes on the slightest phrase seemingly uttered by a witness in an offhand way and tries to probe into it ... the courtroom fills with laughter and the master actor flashes his smile back at the audience.

One of the polished techniques of Milt Harradence was the ability, rare in the courtroom, to simultaneously lighten the proceedings, disarm the witness, and unnerve the witness's counsel. Here is a perfect example, again from the Laycraft Inquiry:

The proceedings had to do with a police investigation into alleged activities of a corporate midway in Western Canada, and also involved was an investigation into alleged income tax evasion. The investigations were conducted by the major municipal police forces on the prairies and by the Royal Canadian Mounted Police. I will use pseudonyms for the immediate parties in this example.

It was the policy of the Department of National Revenue to communicate information with respect to income tax matters only to the RCMP The municipal police forces were denied this information. A member of the Department of National Revenue who was liaising with the RCMP for this purpose we shall call Aardvark. A very senior member of the Income Tax Department from Ottawa (Jones) was on the witness stand and he was led through his evidence by commission counsel. In his cross-examination, A.M. Harradence began:

Q: *Mr. Jones, you took over from Mr. Fish, did you?*
A: *Yes, I did.*
Q: *And when did you take over from him?*
A: *About the first of May, 1975.*
Q: *You were working with Mr. Fish, were you, on this project?*
A: *Prior to that date, yes.*
Q: *And you were aware it was a combined project?*
A: *Yes, I was.*
Q: *And by combined, I mean that the major municipal police forces in Western Canada would be concerned with this probe or investigation?*
A: *That was my understanding.*
Q: *Yes. And in fact they had representatives at the meetings in Regina on May 13th and 14th and also in June?*
A: *Yes.*
Q: *And you are also aware that perhaps while the primary thrust was criminal investigation, there was also certainly an effort to see whether or not there had been infractions of the Income Tax Act?*

A: *This was one of the objectives.*
Q: *One of the objectives. And that all forces combined would be assisting in achieving those objectives, were they not?*
A: *This was the purpose.*
Q: *Yes. And I take it, sir, that the tax information that you were to disseminate, or Aardvark was to disseminate, to the Royal Canadian Mounted Police, would come from your office, would it?*
A: *... the District Office.*
Q: *I see. And at that time, as I understand it, your instructions to Aardvark were that he was to communicate that tax information only to the Mounted Police?*
A: *That's right. On a need to know basis.*
Q: *On a need to know basis. And there was a need to know because you were looking into tax problems, were you not?*
A: *Yes.*
Q: *And he was instructed then strictly—or by implication—not to communicate any tax information to the municipal police forces?*
A: *I think more by implication.*
Q: *An implication could be as effective as a direct instruction, can it not, sir?*
A: *I hope so.*
Q: *Yes, I am sure you do. So we have this situation then, do we not, that Aardvark can talk to the Mounted Police, the Mounted Police can talk to Aardvark, and perhaps Aardvark can talk to you? Is that about the situation?*
A: *In respect to . . . tax information, yes.*
Q: *It is a little like that parody, isn't it, of J.C. Bossity, about Boston? "And this is good old Boston/the home of the bean and the cod/where the Lowells talk to the Cabots/and the Cabots talk only to God."*
Mr. MacDonald: "*With respect, I don't think the witness should be called upon to answer that.*"
The Commissioner: "*I do not think Mr. Harradence expects him to comment.*"

It is to be remarked that the names Asa and Milton have Biblical connotations, "Milton" carrying the additional aura of pureness of mind and heart; witness the poet's anguished exclamation, "Oh, Blot on Honour and Religion!"

Harradence started his cross coldly polite, respectful but not by any means deferential, stern of visage. In his demeanour was the ominous suggestion that inaccurate or mendacious testimony would be visited by fiat and sanctions of a vengeful Old Testament God; with Harradence, this was not an idle threat. He rose ponderously, with unblinking, burning eyes boring into the soul of the witness, thunderous brow, the set jaw of Fearless Fosdick, as if viewing for the first time the Philistines pouring over a hill to invade his peaceful, God-fearing and law-abiding fellow citizens; to rape their wimmin folk; to plunder, to pillage, to lay waste. "Bear witness, witness! No man shall give an inch. Get those women and children into a circle. With God's grace we shall win this day." And so on.

Few citizens could withstand his assaults. In cross-examination, he was scrupulously courteous to a fault, but there was ever in his polite mode the veiled suggestion that at any minute he would leap upon the witness and tear him or her into little pieces and send them in envelopes to their friends. Even young, bumptious witnesses were attentive and respectful in turn to Mr. Harradence. He was particularly polite to women. He would begin, "Now, ma'am (pronounced marm)…." To waffle, hesitate, or blurt out nonsense was to invite instant retribution. Most witnesses, when Milt was finished with them, looked as if they had just spent three days in the stocks being pelted with eggs and offensive material by upstanding citizens. The odd one collapsed. Witnesses knew that Harradence could smell their fear, and he knew when he was getting close to the truth. As the *Alberta Report* observed, "The results are sometimes too horrible to watch."

This sixth sense served his clients well on many occasions. A typical occurrence was during a fraud case; Milt's junior of the day, Terry Semenuk, had painstakingly prepared a number of colour-keyed charts depicting the movement of monies between accounts and institutions, for the purpose of cross-examining some shiny-assed accountant. Semenuk had taken great pains to brief Milt over the lunch hour, as the master wolfed down his usual bacon and eggs ("the bacon crisp, ma'am"). Milt impatiently brushed aside the proffered charts, and thundered to the witness:

"Were you in Baffin Island in 1957?"

The witness collapsed.

The Alberta Bar has not seen his like as a cross-examiner before or since.

Chapter Two

First Encounters of the Close Kind

I SAW HIM STRIDING with frowning purpose from the front doors of the Alberta Supreme Court, the eyes intense and the jaw set. At six foot plus, powerfully built with broad shoulders, impeccably dressed, known to be packing a concealed firearm, with a fearsome reputation, and the physiognomy of a matinee idol with a name to match, Milt Harradence was everything I was not.

I ran after him and breathlessly addressed this great man. "Mr. Harradence. Uhhh, I'm . . . uhhh . . . Christopher Evans." I was self-conscious, tongue-tied, embarrassed at announcing myself, because I suspected that I probably looked like an asshole. I was an asshole, a large firm minion, wearing an execrable young lawyer's suit of some bilious green shade chosen by my too-ambitious first wife, dragging the obligatory young lawyer's briefcase bulging with the firm's land titles and court registry dreck. That day, as with most of the dreary days of my articles of clerkship, I was doing the courthouse "beat." I was sure that Milt Harradence could never have plied the courthouse beat; he probably went straight from law school into major homicides. I doubted, moreover, that A.M. Harradence would allow himself to be driven about the back garden of a suburban split-level like a pulpy hoofed nag, harnessed to a Weedex Wonder Bar by the said martial spouse. (Shortly thereafter, I dropped the Wonder Bar, the split-level, and the wife.)

On balance, I have concluded that Milt's early experiences in practice were similar to mine. I am not entirely sure how he looked back upon his articling days at the sonorously omnipotent law factory Chambers Might Saucier and Company of Adventurous Rotarians Trading Into Calgary Bay, as it then was. Our early careers are strikingly parallel: it is rumoured that he, who yearned for combat to his very core, was cruelly shunted into the mortgage department. When he left to join the criminal bar, it is said that the latest mortgage files were found stuffed in his desk drawer. That's the sort of myth that goes around, but one has to be suspicious because Harradence was too conscientious a lawyer to leave work for others. I am confident he left the files in a pile on top of his desk.

I still look back upon my two fledgling years at Macleod, McDermid, Dixon, Burns, Love, Leitch & Lomas with fear and loathing. I, who also wanted to get into a courtroom more than anything, was ignored by most of the litigation section and assigned to wills and estates under a mellifluous solicitor, who billed me to his clients as his "executive assistant." This galling ignominy was compounded by the fact that his highly capable secretary ran me and the department. This was an "old boy" firm and it hived off all the big estates of this or that generallisimo of industry or powerful cattle baron, all of whom were badly wanted in heaven. The end came when my senior treated me to a rare luncheon at the sonorous Ranchmen's Club (later immortalized by me in the *Albertan* newspaper as the "Paunchmen's Club." See Appendix.) He notified me over the famous cheddar cheese that I had some rough edges, but nothing that couldn't be smoothed out by assiduous devotion to abject mediocrity. He then importuned me with the admonition that I should read the Royal Bank of Canada monthly letter, in particular the edition he then thrust at me: "Attributes of a Junior Executive." Stunned by the suggestion that he, the firm, and I might benefit from my perusal of this load of smarmy codswallop, I thanked my mentor and told him that I thought I might be happier elsewhere. My senior was a kind man, although obviously not my kind. I spared his feelings as best I could, then made for the lower ground at the first reasonable opportunity. Being the very model of a junior executive was not my idea of career fulfillment.

If Milt had similar experiences, he said little; but I got the distinct impression that we had something in common, that is, a dislike of hollow privilege and a healthy disregard for cardboard authoritarian figures in a cowtown landscape.

So I tentatively addressed him in the street in this first encounter. And his face burst into that big, generous smile that slipped out in his unguarded moments as he thrust his hand out and grasped mine. I tried to squeeze hard because I knew he would expect a manly grip; unfortunately, my Navy ring got wedged by *his* manly grip and I went suddenly to the pavement in a spasm of pain. Milt was alarmed, "Are you all right, son?"

I managed to regain my feet, and stammered out that I had met him once, that I was in slavery at Macleod, McDermid, and that I wanted to be a criminal lawyer.

"Yaas. Where was that?"

"At your office, sir. I was looking for articles."

"Yaas."

"You asked me what my politics were."

Now he frowned. "I did?"

"Yes, I mean yaas."

"What are your politics?"

"I don't have any."

"We'll have to do something about that. Who's your principal?"

"Mr. Leitch."

The big smile again. "A very good friend of mine. You'll give him my compliments."

"Yes, sir."

"Now you call me up, you hear, and we'll talk about criminal law."

"They don't talk much about it at Macleod McDermid."

An even bigger smile. "I'm sure they don't, m'boy. Is it Cliff?"

"No, Christopher."

"Oh, Chris. Good. Well, nice talking to you. Very nice. Call me, now, Cliff."

He marched away, leaving me awash in admiration, more conscious than ever of the horrid suit and the egregious briefcase and the dismal prospect of more of the same at the Big Firm.

From that first, inspiring encounter, one irrevocable error has persisted: in all the years that we have been close friends, Milt has always insisted upon calling me "Cliff." In mischievous retaliation, I would call him "Merv," to his great discomfiture.

People get stuck on misnomers: the late Honourable Judge John Gorman insisted upon calling John James "Mr. Fisher," no matter how many times James appeared before him and announced himself correctly. James would stand up: "John James defending, Your Honour." "Thank you, Mr. Fisher."[1]

A year or so after the first encounter, I had Macleod McDermid and Company up to my yang and they had me up to their ying. It had been a period for me of intense misery, and we quitted each other by mutual consent, but not before one of the partners warned me, ominously, "You realize that if you leave this firm, you can never come back?" That seemed to me to be the best reason for leaving. I said goodbye to a couple of the lifers in the place. I told one cold fish, all transistorized and made in Japan, "I'm going to do litigation." He responded, with a downturned mouth, "We shall all live in constant trepidation." A partner named Cuthbert shook my hand warmly: "George, it's been great having you here." I replied, "Sam, it's been a slice."

I then served a two-year stint doing civil litigation as junior to Thomas Duckworth, Q.C., in the days when Burnet, Duckworth was six lawyers; not so many years later, it achieved mega-status. Tom and I disagreed on just about everything except a mutual devotion to Guinness Stout. Tom was the most tenacious civil lit-

---

1. Judge Gorman's comment to (now) the Hon. Suzanne Bensler (nee Manolescu) is the classic of all time in our jurisdiction. Crown Prosecutor Ms. Manolescu, who had appeared for the Crown for years, married Dr. Bensler. Dwayne Rowe and I christened her Mercedes Bensler for having the good fortune to marry a doctor. In any event, shortly after her marriage she appeared before Judge Gorman. "Mrs. Bensler for the Crown," she advised the court. Judge Gorman looked at her intently; the afternoon's list proceeded; every so often, Judge Gorman would start abruptly and lean forward and fix Mrs. Bensler with a searching gaze. Finally, he abruptly interrupted her: "Do you know something Mrs. Beezler? You look uncannily like a lady prosecutor who appeared before me for years named Miss Manolowski!"

igator I ever knew, with the possible exception of my late dear friend Patrick McCaffrey, Q.C. They could both project a remarkably well-feigned air of injured innocence on behalf of their clients.

The Harradences and the Duckworths were close neighbours on 14A Street Southwest in the upscale part of town which housed the upward mobility. One of the major differences between Milt and me is that he sought influence in high places and I sought influence in low places, which is where the real influence is. As the years went by, I maintained a somewhat unique accord with both families, best described as that of a prodigal second cousin who was a bit too far off the wall for their steady diet but who was always warmly welcomed, plied with hospitality, then set loose again, partially but not permanently rehabilitated. There is a poignant footnote to my relationship with the two families that I shall talk about later.

I had but one criminal case between 1963 and 1966 when I hitched up with Jim Cox and Mike Farrell, eminent solicitors who elected to harbour a barrister. The one case came my way via the meticulous R.A.F. Montgomery, Q.C., at Macleod, McDermid, McDixon, McEtcetera, McEtcetera. Mr. Montgomery had a defence in law for some traffic violator. He was aware of my unrequited longing for crime and kindly kept a lookout for briefs for me. He instructed me to go to the (then) Magistrate's Court, sit through the Crown's case without saying "boo," wait until the Crown Prosecutor said, "That's the case for the Crown," *then*—and only *then*, he emphasized, only *after* the Crown Prosecutor said those magic words (I had not the slightest idea what they meant)—to move for dismissal on the legal point that his secretary typed out for me on a card. I was to recite it verbatim.

My heart pounding, I repaired to my first criminal trial. Well, it was a traffic trial but quasi-criminal. All the careful instructions I followed to the letter, except one: after the second Crown witness had testified, His Worship Magistrate Fred Thurgood, Q.C., asked junior Crown Counsel, Paul S. Chrumka, "Have you got any more witnesses?", probably because it was close to coffee time.

"No," quoth Chrumka.

I thought that was my cue. I rose hurriedly and read the litany from the Montgomery secretarial card with a quavering voice. The Magistrate interrupted me: "He (indicating Chrumka) hasn't closed his case yet. Siddown."

Chrumka was on the bit. He asked for an adjournment to consider the Crown's position. I was petrified and speechless. The adjournment was granted.

Trembling, I reported this unfortunate development to Mr. Montgomery. He had a mild shock and staggered off to his chambers to seek solace in *The Naden Gazette: The Seaman's Magazine.* This was a double blow to my career, as I was aspiring to the first lieutenant's berth at HMCS *Tecumseh,* the local naval reserve "ship," and R.A.F. Montgomery was rumoured to be her next Captain. It was not an auspicious start.

On the adjournment date, as it turned out, the Crown threw in the towel in a most sporting manner, deferring in any event to Mr. Montgomery's defence in point of law. But it was, in view of my blunder, a Pyrric victory at best. Mr. Montgomery, however, was placated to a point. Nevertheless, I wisely transferred forthwith from the active reserve to the inactive reserve, whatever that means, and hung up my gaiters and sword. Canada, I decided, could get someone else to stand on guard.

That—such as it was—was my first almost criminal case. The second experience was to be a more heartening enterprise due to Milt Harradence.

In 1966, I set up shop with Mike Farrell and Jim Cox and put my name down for Legal Aid. I say "for" advisably, the initials L.A.—then, as now—standing for "lawyer's assistance." The Alberta Legal Aid Plan, established under the benign auspices of the Law Society of Alberta and the Attorney General, was in its fledgling years. Prior to Legal Aid, which ushered in decades of guaranteed modest fees for struggling criminal and family lawyers, there was a volunteer arrangement called the Needy Litigant Committee, sort of an Alberta version of the Dock Brief, for indigent civil (and some criminal) clients. One could also be appointed by the court to defend the odd miscreant who was without counsel on a serious charge: that was without pay, but a great honour.

It would be appropriate here to insert William V. Stilwell's description of the pre-Legal Aid Criminal Bar in Alberta, which description cannot be improved upon. In retrospect, that system cannot be improved upon either. This excerpt was part of a letter Bill wrote to the Law Society/CBA Hindquarterly in March 1996:

> Before 1964 there was no Legal Aid in Alberta, no duty counsel, nothing.
>
> An arrested person did not get bail unless he applied for it, and the onus was on him.
>
> It was routine for a man to be arrested during the night, to appear in Court at 9:30 *a.m.*, plead guilty and in a few minutes be on his way to the penitentiary for a term of years, all without ever speaking to a lawyer. We thought nothing of it.
>
> In those days, there was a small group of lawyers whose practices were almost completely confined to the magistrates' courts. Some were old and some were young; many were heavy drinkers and others not. What they had in common was the ability to judge to a hair's breadth just what would fly and what wouldn't and just what each magistrate would do in a given case. They knew when to cross-examine and when not, when to argue and when to shut up. They knew what many lawyers learn late in life and some never: the essence of advocacy is knowing what to leave out. They were generally regarded as just slightly disreputable.
>
> But prosecutors liked them because they were absolutely trustworthy. In those days, crown and defence counsel didn't write letters to each other. There was no need to. When you said you'd do something, and the day came, you'd do it.

Anyway, along came Legal Aid and the social welfare net era of criminal defence. I am hardly knocking it: I cut my teeth on Legal Aid cases, as did every one of my contemporaries. In the course of time, the plan bogged down into the usual bureaucratic morass. I took Legal Aid appointments for twenty years, including while I served as a Bencher. In those days, my fellow Benchers waxed windily upon the contribution required of the "profession" (translation: the Junior Bar who were not in large firms) to defend the indigent criminal or financially embarrassed divorcee. I had enough of this horseshit by 1982 (my fifth year as a Bencher) to interrupt the oratorical excesses that always accompanied the Legal Aid budget debate with a Point of Order: "Mr. Chairman," I thundered, "hands up any Bencher who has accepted a Legal Aid certificate in the past ten years!" My recollection is that two hands went up: mine and that of Hugh Landerkin, the prominent divorce lawyer. I would be pleasantly surprised to learn if any one of the other eighteen Benchers had ever done a Legal Aid case or was minded to do so.[2]

My first criminal client was a young man who told me, in tones of shocked disbelief, that he had been charged with "gross" (he rhymed the word with "loss") indecency. The allegation was that he and a male friend had had carnal conversation with an adult female. His co-accused, being more flush, or who had a family who were more flush, retained the services of the eminent Milt Harradence. I had not the slightest idea what to do for my poor client, who seemed a thoroughly decent lad who had got carried away in an escapade where boys will be men. (One was allowed to make cracks like that in those days.) I have little independent memory of the conduct of my client's defence, except that I do remember the unstinting assistance and encouragement given to me by my learned friend, Milt. Of course, one defending a joint accused has to save the last bullet for the other defence counsel, but there is meanwhile a common enemy, the massed pipes and drums of the Crown and the cops. In my first criminal case, I learned that from Milt. "M'boy," he said to me, glowering, "if it

---

2. This is the same bunch that voted almost unanimously not to subsidize the flagging Legal Aid budget from the deep coffers of the Alberta Law Foundation. The Foundation got its lucre from the interest on the trust accounts of solicitors who did not accept Legal Aid appointments; it was always quick to fund some ennobling and aggrandizing obscure project. Curiously, it was also Landerkin and I who were the only Benchers to vote against the stupid rule that prohibited national law firms; the Benchers proposed and passed the rule on the specious pretext that they could not oversee disciplinary matters of national firms, but the real reason was crass Alberta protectionism for fear of the greater talent elsewhere which would rabbit off their major clients. Then the Benchers chose to litigate this to the Supreme Court of Canada at a cost to its members of thousands of dollars and *lost,* plus costs. This was an obscene abuse of power. Why the rank and file members of the Law Society have not risen periodically in revolt and terminated the Benchers with extreme prejudice is quite beyond me. However, it is never too late.

comes down to pointing fingers, it's every man for himself," (you could say that in those days, too) "but let us combine forces against those sanctimonious bastards [indicating the Crown]." In the result, the sanctimonious bastards prevailed and the two accused were taken down to serve their six months each.

That trial to me had all the excitement of the Crossing the Line ceremony: I knew before it was over, notwithstanding the odds, the archaic law, and the loaded facts, this was what I wanted to do, to get up on my hind legs and make the other side *work* for their living. Milt led for the defence, of course, and to me he was the fastest gun since Hoot Gibson. I was then but a poor second. But we gave the Crown a fight, by God, we did!

After the sentencing, Milt treated me to lunch at the York Hotel, which had a passable dining room. He was the most impressive and the most thoroughly decent lawyer I had ever met, and when he insisted on my calling him "Milt" and said he looked forward to our doing other cases together, my cup was overflowing.

Another thing that stands out as an occurrence at that luncheon—I recall clearly—was a curious phenomenon: after some initial pleasantries, Milt suddenly addressed me intently upon a matter where, it appeared, he was starting at a point halfway through a detailed polemic, assuming that I had been privy to the first half. I had not the slightest idea what he was talking about from beginning to end of this segment of the luncheon. The best I could do was to abide the admonition of Chairman Mao and try to appear "united, alert, earnest and lively." Much later, I was to discuss this singular eccentricity, which re-occurred with alarming frequency, with Jack Major, Q.C., who offered his usual practical and pithy insights into our friend Harradence which will require further elaboration.

Coming hard on the heels of this first experience in the criminal courts was my next case the following week, which was the guilty plea of a sixteen-year-old client who stole a car. I got it down to "joyriding," as it was then called, and the accused copped a plea and got suspenders. I felt it my duty to go back in cells to admonish this youth about further antisocial behaviour. "Let this be a lesson to you, young fellow," I counselled, with upraised finger. "Fuck you," is what the ungrateful lout said back to me.

Stung by this reproof from that ingrate, I related the encounter to Milt. "Welcome to the Criminal Bar, Cliff," was all he said, and from that day forward I never again confused the calling of the criminal barrister with the trade of the social worker.

My career at the criminal bar was launched, as was the beginning of an extraordinary friendship.

Chapter Three
Aftermyth of War[1]

"Mad is he?" George II is reported to have said of General Wolfe, "Then I wish he would bite some of my other Generals."

– *Michael Howard,* Over the Top

THE LATE Honourable John Sopinka, Justice of the Supreme Court of Canada, fondly recalled *his* first encounter with A.M. Harradence, Q.C. The contest was a labour case, somewhat uncharacteristic for Milt's practice, but on occasion the sort of eclectic exercise he would undertake. This matter had to do with certification of a union, or something equally esoteric, Harradence and Sopinka opposing. The important point is that Milt called his client to give evidence before the tribunal. We must assume that the client was a material witness. Sopinka, J. recalls that Milt's first question of his client was remarkable:

Q: *"Sir, I understand you were present at the crossing of the Yalu River!*

Sopinka, Q.C., (as he then was) found this opening gambit most amusing; the tribunal, probably the usual gaggle of labour lawyers, probably found it puzzling.

Jack Major explains: "To Milt, that was how he established his client's credentials. His client's evidence from then on, presumably, was unimpeachable." Milt's ascription of instant credibility

---

1. Title borrowed with grateful acknowledgement to the brilliant 'Beyond the Fringe' review, 1962, copyright Miller, Moore, Cook, and Bennett; Capitol Records of Canada Ltd. registered user, copyright.

to those who had fought for Queen and country in this or that passage of arms surfaced periodically in his defence of the innocent. He naturally expected that any Court or tribunal with any sense would similarly defer to such a credential.

I had occasion to prosecute a prominent physician who had been nailed for allegedly operating a motor vehicle while his ability to do so was impaired by alcohol. Milt defended vigorously, but the client was duly convicted of this delict in the then Magistrate's Court. Milt automatically appealed, and it was fortunate for his client that the matter came on for a *trial de novo* before His Honour Judge E.R. Tavender of the then District Court of Alberta. The District Court sat on appeal of Magistrate's decisions in summary conviction matters; sometime later, the Trial Division of the Supreme Court of Alberta and the District Court of Alberta were squished into the Court of Queen's Bench after vociferous debate pro and con. The ever-witty Buzz McClung, J.A., summed it up pithily:

> The merger of the District Court with the Trial Division has raised the mean I.Q. of both courts.

In defending his client, Milt placed him on the stand. His first question of the doctor was a classic of the Yalu River genre, and the following court dialogue ensued:

Q: *Sir, I understand that you served as a Canadian Army physician in the last war, and that you made several parachute jumps with the troops in combat conditions?*
[Judge Tavender leaned forward, engaged.]
A: *Yes, Mr. Harradence.*
Q: *And I further understand, doctor, that as a result of these parachute jumps in the service of your country, you suffered and continue to suffer periodic pain and stiffness of the limbs?*
A: *Yes, sir.*
Mr. Evans: *Your Honour, the Crown will concede as a fact that the witness suffered discomfiture and possible permanent partial disability, particularly if the parachute did not open.*

Mr. Harradence: *Your Honour, this is not a matter for levity.*

His Honour frowned at my inappropriate observation.

The evidence-in-chief continued, but the case was lost for the Crown: so much for "he staggered when he walked," which was the prime prop in the cops' arsenal of indicia of impairment by alcohol in pre-Breathalyzer days. His Honour Judge Tavender rose solemnly after acquitting the appellant. He always presented a grave mien and there was no tomfoolery in his court. On this occasion, as he departed in his usual dignified manner from the Bench, he turned slightly toward me with a nod, and stated, "Not much coal falling in the Guild Halls today."[2] *Exeunt omnes.*

Also of note is *Regina v. P* (1981 Alta. C.A.), which was a Crown appeal of my client's sentence before Laycraft, C.J.A., Arnold "Spud" Moir and Prowse, JJ. A. I had represented Mr. P on a guilty plea before (then) His Honour Associate Chief Judge Kerans of the District Court. The accused had made off with a considerable amount of his employer's money, which defalcation was discovered only after he had retired and received his gold watch. A routine audit disclosed the villainy, and Mr. P did the right thing and marched into court at the earliest reasonable opportunity to plead guilty. He had an impeccable background and in particular had served in the U.S. Forces in the Korean War. There is no doubt in my mind that that was probably the major factor in my being able to hold the two-years-less-a-day sentence in the Court of Appeal. The Crown's appeal was dismissed, the court observing, *inter alia:*

> The Crown seeks leave to appeal a sentence of two years less one day imposed by the learned trial Judge for a series of thefts by the Respondent from his employer. Over a period of five years by means of 49 improper cheque requisitions the Respondent stole nearly $292,000. It is clear that throughout the five year period he was guilty of a gross pre-meditated breach of his employer's trust. The thefts were discovered only after his retirement on pension.

---

2. Another classic from "Beyond The Fringe," supra., "Sitting on the Bench."

> Having emphasised the enormity of the offence we observe that a great deal can be said on behalf of the Respondent. He is 52 years old. Following distinguished military service in which he was decorated for valour he had a long and respected professional career. His reputation was such that all who knew him including members of his family reacted with shock and amazement at the disclosure of his crime.

I had thought to emphasise the military service, remembering the jury opening of Sir Wilfred Robarts, K.C., in *Witness for the Prosecution*, making an artful referral as if in passing to his client's "distinguished war record." Chief Justice Laycraft and Mr. Justice Prowse had both seen active service in World War II with the Canadian Artillery and the Royal Canadian Air Force respectively.

There is a significant, perhaps nostalgic, point to be made: today, the end of a violent century, that plea would now fall not so much on deaf, but on non-comprehending, ears. A "war record" was always mitigating, sometimes partially exonerating, as to culpability in the two decades following the Second World War; even Korea was worth quoting in sentencing submissions. But following the bitter legacy of Vietnam, the peacenik movement, the emotionally loaded celluloid portrayals of those events, and then the "unification" and denigration of the Canadian Armed Forces including the dismemberment of some Regiments in Canada, and then the fall of the Berlin Wall, such a distinction was as irrelevant as the plea of Othello that he "had done the State some service." In some callow courts, an unblemished service record would today be an aggravating factor; in the United States, it is probably grounds for suspicion that one is anti-government. In Canada, conscientious objectors, peace-mongers, as well as those who actively oppose the annual seal hunt or chain themselves to trees in Clayoquot are a cert for an absolute or a conditional discharge without more. If one got up in court today and stated, "My client is a Vet," the court would think the client was an animal doctor.

Milt was very big on military service as a distinction to be worn for life, if earned. I cannot say I disagree. Initially, I was not aware that he shared my appreciation of the absurd in the ramrod-backed blockhead mentality, or worse, the ass with the delicate air who wore a white handkerchief shoved up the left sleeve of his uniform and would say loudly and plonkingly to the barkeep in the Wardroom at Weepers: "I'll have a glass of my wine." I have remained uneasy at claiming a privileged position in society by virtue of my past military service or this or that minor accolade, remembering the admonition of T.S. Eliot that one should do more with one's life than end up an empty vessel hung with empty honours. One has only to pick up the telephone book to marvel at certified nincompoops who still list themselves as "Sqdrn. Ldr. (ret'd) J. Bloggs."

I had a singularly undistinguished career in the Royal Canadian Navy, but to Milt the fact that I had served two years at Royal Roads, Victoria, provided my "credentials" and an entree to his confidence and his service memoirs. I empathize with Sir Frank Kermode in *Not Entitled: A Memoir* (quoted by Michael Wood in the *London Review of Books*):

> At the age of twenty-six, he tells us, he left the Navy with "no idea of what I was going to do, except for the negative certainty that it wouldn't be seafaring. A little more positively, I was fairly sure that it would involve writing of some sort and reading, if I could buy the leisure to do it."

Royal Roads was so tough that even the Chaplain went over the hill. Regrettably for my family but happily for me, I had been released from active service in 1958 under the unambiguous subsection "compulsory withdrawal of subordinate officers due to academic failure"; even so, the academic standards at Roads were so high that I was able with alacrity to gain admission to the second year of the three-year Bachelor of Arts program at the University of Alberta, Edmonton; in the result, achieving my B.A. by osmosis in 1960 (third class), I secured a reserve Commission "with seniority of September 1960," thus beating my military college "Term of '56" to the rank, and rushed out to the College to enjoy the spectacle of them having to salute me. I considered it important over the next six or seven years to maintain my association in the "active reserve," an oxymoron. I had never been successful with women, and the uniform added cachet to an undistinguished phizzog and gangly body; the old song "all the nice girls/love a sailor" is dead wrong; the happy fact is, all the wrong sorts of women love a sailor. Make no mistake. I cite the great Proust in *Swann's Way: "Even those women who claim to judge a man by his looks alone, see in those looks the emanation of a special way of life. That is why they fall in love with soldiers or with firemen; the uniform makes them less particular about the face."*

Because I knew army sword drill and had a loud voice, at both HMCS *Nonsuch*, Edmonton, and subsequently at HMCS *Tecumseh*, Calgary, I was the officer of the guard and the ships' drill instructor. This, to me, was all showbiz. To my friend, Milt, it was the mark of the Warrior; his friend, Evans, commanded the Men under Arms!

I think that the common experiences we shared of youthful service in the armed forces contributed much to our rapport from the outset. Further, although Milt was far more an observer of military punctilio and jargon and the virtues of ceremony and uniforms, medals, etcetera, than was I, I became aware that he as a young subaltern was alert to the attendant preposterous fopperies and excesses of the pseuds and poseurs who also were attracted to the military mindset. Thus, in differing degrees and circumstances, but within the same oppressive context, we shared a powerful dislike for abuses and abusers of authority. This caused him major headaches and setbacks in his war service, and me similar disaffection in peacetime service and prejudiced both of our service careers. As time went by, however, he managed to some extent to anaesthetise his bitter experiences, while mine intensified.

Milt's bitter experiences included stiff-backed, small-minded opposition to his being posted overseas because he had managed to alienate some of his less gifted superiors. Milt's Air Force career ended in Lethbridge as a result of a basic philosophical disagreement between him and the Commanding Officer on the care and handling of His Majesty's aircraft. Harradence's approach was that the Bolingbroke was fully aerobatic; the Commanding Officer held the opposite view. Says Milt: "When that dispute became irreconcilable, the Station wasn't big enough for both of us. As he was a Group Captain and I was a Flight Sergeant, it wasn't hard to predict who was going to leave the Station and the Service."

All that is known is that Harradence ended up for the balance of the war as a corporal in the Army, banished to Alaska. He bore this banishment stoically. That's another great attribute of Milt: I have never known him to bear grudges. I am the opposite: as J. Paul Getty is reputed to have said on receiving his grandson's ear from alleged Italian kidnappers, "They don't know the meaning of the word 'vendetta'!"

From those disappointing years emerges a true story that aptly illustrates the typical generosity and selflessness of this man. Most of the old crates used for training by prospective Air Force bomber crews were held together by string, piano wire, a wing, and a prayer. One of these fine behemoths was piloted by Sgt. Pilot Milt Harradence who was posted to a bomber reconnaissance squadron in Vancouver at Seal Island. The role of bomber pilots did not really appeal to Harradence, who preferred fighters. In order to maintain operational efficiency, Milt was out flying and observed a farmer unloading hay into his barn. In a spirit of cooperation, he went down to help the farmer blow the hay off the rack. As he went around the corner of the barn, he came upon a tree that had escaped his notice. He pulled up sharply to avoid it, but the port wing and motor absorbed a great deal of the wood. Said his navigator: "What are we gonna tell them when we get back to base?" Replied Milt: "We'll tell them we hit a fucking tree," which he did. As this was not part of the training syllabus, and the Commanding Officer lacked a certain sense of humour, Harradence was court martialled, fined $50, and his promotion was suspended for six months.

Years later, Milt—now ensconced comfortably in private law practice in Calgary—received a letter from the Bureau of Pensions Advocates on behalf of one of the crewmen, purportedly injured in the manoeuvre. This veteran was now making a disability claim related to his World War II service, with specific reference to this incident:

> The records show he was involved in a flying accident on 13 October 1942 when some damage was done to the Bolingbroke Aircraft,

> but the report indicated 'Nil' injuries to the crew. X claims he was thrown violently against the framework of the crawl space over the bomb bay, striking his head and jaw against the metal framework, but did not report this 'injury' because the pilot was in some difficulty in connection with the incident. The veteran is now totally disabled by the motor neuron disease and I am seeking some confirmation of possible injury at the time of the accident.
>
> Accordingly, I would be grateful if you could send me a statement of your recollection of the incident with particular reference to whether X complained of or otherwise mentioned being thrown about when the aircraft struck a tree in flight... your statement may prove very helpful in seeking the award.

Milt responded at once. What may have caused the injury was the sudden G force caused when he tried to avoid hitting the tree. It would occur to most of us to perhaps confirm that X was a member of the crew only, then to make no other comment, considering the allegations. That, of course, was not Milt's style. In a response that was so typical of his character then as now, he wrote:

> I recall very clearly the incident referred to in your letter, but I have no recollection of any member of the crew complaining of an injury. However, it is quite conceivable that if X did not have his safety harness secured, he could have struck his head, not from the impact of the aircraft with the tree, which was very slight, but from the evasive action taken in an attempt to avoid striking the tree. Mr. X is quite right in saying that I was in some difficulty, as I was subsequently court-martialled for unauthorized low flying, and he, for that reason remains silent with respect to any injuries he may have sustained.
>
> If I can be of any further assistance please contact me and I certainly hope that Mr. X is successful in obtaining his pension.

This is gallantry and the art of being a gentleman "in all things instant" (to quote the late J.E.A. MacLeod, Q.C.), the sort of high-mindedness that went out with the First World War and "The Shooting Party."

After the war, Milt was Commissioned in 403 Reserve Squadron at Calgary, and became its deputy flight commander. As such, he attended Air Force "summer camp" at Ottawa in 1953. There, at

Rockcliffe, a Royal Canadian Mounted Police station was located right next to the air station. As a tribute to the astute planning efforts of the Department of National Defence and the Solicitor General's Department, a parade ground was located right off the end of an active runway. How like the Government of Canada! Milt and his winger, Flying Officer Greg Forsyth, had the first flight one morning, a formation takeoff. The Mustang aircraft is blind on takeoff—as the nose of the plane comes up, one achieves full frontal vision. Much to Milt's "shock and dismay," there, in front, was a full-dress parade of several hundred Mounted Police. That created a problem. Milt explains: If an engine failure occurred on takeoff, they would end up in the middle of the parade. The only way to avoid the cops was to get sufficient speed to clear the parade square. The only way to get that speed was to hold the aircraft down until the last possible moment, which of course Harradence did. Therefore, they joined the parade. This caused a stampede to the fringes of the parade square, consternation, and Questions in the House. Relations between the RCMP Brass and the RCAF Brass were "strained." Milt said later: *"You could fly for one hundred years, and never get an opportunity like this!"*

In matters military, Milt also had a delightful sense of humour. One of his most inspired invented characters was the Honourable Colonel Ridge-Drawers, C.D., O.B.E. (Other Buggers' Efforts) (Ret'd). In the guise of this purported ageing pomposity of rigid military aspect, Milt would phone and harangue selected targets and scare the living be-jeezus out of the recipient of his diatribe. Indeed, I have reason to believe that he actually fooled his own Chief Justice on the Court when he contrived to telephone the Chief during a dinner party at his (Milt's) residence. Harradence was on the downstairs phone and managed to have the Chief Justice called to the telephone, whereat he delivered an explosive comment on some recent decision of the court that had the Chief stammering and stuttering and endeavouring to engage this obvious lunatic on the other end of the telephone in a semblance of polite conversation. The true identity of Colonel Ridge-Drawers was only revealed at a later date, to the amazement of the recipient. At least two of my learned juniors were importuned by

Colonel Ridge-Drawers, reporting his unreasonable demands to me still unnerved by the experience. The best sally of the Colonel followed the publication in the eminent *North Hill News* of my column that I fancied to be extremely funny and thoroughly insulting to the Calgary horsey set, particularly the strutting termagants who march around in jackboots wearing chamber pots on their heads and lording it over the peasantry. The article was entitled, "They Shoot Horses, Don't They?" and the opening paragraph began: "The horse is the stupidest animal made by God. The only stupider animal is the creature who habitually rides the horse. Put them together and you have a double horse's ass." The article went on to excoriate horse-faced women riders, who had dropped bottoms in their jodhpurs, and their escorts who wore ill-fitting tweed jackets and smoked vanilla-flavoured pipe tobacco. Colonel Ridge-Drawers was infuriated and phoned my residence and poured a torrent of abuse and denunciation upon the vulnerable head of my wife. Even the redoubtable Bernice Evans, who has never been backward in coming forward, was stunned to silence by this attack, which ended with Colonel Ridge-Drawers threatening "to come 'round to your establishment forthwith and lay onto that fellow with a horsewhip!" This was duly reported to me, and we spent a couple of uneasy evenings hiding under the bed, loaded revolvers at the ready. When Milt, with great guffaws, in due course revealed the identity of the Colonel, we contrived a copycat revenge which involved calling his residence as Sir Jodhpur Boot, and inviting him to join the Society for the Preservation of the Hunt. Milt did not fall for that one. The two of us subsequently planned to try out Colonel Ridge-Drawers and Sir Jodhpur Boot, as a duo, on our mutual friend, Roy Farran, who had become Solicitor General in the Lougheed Government. Roy Farran was an ardent horseman and hunt enthusiast, also a respected military hero and the author of a highly readable reminiscence, *Winged Dagger.* We phoned his office on a couple of occasions, Milt on the blower and me on the extension, giggling like school children, demanding to speak to "that fellow Fahrenheit," but we never could catch him in.

A sense of humour can get you into a lot of hot water in the military. I was standing a miserable, bedraggled wet watch on the open bridge of an old tub c. 1945, HMCS *Ontario*, at sea in a storm. I was a dogsbody called Cadet of the Watch, whose principal duty was to stay out of everyone's way. I was trying to hide and shelter in a partially covered section when the bridge phone let out a horrendous squawk. I grabbed it but was so unnerved by the sudden blast that, instead of announcing, "Bridge, Cadet of the Watch," I stammered, "Hello?" A gruff voice demanded, "Who's the idiot at the end of this phone?" "Which end?" I asked. As the interrogator turned out to be the Captain calling the bridge from his sea cabin, I spent the balance of the training cruise chipping slag out of the boilers.

Thus it was somewhat incongruous to me that Milt always insisted upon the formality of military rank and precedence and marks of respect at appropriate conspicuous national events. For example, on one soporific occasion of the Right Honourable Sir Winston Spencer Churchill Memorial Society dinner (by the time one finishes the title, one is asleep), he introduced me stiffly to Lieutenant General (Ret'd) the Honourable Senator Stan Waters as "Sub-Lieutenant Evans." (I corrected him to "Lieutenant," but he persisted with the demotion as he did with "Cliff.") I always found this humorous, and later, through the wily connivance of a mutual acquaintance, arranged to have that third party casually show Milt my erroneous designation in the Royal Military College ex-cadet list as "Capt. (N) Evans, C.D." my transposed initials inadvertently conferring upon me the Canadian Forces decoration which I had never earned. ("Captain" is the current Forces universal designation of rank using Army nomenclature, equivalent to Naval Lieutenant.) Milt was mightily impressed, thinking that I had somehow along the way got command of at least a light cruiser on Chestermere Lake. I have never disabused his mind of this false impression. Now, on occasion, he introduces me as "Colonel Evans, C.D." We had not to 1994 resolved the question of who saluted whom.

In that year, A.M. Harradence was honoured by 416 Tactical Squadron of Air Command at Cold Lake, Alberta, battle honours including the recent Gulf War, and the Base Commander Colonel (now General) Ed McGillivray, with the appointment of Honourary Colonel. I must say, he looked absolutely splendid in the wings and strings and Fort Knox knickers of the ceremonial uniform, with scrambled egg on the cap, and it was with difficulty that the Honourable Chief Justice Catherine A. Fraser enjoined his wearing the uniform during Sittings of the Court of Appeal. I advised him that I was now obliged to defer to his seniority and rank, and he accepted this appropriate chain of command with grace.

Milt's military mindset was always in overdrive: one night in mid-trial we were signing in at the courthouse on the way to the law library (the then Chief Justice did not want the "wrong sorts of people" in these sacred precincts). Milt glowered at the sign-in ledger's "time in" column, and the pathetic scribble of civilian time designations. He wrote, with ostentatious flourish, "1830 hours," and looked meaningfully at the hovering Commissioner and at me: "That'll shake 'em up!" The Commissioner was mightily impressed. One asks, "Shake up *whom*? *Why*?"

As I have earlier noted, Harradence had been a "Colonel" for some years, albeit a Colonel in the Confederate Air Force, the cadre of enthusiastic lunatic stunt pilots who publicly barnstormed about the United States and environs in vintage and/or bizarre aeroplanes. Their dangerous peregrinations discouraged insurability by even disreputable life insurance companies. From the time that Milt joined this elite Kamikaze Squadron, in the early sixties, his family remained vulnerable to zero proceeds on his untimely demise in this or that fringe air show. This did not contribute much to the harmony of the Harradence household, although his wife, Catherine, with her usual admirable equanimity tried not to think too much about it.

Every so often the members of the Confederate Air Force had a free-for-all. On one occasion they gathered at "Rebel Field," somewhere in Texas on the Rio Grande. On this occasion, Catherine came down and joined the Squadron's ladies who were observing the antics from the second floor of the headquarters building. Milt, piloting the Mustang, flew by *below* her level. Catherine had a few words with Milt about that. This was the only time she ever demurred. Testimonials to Milt's superlative flying skills are included in the Appendices.

The extremities to which the members of the Confederate Air Force habitually exposed themselves naturally attracted international notoriety. It was not surprising that the producers of *The Battle of Britain*, one of those cinemascope extravaganzas dramatising the Glory of War, enlisted some squadron members as stunt fliers for simulated air combat film footage to be shot in Spain.[3] Only certified fellows of the Confederate Airforce would be mad enough, and skilled enough, to pilot the rickety World War II Spitfires, Stukas, and Messerschmitts assembled for the aerial combat sequences.

Milt answered the call with the alacrity with which, in 1940 at the age of seventeen, he answered his country. Perversely, and to his secret delight when he recalled the unfair indignities to which during the Real Thing he had been subjected, Milt ended up in the film flying a German fighter against the R.A.F. He was offshore for eight weeks for that caper, and returned, in effect, a war hero. When *The Battle of Britain* had its Canadian premiere at the Grand Theatre in Calgary, the local promoters deployed search lights and a celebrity motorcade for the screening of the film, the highlight being the arrival by stretch limousine of Milt and Catherine in formal attire at the entrance to the theatre, to the adulation of the masses. There is a gentle irony in all of this; it is the stuff of desirable myth.

Regrettably, all or most of Milt's aerial fighting footage was left on the cutting-room floor, prompting the ever-witty Assistant Chief Judge Brian Stevenson to remark, "Milt's the only combat pilot to have missed the Battle of Britain twice."

Milt's return home to a hero's welcome was bizarre, considering that, heroic as he was and is, wartime heroism was not in the cards. No one knew this better than he; witness his genuine deference to those anointed Few (bringing to mind one of the best

---

3. It is not unusual to be shot in Spain. Ask any member of the International Brigade, c. 1936. Even today, the cops carry carbines. Well, as Steven Potter sniffed, "I never thought Barcelona was much of anything since the Anarchists liberated it in 1937."

deathless lines from *Beyond the Fringe*: "Please, Sir, I want to join the Few." "I'm sorry. There are far too many.") Thus it is all the more curious that he allowed himself to be the guest of honour at this Great Canadian Premiere in Calgary screening this utter bilge, with Sir Lawrence Olivier as Chief Air Marshall Somebody-or-Other and all of the Usual Suspects, Hollywood-style with search-lights and limousines arriving before the gawking peasantry and disgorging swells. Quoth the Mob: "Oooohh and Aaaahh!"

John MacPherson called me a couple of days before the event, asking if he could borrow my tux. The only garment I had approaching a dinner jacket was a facsimile I got for thirty-five dollars in Barbados on my first honeymoon. Mac said Milt had decreed his presence and black tie was obligatory. He had demurred. "Have you forgotten the Scriptures?" I reminded him, "'Friend, where is thy wedding garment?'"

Apparently, this vulgar extravaganza actually took place. Of course, I was not invited. Milt well knew the drubbing he and the Occasion would get in my *Albertan* newspaper column, and he was not taking any chances.

Jack Major has remarked upon Milt's unabashed respect for those who had gone "over there" and experienced actual combat. They are in a class by themselves, he says, and he is—and has always been—reluctant to share either a stage or a spotlight with former active combatants. One of his personal heroes, and a hero to many of us, was the legendary Group Captain Douglas Bader, the famous R.A.F. pilot shot down in the Second World War. Bader lost both of his legs in a peacetime air crash and was invalided out of the Royal Air Force. When war was declared, he persuaded them to take him back. He became the "legless ace" of the R.A.F.: twenty-one enemy aircrafts destroyed. He collided with a Messerschmitt over France and managed to bale out, without his tin legs. The Luftwaffe offered free passage to the R.A.F. to deliver a new set of legs to Bader. The R.A.F. indeed delivered the legs as invited and dropped them together with a load of bombs. Bader got his new legs and promptly escaped from the Prisoner of War camp. He was apprehended and confined to Colditz. Milt and Catherine became close friends of Sir Douglas and Lady Joan

Bader. Milt's 1982 letter of condolence to Lady Bader on the death of Douglas Bader is included in the Appendices.

That, of course, points up the difference between the blockheads who ran the Canadian show and those in England who were more attuned to the dividends of good theatre. Whereas the powers authorised Bader to re-commence his sorties subsequent to his thrilling escapades, it was the practice of their Canadian poltroonish cousins to recall their heroes and send them around the country trying to drum up sales of war bonds. Group Captain Bader came to Calgary to address the Sir W.S. Churchill (etc., etc.) dinner, and Milt entertained him as the guest of honour at a memorable dinner attended by several Calgarians who had distinguished themselves as flyers "over there."

The fact is, Harradence was as daring and brilliant a pilot as he was a barrister. He indeed bore the Mark of the Warrior. His courtroom performances were consistently outstanding, as were his mad flying activities in a variety of very fast single-seater aircraft.

In the air, his acrobatic exploits matched the derring-do and recklessness of an Errol Flynn. There is no doubt in my mind and that of many of Milt's contemporaries that, had he simply headed south to Hollywood after the war, he would have in short order—with his matinee idol's stunning good looks, that toothsome grin, that gregarious charm, and six foot plus inches of beefcake—become a blockbuster star who would have relegated the likes of Flynn, Clark Gable, Valentino, and their ilk to perpetual soda jerkery.

There is in existence—and known only to a few—perhaps the Few who were at Biggin Hill—a bootleg film of Flight Lieutenant Harradence, R.C.A.F. (Reserve), c. 1950, putting a World War II Mustang fighter through its paces in a spectacular display of aerial stunt flying. It leaves the viewer breathless, shaking. Prominent in the cast of this swashbuckling documentary are the late William (Bill) Gill, Q.C., and G.R. (Greg) Forsyth, Q.C. (as he then was), Milt's wingers in the Calgary RCAF. Reserve squadron and themselves Air Force veterans. It rivals the best of Hollywood or the Rank studios.

The Mustang was the first of Milt's private airplanes. This was followed by his very own Vampire jet fighter. Subsequently, as part of his never-ending quest for superior air power, he located a decommissioned Canadian Forces F-86 Sabre jet destined for the old jet's knackers yard, the Aviation Museum. The Sabre had seen service with the acrobatic Golden Hawks and had been overhauled. He negotiated the purchase of this formidable flying machine from the Air Museum. Horrified at the prospect and undesirable precedent of a private citizen flying a sophisticated war plane about the continent, Federal Government bureaucrats of a more sedentary and retiring frame of mind than Harradence refused to issue the requisite Certificate of Airworthiness. They unwisely chose as their adversary the most formidable advocate of his day and as the forum to decide the issue the Trial Division of the Supreme Court of Alberta. The forces of reaction were duly put to ignominious rout by a Court of Competent Jurisdiction, A.M.H. won his Certificate of Airworthiness, and the citizens of Calgary were treated to the frequent spectacle of a glittering gold Sabre Jet sporting the Confederate Flag streaking across the prairie skies. The cost of putting the thing in the air, prohibitive to the average gaping yokel, was staggering. Colonel Milt Harradence proudly piloted the fastest private plane in the world.

One of the most delightful reminiscences of the late Alan Cullen, Q.C. (later the Honourable Mr. Justice) was of a meeting with his opposing learned friend Harradence at Lethbridge. Milt flew down to confer with Cullen on a case. At the conclusion of this barristers' conference, Cullen drove Milt to the local airport, where Milt mounted his silver Mustang. As Cullen recalled to me with that infectious enthusiasm with which he coloured his wonderful stories, "[T]here was a mighty barrooom followed by a tumult of gathering of the energies of all Hell, and this magnificent plane and its magnificent pilot roared off the tarmac and straight up into a menacing prairie storm. I could muster only one descriptive word for this awesome spectacle: *Gotterdamnerung!*"

One court day ended early in the afternoon, following the usual fight to at least first blood, and Milt graciously suggested that I accompany him for a viewing of the Sabre. As we drove to the airport hanger in his custom block-long Cadillac, he waxed poetic upon the glories of the freedom of flight, this being the first time he had shared with me his exhilaration at his obsessive pastime: "Oh, I have slipped the surly bonds of earth . . .," he recited Pilot Officer John Gillespie Magee. When we got to the hanger with his golden jet in all its glory, he insisted that I sit in the pilot's seat and don the golden helmet with the cheeky Confederate Flag thereon emblazoned. I humbly complied, feeling a bit of a clot. But Milt was absolutely delighted. He loved to share his happiness with others. I kept the cracks to a minimum, and looked duly overwhelmed. It was overwhelming. The flight deck of this behemoth resembled the set of *Star Trek.* "Any questions?" asked Milt, beaming upon his newest disciple from the foot ladder athwart the fuselage. "Yes," I responded, "where's the 'eject' button?" For a moment, Milt gave me a hard look. I was not taking this event as seriously as the occasion warranted. Looking back, I know that the biggest disappointment Milt had with me from time to time was that I let my cruel sense of humour take precedence over matters close to my friend's heart, a failing that earned me at least one negative note in my service evaluations.[4]

Among the memorable experiences that Harradence had in his flights willy-nilly about North America in his private fighter planes, no story matches the spectacle of his unscheduled landing at a top-secret Strategic Air Command base in the early sixties. One will recall that that was a time of intense North American paranoia about the Red Menace and the pervasive fear that "them Rooskies" would pull off a pre-emptive nuclear strike on selected North American targets.[5] It will be remembered that Milt, as a loner criminal lawyer archetype, found roaming the skies comforting, and Major reports that he frequently would get up in his crate and pop over to Montana or North Dakota so that he could just

---

4. I remain unrepentant. What are friends if they cannot take the piss out of each other?

5. I remember this era particularly well. My older sister had married an entrepreneurial Seattle businessman who had a grand mal if one as much as mentioned "Red China" in his living room. "Don't mention that country in this house!" he would cry. "Children, children, leave the room." My sister confided in me that Seattle had been designated by the Reds as a "prime target." "We're so proud!" she said, stifling a sob.

drop in on pilot pals at obscure hangers in weird one-horse U.S. locations. He liked the company of other men of the air. Frequently, he would fly many miles, land his plane, have a coffee with this or that pilot or aircraft mechanic, then fly his lonely way home again, his innermost psychic dialogue refreshed. On one such foray, of a sudden, he noticed his aircraft to be dangerously low on fuel. He scanned his chart for the location of the nearest airport in order to make an emergency landing, and broadcast a "May Day" alarum. He noted that the nearest landing strip was a classified S.A.C. airbase. Harradence broadcast his intention to make an emergency landing on the emergency frequency over the base and was specifically warned off by the military, in no uncertain terms. He was directed to a small civilian airport which was a feasible landing place. Deaf to compromise, Milt set down at the S.A.C. base. He made the landing successfully. He had barely taxied to a halt when his Mustang fighter was completely surrounded by armoured, tracked carriers mounted with .50 calibre Brownings, which in turn were pointed directly at him by helmeted security personnel. "Get up outta thar with yer hands in the air!" a loud hailer barked at him. Milt demonstrated that he was unarmed, and he and his plane were escorted by this armed convoy to the top-secret aerodrome building. Milt was marched in armed custody to the office of the Commanding Officer. He was a Southern gentleman of charm and experience, and he took an instant liking to Milt. When it was finally established that Harradence was who he said he was, the following dialogue ensued:

Milt: *"I'm headed for Harlinger, Texas."*
Q: *"What are you going to do there?"*
Milt: *"I'm going to take part in an air show."*
Q: *"Who is sponsoring it?"*
Milt: *"The Confederate Air Force."*
(They looked at each other as though they thought he might need a saliva test.)
Commanding Officer: *"Why didn't you land at Union Airport?"*
Milt: *"Sir, would you expect a Confederate officer to land at a Union base?"*

They repaired Milt's navigation equipment and fuelled him up, then drove him into town for the night. The next day, there was a parade back to the P51: a lot of the pilots had flown this aircraft previously and wanted to see it.

On one occasion, Milt convinced his partner, the late John MacPherson, also a formidable barrister, that Milt should fly the both of them to a meeting in Edmonton in a rented two-seater crate. Milt delighted in telling me the story that the nervous MacPherson, strapping himself into the co-pilot's seat, was horrified as Harradence, receiving the go ahead from the tower, cried "Okay, m'boy, here we go!" as he covered his eyes and bore down on the throttle. MacPherson survived the trip, but took the Pacific Western Airbus back to Calgary.

I did a similar jaunt with Milt a couple of years later. It was a single-engine job, and we were going from Calgary to Edmonton for a meeting. I confessed to some considerable nervousness at being up there in the wild blue yonder with my mentor at the controls. I had no doubt whatsoever of his skills and experience as a pilot; what concerned me was that he was a prodigious inhaler of bacon and eggs, and I was struck by a sudden pang of fear at the thought that all that cholesterol might suddenly finds its mark, clog the warrior's arteries, and I would be left "up there" like David Bowie's *Major Tom*. As we were passing over Sylvan Lake, I said to Milt, "You know, what would happen if…? I mean… you're feeling okay, aren't you?" "What d'you mean by that, m'boy?" "Well… suppose you were to get sick up here, or something…?" Milt scoffed. "Not a problem. They'll talk you down." Would they, indeed? Fortunately, the theory was not put to the test.

I observed elsewhere in these pages that A.M. Harradence was a devotee of the late and great General George S. Patton, Jr. There are uncanny similarities between Harradence and his idol. Both had the romanticized Napoleanic fixation that their manifest destiny was victorious combat: they were War Lovers. They were fantastic poseurs: Patton's ivory-handled pistols and Milt's arsenal of personal sidearms. They revelled in the dandyish sashes, baldrics, ribbons, stars, and garters of Heroic Office: Patton's four-star full-dress cavalry accoutrements and Milt's Honourable Colonel's gladrags. These were star-spangled men. Both derided "pansies" and cowards, detested the bureaucratic mindset of dotty or more cautious superiors. Each in his own unique, gawdy style was flamboyant, munificent, courageous, madly ambitious, self-aggrandizing and, when put down or reprimanded, full of injured innocence and madly suspicious of the perceived conspiracies of inferior men being mounted against them. They were indeed larger than life but also, at their most dramatic, in those moments of full flight, quite hard to take and impossible to reach with reason.

Milt's favourite film of all time was and is *Patton* starring George C. Scott. There were indeed memorable occasions upon which one has been hard put to distinguish Milton Harradence from George C. Scott from General Patton from John G. Diefenbaker. Milt has actually been mistaken for George C. Scott on several occasions, both the *voice* and the *look*. A.M.H. was in good or bad company, depending to some extent upon your view now of Richard Nixon then.

In his article in the February 8, 1996, *London Review of Books*, "Over the Top," Michael Howard reviewed Carlo d'Este's *A Genius for War: A Life of General George Patton*. Mr. Howard notes that that particular film "brought Richard Nixon great consolation during the lonely watches of the Watergate nights." He notes that "for many in the United States he [Patton] remains the Great American Hero, who like all such heroes (including Rommel) was underrated and betrayed by an incompetent and politicised High Command." Sound familiar?

Other passages from this article are worth quoting:

> Even as an infant, George could hardly wait to gird on a sword and join them in Valhalla ... from the very beginning Patton forced himself to succeed... to fulfill what he increasingly believed to be his destiny — to exercise the highest of commands. He had to create an artificial persona, and he spent his life doing it. The courage had to be constantly displayed and tested....
>
> His sanity was seriously in question. As S.L.A. Marshall, the most judicious of American military historians, put it: "any man who thinks that he is the re-incarnation of Hannibal or some such isn't quite possessed of all his buttons."

Howard notes:

> ... the undeniable fact that Patton was a fascinating, complex, odious, loveable, highly intelligent, foul-mouthed, courageous and unique monster, who but for the two World Wars would have drunk himself to death, broken his neck on the hunting fields, or ended up in an insane asylum. The British (especially the Scots and the Irish) produced figures like that in the 19th century. Few survived the First World War.
>
> Not only did he need a war: perhaps the United States needed a war as well, to provide a legitimised outlet for his ferociously destructive energies.
>
> He has, alas, left his avatars; not many persons in the United States Army but plenty on the fringes. With the end of the Cold War their occupation is, also, dangerously gone. All are mad; but none can possibly be so splendidly, gloriously and, in his context, usefully mad as was George Patton.

Mr. Howard also observes that the young George Patton had "neither the physical courage nor the commanding presence that he would need" for his later accomplishments and exploits; Milt Harradence had both the physical courage and the commanding presence in spades *ab initio*, but not the opportunity, being thwarted by first cousins of those who did dirt to General Patton. In retrospect, it is too bad that Milt did not bite a couple of his commanding officers. I am sure that today he wishes that he had.

With the advent of television in the fifties, the hilarious Sid Caesar became a household word, as they say.[6] Among Caesar's weekly offerings on the goggle box was quite often a parody of a silent movie. One such, and the funniest of the genre, was his and Mel Brooks's send-up of *The Four Horsemen of the Apocalypse* and *All Quiet on the Western Front*, wherein the wretched protagonist, portrayed by Caesar, is condemned to the World War I trenches and is part of a doomed squad who are to propel themselves "over the top" and into the face of the enemy's machine guns. The men are admonished by their officer: "Alright, men, get ready to go over the top. We'll do this in alphabetical order. You first, Aard-

---

6. Actually, as Shakespeare said, of course. See Hank the Cinq.

vark!" Caesar gnashes his teeth in the silent movie tradition, and mutters some desperate last words, which flash on the screen: "Lucky Zazzlefratz!" He pulls himself over the rim of the trench, starts to run, and is mowed down. Well, if Milt had been in that squad, I have no doubt that he would have jumped ahead of Aardvark, would have considered *himself* lucky: Death or Glory for King and Country!

As with many an intrepid commander of men at arms in times of turmoil, Harradence was a conspiracy theorist of the classical school. He had another memorable experience in skies across the border: this time, he had popped over to Montana when his single-engine fighter developed "engine trouble," significant engine trouble. He was in the Vampire jet, on his way to join his biker friends and planning to land at Billings, Montana. On the downward leg, as he dropped his landing gear, the whole aircraft started to shake and the cockpit filled with smoke. Milt shut down the engine. There is no ejection seat in the Vampire, and one cannot bale out because one's legs would be removed by the stabilizer bar.

In a feat of pilotage, Milt was able to dead stick the plane and himself safely to land. Subsequently, Milt and his American allies examined the engine for the cause or causes of its sudden failure in flight: the bearings had let go, dropping the turbine blades down into the shroud. Later on, not having any intelligence in the matter volunteered by a tight-lipped Milt, Major enquired of him as to his conclusions.

Milt looked grim, his eyes narrowed; all he said was, "they knew exactly what they were doing."

CHAPTER FOUR
Death or Glory

The difference between death or glory is often but a fraction of a second.

– *Introduction to* The Gunfighter *starring Gregory Peck*

TO DO JUSTICE to the heroic aspirations and tragic ironies that permeate the Harradence chronicles, both reality and perception—or, if you like, man and myth—require the lush scoring, fortissimo, of the *Ring of the Nibelungen*, in particular, *Gotterdammerung*. Wagner's masterpiece, twenty-eight years from conception to completion—it seems to take that long to listen to it—is the only epic whose scale and majesty could provide the appropriate context. Milton Harradence would be right at home hob-nobbing with this or that god or hunking down to a mess of victuals and a friendly assay-at-arms or two with other warriors, all wearing those smashing horned helmets and tin vests, brandishing anti-personnel axes, spiked clubs, and a variety of sharp striking instruments, the while being waited upon by adoring Amazons wearing tin breast plates and braided plaits.

Milt's *leitmotif* was, "We've got no choice!" With that, he rushed into the Jaws of Hell, which were guarded by this or that draconian old brute of a Red Judge, Alberta version.

To carry the analogy to its logical end, no one who knows Milt could envision his going gentle into that gathering gloom. Rather, still fulminating "Death before Dishonour!" although mortally wounded, he will be borne on a flag-draped battle shield by eight captains (four more than Hamlet, the sad Great Dane, and two more than Siegfried) to Valhalla, roses all the way, while the Universe blows up like Chernobyl to the hundredth power. A great panoply of northern lights, courtesy of Loge and Calgary Power, will illuminate the western reaches of the universe, larger than the Toronto Skydome's roof and eclipsing the milky way and spelling out *Per Ardua Ad Astra* ("through adversity to the stars," the RCAF version of *The Ride of the Valkyries.*)

The other analogy that naturally comes to mind, given the western setting, is that of the *High Noon* breed of principled loner.

The way of the criminal lawyer is lonely. It is the way of any solitary gladiator. They tolerate the company only of other like-minded loners. Thus would Milt fly his fighter plane alone, like a knight errant on a sacred quest, to Great Falls. There, he would land and have coffee with other knights, then fly home. The round trip probably cost him four to five hundred dollars a sortie.

I call this "combat loneliness." I think of my friend going there all alone, and sometimes I wish at the time I had been more sensitive and less derisive, and simply—once in a while—let him talk about it, so he would know he was not the only one who suffered from the syndrome. Only those who engage habitually in combat for a livelihood can recognize this and understand it. Lonely indeed are the brave.

But not *completely* alone. One remembers a comment by Morley Callaghan, quoting Ford Madox Ford: "'No writers can go on living in a vacuum.' It took me some years to discover how true this was; not just for writers, but of all men who would stay alone in their hearts. There must be someone somewhere you count on for approval, someone whose praise would be dear to you. When finally there is no one you might as well hand in your ticket."[1] For Milt, there was Catherine. For me, Bernice. Thus, our innermost psychic dialogues had common cause. That is why he of all individuals I would want to call "friend" struck such a deep and responsive chord in me from our first meeting.

The most charming story about Milt is of his first meeting with his future wife. In Calgary at the end of the war, a group of kindly matrons sponsored a soiree for the young servicemen who had

---

1. *That Summer in Paris, ibid.*

volunteered. We have already noted that Milt had immediately volunteered to join The Few, but had to wait in Canada because, as Allan Bennett observed, there were far too many.

The band struck up a sedate schmaltz. Spotting the lovely Miss Catherine Richardson sitting with her mother across a vast expanse of ballroom floor, the uniformed Milt marched stiffly over to her, bowed, and asked, "Ma'm, may I have the honour of this dance?" Her mother refused the invitation on Catherine's behalf. A formal introduction, however, was made and accepted. Milt was later invited for tea. I am sure that he proposed on bended knee, but only after asking for his intended bride's hand in marriage from her father, Dr. Richardson.

Knowing my friend, I think how smitten he must have been, that shy young soldier who did not like social settings, and how excruciating it must have been for him to negotiate that entire ballroom floor in his new, squeaky boots, to meet his future bride, only to be refused the honour of the dance. Life's like that, sometimes. But it all turned out well in the end.

Milt and Catherine Harradence have always been as devoted to one another as Captain Sir Richard Francis Burton and his wife, Isabel Arundel. Captain Burton never went anywhere without his life's companion and soulmate, Isabel, "a clever, capable woman, self-reliant in difficulties, with a pretty sense of humour … "[2]

Theirs was the type of devotion we see in a letter of Oliver Cromwell to his wife, in one of his "rare expressions of personal emotion": "Thou art dearer to me than any creature."

People like Harradence are born out of place and time, in his case about a hundred years too late.

Born sixty years earlier in England, he would have ended up in Captain Scott's forsaken tent, all hope almost gone. His feet so badly frost-bitten, and mindful that his selfishly remaining alive deprived his stalwart uncomplaining companions of needed rations, Milt would surely have ducked out of the tent into seventy below and gale force winds with Captain Oates: "I may be some time." One line in his diary would be addressed to his parents: "It

---

2. Edward Rice, *Captain Sir R. F. Burton*, Chas. Scribner's, New York, 1990.

is a far, far better thing I do now than I have ever done. It is a far, far better rest… " Here, mainly because his frozen fingers fell off, the message abruptly ends.

Born a century earlier, Milt would have fought with distinction in the Civil War—with the Confederates, of course—earned a field commission, harried Sherman's flank as he burned and bruited his way South, then headed out West with his motley band of renegades. Following a stint of buffalo hunting, robbing the odd bank with generous distribution to the poor, and learning the Way of the Pawnee, the Colonel would have turned up in Dodge City with Masterson and Earp. When the showdown came at Tombstone, Milt would have strapped on his pearl-handled peacemaker with "We've got no choice!" and ended in a blaze of glory at the O.K. Corral. Alternatively, taking the left fork out of Atlanta, he might have teamed up with The Man With No Name or even with Yul Brynner in Mexico. The simple peasants would have planted him with all due ceremony at Boot Hill while a Mariachi band played *Requiem for a Gunfighter.*

Another way of characterising Milt—if one were to be swayed by the romantic school, which puts more emphasis on the chivalric and less upon the mercenary aspects of the Profession of Arms of the Medieval Knight Errant—would be to draw the parallel of the impoverished, landless, third or fourth son of a robber baron of the feudal caste who, by distinguishing himself in battle and tourney, faithful service and god-fearing uprightness (with a relaxation of these rules if rapine and pillage of the peasantry was all that was at hazard), rose to become a peer of the realm.

The role model for the aspirant is given by Philippe de Navarre in *Les Quatre Ages de l'Homme,*[3] which informed the progress of Milton's ancestral clones:

> In his youth, a man should use without laziness or delay, his prowess, his valour, and the vigor of his body for the honour and profit of himself and his dependents; for he who passes his youth

3. Ed. Marcel de Freville, Société des Anciens Textes Francais, cited in Painter, Sidney, *William Marshall, Knight-Errant, Baron, and Regent of England,* Barnes and Noble, New York, 1995.

> without exploit may have cause for great shame and grief. The young nobleman, knight, or man-at-arms should work to acquire honour, to be renowned for valour, and to have temporal possessions, riches, and heritages on which he can live honourably ...[4]

In practise, this Prince's admonition to the squire or novice to place emphasis upon adherence to the teachings of God and the Christian Church and upon the honour and protection of women (translation: rich female heirs to landed domains), was observed more in the breach than the performance. Indeed, the embattled Henry II and his suzerain, Louis VII, had barely kissed and made up their unhappy differences and both taken the Cross in a joint vow to rid the Holy Land of the *disbeliever* (translation: the people lawfully entitled to it), when they once again declared war on each other. This for our purposes is irrelevant, but like Phillippe de Navarre, I never miss a chance to educate my readers.

In regard to the god-fearing and women-protecting aspects of Knight-Errantry, A.M.H. was actually a paradigm of the idealised Galahad-Lancelot-Percival School. War and combat was his great business, but he conducted his vocation with more than a due regard for the traditional moralities, civilities, and courtesies.

With Harradence, chivalry was far from dead.

A typical day in the life of the Knight-Errant's vocation is described graphically by the biographer of Don Pero Niño, a knight of the fourteenth century:[5]

> Knights who are at the wars... are forever swallowing their fear ... Ware! Who goes there? To arms! To arms!
>
> With the first drowsiness, an alarm; at dawn, the trumpet. "To horse! To horse! Muster! Muster!" As lookouts, as sentinels, keeping watch by day and by night, fighting without cover, as foragers, as scouts, guard after guard, duty after duty. "Here they come! Here! They are so many—no, not as many as that—this way—that—come this side—press them there—news! News! They come back hurt, they have prisoners—no, they bring none back. Let us

---

4. Having, in the case of the average baron, acquired them dishonourably.
5. Cited by Barbara W. Tuchman, *A Distant Mirror: The Calamitous Fourteenth Century*, Ballantine Books, New York, 1978.

go! Let us go! Give no ground! On!" Such is their calling.

Well, on balance, not unlike a typical day in the life of A.M. Harradence, Q.C., courtroom warrior. Such was his calling. He also bore an uncanny resemblance to the grim-faced twelfth century warrior fief-holder portrayed by Charlton Heston in one of his better films, *The War Lord.* Certainly, when Milt was at the helm of his golden flying machine, he imitated Charlton Heston's navy pilot in *The Battle of Midway* to the life. (The probability is that the scene was staged with Heston strapped to a chair in the studio which was, the while, being agitated by a couple of stagehands. He was told by the director to look up, down, left, and right, similar to the instructions barked at one by an ophthalmologist's tortureagent as she administers the pre-examination eyedrops.)

It should be noted here that Milt's philosophy of Death or Glory, particularly the self-destructive aspects, reared up in the business world. The lure of the corporate boardroom—principally its power—had a transient but intense appeal to Milt over a brief couple of years. I mention a couple of his ventures only *en passant.* I remember seeing Milt's phizzog one ear, one nose, grim and corporate—held forth in the public prints as a new director of some short-lived steel company. He also served on the board of a life insurance company. Both these corporate honorifics pale in comparison to his investment in a factory that produced vibrating easy chairs, those indecorous monstrosities that never made it into the Metropolitan Museum of Modern Art. This last was a source of great amusement to Milt's acquaintances, particularly as he set one of these things up in his office and insisted on demonstrating it to visitors.

The heady world of commerce was ill-suited to his reckless temperament, and *vice versa.* Also, Milt could never survive in a dog-eat-dog milieu; he was far too honest and far too trusting. The commercial ventures that he did invest in were often disasters. Milt had a tendency to embrace the pitch of this or that anxious huckster for a completely improbable adventure in the nature of a trade and arrive home not merely excited but transported. It was the *adventure* part that appealed to him. Again, he was born a hundred and fifty years too late. One can readily envision him, with coonskin cap and long Brown Bess musket ("Hawkeye" to his confidantes), piloting his caracel of hides out of Hudson's Bay or striding across the plains with Anthony Henday ("My dearest Catherine: today we saw more lilac trees. Here, we shall found a metropolis. The ways of the Plains Indians are instructive. As ever, your loving, etc."). The commercial side of the transactions was best left to others. Milt would have been better off financially had he restricted his economic adventurism to purchasing lottery tickets.

Milt's frequent nemesis in the criminal courts was Chief Crown Prosecutor Edward P. Adolphe, Q.C. They enjoyed a symbiotic relationship similar to that of Pat Garrett and Billy the Kid, Sam Peckinpah version. Or, in similar vein, the wily *Chauvelin vs. Sir Percy Blakeney* (see Chapter 6). They both did a deal of glowering and growling at each other, but there is the genuine mutual respect of the professional gunfighter to their long adversarial relationship. When Edward Adolphe's daughter was called to the Bar, it was the Honourable A.M. Harradence, Justice of Appeal, who presided, and sitting with him *en banc* his old friend/enemy the Honourable Judge E.P. Adolphe. There was a brace of barristers, the stuff of legends, a professional pride of lions!

In selecting and commenting upon a number of A.M.H.'s cases for this book, I did not necessarily choose only those that were his "greatest," as do burnt-out musicians their "greatest hits album." What I looked for was a cross-section of combats worthy of this record. Milton Harradence was programmed equally for brilliance and for disaster. This was also said of Edward Marshall Hall, K.C., whom Milt resembles in some superficial and other more significant ways. Certainly, like Hall, K.C., Harradence, Q.C. trained and prepared for any case he undertook as assiduously as for a major military offensive: his vigour and determination often in the teeth of certain defeat were Churchillian, and even if the cavalry did not arrive on time he always soldiered on. It is truly a pity he was not given another war of some sort early in his life.

I repeat Milt's famous expostulation, "We've got no choice!" There was an ethical position behind this unequivocal statement.

This was not a mere rhetorical device for dramatic emphasis. This was commitment to the cause of the client, no matter how uncomfortable or unpopular.

That being said, to be honest, I always thought we had a *number* of choices. One was to plead guilty. But the client was always "innocent until proven broke," which phrase Leo Collins enjoyed putting to Milt. Further, in the early stages of a criminal litigation the suggestion to Milt that the client or clients should "cop a plea" almost affronted my leader. There were, of course, exceptional cases where an early guilty plea at the first reasonable opportunity was the best strategy and one at which Milt was also a master.

Going into combat with Milt was about as close as one got to siding with the English at Agincourt with Henry V. Here is an apt parallel to the might of the Crown against a rag-tag band of the defence; not only the might of the massed fifes and drums of the RCMP. or the Calgary Police, but the bias of that instant credibility that any Crown Prosecutor has with an Alberta Judge arising out of the "long-standing love affair between the Crown and the Bench."[6] Crown counsel and Crown witnesses were always well briefed and well fed. Everyone was spoiling for the blood of the accused, who has lied in any event to his counsel and who is done like a dinner. So everyone would be against us from the outset. And I would say to Milt as we would be struggling into the battered armour and the rusted chain mail in the barristers' robing room, "I don't know, I don't like this one, Milt. It doesn't pass the smell test. I think we're in trouble."

At that point Milt would jump on top of the locker, and deliver the following peroration:

> He who hath no stomach to this fight, let him depart/His passport shall be made and crowns for convoy put into his purse/We would not die in that man's company/ For he today that sheds his blood with me shall be my brother!

Of course, we won all the battles and lost the war. The accused

6. John Mortimerism.

were almost invariably convicted. As Balzac said, "In times of adversity intelligent men turn to philosophy." And Milt was always philosophical. "Well," he would say, surveying the wreckage and the carnage in the wake of the last futile charge, "look on the bright side, m'boy. It took those two crooks four years to steal the money. It took us four days to get it from them. They went to jail, we didn't. Never lose faith in the system, m'boy!"

So we regrouped the forces and we lived to fight another day. I lived to fight another day with the man who was and still is the fastest gun in the West, this quintessential barrister who continues to be an inspiration as a hero to all members of the Criminal Bar, both senior and junior.

In an era when it was less fashionable to have heroes and more correct to have some wishy-washy nerd as a "role model," Milt still had his heroes. Prominent among these was the superlative legal showman, Gerry Spence, who wrote *Gunning for Justice* and posed for photographic studies of his grim phizzog surmounted by a huge twenty-gallon cowboy hat capping the locks of Wild Bill Hickok, his upper superstructure draped with a fringed buckskin jacket of the mountain-man genre. His own accounts of his exploits rendered the likes of Belli and Bailey mere shrinking violets. Milt used the same scowling countenance to telling effect, as I have recorded.

Milt had heard Gerry Spence speaking at an advocacy seminar in Toronto and often repeated Spence's put-down of state prosecutors, whom he called "sanctimonious pukes." Roared Spence with derision: "Every night that poor state-employed sap goes home and crawls into bed with his fat wife who rolls over away from him saying 'you let Gerry Spence beat you again!'"

Milt loved that line. He would never call one of counsel instructed by Her Majesty the Queen a "sanctimonious puke," but he must have thought it from time to time. At the height of combat, there is nothing worse than an opponent who whines and snivels his way into an argument. One wants a warrior on the other side, in accordance with the Samurai tradition. When I was a junior Crown, then working my way up in the civil service to the coveted Solicitor Four with the title Chief Crown Prosecutor, I seldom encountered sanctimony among my fellow prosecutors. The Alberta Crown had a reputation for fairness and objectivity; nobody was rolling over, but one put the facts before the court, assisted the court with the law, and then one sat down. From my early days with the Crown, I hope that I was able to learn from my leaders the full significance of the phrase "the Queen is the Fountain of Justice." That is, the Attorney General has as much a duty to stand between the citizen and the State as he/she is responsible for the public's observance of the Rule of Law. I wish that today's young prosecutors could sit in for a day to hear the Stilwells (Bill and Dave), Edward Adolphe, or Paul Chrumka put in a case for the Crown. How vividly I still recall Francis O'Sullivan as the Attorney General in *The Winslow Boy* accepting the Petition of Right from the defendant's counsel, Sir Edward Carson, with the words "Let right be done!"

I suppose today's smart young advocates, particularly the anxious fledgling Crown Prosecutors who are resembling and emulating more and more their U.S. cousins, would find these remembrances of things past to be quaint or even risible. Sometimes when I speak on advocacy to various groups of law students or young lawyers, many of them look at me and shake their heads: "Poor old boy. I think he's losing it." But that was the milieu in which Milt and I practised.

That era up to, say, the mid-seventies, was captured in a more down-to-earth way by Bill Stilwell in his letter to the *Law Society, C.B.A. Newsletter* of April 1996, which I have previously quoted in this book. Mr. Stilwell's comments on the acumen of and honourable conduct of the members of the criminal bar of that day are apposite here. And I quote further:

> While we are on the subject of ancient history, let me digress. In those days there was a known and recognizable criminal class. They knew they were criminals, and the police knew it, and the Crown knew it. When we met on the street we would greet each other and sometimes stop and talk.
>
> And, lest it be forgotten, let me record that in those years young police constables patrolled the streets and back alleys of Calgary and Edmonton at night, on foot, alone.

> The big difference is that drugs were almost unknown then. By 1969 there was a large number, almost a class in fact, of young middle-class offenders against the drug laws. The conventional wisdom, particularly as dispensed by the R.C.M.P., was that smoking marijuana led directly and inevitably to heroin addiction and death. I've been told, by persons whose opinions I value, that this kind of dogmatism produced a generation of young people who had lost respect for the law.

This was the reasonable time before Crowns became victim's advocates and defence lawyers became conspiracy theorists. It was an era in which both the Crown and the accused were better served by real professionals who left their own personal hang-ups and psychoses behind in the locker room before they went into court.

Between 1966 and 1968, I did a fair amount of crime. I received much encouragement, particularly from Milt, who went out of his way to refer clients as well as to bring me in on cases. From early on, he would discuss the details of prosecutions he was defending, trusting me with his confidence and respectful of my views. In this, I was greatly honoured, especially as I was never associated with him in practice or employed in his office.

In October 1968, I joined the Crown Prosecutors' office at Calgary, which then was staffed by the following *illuminati* of the Calgary Bar: Edward Adolphe, Q.C.—El Supremo; Paul S. Chrumka, Q.C.—El Secundo; E. Leo Collins—my Best Man in 1969; Daniel C. Abbott, Q.C.; Louis Charlebois; Walter R. Christensen; and me. The not-so-magnificent seven!

For the five ensuing years, I learned my trade and the rules of evidence on my feet in the criminal court five days a week. I served only six months in traffic, whereupon Adolphe, Q.C., assigned me my first homicide as a Crown. In those days, seven or eight trials or preliminaries per day was not an unusual load. Moreover, the Magnificent Seven prosecuted all causes in Calgary and a number of towns within our judicial district, latitude from Banff to Gleichen, longitude from Olds to High River, and all the circuit points in between.

For four of those five years, I met Milt in combat two or three times a week, sometimes more. This was mortal combat: the engagements were violent, often to the professional death. First blood was never good enough. And he was good. He is the best I have ever known. And out of that period came a cherished friendship and a comradeship that does not require description. I do not think I could describe it. In this business, one starts out fearing one's chief adversary; as things go along one then respects and admires the adversary; in the fullness of time, the toughest adversaries become close personal as well as professional friends. That is what advocacy is all about to the barrister.

In the fifth year, after a brief stint of cleaning up the crime in Medicine Hat, I ended up as Chief Crown Prosecutor at Red Deer, gaining an office with a rug and two subordinates. I clashed with Milt less frequently, but on occasion he drove menacingly into town in his latest block-long motorized extravagance to conduct the defence of a high-profile case. Harradence kept a frenetic schedule and seldom if ever arrived anywhere on time, and particularly not for Magistrate's Court. However, he was always prepared, always resplendently attired, and always had a unique argument or spin on the law or facts which, if not persuasive, were usually well received by summary Courts not noted for patience or innovation. Above all, Harradence was impeccably courteous to the Court, to witnesses, and to opposing counsel no matter how junior. Everybody noted this. I recall three of the last old-style police magistrates in Alberta, Judge Wulliver of eastern circuit, Judge Yates of Drumheller, and Judge MacDonnell all remarking to me on separate occasions upon the unfailing courtesy with which this top Alberta Q.C. always addressed their Courts.

Cross-examinations by Harradence were always instructive, usually effective, and sometimes awesome. One practice I learned from him was *never* as a cross-examiner to seek an adjournment even if the evidence-in-chief has been totally unexpected. As soon as the Crown Prosecutor said, "Thank you. Answer my learned friend," Milt was up and immediately put his first question, the question that told the witness, "I know something about you that you did not think I knew." The effect upon the trier of fact, whether Judge or jury, was always positive. There was no dithering, no pausing, no fussing with papers or looking about for help: Harradence was up and at the witness right now. Death or Glory.

This is a practice that I have followed for the balance of my career at the Bar. I have the greatest contempt for counsel who seek adjournments to cross any but a surprise expert witness. Plotting the strategy and content of cross-examination is the most arduous of the hours one puts into pre-trial preparation. All reasonable permutations of the evidence of the opposing witness must be anticipated in light of the facts of the case and the client's instructions which must be put to that witness. The test is *not* that tired old cliché, "never ask a question unless you know the answer;" the test is "never ask a question where you cannot *handle* the answer." The cross-examiner must be ready, *instanter*, and for all possible dodges and wheezes, prevarications and inventions. I learned that, too, from A.M. Harradence. It helps also if you can play chess.

Milt did not like juries. This must be a surprise to those who have been impressed by his presence, sense of timing and theatrics, movie idol looks, voice delivery, and wardrobe. There are three reasons for his reticence to commit his client to the tender irrational mercies of twelve *National Enquirer* readers:[7]

First, Milt always got a sympathetic hearing and often spectacular results from most Judges sitting alone. The reason for this is that Judges of the day, both High Court and Magistrates Court, were of a much higher calibre and astuteness than today's crop of bar politicians and obscure solicitors.[8] The Alberta Supreme Court Trial Division, in particular, with one or two lamentable exceptions, was manned by astute former barristers who had practised with distinction for years in the Courts. Milt could play them like an old violin, as could his Edmonton opposite number, Buzz McClung, Q.C. These Judges were as experienced and canny as they were able; you got right to the point before them, and if you had a point they took your point. If you did not, it was best

---

7. Another apt gem from Stilwell the Younger.

8. See my forthcoming diatribe *The Judicial Image*, coming soon to a book store near you.

to save your breath and speak to penalty.

Getting to the point in Court is illustrated by the following appearance by Harradence before Mr. Justice Cairns. Things had not gone well for the defence.

The Judge: *Mr. Harradence, I'll listen to you on conviction. But what I really want to hear you on is sentence.*
Milt: *Very well, M'Lord, as to penalty.*
Judge: *Well now, Mr. Harradence, I know perfectly well what you're going to say. Why don't you let me say it for you...* (whereupon the Judge set out the mitigating factors).
Judge: *What did you think of that?*
Milt: *Excellent, far better than I could have done.*
Judge: *I don't know about that, but it had a lot more authority.*

Second, there were very few juries in criminal causes, and virtually none in civil cases. That is because the then Chief Justice of the Trial Division in the fifties and sixties decades, tough but brilliant, went out of his way to discourage juries. They were expensive and cumbersome, and it took far too much time for his Judges to care for them, feed them, instruct them in the law and on their duty. In short, it was worth your life to elect trial by jury. If you did, you could count on the Chief, assigning the trial to himself or to a like-minded hardrock and the jury being instructed accordingly. Three examples of judicial influence on the unwelcome defence jury election are as follows:

(1) In a jury trial, the trial Judge, unimpressed with the Crown's first witness, said to Leo Collins who was prosecuting, "Have you got anything better than that, Leo?" Leo responded that there were more witnesses for the Crown, and called his second witness. Halfway through that second witness's testimony, the Judge winked both at Leo and the jury and said, "I see what you mean!"

(2) Some trial judges were particularly astute at seeming in transcript hindsight to be charging the jury dispassionately, but you had to be in their court to not only hear but see them

reviewing the evidence for the jury in the charge. "Of course," they would say, as if tolerantly, but rolling their eyes, "you've heard the evidence of the accused. Now you can give it such weight as you see fit." This was usually the kiss of death. Of course, the latter sort of sneer read innocuously in the appeal transcript, thwarting any bid for a new trial.

(3) A homicide I was prosecuting, defended by Web MacDonald, Jr., was put down before an experienced Judge. Webby had elected a jury to try this case of murder. The Judge called us in the backroom. "Webby," said he, "do you intend to stick with this jury?" Web allowed as how he would. "Very well," said the Judge, meaningfully, "but if he is convicted the sentence will reflect the solemnity of the election." Webby thought for a minute, then said, "Come to think of it, Judge, I think I'll re-elect to Judge alone." I jumped in, "Oh, I think this is a good case for a jury, Judge." The Judge was having none of that. "Bag your lip, Evans," he said, "Webby, you've just made the first smart move in this trial." The accused was convicted of manslaughter after a brief trial and given a reasonable sentence.

Harradence well knew the views of the Supreme Court Trial Division on juries, and to my knowledge in the time that I practised against or with him, he stayed away from juries. In fact, most defence counsel wisely shunned juries for a couple of decades, and it was really only in the late seventies that criminal juries in Alberta became a common affliction for the new Court of Queen's Bench, which they both richly deserve.

Third, and personal to Milt, he had as a young lawyer elected a jury in a case of what was then called rape. Edward Adolphe prosecuted. It was an all-male jury. Milt was full of enthusiasm for the cause of his innocent client and gave the jury a blockbuster address. He threw in Lord Hale's famous admonition, "Rape is a charge easily to be made, and hard to prove, and harder still to defend by the accused be he ever so innocent," and all the usual uplifting boilerplate about presumption of innocence and reasonable doubt, wrapping his client in the Canadian flag, and ending with the thunderous peroration: "If you're men, you'll acquit!"

The jury went out for about half an hour and came back with a verdict of guilty. Milt's flabbergasted reaction could be heard all through the courtroom: "Pansies!"

If *that* isn't Death or Glory, nothing is.[9] From then on, Milt was very leery of juries in any event. Even capital murder in Alberta could in those days be tried by a Judge alone, and Milt stuck with that preferred mode of trial.

In fact, it was a lengthy out-of-province jury trial in 1978 that tilted him toward the Bench. Milt and Allan McEachern, Q.C., defended a massive fraud case in Vancouver which went almost eight months—February to October—in front of a jury. Most cases of that nature in that jurisdiction were set down before juries and the Crown could insist on a jury for that level of offence. Milt thus reluctantly found himself commuting from Calgary to a protracted jury trial over an eight-month period. The jury convicted. Milt had become quite ill with the flu during the trial, and it took a great toll of him, as away-from-home games always do. Thus he was ripe for the telephone call from a flunkey for the Justice Minister which I deal with in detail in Chapter 10.

The philosophy of winning the day spectacularly or, if defeated, going down fighting with all flags flying, permeated all of Milt's efforts, both within and without the Courtroom. My previous analogy of Don Quixote is apt, for frequently the causes undertaken with the highest motives were as misdirected as they were hopeless. Thus in his political life he flailed away at the people he should be supporting and aspired to join forces with the gang he should be attacking. The death-or-glory mentality rides either with the Light Brigade or with Marshall Blucher: Here comes the cavalry!

The Harradence tradecraft visage of the classically clenched jaw, piercing unblinking eyes, and thunderous Old Testament brow most probably started off as pure theatre, appropriated from any number of Hollywood dreadfuls or military or political poseurs who are an easy guess. However, it is too facile to dismiss

9. A celebrated Toronto defence counsel and close friend of Milt's, David Humphrey, once gave a one-line address to a jury on a similar charge: "If that's rape, I'm a monkey's uncle!" He added, "While the resemblance is amazing, I ain't." The jury acquitted.

this smouldering look as a theatrical prop turned on and off at will like a politician's smile or a woman's tears. Milt did indeed view certain events and behaviour with genuine approbation: any disrespect to women, loose morals generally, denigration of the Royal Family, contempt of Parliament, "pansies," cowards, quislings, academics (see "pansies"), conscientious objectors (see "cowards"), perceived threats to his family, the evils of drink, people who were "out-of-shape." There is too long a list to list.

He vigorously defended all manner of genuine villains, and would literally defend to the death their rights to the presumption of innocence and a fair trial with proof beyond a reasonable doubt the never-shifting burden of the prosecution. Having noted that, I observed that Milt, too, was human: I remember a conversation he had with Leo Collins. Leo was prosecuting a particularly vicious rapist whom Milt was defending. During a break in the trial, over coffee, Leo asked Milt: "What if the victim had been *your* daughter?" Milt's reply, accompanied by that trademark wrathful look, was as chilling as it was sincere: "There never would have been a trial!" He was dead serious. They finished their coffee and went back to the fray.

Because Milt was portrayed in the public consciousness as the champion of the underdog, lunatics presented themselves at his office with alarming frequency, seeking advice and direction—and possibly a cure—from the Oracle. He was courteous to such pests, and even kind to them. He went out of his way to direct them to agencies that might be able to assist them. On occasion, he referred them to lawyers specializing in the field of their problem. Most of them simply needed psychiatric help or intervention and probably incarceration at the local nuthouse. Still, Milt had tremendous patience with the botched, which forbearance I did not share. Once or twice, with the best intentions, he referred a troubled paranoiac or schizophrenic to me, and I lasted but a few minutes before I threw them out of the office and put the dogs on them. Of course, there were times when Milt had to take a firm hand with a potential client spouting abject prevarications: I remember in particular his rising wrathfully from his chair while some lout recited a tissue of fabrications, took him by the front of the shirt and said, "You little bastard, you tell me the truth or your head is going through that fucking drywall!" The truth then proclaimed itself.

I particularly note that A.M.H. always had the courage to speak out loudly on controversial issues where more prudent poltroons or socially/politically ambitious sycophants were content to remain silent. An example is his famous letter to the Chancellor of the University of Calgary. (Appendix.) I have tried to follow his example and have preached to law students that sometimes it is the duty of a barrister to speak out for unpopular causes and it is equally the duty of the Bar to stand in support of that principle, even if they disagree with what he/she has said.[10]

That is particularly applicable today where the citizen who speaks with courage and conviction against the received ideas and collective ignorances that constitute "politically correct non-thought" is immediately branded a pariah: always by wacky or self-serving pressure groups but never by the too-silent majority.

Milt knew all about professional glory, and about professional death. He said, "You leave a piece of yourself in the courtroom every time you walk out at the end of a criminal trial."

Sometimes, you leave a really big chunk. Haemorrhaging, you stagger about the streets, maybe a bit pissed, incredulous that other citizens go about their boring functions and boring lives, that "life" at large carries on, all apparently oblivious to you and to the contest you just finished, or, rather, that just finished you.

I have had a few cases like that. We all have, those of us who fight so hard and so alone.

In one of my earlier cases I had gone toe to toe for fifteen rounds with the best counsel (save Milt) that I had ever encountered. My client was convicted. As with a number of typical cases, with similar allegations of fact that demanded more than a mere supreme effort, I had laboured late at night and toiled in Court all day without let-up for several days. I was exhausted, demoralized, broken. After the conviction, I had visited my client in the city cells, known as the "bucket," and amid the screams of the derelicts

10. See "Fear and Loathing in Edmonton and Camrose: *Law Society of Alberta v. Harry Midgley*," vol. XVIII, 1980 A.L.R., p. 520, by this author, if you are serious on this point.

in the tank and the stench of vomit and urine and feces and the indifference of the lifer guards, I tried to be as optimistic as I could in the face of the several years he was looking at. Before he was led off to those years of penal servitude, he thanked me for my efforts.

Later that evening, about 9:30 *p.m.*, I found myself wandering the streets alone, totally wired on caffeine, mumbling to myself. I had simply stalked out of the cells and walked about in a circle and in a semi-stupor. I had an aching discomfiture of guilt, that I should be in the office, working all night, again, still. Bernice had to go to some soporific university function that she couldn't duck. At the LRT station at First Street, puke boulevard, I spied a pay phone.

I called Milt at home.

"Yaas?"

"Have you eaten?"

"Yaas."

"Do you want to eat again?"

"Why not."

"I need to talk."

"Get over here."

I got over there. Milt took one look at me.

"Have you been drinking, Cliff?"

"No, but I'm about to."

We went in his Caddy to Mamma's, a table in the corner, coffee for Milt, a pail of dry red for me, and Milt let me talk while he listened. I didn't have to explain anything. He knew all too well. The only person you can talk to when this sort of thing happens is another criminal lawyer, someone who's been there, someone who's taken the punishment and got up and been knocked down again and again, but who remains standing in the ring at the end, bloody, disoriented, weaving, wounded.

Then he spoke and I drank—and listened. Then he took me home. "You'll be all right, m'boy. This, too, will pass."

It did. But I never forgot that evening, never forgot that he was there when I needed him most. If I had called him from Toronto and he had been in Calgary, he would have hopped the next plane. That's the kind of man, the kind of a lawyer's lawyer, that Milt Harradence is.

It wasn't all losses. The turning point in my career came in 1979 when A.M.H., unable to accept a brief due to a conflict, recommended me to Allan McEachern, Q.C., who sent me a client and the most challenging case I had yet encountered. In 1983, following commission evidence in Bermuda and a six-week trial with a jury, my client was acquitted of fraud by a jury of his peers. The complainant was a corporate citizen whose name ended with the suffix "ex." My then law partner, Dwayne Rowe, called it "______ Exlax," because "if 1.2 million of your alleged money ended up in a numbered Swiss bank account, you'd shit too!"[11]

Early on, a sonorously omnipotent drone factory, acting for the alleged corporate victim, moved against my retainer. Its taciturn counsel and some four-eyed student attended without notice at my Chambers, the latter scribbling notes, while Mr. Big Time importuned me that I harboured "tainted funds." He wrote me a Big Firm prototype snotty letter, stating "you use these funds at your peril." I retained Jack Major, who wrote Mr. Big Time and told him in no uncertain terms that he threatened me, his client, at *his* peril. Of course, the snotty big firm ran the other way as soon as the big boys brought out the baseball bats. Nothing more was heard from Mr. Big Time and his henchmen until months later when he telephoned me to tell me that I was going to be named as a defendant in ______ Exlax's lawsuit, and I reminded him that the Law Society rules prohibited a solicitor calling a party represented by counsel, and he could take the matter up with my lawyer. Of course, they never did sue and it was the usual big firm bully threat which they never carry through. Meanwhile, one of Mr. Big Time's sleek partners stuck his patrician nose in my office one day. "Slumming?" I asked. "I understand you'll be reversing some fees soon," he sneered. I marked him for the first snot to be put to the wall in the New Era.

Subsequently, my client was acquitted at trial. Very handily, I might add. I wrote Mr. Big Time a letter:

---

11. Nothing that Dr. J. Colis Browne's 'Chlorodyne' won't cure; it was used by the Nazis as a 'truth serum' in *The Falling Sparrow*, copyright R.K.O. Radio Pictures, 1940, starring John Garfield and Maureen O'Hara. I commend this terrible film, and the cure, to their lawyers.

Dear Sir or Madam,
Re: 'Tainted Funds'
Well??
Yours truly.
P.S. Fuck you.

The Big Firm has no collective or individual sense of humour. There was no reply.

Milt, now on the Bench, called me after the acquittal:

"You know I can't talk about this case."

"I know."

"Savour it, m'boy!"

I did.

Chapter Five

The Loneliest Man in the Courtroom

The harbour gapes, but not
For you; arms open, but they are not yours.
Along your road you will meet no great crowds
Going with gongs to greet you returning
With your gains to an ungrudged conclusion.
Only expulsion, obloquy, and shame
Watch for you. Welcome them. Welcome too
Smooth malice, smarmy enmity, these things
Will shape and sharp your purpose, stroke and strop
Your temper, point your passionate aim. So,
Gay in the midst of growling things, you'll go
Tip-toe, songs in your ears, sights in your eyes,
That blind and deafen you to compromise.

Direction to a Rebel
By W.R. Rodgers

PART ONE
One Of, But Yet Above

MILT WAS A UNIQUE criminal lawyer. Everybody knows that criminal lawyers are loners, secret boozers, womanizers, rebels without causes, bullied kids at school now getting their own back because they were always picked last for the team due to their athletic incompetence, crippled survivors of broken homes, losers, or "cherries" who could not get dates even with dogs ("Fuck off, asshole!"), recluses, misanthropes, curmudgeons, misfits, wackos, and other extracts from the encyclopaedia of solicitors' received ideas. Harradence did not fit into any of these categories.

Except one: the criminal defence lawyer *is* the loneliest man/woman in the courtroom.

Where *does* A.M. Harradence fit into the scheme? What forces in his youth and early development drove him inexorably to the top of the Criminal Bar? We know he shared our revulsion for the team mentality and for playing team sports. Milt was a boxer, a light heavyweight champion of Saskatchewan; I was a fencer, sabre the weapon of choice (if one could not kill the opponent, one could hope to at least maim or mark him for life). Milt's idea of a workout was a daily solo pounding of "the heavy bag." Major and I ran, alone, miles every day (Major has solemnly recorded his mileage for the past fifteen years; he has circled the globe at the equator once, plus or minus.) Milt detested golf and the golfing mentality, which loathing he and I share. Milt has eschewed service clubs and imbecile lodges; we are agreed that members of those infantile organizations do themselves a lot more good than the purported good that they do, as they hand over cheques to politicians and grin for the photo ops. I have already pointed out that all of Milt's personal aeroplanes were single-seater fighters. His idea of a good time was solo stunt flying. His calling was combat. His recreations also were *mano a mano.*

> ... [Hemingway] had never been really good at team sports. He liked skiing and boxing and fishing and shooting, the solitary sports. The things a man could do alone.[1]

Now, that is interesting. Can you imagine *Siegfried* playing on a *team*? As I recall, A.M.H. never required his mates to be team players. He could not stand such nincompoops. He was, as I say, the classic loner. That is why his apparent need for political office, for leadership in politics, is inexplicable: it is contra his entire nature. It is another inconsistency.

The best example of the attitude of Milt and his brother, Clyne (as at this writing, a pre-eminent Q.C. who has practiced forty-six years at the Criminal Bar in Saskatchewan) toward team sports was the fateful day that a two-seater light plane buzzed the half-time entertainment at a packed university football stadium and a life-sized dummy stuffed with ketchup was dropped from the air with surgical precision into the midst of the strutting majorettes. Years later, William Stilwell was to pronounce this daring dive-bombing a fitting epiphany for "small town baton twirlers" and for the sorts of morons who go to—or worse, play at—football games.

One hears the term "lawyer's lawyer." It is used and sometimes over-used by lawyers to describe a few other lawyers who are a select breed. It is a self-defining term of the highest approbation, somewhat akin to the now obsolete "ornament to the Bar."

Harradence most certainly was a lawyer's lawyer. It is indeed a compliment to the ability and ethics of a professional that other professionals of the same discipline turn to him or her in times of their own personal jeopardy.

Having said that, and having been myself so complimented from time to time, I must also stipulate that fellow lawyers are among the most demanding, aggravating, and myopic of clients. I have had a bellyful of bent or stupid legal brethren, always rationalizing and explaining, and I now think twice and carefully before accepting such a brief. Lawyers in trouble, particularly lawyers in

---

1. Callaghan, Morley, *That Summer in Paris*, Stoddart P.C.L., 1992, Toronto.

trouble with the criminal law, are, generally speaking, the first to complain about you and the last to pay you. And they almost always did it.

There is a third category of lawyer who seeks legal advice, usually too late, although the sub-group is not discrete and slops over into the first two categories. This is the theretofore purportedly high-principled and certainly highly successful, highly placed and highly paid solicitor who has been caught and accused of villainy by the gendarmes or by the Law Society. Social friends and business and professional associates, co-religionists of his church and fellow swells of his exclusive clubs, his partners at the Big Firm—if any of them know yet—are all aghast and unbelieving: "Smedly? Screwing a goat? Egad! *Completely* out of character! (It *was* a nanny?)" The client is tearful, remorseful, in denial, innocent, framed! "Do they know who I am?" Unfortunately, they do. His wife, the usual country-club model with the "Mount Royal" bob, Chanel suit, and expensive accessories is "fully supportive." She conducts herself reservedly in his presence as if he had just contracted some loathsome and contagious skin disease of venereal origins. She tries to smile gamely, the while silently lamenting the blow—not to *his* career and fortunes, of course, but to hers.

All of this points up the accuracy of H.L. Mencken's aphorism: "Self-respect is the sure feeling you have that no-one, as yet, is suspicious."

When one or other of these poor fish lands on my doorstep crying for help, my first consideration is whether he (or she) had ever snotted my wife or myself in their other life. If so, the hourly fee is increased exponentially. Then one listens to the entire story, sitting Sphinx-like with hooded eyes watching the wife's face. Then one leans back, folds one's hands together, pulls one index finger sharply so that it makes a sickening "crack," and one then intones, "these charges, if proven, could have grave repercussions." One owns the moment, their wallets, and their futures.

I observed to Milt Harradence, on occasion, if I enjoy this fringe benefit to the practice of criminal law, we warriors being so reviled by those proper solicitors and their ambitious, suburban, prototype wives with the upturned noses and the latest trendy fashions, surely he must revel in it. But Milt, such a kind and compassionate man, demurred. I am sure that he seldom if ever charged a colleague for legal advice.

In one notorious case, he brilliantly defended a fellow lawyer on a serious charge, spending large amounts out of his own pocket in preparation for the trial. The member was acquitted handily. In or about 1963, A. Webster MacDonald, a colourful larger-than-life character at the Criminal Bar, was arrested and charged with fraud. Web had stepped on more than a few establishment toes since his arrival in Calgary in the late fifties from Nova Scotia, and he had made the worst kind of enemies: pedestrian-minded local poobahs. He undertook many unpopular causes and defended with vigour a disreputable class of clientele for whom no one else would act, Clarence Darrow's "damned."

The charges arose out of some alleged corporate maneuverings. The facts are fully described in the late A. Webster MacDonald's own autobiography, published in 1994. Web died untimely, but he had a full and exciting life. He was expansive, outrageous, a raconteur, a poseur, and—at times—exercised questionable judgment. For all that, he was kind, hospitable, well read, with a charming wife and delightful family of redoubtable sons. He loved the law, he loved life. He was always very kind to Bernice and me.

The case was a local sensation. I had just commenced articles after law school (see Chapter 2 for the flavour of the horror), and the arrest and pending trial were constant subjects of firm gossip, most of it denunciatory of Web and no doubt declaimed with downturned mouths. It was rumoured that the cops in the bunco squad drew lots as to who would get the fun of arresting Web, and the four exultant winners elected to descend upon this desperado at his office in broad daylight without prior warning. If this is true, it is a blot on the escutcheon of the cops. The arresting officers also took the precaution to block the rear entrance of Web's office with a squad car, presumably to prevent flight.

Web always kept his keen sense of humour, even in his darkest hour. At the ignominious booking-in procedure, he responded to the usual cryptic questions from the grizzled desk Sergeant:

Q: *Any marks?*
A: *No.*
Q: *Any scars?*
A: *No.*
Q: *Any moles?*
A: *No. Gentlemen, you see before you the perfect physical specimen.*

Harradence undertook the defence of his beleaguered colleague. To prepare for the trial, Milt closeted himself for a week in the Palliser Hotel, sacrificed his wedding anniversary, and literally memorized the myriad documentary exhibits and the corporate minute books. At the trial, before Mr. Justice Milvain and prosecuted by Edward Adolphe, Q.C., Harradence's cross-examinations of various corporate drones and solicitors were as close to brilliance in technique and mastery of subject matter as one could ever come in a lifetime of counsel work. He simply demolished the Crown's star witnesses. A. Webster MacDonald was acquitted, Milvain, J., holding there "was not a tittle of evidence" implicating Web at the end of the day.

Harradence charged no fee to Webster MacDonald. Professional courtesy, he said.

On another occasion, Milt made an absolutely incredible deal for the son of a prominent colleague. The scion of that patrician family, a recently qualified solicitor who had struck out on his own (so to speak), had been criminally charged with theft from his trust account. Milt convinced learned Crown counsel that, provided he entered an unequivocal plea of guilty before the judge of his choice, they would take their chances in that forum and the Crown would not appeal. The prosecutor, being an agent, bound the Attorney General. In short order, Milt had the client up before a compassionate beak, entered the plea, and despite the admonitions of the Crown reminding the court that a prison term invariably followed the event of conviction in these circumstances, the accused solicitor got off with a suspended sentence. The Crown, bound by the deal, could not appeal. Public criticism was exacerbated by a concomitant case proceeding at roughly the same time in Edmonton, wherein another top Alberta litigation counsel pled a similar accused lawyer guilty, won a suspended sentence from a sympathetic judge, and was met with an instant Crown appeal resulting in a sentence of one-year imprisonment. It says much for Milt's ability and persuasive powers that he was able to accomplish this miracle, the client virtually walking. Milt was not only the master of the courtroom confrontation, but as well the most accomplished practitioner I have known, along with Buzz McClung, of the timely guilty plea in the appropriate court.

I have no doubt whatever that the parents of the client were suitably grateful. There is a personal footnote to add; however, I shall not mention the name of the accused, to spare his family and particularly his father, whom I greatly respect. Sometime prior to the events I have described, I knew the client very slightly; he had always purported to move in Calgary's version of the better social circles. He was finishing law school or had just started in practice when my wife and I encountered him by chance at a trendy but tasteful Vancouver restaurant. As we arrived, this person and his entourage were leaving. He stopped, nonplussed: "I didn't expect to see you in a place like this." He was absolutely serious. The fact that peasants like ourselves had the effrontery to presume to dine at a restaurant favoured by clientele of his class was clearly outrageous to him. I took no satisfaction at his conviction, although the irony of his becoming clientele of a different class was not lost. I made a point of attending in the courtroom to watch the proceedings, the Harradence technique always part of my learning process. Later that day, quite inadvertently, I attended at Milt's chambers for a meeting, and there was the client, sitting in Milt's office as I entered. "Oh," said Milt to his client, "do you know my friend Evans?" The client nodded shortly but would not look at me. "We've met," I said, giving him a hard look. That was our last encounter.

Robert Black, Q.C., one of the most able and eminent members ever to practice in Alberta, on receiving his fifty-year certificate from the Law Society of Alberta at a brief ceremony, said: "All that you have at the end is your family and your reputation." So true. The client was lucky he had his family. How frequently we find that the sons of exceptional men are bent, weak, or churlish; they come "misshapen from the potter's wheel," with faded genes.

One of the crueller myths about Milt, stoutly refuted by his brother, Clyne, is the fairy story that Milt charged exorbitant fees. In fact, ironically, that sort of lie can only enhance a criminal lawyer's reputation; I have always taken the greatest pleasure in similar myths about my fees.[2] But the fact is, criminal lawyers do not make a fraction of the earnings of the robber barons who populate the upper echelons of the large law firms, who routinely hammer their clients with "success" fees or "premium billings," which is just a fancy form of larceny. The fact is, also, that Milt Harradence took on many cases and causes where his remuneration was a big fat zero. No one ever gives credit for that sort of contribution to the law, especially the envious and small-minded non-Criminal Bar. But his colleagues knew the truth.

It was Milt who told me that a judicial brother of his on the Court of Appeal expressed not only shock but dismay—to anyone who would listen—on hearing about my alleged fees in a homicide case. How he heard, and why he lent an ear, is a mystery, it being none of his business. This judge had been a civil litigator in, of course, a large firm. Milt took exception to these defamations and advised that he straightened his fellow judge out, on my behalf, and I am confident that he did. But just for good measure, when I heard that at long last my prayers were answered and that sanctimonious pomposity was dead, I found out where he was planted. Early one morning, picking my way through the markers and sepulchres of assorted stiffs in the graveyard "... waiting for afterlife to begin. Dressed in Sunday best, arms folded across chests, blessed and waiting,"[3] I found his grave so that I could be sure that the gentleman was dead.

Milt once got $50,000 for a guilty plea from a grateful client, and he earned every penny. But for every large fee that he was entitled to command, he gave his time away to others on many

---

2. I once charged an accused about $4,000 for a five-minute application, and I was underpaid. This person duly complained in a public courtroom to the judge about my fee, which was widely reported, doing my reputation no end of good.

3. "During the War" by Shannon Borg, *London Review of Books*, 9 May 1996 edition.

occasions for nothing or for a pittance. This petty scandal-mongering about criminal lawyers' purported fees underscores a fact of law practice: the criminal lawyer at best experiences an ambivalent relationship with the self-styled social leaders of the Bar. On the one hand, the criminal lawyer is at bottom always mistrusted by his or her other colleagues, simply because he/she acts for criminals, and this is perhaps understandable: it is difficult to esteem one who habitually represents thugs. On the other hand, there was a wart: there is a grudging admiration of the criminal lawyer by the rest of the species, because it is common knowledge that it takes a particularly independent person and a remarkably tough-minded and just plain tough person to make a career of defending the pariahs of society.

To know this man, Harradence, was to like him. First and foremost, he was a gentleman, and I mean a *gentleman* of the old school, who was courteous to his elders and scrupulously polite, courtly, in fact, to women. He had great respect for those who had earned their way, more than what he mustered for those who were in positions of power but whom he knew to be poseurs and pseuds, although he was actually too kind as well as too courteous to give that lot the back of his hand. He had reverence for institutions such as Parliament, the Legislature, the Court (and, by implication, some of the obvious boneheads who populated the court; nevertheless, they were judges, and deserved respect), the Armed Forces, and, for all I know, General Motors. He had heroes (more on this). He believed in the Rule of Law. He believed in discipline, self-discipline, and the imposition of discipline to bring out the best in a man or a woman. He was a staunch traditionalist. He was a devoted husband and family man. He was the most loyal and true friend that a man could have. He was, indeed, a man's man and a woman's protector, quaint as that notion may be today, and even heretical. He was passionate about the issues that Canadians are expected to be passionate about, including freedom, free speech, straight talk. Most importantly, in pursuing his profession he genuinely believed that every person no matter how base had a right to be presumed innocent and to be vigorously defended.

It was easy for me in our early associations to conclude that he had perhaps too much respect for authority, but the more I got to know him the more I realized that he had a healthy disrespect for *blockhead* authority, which I shared.

There was, however, one thing about my friend that has always concerned me, and I have told him so on occasion: he had (as I note in Chapter 10) a need for the affirmation and approval of others, but too often sought it in the adulation of the mob or of his inferiors. He never had any problem gaining the respect of others, but he always seemed to want more. I cautioned him, I'm sure with presumption being his junior, that he should guard against seeking the respect of others because frequently all that one achieved was respectability. And that could be a curse that would dog one to the grave. See, for example, Charles-Joseph Panckoucke, pre-revolutionary publisher in Paris who was "always torn between commercial acumen and a yearning for respectability."[4]

Lady Wilde, upon being asked to receive a young woman said to be 'respectable,' replied:

> You must never employ that description in this house. Only tradespeople are "respectable."

As to Milt's need for the adulation of others, two incidents will suffice as typical illustrations:

For some reason I had to meet Milt at a hostelry south on Macleod Trail about noon one day, and he suggested we have what the lower middle class calls 'brunch'. We had our discussion and something to eat, and as we were leaving, a prole rose from a nearby table, approached Milt, and said, "I just want to shake your hand. You're the greatest." At about the same time, Milt noticed someone at another table giving a sort of wave, yelling, "Best to you, Milt. Go get 'em!" This was at the height of the separatist nonsense. Milt blew up like a balloon, and as we left the hotel, he took my arm excitedly and exclaimed, "They know me. They know me!"

On another occasion I was with Milt at the courthouse coffee shop in Edmonton. He was engaged in defending a much publi-

4. Schama, S., *Citizens*, ibid., at p. 177.

cized case, the trial of an Edmonton lawyer charged with chicanery. Jim Redmond, Q.C., a very prominent Edmonton trial lawyer indeed, came up to the table and greeted us, saying to Milt, "From the news reports I see you're working your usual magic." When he left, Milt whispered to me excitedly, "Did you hear that? They know me up here, too."

Now, there is nothing wrong with being complimented and recognized. In Milt's case, such recognition was well deserved. However, he never suffered much from humility, and such encounters did not encourage him in his later years to renounce ambition and pursue the verities.

What was totally unique about Milt Harradence is that he was always able to function brilliantly with a foot planted firmly in both camps: the Establishment (which he coveted) and the Outlaws (of which he was the clear and undisputed top gun). This was not a case of him being Heathcliffe Milktoast by day and Zorro by night: Milt belonged to both groups as a charter member, twenty-four hours a day. This presents as a curious and unprecedented contradictory phenomenon.

I think I can explain this perplexing contradiction. No esoteric analysis is called for, and my initial diagnosis of societal schizophrenia may be erroneous. Brian Beresh, who introduced me at the 1995 Edmonton Criminal Trial Lawyer's Association dinner in honour of Milt, was shrewd enough to observe that I probably knew Milt better than anyone in that crowded room. That was not taken by me as a compliment; I think it was fact. Assuming it is fact, I shall give my views. In my view, Milt Harradence is a very private person. I believe, moreover, that he is in the social context a shy person. He presents as far more at ease in the company of men than in mixed company. The company of groups of women was simply anathema; witness his dislike of summer residence at Gull Lake and all that that entailed. I think that social obligations are a chore for him as they are for me and most criminal lawyers. People liked Milt and were drawn to him, but he seldom if ever wished to listen to them and did not consider the average human blank an appropriate recipient for what he had to say. Milt has always been an engaging conspiracy theorist, and one simply cannot make loose conversation on matters of national security with coffee claquers. Milt felt out of sorts among jolly crowds of fun seekers, and thus avoided holidays and holiday groups. He has never been able to relax among people and would ostracize himself. Every time, over years, that I have attended a mixed social function and encountered Milt, he and I have always ended up in the corner for the duration, plotting in low tones. Milt arrived not always on time, as he liked to make a dramatic or at least an imposing entrance. He would shake hands stiffly with the hosts, then would invariably be searching for exits like a trapped tiger. If I was around, he would gesture meaningfully to me, and I would drop what I was doing or saying and get over there, the same way he expected me to jump out of bed at two or three *a.m.* when he called and ordered, "This is big. Get down here." At once, Milt would abruptly break off whatever he was doing and steer me into the nearest corner. Milt always wanted his back to the wall. There, we would happily plot for the balance of the evening, until he would suddenly say, "Let's get out of here." If any third party ever approached our huddle, Milt would make it clear he or she was intruding on urgent affairs of State. I have no reason to believe that Milt behaved in any other fashion at other social functions, whether or not I was there.

He was always notorious for tardiness or even the occasional inexplicable no-show at his own home when he and Catherine were entertaining. On one such occasion, pre-occupied with a case, Milt arrived for his own hosted dinner as the guests were retiring to the drawing room for coffee at about ten *p.m.*, stalked through the circle of close friends to the kitchen, asked for and wolfed down a plate of bacon and eggs, then departed at once for the office. He said not one word to anyone.

I am firmly of the view, however, that Milt did not attend social events because of societal or family pressure. A phrase he often used was, "You've got to be *seen*." Therefore, he wanted to go, but he hated it when he got there. This paradoxical tug-of-war also permeated his need to seek political office. He was elected an Alderman of the city, and detested the job. (Milt would not be the type you could call at night because the garbagemen were late or there was an unfilled pothole on your street). He was elected a Bencher of the Law Society four times; he had no time or tolerance for the detailed committee work, the endless convocations with tedious windbags eternally debating the Law Library closing hours or yet another amendment to the rules respecting solicitors' trust accounts. But for the cut and thrust of discipline hearings, Milt had no truck with any of it, least of all the obligatory social side. He had to run, he had to be elected, he had to win: but he always knew in his heart what H.L. Mencken had articulated about seekers of success, particularly seekers of public office, "Most... are miserable both along the way and at the goal."

In sum, Milt was a textbook renouncing achiever. The Harradence ambitions in the larger political sphere will be canvassed in their own chapter, *poste,* but Shakespeare is always instructive: "Enjoyed no sooner but despised straight/past reason hunted; and no sooner had/past reason hated, as a swallowed bait."

So what is the conclusion? Milt Harradence *was*, and *is*, Bicycle Repair Man.[5] He could handily be cross-examining a star witness, hear a fire alarm, note children cowering on the roof of an adjacent burning building, leap from the courtroom to the other building with a single bound, carry the children to safety on his back, deliver them to their weeping mother with an "aww, shucks ... (saluting)... all in a day's work, Ma'am (pronounced 'marm')," return to the courtroom and apologize to the judge for his unscheduled absence, win the case, donate his fee to the Kiwanis apple drive, and still be fresh and impeccably turned out and sartorially splendid when he met Mrs. Catherine Harradence and the Ronald Reagans or somebody else important at the Glencoe Club dining room, sip a half glass of wine the entire evening, deliver a riveting speech on Western Alienation, then retire early, to be awakened at two in the morning by an anonymous client claiming to be the Pretender to the Throne of Ruritania so that he could then call me with, "This is Big!"

That is a typical day in the life of A.M. Harradence, Q.C., before he went to the Bench.

---

5. See Monty Python: "And now for something completely different!"

PART TWO
The Harradence Gang

MILTON HARRADENCE was the top gun. He was Number One from the time that he first strapped on his Colt 44 long barrel to the time that he hung up his spurs and took the judicial ermine.[6] This, to a professional gunfighter, is the equivalent of taking the gaspipe rather than going down on the street and out boots first.

Milt has many genuine friends and a huge overwhelming circle of acquaintances and admirers, both within and without the profession. It is my personal opinion that very few people really knew Milt in the sense that they took any trouble to enquire as to what made this magnificent man tick, what made him run, what drove him to Death or Glory, what were his true colours, what were his secret fears. He was very close to his immediate family, of course, who all loved him and knew him intimately as husband and father, a side of him that is very private and is no one else's business.[7] The great majority of all of the others were on the periphery, always open-mouthed and openly admiring but also perplexed: they might be his clients or his partners; they might do business with him or belong to the same club; they might preside over his trials; they might sit with him on the Court of Appeal and sometimes achieve a consensus; they might also fly planes or shoot guns or work out or whatever. The shrewder or more perceptive of them might discern this or that superficial characteristic of this man. But, by and large, they did not know Milt at all.

The barristers described in this section are the only persons of all of the above who, in my view, were properly recognized as members of what we still call "the Harradence Gang." These people knew Milt Harradence. None of the rest qualify for this exclusive club. I'm not sorry about that; you can't have opinions about facts.

---

6. When news that A.M.H. had been appointed to the Court of Appeal hit the street, an eminent contemporary is reliably reported to have cried out, "That makes me Number One!"

7. One of the few times that Milt actually said anything about the toll his career took on his family was at his gala retirement, when he said that he had only one regret and that was that he had not spent more time with his family and if he had it to do over, he would make that time.

The test for membership is the same as that which entitled one to wear the Colours of any biker club: the following persons, briefly described, were the guns that A.M. Harradence would have called upon to back him at the O.K. Corral.

1. THE HONOURABLE J.C. MAJOR

Jack Major appears often in these pages. He and Milt had parallel careers. There are two fundamental quintessentials of advocacy: knowing when to keep your mouth shut (see Chapter 4) and accurately defining the lynch pin issue in the case. Major has always been an examiner-in-chief and cross-examiner of few but effective words. Further, he is the most accomplished and confident reductionist I have ever encountered. Both of these qualities are in evidence in his terse, focussed judgments on both the Alberta Court of Appeal and the Supreme Court of Canada. Would that some of his colleagues would line up for lessons.

Major was Milt's contemporary at the Bar for twenty-eight years. They were also close friends. They articled at the same firm. Major practised for his entire career of thirty-four years with the sonorous successor to Chambers Might Saucier etc, etc. (later the pre-eminent Bennett Jones Verchere, also known to me as Bennett Jones Versailles), becoming, along with Don Sabey, Q.C., the head of its litigation department and one of its principal rainmakers. He was equally at home in civil litigation, criminal litigation (acting as special Crown Prosecutor for the Attorney General's Department as well as frequently acting for the defence) and administrative and disciplinary tribunals. In that sense, he was in his day simply the best all-around advocate in Alberta. A few others have come close in certain spheres, but no one else could combine those abilities with the down-home practicality and cruel wit that he added to the combination.

Major, who wrote the introduction to this book, deserves his own book. I am confident he thinks so, too, and as J.C.M. always gets what he sets out to acquire, he will get his book in due course. I hope it is not written by some sycophant, because there is much about Jack that provides one with great amusement. This is warm humour, because Jack Major in his time has been my mentor, my colleague, my lawyer, my neighbour, and my not uncritical friend. I hold him—as I do McClung and Milt—higher than most men.

His one visible vice is golf. I fear it will be his undoing. He refuses to heed my admonitions that the pursuit of this stultifying pastime destroys brain cells.

Three professional colleagues have always been there for me when I have needed help or a sounding board or an ear (not necessarily sympathetic, but empathetic): Milt Harradence, Jack Major, and John W. McClung.

2. WILLIAM V. STILWELL

William Stilwell, certainly the most brilliant criminal lawyer ever to practice in Alberta, has always been one of Milt's very closest confidantes. He was a contemporary of A.M.H. and a counsel worthy of his steel, as well as a charter member of the Harradence Gang. Stories about Stilwell are also the stuff of legend. Stilwell, it must be noted, has always been the classic loner, an old-style gunfighter right out of Jack Palance's finest cinema portrayal *The Lonely Man.*[8] He was and is madly eccentric, aloof, dismissive of fools and hearty fellows, a devotee of H.L. Mencken, a world-class recluse (the sign at the entrance to his bleak northern ranch reads: "Visitors are not welcome; Trespassers will be shot"), a "doctor of broken hearts" self-styled. He dislikes television, computers, children, noise, stupidity. He lives alone on a remote half section at Dapp near Slave Lake, Alberta, where he repairs the roof and writes poetry. He is the best amateur flat picker I have known. He drinks his sippin' whiskey neat, no ice. He raised and trained quarter horses. His co-enthusiast in matters *Equus caballus* was the laconic loner, ex-Communist, and scholar of the arcane, Jack Pecover. The following dialogue is typical of Stilwell and Pecover:

---

8. Dwayne Rowe and I got in an elevator with Jack Palance in Bermuda in 1981. He looked big and mean. Rowe said, "I've got a question." Palance growled, "What's the question?" Rowe asked, "How come a big guy like you let a little runt like Alan Ladd beat him?" I didn't know whether Palance was going to attack us. Thank God, he smiled. "I think it was in the script," he said. As I recall, the next time Rowe and I were in the bar, Palance sent him a drink.

Stilwell: *To what do you attribute your skill in harnessing solid-hoofed perissodactyl quadrupeds?*
Pecover: *Rigid adherence to principle.*

Bill Stilwell was the youngest Chief Crown Prosecutor ever appointed in Alberta. He met early on in combat with Milt. A close friendship based upon mutual respect developed over many years. Stilwell on campus at the University of Alberta was a card-carrying communist who experienced Arthur Koestler's conversion about the time he married the daughter of a clothing manufacturer. His first major case was *Pecover v. The Board of Governors of the University of Alberta and Bowker* which he conducted on behalf of his fellow communist, Pecover, when Pecover was refused admission to the law school on the ground that it was a privilege and not a right. There are doubtless other ramifications to this case, but I have as much enthusiasm for reading it as I do any civil case. Pecover and Stilwell, as they say, won the battle but lost the war: Pecover gained admission to the law school but was flunked in his second year, leaving him without the second third of the law degree, and he had to finish his law degree at the University of Saskatchewan.

Throughout his career, Stilwell remained aloof from and disdainful of the mob. Commie or not, he had no time for proletarian entertainments. He did not suffer fools gladly or at all. (Other true stories will be saved for my own memoirs after Stilwell shuffles off this mortal coil.) If Milt was George C. Scott alias Patton, Stilwell was Tom Courtney's Strilnikoff. That's not a bad analogy, either: Stilwell was also a charter member of the Communist Party in Alberta long before denouncing Lenin and embracing anarchy, cash retainers, and Milt's mercenary (with bursts of *pro bono*) metaphysic. As to whether he ever abandoned Trotsky, the jury is out.

Stilwell became a Police Magistrate at a time when they were still called that, and did not take themselves seriously as do today's mostly callow Provincial judges. Elsewhere in this history I quote from Stilwell's recent description of those days. After a number of years on the bench, Stilwell went back to the Defence Bar and undertook quite a number of criminal cases as co-counsel with his friend, Milt Harradence.

Stilwell was a fearless advocate, and I had the pleasure of seeing him tell off the Court of Appeal on more than one occasion. Once, he was so fed up with their thick-headed inability to appreciate his simple point that he threw down his papers and said, "I'm just wasting my time," sat down in his counsel chair, and turned it so that he sat with his back to the Court.

He took little notice of the snivelling of his clients. For example, during a preliminary inquiry his legal-aid client, charged with homicide, kept pestering him from the prisoner's dock with "How does it look?" and finally Bill barked at him, "It looks more like murder every minute."

About 1987, Stilwell resigned from the human race and barricaded himself on his farm at Dapp. He remains incommunicado.

3. JOHN A. MACPHERSON, Q.C.

"Johnny Mac," known to his envious detractors as "Mini Milt," articled with A.M. Harradence in 1964 and later became his partner until his untimely death in August 1986 in a motor vehicle accident.

We were a year apart in entering practice and three months apart in age. We had parallel careers, somewhat like Jack Major and Milt.

I met Mac in combat as often or perhaps more often than I did Milt. Like his partner, he scorned notes, files, appointment diaries, keeping all the essential information on the inside flap of a match cover. He smoked heavily and boozed with equal gusto—a marked contrast to Milt—and was not averse to engaging in fisticuffs with yokels in this or that disreputable tavern. He liked fast cars and he drove them fast, which was probably his undoing.

Mac was an animated, eccentric, frenetic swashbuckler whose ability on his feet in the courtroom was formidable. In those traits and attributes, he did to some superficial extent resemble Milt. This was neither imitation nor mimicry. Johnny Mac's style was personal to him and he had worked it out on his own. Early on, he had branched out into his own area after seconding Milt for a couple of years. He was much his own man, with no respect for authority or seniority. If A.M.H. called him at two *a.m.* with an imperative summons to the ramparts, Mac's usual response was, "Milt, I know it's all very interesting, but fuck off!" This was said with the greatest respect and affection, of course, but Mac was having none of Milt's nocturnal adventurism.

He had a terrific ability to make lots of money and became the consistent top litigation biller of the firm, even eclipsing his learned senior partner. Mac's great facility was in defending most of the impaired and drunken drivers of Southern Alberta. So busy and so successful was he with this speciality that he eschewed most other briefs, and I was the frequent beneficiary of major cases that Mac would not touch: "Not interested, m'boy. It's all yours. Take a big dollar from the bastard. He's in trouble." In most cases, the client was, and I did. I would always acknowledge the referral: "Dear Mac, re: *R. v. Snodgrass*: Thank you for this referral. I thank you, my wife thanks you, my tailor, agent, and landlady thank you also."

We had a close personal and professional relationship over many years, and everybody who knew Mac and practised with him thought much of him. He was brash and a bit of a hip shooter, but a devil-may-care exterior and a flip attitude masked a consummate professional. He was one of the best in the business.

Mac's relationship with Milt was very much closer than most people thought or knew. He was in many ways a surrogate son to Milt, and his death, coming as it did hard on the heels of Milt's loss of his eldest son, Rod, was a double blow that was almost mortal for the then old warrior.

4. THE HONOURABLE BRIAN C. STEVENSON

It is to be remarked that all of the members of the Harradence gang were persons notably free of pomposity, self-importance, and self-delusion.

Assistant Chief Judge Brian Stevenson of the Alberta Provincial

Court is not much impressed with his "Honourable," nor does he take himself too seriously. Also in common with Major and Stilwell, he is dismissive of toadies and twits. Like them, he can be funny and his honed wit can be cruel.

Stevie B. professed to be a Liberal—both small and large L—but I always found his personal political ideology, for want of a better term, to be far to the right of the ubiquitous centre. He spent a lot of his younger life in the fruitless politics of Alberta liberalism, when it was worth one's very life to be left. Stevie actually ran for public office, most notably in the Provincial election against the surging Peter Lougheed in Calgary South, which is as close to a kamikaze plunge as one can get. He made a good account of himself, with his folksy manner, superior speaking ability, and "plain talk" pamphlets depicting him in various snarling poses. I have reason to believe Premier Lougheed respected Stevie for that and for running an ethical campaign and debating real issues. Certainly when Brian applied at a relatively young age for the Provincial Bench he was handily appointed. That appointment was in the gift of the Provincial Progressive Conservative Party, who then as now are not celebrated for appointing their enemies to anything.

B.C. Stevenson made an early reputation at the Criminal Bar and caught Milt's attention. I have earlier observed that Milt was always welcoming and generous to new, young, aspiring criminal lawyers, and went out of his way to help them and to refer work. In addition to defending criminal cases and co-defending with Milt, Stevenson also landed an appointment as Special Prosecutor in narcotics for the Federal Department of Justice. That appointment was in the gift of the Federal Liberal Party, who maintained power in Ottawa for years, and who were also not noted for appointing their enemies to anything.

For a number of years Brian Stevenson, together with Gib Clark and Sandy Park, Q.C. (known as "Clark and Park the Narcs"), prosecuted teenagers for possession of or trafficking in the dread Cannabis and other illicit and contraband substances, including a variety of illucinogens. Business was brisk, Calgary having emerged in the post-Beatles seventies as a gaining drug distribution centre.

Brian made short work of most defence counsel, but A.M. Harradence was his most challenging opponent, as he was mine when I prosecuted. They, too, became good friends from their frequent court clashes.

The while, Stevenson kept his hand in at the Defence Bar. One of his most sensational retainers was the defence (along with Haradence and Stilwell) of *The Barbeque in the Badlands* prosecution. Chief Judge Stevenson told the story to the senior Bar of Calgary at a 1996 reception.

From the text of that address I have extracted the following brief examples of the Milt Harradence style of cross-examination, on that occasion the ruthless frontal attack on a medical doctor at a preliminary inquiry into homicide charges arising out of the untimely death by burning of a penitentiary inmate. As Judge Stevenson reports, Milt decided to question the doctor's professional qualifications:

Milt: *This B.S.c., M.D. F.R.C.P.S.—what are those? Music degrees?*
Doctor: *No, they are not.*
Milt: *Do you have your degrees with you?*
Doctor: *No, they're on the wall in my office.*
Milt: *Pity!*

Over the lunch hour, as part of the theatrical entertainment of the mob in the courtroom, the hapless doctor had to lug his degrees from his office wall into the courtroom to prove he was who he was.

Subsequently, Harradence attacked the doctor's Court identification of the body that he purported to have examined at the hospital and pronounced dead:

Milt: *Now, doctor, looking at this police photograph of the alleged deceased person, are you able to swear that that is the person that you pronounced dead on that occasion?*
Doctor: *Well,...* (hesitates)... *perhaps if I could see the body from the other side.*

At which point, Harradence flipped the photo to the blank obverse and showed it to the doctor:
Milt: *Does that help you, doctor?*

Milt loved to attack medical doctors as well as other "experts." For them, he had the advice of his oft-quoted Judge Irving Younger: "Get yourself a stethoscope, a good supply of tongue depressors, and never go to court."

For some years in our early days, a solemn barrister who shall be nameless, stodgy but very able, appeared for the defence. One time when he was winding up for the "zinger" question to some civilian witness in a homicide, he fired off the tough question with menacing tone and a stabbing stubby forefinger, but somehow the words got spoonerized. I, prosecuting, laughed cruelly. Stevie was sitting beside me waiting for his case, and whispered to me "Solicitor Boot!"

Now, whenever I appear before Stevenson, A.C.J., I rise solemnly and say, "Solicitor Boot for the defence." Stevie nods with equal solemnity, and intones, "Solicitor Boot." We then rollick and wisecrack our way through the case, until at the end stern Judge Stevenson often convicts and slams my lad off to the common gaol.

We still meet occasionally for lunch, which usually consists of a quart or two of Wild Turkey.

5. ASSORTED JUNIORS

Harradence had a knack for singling out a likely prospect from a myriad of applicants every year. Every aspiring trial lawyer wanted to article with Milt. Milt knew what he was looking for in a junior, and most of those legal eaglets fresh out of law school that he chose to work with him went on to distinguished careers at the Criminal Bar. I name the exceptional of them—Alain Hepner, Q.C., Larry Ross, Q.C., Noel O'Brien, Q.C., Terry Semenuk, Q.C., Joe Markey—who carry on and pass on the techniques and the traditions they learned from Harradence, Q.C.

6. PETER TARRANT

As *uber*-gumshoe Paul Drake was to Perry Mason, Peter Tarrant was to A.M. Harradence. This was one of those truly unique working relationships, based on mutual trust and respect, that actually could have been put in a movie. Between 1971 and 1979, there was hardly a case that Milt undertook that did not involve the professional services of supersleuth Peter Tarrant. From the time that Milt went to the Bench in February 1979, Peter and I developed virtually the same relationship respecting the defences I undertook. Tarrant had experience, investigative skills, street smarts, and a perceptive sixth sense that served those who retained his services well. Indeed, Milt's m.o.—and mine as well—was, in many cases, simply to instruct Peter Tarrant at the outset to do a complete investigation in his discretion. We would then await his interim report which, in addition to detailing his interviews with the client and all significant witnesses, developed defence theories and made important recommendations. We were wise to follow his suggestions. In the result, many a sow's ear was turned into a silk purse defense, and both Milt and I can recall many putatively hopeless cases that were pulled out of the fire due to the invaluable information and intelligence unearthed by Peter Tarrant.

Tarrant served in the London Metropolitan Police for five and a half years, and then the Calgary Police Service for ten years to January 1970. Through that period, his twin brother, Ron Tarrant (they were distinguished the one from the other by Tarrant Wet Look and Tarrant Dry Look) accompanied his brother through their mutual police service careers, Ron Tarrant eventually rising to the rank of superintendent in the Calgary Police Service. Peter left the service in 1970 and set up as a private investigator and then hooked up with Milt Harradence, as well as serving an impressive number of other clients, including major corporations.

In 1984, Tarrant was named International Investigator of the Year by the Council of International Investigators. Another major highlight in his career was that in or about 1977, Sir Peter Matthews, Chief Constable of Surrey, U.K., and for two terms the head of Interpol, presented Peter with a Bobby's helmet, which he proudly displays with his memorabilia.

7. OTHER CONFIDANTS

Other confidantes of Milt have been referred to in this narrative. Some had great influence upon him.

Milt's relationship with his long-term partner, Gordon Arnell, Q.C., for example, was unique in that Milt often sought Gordon's counsel on aspects of a criminal cause, even though commercial and corporate solicitor Arnell was not at all engaged in that discipline. Arnell was a quick study and had sound judgment coupled with practicality plus encyclopedic knowledge of law. He was throughout a mainstay of Milt's mercurial career from early days and a close friend.

The Honourable Allan McEachern, the Chief Justice of British Columbia, was present at both Milt's swearing-in and at his gala retirement dinner. The Chief Justice was also present at other major events in Milt's life, including Milt's last major case. Harradence struggled with an uphill-on-broken-glass defence of a mutual fund manager, and McEachern vigourously defended the co-accused, the president of a trust company. Both clients went down for three years, but not before McEachern had penned a series of perceptive limericks commemorating the more vivid skirmishes and personalities of this lengthy and demanding trial. Some of these he read at Milt's swearing-in.

McEachern was also one of those rare barristers we call a lawyer's lawyer. He, like Major, was equally at home in civil and criminal litigation, and after a brilliant career that saw him the undisputed top gun in Vancouver, he went straight from the street to Chief Justice of the British Columbia Supreme Court, and later from there to Chief Justice of British Columbia. As with all such men and women who excel far and above their fellows in their professions, Allan McEachern remains a humble and self-effacing public servant who has dedicated his life to the law. We need about a thousand more of him at any Bar in Canada, but—of course—his breed is all too rare.

He remains a true friend and great admirer of A.M. Harradence.

Milt's brother, Clyne Harradence, Q.C., at this writing has practiced at the Criminal Bar for over forty-eight years. He, too, has embraced that side of our calling analogous to the Profession of Arms, and his numerous courtroom combats in Saskatchewan have been as compelling and remarkable as those of his brother. He has earned as prominent a reputation in his bailiwick as has Milt in Alberta. The Harradence brothers, indeed, as a prairie phenomenon are often spoken of as the dynamic duo (not to be confused with *folle a deux,* although jealous detractors carp in those terms). When the two of them served on the faculty of the National Criminal Law Program,[9] they were a strong draw for registrants eagerly anticipating more showmanship than law. With the Harradence brothers, they got both. The principal antics of the two, which over the years have achieved legend status, arose during their undergraduate days at the University of Saskatchewan. More on this, *poste.*

Mr. Justice Jack Waite ran the civil litigation end of the Harradence Chambers. He always looked upon the Harradence intrigues and accompanying shenanigans with *sang froid,* although from time to time a certain suppressed incredulity glazed his eye, however briefly. After all, Milt's fame and reputation, together with the theatrics, were good for business. Waite built a busy civil end, mostly insurance litigation, which together with a couple of experienced commercial solicitors rounded out a very successful firm.

Notwithstanding that fact, I had always wondered aloud to Milt why he and MacPherson did not simply decamp to the penthouse of the Cosmo Slotnik Building with their entourage of juniors, students and staff, and, like robber barons, fleece the public grandly from such an aerie, unhampered by the larger staff and overheads that burdened the big and medium "all service" mills. But Milt demurred. He *had* to have a *firm,* that is, barristers and

9. Also known as "criminal lawyers' summer camp," the best C.L.E. program in Canada, chaired by Mr. Justice David Watt, under the umbrella of the Federation of Law Societies.

solicitors, all moiling away at all disciplines, even if the simultaneous attendance of serial rapists, fraudsmen, bank managers, and captains of industry in the reception area was as disquieting to the two last categories as it must have been to their attorneys. Of course, the purported distinctions may be entirely academic: bank managers and businessmen are probably right at home in the company of crooks, adhering to the same essential philosophy. I do think that this necessity for the large firm approach in Milt had much to do with his need for peer approval and for respectability, both pre-requisites for entree to Calgary café society and the likes of the "exclusive" Paunchmen's and Golf and Country Clubs. That said, the firm set-up was not seen as a pre-condition for Appointment to the Bench: so far as I am aware, the last thing that anybody thought the great barrister would accept would be a judgeship. Indeed, I recall him to be openly derisive of any such suggestion that he should hang up his spurs. He was one of the princes, probably by universal edict the king. Why give all that up, plus one's hard won independence, to become a common public servant! As Carson, Q.C., advised Wilde, ominously: "We shall come back to that."

PART THREE
A Bencher of the Law Society of Alberta

A.M. HARRADENCE, Q.C., was the first criminal lawyer in Alberta to be elected a Bencher of the Law Society, signalling a breakthrough for the real lawyers in 1970. The Benchers, the po-faced governors of the profession, presented theretofore in successive group photographs as stuffy, poorly tailored, and in most cases unhealthy: too much rich food, too many *matters of grave import*, too little exercise. Milt went on strength by popular vote of the members at a time when the Old Boys probably required their ladies to retire after their black-tie dinners (at the expense of the Profession, natch), then deployed cigars and port and shook their collective jowls over the way the Calling was going to Hell in a Handbasket.

Milt must have been a shock to their sensibilities, not least because he wore suits that fit and did not need two pairs of pants as a selling point. It will be remarked that most of our betters in those days were from the peasant class, but had come up fast in the egalitarian years following the war. This fact, well hidden, made them the more pompous. Christopher Isherwood surely had Western Canada in mind when he defined 'landed gentry' as "farmers who made their money so long ago that their origins have been decently forgotten."

A.M.H. was certainly the proverbial breath of fresh of air to the rest of us, including a breakaway Calgary collegial association of criminal defenders and sole general practitioners styled "the Little Bar." The Benchers broke bread at the Paunchmen's Club with pomp and circumstance; the Little Bar met once a month or so over a soup and sandwich at the Wales Hotel and fumed over, *inter alia,* the depredations and excesses of the Benchers. A Senior Bencher, Q.C., Divers Honours, who had held in his time what Tom Walsh called "the Triple Crown" (that is, President of this, President of that, and President of the Other) once addressed the Little Bar to "respond to their concerns" about some draconian new rule or other. ("Responding to concerns" of the little people was a favourite of the Western barnyard aristocracy, and a big catchword for the Lougheed government as its big credibility booster.) The Little Bar had none of it: when, in response to a telling jibe from the superb (and greatly amusing) barrister Derek Maguire, the Senior Bencher intoned, "Let me say this to you as a former President of the Law Society and of the...," he was booed to silence.

The Calgary "Little Bar" was held in contumacy by the fops and doyens of the large firms. Perhaps the Little Bar were *true* revolutionaries: in the teeth of our betters' mission to have "the great laugh at the expense of the small," at the modest proceedings of the Little Bar, for a short period of time in the history of the Calgary Bar, "the lowly could laugh at the expense of the great."[10]

In contrast to their rich pompous cousins at the large firms,

10. Schama, quoting the author of *Correspondence Secret, Citizens,* ibid. at p. 141-2.

many young criminal lawyers and general practitioners of the day flying solo had modest practices in poor surroundings. Yet the Criminal Bar was always an aristocracy: "... a rich man had no distinction and no real power." Nobody could buy his way into the Criminal Bar the way mediocrities bought their partnerships in the big firms like second sons buying British army commissions, c. 1750 *et seq.*

Prior to the Harradence breakthrough, the Benchers had been a closed shop of old boys (N.B. no old girls) dominated by the large legal mills, who all adhered to an unspoken conspiracy: "You vote for our old boy, and we'll vote for your old boy." Voting for Benchers has always been a loaded sort of popularity contest, with the current differential in favour of the botched having come about only because of the demographic shifts in the backgrounds of the members of the Law Society together with politically correct biases and the gender factor.[11] The system in the bad old days worked the best when the word went out to all partners, associates, and juniors of the large firms from the other large firms: vote only for the large firm slate; do not waste an X on any other candidate, as the less votes for third parties (i.e., those who are not Members of the Club) the larger the aggregate for the slate. The only thing that could break the monopoly was the aberration of a candidacy by a lawyer popular with everyone and throughout the Province; thus Milt was elected on his widely revered reputation for ethics and for successful courtroom combat. Bill Stilwell damned him with faint praise: "Milt, I believe your reputation now extends to the very borders of Saskatchewan."

Some firms fielded the less dynamic partners for Bencherdom. If he wasn't making big dollars, he could at least show the firm flag in the corridors of power. History repeats itself: when my father was adjutant of an artillery regiment in the Second World War, they used to receive communications from headquarters respecting this or that hush-hush big project: "Send your brightest young officer." They always sent the biggest dweeb in the Regiment, just

11. Although it is a notorious truism that so-called empowered women are loathe to see another so-called empowered woman get ahead, they do close ranks against the common enemy, the abusive and rape-prone male.

to get rid of him. That no doubt was the philosophy of some of the firms.

It is important, however, to note that there were other clear exceptions to the old boy rule besides Milt Harradence, for example, Bill McGillivray and Herb Laycraft, who were also the two pre-eminent civil barristers of their day in Western Canada, lawyers *par excellence* and 'lawyer's lawyers,' both of whom became respectively Chief Justice of Alberta. I had a warm relationship with the former and a formal relationship with the latter, but respected them equally as the best of all of us.

One should add in fairness that otherwise on occasion the large firm's nominee coincided fortuitously with a leader of the Bar. Indeed, let us be blunt: the prototype Bencher of the old boy network was probably a better specimen than the mixed windbag of today. There is one thing worse than an old fogey and that is a young fogey. Yes, yes: there are—of course—some honorable exceptions.

Milt burst upon the Bencher's scene like an anarchist's bomb. First, he was a magnificent physical specimen, and kept himself "in shape" by "punching the bag." Men's health clubs were not *de rigeur* in those days, which preceded cholesterol and stress scares, and the Benchers of the day always looked baggy in their off-the-rack suits. Milt worked out every day at the gym. He eschewed tobacco and alcohol. His best friend at the Bar was Jack Major, who ran seven to eight miles a day in all weather at a time when runners were considered both deranged and dangerous, and dedicated marathoners like Major had to sneak down alleys in their plimsolls and baggy shorts for a run, to avoid the opprobrium of their fellows, like the kid in the fifties who took violin lessons.[12] Milt was theretofor viewed, nervously, as some sort of lethal combination of religious zealot, criminal sympathizer, mindless jockstrapper, and Caped Crusader for the Underdog. Underdogs were not big with the Benchers in those days, which era also preceded Victimhood as the Gateway to Earthly Paradise.

---

12. Dictum of Quigley, J.: "The only time a guy should run is away from the cops and after a pretty girl."

Milt also set a standard of sartorial splendour that left the others, in their plaid sports jackets and sagging wide-trousered suits, out in hickland. (Milt's tailoring is worth a special chapter, *poste*). All of a sudden, the Benchers were infiltrated by a pistol-packing paranoiac who scared the shit out of them every time he opened his mouth. Such eloquence on opinions fiercely held was novel to the staid monosyllabic governors.

Milt was not a devoted Bencher, any more than I was. If something interested him, for example a disciplinary matter, particularly where some hapless single practitioner was being railroaded by his establishment brethren, he could know more about it in a shorter period of time than any of his fellows: he was what they call "a quick study." But Milt missed out on a lot of the graver deliberations at Convocation. "*Convocation*?" you exclaim. Yes: most ordinary people, even Boards of Directors, meet; the Benchers always "convocate." When he finally blew in, an hour or so late, clutching the foot-thick itinerary as he noisily took his place, it was noted that the pre-delivered "agenda and materials" were encompassed in the same elastic bands that had bound their recondite secrets when they were entrusted to the courier service. Milt would peel off the elastics, then glower around and about as his fellows looked hurriedly away or down. He always had that lot on the defensive. When, however, the time came to speak out on an issue when the more prudent were content to keep their own counsel, that is, to remain silent, Harradence rose invariably to the occasion. He was always his own man; he was always an urgent voice for real reform.

One of the major reforms instituted by Milt was an unintended but effective purge of the venerable Palliser Hotel lobby. In those days, the early seventies, it still displayed that turn-of-the-century decayed elegance featuring potted aspidistras and potty old ladies sipping tea in its sheltered precincts. Harradence had taken to securing his deadly and loaded Walther pistol in a cunningly designed ankle holster that did not work very well. The Benchers in those days "convocated" in a meeting room on the mezzanine floor at the Palliser, and the fastest access was up some broad stairs from the lobby, reached after one traversed the gauntlet of old dolls with the blue rinses and the china teacups. Late—as usual—for a Benchers' meeting, Harradence rushed in the front doors, sprinted through the lobby laying waste to the palm fronds, and up the marble stairs. He was halfway up the stairs, when the pistol became dislodged and, to the shock of the assembled regulars, clattered noisily down the stairs and came to rest on the British India rug. "Jesus Christ!" he cried, swooped down, retrieved the lethal article, shoved it into his belt, and ran back up the stairs. Several old dears fainted away.

I have said that the large Alberta mills dominated and controlled the Benchers for years. This unhealthy despotism was to change dramatically starting about 1985 and then again in the 1987 election, when the fat fap stranglehold was broken forever, thus ending the era of the old boy network.

When the time came that Milt could not stomach another term, having sat through four two-year sessions, he importuned me to run. "Why me?" The Criminal Bar has to have representation, he said, "and you're it, m'boy."

"Are there any options?"

"You've got no choice."

I ran. Inexplicably, I was elected. History records strange flukes, blips, and aberrations: my election to the Benchers by my peers was the equivalent of sober God-fearing American taxpayers of the Christian Coalition electing Hunter S. Thompson to the United States Senate. Think of it: the first Gonzo senator.

I was the first Gonzo Bencher. And the last.

The Benchers election of November 1977 had a few ramifications, best expanded upon in my own memoirs. I shall recite the significant highlights involving A.M.H.

Tom Walsh, Q.C., O.C., my then senior partner and a former Bencher, is endeared to me because his test for the imposition of professional discipline upon members is what we lawyers call a classic: it is the most succinct expression thereof, and it has withstood the test of time. T.J. Walsh said: "I look at the facts of what the guy did, and I look at the guy, and I ask myself, 'is this a wrist tapper, or does the poor s.o.b. get his rubber boots and shovel and line up at City Hall?'"

Milt also liked the folk wisdom of Tom Walsh. Milt's version of the test for professional disciplinary sanction was the requirement that counsel for the Law Society prove the allegations beyond all reasonable doubt; however, mindful of the correct legal test, which was the balance of probabilities, he always tarted up his decisions to turn on the high degree of that balance. I took his lead, and many a borderline rogue was granted clemency. Milt always said—as did T.J.—that if you are going to yank some guy's license, you had to be sure. "Moral certainties" are now out of fashion, but they were good enough for generations of lawyers. Nowadays, of course, they disbar you if you so much as imagine the death of the Master Treasurer.

Like Milt, I considered it my proper function as a Bencher to concentrate primarily on discipline and ethical issues, particularly the adjudication of disciplinary hearings and related matters, and as a further function probably ranking equally in importance, to represent the vilified Criminal Bar as best I could; further, to take the piss out of my fellow Benchers whenever they got too self-righteous or judgmental, which was all too often. I considered that both he and I made a useful contribution to the governance of our profession, although the majority of our peers are of the opposite view. What they probably resented the most, of course, is that both Milt and I consistently topped the polls.

Also, like Milt, I eschewed much of the social side. I was never easy spending the members' money on yearly junkets to Jasper and self-promoting black-tie dinners. Getting up before ten *a.m.* has always been a most uncivilized practice to me, and the Benchers' practice of commencing the day's deliberations at eight *a.m.* sharp so that they (that is, all of them except me) could be on the Jasper or Kananaskis golf course for one *p.m.* tee-off time (or whatever that mindless stupidity is called) was reprehensible.

I took office as a Bencher of the Law Society in February 1978. I was then in private practice. At about the same time, Milt and his partner, John MacPherson, and I had serious discussions about my joining them in practice. I gave this opportunity a great deal of thought, but finally opted to start my own criminal law shop, opening up in February 1979 out of the high-rent district not to save the client's money. I think Milt was a bit hurt by this decision, but I told him that I would rather run my own outfit than be the fifth criminal lawyer in his booming mill, and he took my point graciously. As always, he and Johnny Mac went out of their way to refer work to me. At that stage, I was as needy as I was grateful: I left Walsh Young with four files, one fat fraud and three Legal Aiders. I left behind all the lucrative civil litigation files with Walsh Young as their "property," with no unseemly squabbling. I did not want them. Walsh Young, in turn, refrained from throwing me (without my furniture) down the elevator shaft, which was Walsh and Young's traditional way of dissolving partnerships. On February 1, 1979, I sat on the linoleum floor in my new "chambers" in the old Lougheed Building, c. 1910. The lease said, "as is, where is." Net assets: a telephone (also on the floor), and the aforesaid four files. For the first few days, I wondered where my next meal was coming from. Of course, it came from Milt.

A few months later, as C.D. Evans Professional Corporation was hitting the black, Harradence, Q.C., was elevated to the Court of Appeal. I fell heir to new work. His firm bifurcated, the solicitors heading one way and the barristers to MacPherson and Associates.

It was the end of a dynasty. In that end was my beginning. I know Milt wanted it that way

Chapter Six
Satirical Spendour

Part One
Dressing the Part

POWER DRESSING, contrary to the assertions of the iron-faced females' brigade, is not a new concept. It is true that today women do it better than men, but that historically has not always been the case or, at the least, the fop and the courtesan were contemporaneous blots on the landscape.

There is a school of thought—well, actually, it is a school of non-thought—that the young person on his or her way up must "dress for success." This, to the thinking person, is both specious and vacuous frippery. It is the *content* of the container that invites judgmental scrutiny and evaluation, not the packaging. Under a fashionable hat sits many an atrophied brain. Those who sport coloured stockbroker suspenders suspend both their trousers and my confidence, and raise my suspicions. Indeed, the more stylish the attire, the more likely it is that the stylishly attired is an ignoramus. "One may forgive the male peacock his plumage," I have written elsewhere, "because he is the stupidest of birds." Beau Brummell has never been my kind of man.

The one exception in historical romance fiction is Baroness Orczy's "Sir Percy Blakeney," as egregious a fop and one-dimensional dilettante as ever minced about a salon de société, c. 1790. There is no mention of Sir Percy in Burke's "Reflections on the Revolution in France," and one may safely conclude that Baroness Orczy[1]

1. Baroness Orczy appears to be to Mrs. Montagu Barstow, 1865-1947, as the Scarlet Pimpernel is to Sir Percy Blakeney.

had a fertile imagination, enough to excite that of generations of English schoolboys. Disdain for the creepy and preposterous snob Blakeney transfigured to open-mouthed admiration for his *alter ego,* the Scarlet Pimpernel, sort of an aristocratic English version of John Wayne's "Shucks, ma'am, it's all in a day's work." The issue of whether the useless scions of the French nobility were worth all that frenetic swashbuckling may properly be left to other texts.

Let this testament record that Milt Harradence was another genuine historically romantic exception, non-fictional. I have already noted in earlier pages exploits of his derring-do equal to, or exceeding, those of Sir Percy. Thus, his obsession with his wardrobe and personal toilette may appropriately be relegated to theatrical self-expression, and he may find support in the much quoted aphorism of a similarly flamboyant, larger-than-life character, Oscar Wilde: "One should either *be* a work of art, or *wear* a work of art." (Milt will not appreciate the comparison: his generation abhorred "pansies" and admired and embraced the *Junker* mentality.)

Milt gave great style to his life by his insistence upon elaborate and meticulous dress. He shared Oscar Wilde's instinct for setting himself apart by his outrageous fashion "statements." Therefore, certain superficial comparisons with Mr. Wilde are inevitable, although in most matters the two characters are as unlike as chalk and cheese.

A.M.H., like Wilde's Lord Goring (*An Ideal Husband*) and indeed like Wilde himself, was "the fashion plate and authority on Style, the *arbiter elegantierum.*"

Milt cut a fabulous fashionable figure. The first thing one noted about him was his impeccable tailoring, with all accessories just so, always appearing publicly in a co-ordinated ensemble worthy of Louis Quatorze, the fabled Sun King. One could carp, after Doris Lessing, that the cost of one such splendid outfit could feed an African village for five years, but the example is invidious: it was Milt's money; he earned it, and he could spend it as he wished. Supreme potentates like racehorses and yachts. Thomas de Quincy spent his dough on dope and wrote one good book. Numerous other examples abound, too tedious to relate. Social justice is irrelevant. It is a "hideous fact," writes George Steiner, "that hundreds of thousands could be fed on the price a museum pays for one Raphael or Picasso."

Famous prizefighter Willie deWit, Canada's Raging Bull, vividly recalls his first glimpse of the Great Barrister, by then a Judge, who later was to play such a major role in Willie's career. DeWit, on his way up the heavyweight ladder, was working the heavy bag[2] in a downscale Calgary basement gym. He looked up from belabouring the bag to observe the immaculately accoutred Justice of Appeal sedately descending the rickety wooden staircase from the street, replete with dark herringbone overcoat with velvet collar, striped Court pantaloons, every silver hair in place, with menacing expression. In those days, the deWit entourage was gaining fame and predictably attracting the usual phony "promoters" anxious to get their grubby mitts on a rising talent in the fight game. A seasoned old trainer, noting the looming figure of the grey eminence, removed the unlit cigar stub he was masticating and remarked to Willie: "That guy is either the real thing or a real fake!"

It was critically important to Milt that he always present as if he had just been hatched by Savile Row. Indeed, the best of Savile Row was not quite good enough for A.M.H. My only concession to tailoring in the last twenty years has been two excursions each ten years apart to my father's tailors in that venue, London, to procure the best of the bespoke, a "director's" suit, black waistcoat and all. Milt sniffed: "The trousers are too wide." I responded, "Fashion is ephemeral. Taste is always in style." Milt retorted, "You look *baggy,* Cliff." I reported this to Bernice. "He is right," was her judgment. Stung, I cried, "I'll have you know that my tailors make suits for the King of Sumer." She roared with laughter. "Of course, they look like pascha pantaloons. He probably wears them in the harem!" I sulked, then snuck off to Mirvald's Fashionable Tailoring, on 17th Avenue S.W. opposite Western Canada High School, to get the baggy striped bags narrowed. As to my penchant for the

---

2. One of A.M.H.'s favourite pastimes, lumped by William Stilwell into "mindless jockstrapping."

correct barrister's attire of director's suit, Milt growled, "They're not yet ready for that here, Cliff."

Milt's view was that one could not own nor wear a suit unless one had the appropriate meticulously co-ordinated shirt, tie, socks, belt/suspenders (A.M.H. did not wear *both*, being an optimist; many yoicks of the cattle baron persuasion did), and highly polished footwear, which in Milt's case was always a pair of elastic-sided half-Wellingtons, a legacy no doubt of his military mindset. Milt's half-Wellington had soft leather, zippered tops, and the toes were shone to the nth degree. Oscar Wilde also particularly favoured soft leather boots over "stiff Hessian ones." I dubbed Milt's footwear "winkle pickers," which he found not amusing. He even had a pair of *cream-coloured* half booties!

This exchange in the Judges' elevator, following upon a Sittings of the Court of Appeal presided over by an austere Senior Justice, is reliably reported:

A.M.H. (glancing askance at the other's sensible, dull black Oxford laceups): *Could use a shine.*
Sr. J: *The day I want to look like an Italian pimp, I'll let you know.*

One could not own one suit or ten suits or fifty suits: to my knowledge—and I lost count—Milt had a suit for every day of the year, with some outrageous numbers reserved for what he termed, in modest self-deprecation, "high feast days." One such was made of patterned shiny grey silk and had a *belt* in the back of the jacket that sort of hung down in a swag like those on a lady's cocktail gown. I made much sport of this, and Milt was not amused. Nor was he amused when I announced at a legal function that the Harradence family had to move into the garage to make room in the house for Milt's clothing. It *was* sport to make frequent fun of our friend's fashion excesses. Major would join in, but I had detected also in him the same fatal fascination with male plumage, although he is a deal more subdued than Harradence. Still, Montreal tailoring and Florsheim shoes do not exempt Major from my rod.

The preoccupation with the detail of the Harradence wardrobe extended, of course, to outerwear, and, for all I know, underwear, perhaps even pajamas. Milt exhibited a variety of raincoats and overcoats, and winter greatcoats of a Napoleonic cut. The raincoats were, of course, the Robert Mitchum/Richard Widmark sinister trench coat model replete with epaulettes and secret pockets, with a belt slung rakishly to the rear. An exception was the Philip Marlowe shortie model which flared from the cinched waist like a tutu. The overcoats tended to the subdued grey herringbone variety or the black cashmere, both with velvet collars, tailored *a pointe*. There was a formidable camel hair greatcoat with ferocious lapels, and a brown wool with a wide belt, worn with the collar up for the Robert Redford jaded roué look. An aviator's white silk scarf complemented this foul weather gear.

Milt refused always to wear a hat. In civilian life, he would not countenance a *chapeau*, even in thirty below. There were military exceptions: his World War II forage cap, his leather flying helmet, his jet pilot's golden helm (a compromise of the Bismarkian spiked *Junker* model), his Hon. Colonel's plumed kepi with scrambled egg on the visor, and—of course—the pith helmet he affects for dangerous expeditions, in which he stashes explorers' maps, quinine tablets, salt pills, and lumps of sugar for the horses, for hoped-for guest appearances in Clint Eastwood's *White Hunter, Black Heart.*[3]

(J.C. Major loves hats. He has a huge eclectic collection, including horrid golf hats. I have seen him in every permutation and combination of headgear. On one occasion, at his office, he was reading his mail wearing three hats, one piled on top of the other.)

When I think of it, there was one significant aberration in the hat and coat department of Harradence and Company, Clothiers and Dry Goods Merchants, and it came about this way:

I delighted in repairing from time to time to a military surplus store in an unfashionable area of what used to be called East Calgary. In addition to carrying all sorts of outmoded gear coveted by eccentrics like the writer, the proprietor maintained an intriguing

---

3. Causing one to exclaim, after Mr. Graham Green's letter to *Time* magazine, 18 March, 1957, "Perhaps the inhabitants were mystified by [his] strange attire and eccentric diet." (*Yours Etc.; Letters to the Press 1945-1989.* Ed. C. Hawtree, Penguin Books, London, 1991.)

war museum which even had at one time some bombs, a World War II armoured tracked vehicle, not to mention gas masks, uniforms, Lee-Enfield rifles, and webbing and gaiters. On one occasion, shortly after Milt had gone to the Bench in 1979, I noticed an ad in the paper by that store, indicating they had in stock genuine German navy pea jackets. I hurried over there with Milt in tow. He was somewhat dubious until he noted that the place had a special on simulated World War II flyers' leather jackets with the sheepskin collars. In the final result, we both purchased German navy pea jackets for about forty bucks each. These were superbly made classic pea jackets with striped ticking on the inside, heavy storm collars, double breasted, with two rows of quadruple fouled-anchor brass buttons. These fit extremely well without alteration, but of course Milt had to get his tailor, at that time the meticulous craftsman Mr. K. Bergwall, to alter the thing by taking it in at the waist and, for God's sake, building up the shoulders a bit. I doubted then that he would ever wear the garment, as it was not his usual style and hardly high fashion. However, some months later, Mr. Justice Bob Montgomery (see Chapter 1), now ascended from the Captaincy of the Good Ship *Tecumseh* to the Court of Queen's Bench of Alberta, recruited by the Navy to a P.R. exercise for prominent citizens, gathered a gaggle of his fellow judges for a government junket to Victoria and a day cruise on the latest Canadian Navy frigate. Milt was one of the invitees. He was thrilled, and appeared at my place in the navy pea jacket. Something was not quite right: he needed an appropriate cap. I, like Major, have a great collection of miscellaneous wondrous headgear, and Milt lit upon a battered Greek fisherman's standard model on the hatrack in the vestibule.[4] I cautioned Milt: "It is dangerous to wear a Greek fisherman's hat unless you are (1) Greek and (2) a fisherman." He ignored my advice and wore it anyway. "That'll shake 'em up!" is all he said as he departed. I understand that he was a great hit.

---

4. Of course, I have a vestibule. I also have an etching of the Death of Nelson over a mirror with hatracks on each side, and an elephant's foot that holds a bird-headed umbrella and a couple of walking sticks.

If Milt travelled anywhere, even for a weekend, he took more suitcases and co-ordinated outfits than the wife of an oil-rich Arab potentate. Travelling anywhere with him was like going on safari. One such trip is particularly memorable.

The background is significant: my idea of tailoring was to have a pair of striped baggies and shiny black shoes on hand for appearances in Court requiring one to gown, otherwise I was happy, and presumed everybody else was happy, with a green corduroy jacket and brown corduroy pants and a subdued tie. Also, the forenoted director's suit for funerals and the Court of Appeal, being similar enterprises. No accessories nor articles of personal adornment were necessary or desirable. That was all right, I suppose, as long as I was still a lifer with the Crown. Milt was obviously silently disapproving, but I was on the other side. However, when I left the Crown in early 1973 I found myself increasingly acting in concert with Milt as co-counsel on cases, usually as a result of his generosity in referral. He hinted broadly on a couple of occasions that perhaps I should pay a visit to a tailor or consider buying a suit, which fell on deaf ears. Milt finally took an active role in my tailoring, which to that date had never been a priority with me. "You've got to dress the part," he admonished me, and did what every establishment gentleman does for a friend: he introduced me to *his* tailor, the excellent Mr. Bergwall, who was in semi-retirement in Ogden but who continued to act as gentleman tailor to the likes of Milt and his brother, Clyne, the late Chief Justice of Alberta, Bill McGillivray, and the McGillivray boys. In due course, I was accepted as a client by Mr. Bergwall. He was a professional of the old school, with classic instincts and unerring eye. One of the first suits that I commissioned, a dark navy blue banker's pinstripe, so impressed Milt that he immediately ordered the same suit which was wrought from the same bolt of fine English cloth. It was a worsted and wore well. There was a similar dark grey pinstripe model.

One Friday night, Milt, as was his wont, called me late and said that he was picking me up in the Fishtail 8 at six o'clock the following morning, as we had to see Allan McEachern, Q.C., in Vancouver for a meeting. The next day was a Saturday. I figured this must have been a Federal case, because Mr. McEachern was then the senior partner of the sonorous law firm Russell Dumoulin, one of the biggest and most prestigious mills around. Next morning at precisely 6:00 *a.m.*, I left the house and as I went down the front steps Milt came up the walk. He stopped, flabbergasted, noting that he and I were wearing exactly the same aforesaid dark blue suit, the same shirt, the same tie, black socks, and black shoes (his were half-Wellington's and mine were lace-ups, but this was a distinction without a difference.) "Jesus Christ!" he exclaimed, "We can't go out to Vancouver like this. We look like a couple of assholes!" He ordered me to change. "There's no time," I said, "haven't we got a plane to catch at 7:00?" Milt was beside himself. "We look like the Bobbsey Twins. We can't travel together." I told him, "We've got no choice," which of course provoked a Pavlovian reaction in him from which he could not readily recover. When we got to the airport, he got his trench coat out of the trunk and, although it was a hot sunny day, insisted on wearing it. "We can't let people see us like this!"

It was not only sunny in Vancouver, it was hot. Milt persisted in wearing the trench coat. We went immediately from the airport to the downtown Georgia Hotel, where Milt ordered up a dayroom. On the plane, he had wolfed down his usual bacon and eggs and several gallons of black coffee. As soon as we checked into the Georgia and secured the room (which Milt regretted could not be swept for listening devices) he said that we should go for breakfast, whereupon we went to the hotel dining room and he had another plate of bacon and eggs. I asked him, tentatively, when this meeting with Mr. McEachern was to take place. Milt started suddenly, and then, assuming his "my God, war at any moment" visage, leapt from the table to the nearest pay phone. Apparently, he called McEachern, Q.C. Because Milt had not taken the precaution of advising Mr. McEachern that we were coming out on a Saturday morning in the summertime for a meeting, it is not surprising that Mr. McEachern was not to be found at his office nor was he at home. Milt was right vexed, as I believe he considered even senior Vancouver counsel to be rather too cavalier in avoiding the office on a weekend, even in the summer and even in the sailing season, Mr. McEachern being an avid sailor. As it turned out, we were fortunate in that Milt was able to locate his eminent colleague, who was gracious enough to drop his Saturday plans and meet us at his office. The meeting lasted ten minutes. Milt continued to wear the trench coat, to the bemusement of Mr. McEachern and the ill-disguised hilarity of myself.

As soon as we hit the streets of Vancouver, Milt marched in double time back to the hotel, noting that it was time for lunch. He had another plate of bacon and eggs. I could not imagine what his cholesterol count must have been, but that has never seemed to bother him.

Knocking off the last morsel, he said, "Let's get out of this place." As we were going for a taxi, Milt spied a shirt shop. "Hold the cab!" he ordered, and disappeared, emerging about fifteen minutes later with something like six shirts.

When we got back to Calgary, Milt decided that we should go to a movie. Featured at the time was *Slap Shot.* I was not a hockey fan, and persuaded Milt to see *The Dogs of War*, a slick production about mercenaries in an unnamed but malevolent African dictatorship. Milt loved it and even forgot that he was still wearing his trench coat in the heat. "Do you think they could use a pilot with his own jet over there?"

After that incident, Milt insisted that we check at least by telephone the day before travelling anywhere or appearing in any court together to make sure that we did not inadvertently wear the same suit by the same tailor from the same bolt of cloth. That tradition has subsisted to this day, although in these last few years I've gone back to baggy corduroy misfits, where the jacket and the pants have never been introduced, justified by the precept that by the time a client comes in to see me he or she is in so much trouble they don't give a damn what I'm wearing. And I'm certainly not going to dress up for some judge. This decline in deportment to Milt is deplorable, but I believe he has finally given up. The rough edges noted by my kindly mentor at Macleod Dixon have never rubbed off, thank God.

I took silk in January 1978, which had everything to do with my being elected a Bencher of the Law Society, having run at the insistence of Milt, and very little to do with my ability as a Barrister. However, I have always been somewhat philosophical about this appointment, considering that I earned mine on my feet in the courtroom in any event, as did Harradence, Major, and John MacPherson. The fact that a barrister as learned and able as William Stilwell has never been appointed Queen's Counsel is simply affirmation of the egregious system of preferment that has always existed in this province. I telephoned my father in London to advise that I had been selected to join Her Majesty's circle of advisors, and his comment was, "Well, over here they double their fees and take half the work." I did both immediately. It was obligatory to purchase a new silk gown and a vest that had fancy double sleeves like those found on 18th century English gentry. As with most Canadian Q.C.'s, I had to settle for the poor Canadian imitation, but this was dramatically corrected by a dear old professional friend of both Milt's and myself in the summer of 1987 in London.

H.A.D. "Bertie" Oliver, Q.C., was much my senior, a close friend of Milt's and a Vancouver barrister of renown, noted for his booming voice, mastery of courtroom theatrics, and his cutting cross-examinations. Like Milt, he was courteous to a fault with his victims. He drove a Bentley, a Rolls Royce being "far too vulgar." Anyway, there was Bertie, sashaying up Pall Mall like a battleship in full sail, looking like he held the first mortgage on the place, which is the way he and Marshall Hall and Harradence walked into a courtroom. Bertie was, as usual, pink-cheeked, expansive, and sartorially splendid, and he greeted me effusively, notwithstanding my garb of blue jeans and biker jacket and my furtive look of one who has just slunk out of a pornographic movie, which I had.

"My *dear* Evans!" he cried, wringing my hand heartily, "How nice to see you, my dear Sir. I'm staying at my *Club*; I've just come from my Savile Row *tailors* and my legal robemakers: Ede and Ravenscroft, Chancery Lane, of course. I needed a new silk gown. They told me, 'Mr. Oliver, we have *real* silk and *artificial* silk.' I told them 'I'm *not* an artificial silk!' Cost me dearly, dear boy, but worth it! Well, I'm off for a few days to the *Cotswolds*. Cheerio!"

All of this was delivered at a stentorian volume, causing heads to turn and traffic to swerve, and Bertie then cruised serenely into the crowd and posterity.

In one of our earlier encounters, I had asked Bertie, "To what do you attribute your great success and fearsome reputation?" He responded at once: "My dear Evans, bombast baffles buffoons!"

After this encounter on Pall Mall, I, too, then procured a real silk gown from Ede and Ravenscroft and, in addition a swallow-tailed Court coat, Q.C.s for the use of, one each. It was the least that I could do, the master tailor having advised me breathlessly that, in addition to exclusively tailoring legal furnishings for prominent Q.C.s, he had just finished Lord Hailsham's trousers.

I wore my new court coat in the Court of Appeal before a Court presided over by Mr. Justice Sam Lieberman. During the break, I received a summons to the back room from the Court. When I went back, Sam insisted on knowing where I had got the Court coat and the silk gown. I told him on condition that he not tell Milt. Sure enough, Sam acquired his own Court coat from Ede and Ravenscroft, and waited until he was presiding in Milt's company. Milt was simply knocked over that Sam had such splendid Court attire, as did his friend Evans, but no one had told him about it.

I told Milt I would make it up to him and subsequently sent him two missiles, respectively dealing with dialogue from Becket's *Homecoming* and a classified ad in the *CBA/Law Society newsletter,* as follows:

> (1) There's an advertisement in the paper about flannel vests—cut price —Navy surplus—I could do with a few of 'em.
> (2) Designer label men's wear. Consignment store offers opportunity to consign suits, sports jackets, mens's wear by Boss, Armani, custom designed, etc. receive 40% of resale. Garments within 3 — 4 years, like new condition. Call today Dress to Suit (telephone #).

Milt found both of these cheeky references as funny as Pierre Mousseau's reminiscence of a lengthy preliminary inquiry that he conducted as Crown with Milt defending, where he publicly upbraided Milt for wearing the same suit on two different appearances in the court. Milt was devastated that his lapse had been noticed and never let that happen again.

In pre-revolutionary France, c. 1785, the apparel of the "honest man" of the underclass was a sober black coat and breeches and no wig. Milt Harradence would surely have been judged to be of the "military courtier" type: a rose-coloured coat and plumed hat, and carrying a sword. See *Pernot-Duplessis (plaintiff) v. Le Comte de Moreton-Chabrillant*, reported by Simon Schama (ibid), p. 137. Milt was a radical in politics, but he was no *sans-culotte* radical.

Mr. Bergwall eventually retired, and Milt was obliged to seek a new tailor. A craftsman with the skills that could even approach the demands of a client like Milt is a rare bird. Enter Klaus Stachow, gentleman's master tailor. Here was a true professional, in more ways than one. Stachow had flown with the Luftwaffe in the Second World War. He and Milt therefore quickly developed a rapport based on the mutual respect that true warrior professionals have for each other, no matter what side they are on. This is so whether the combat is in war or in the courts. Both of them having served on opposing sides in the former conflict, they would appreciate the words of Thomas Hardy:

> Yes; quaint and curious war is!
> You shoot a fellow down
> You'd treat if met where any bar is,
> Or help to half-a-crown

In the final analysis, I would attribute A.M.H.'s dress excesses less to vaunting peacockery than to satisfy the need in all who lead exciting or disruptive lives for a stabilizing routine. A meticulous attention to superfluous detail, be it one's toilette or the winding of a clock, can soothe the psyche in periods of even intense stress. One constant that I can recall with Milt was that, no matter how great the pressures of a defence, of political machination, of the run up to a bold attack, even of personal grief, he was always impeccably turned out: the pressed, tailored bespoke suit, the shiny half-Wellingtons, the shirt and socks and tie and breast pocket kerchief perfectly colour and pattern co-ordinated, the silver hair brilliantined and set in place, the ornate cufflinks, the manicured nails, the man's scent: "that'll shake 'em up." It did. Nothing could make Milt appear *unruffled*. I think he needed that inner feeling of serenity far more than the outward show of sartorial splendour that was its superficial concomitant.

In my view, Milt's preoccupation with Style and Fashion also mirrored, to some extent, his approach to the edicts and suasions and social pressures of society at large. He followed the dress fads of the day—adhering to what Lady Wilde (Oscar's mommy) damned as "the frivolous mutations of fashion"—to the letter, and—I fear—he conformed in like degree to other societal pressures. For example, he was scrupulous about all social niceties and proprieties. This may be attributable to his need to *belong*. The only substantial exceptions were his courage in individualistic courtroom conduct, in which he was often brilliant, and his politics, in which he was both a maverick *and* a disaster. Only in the courtroom was Milt's soul ever free. In those other non-essentials, he should have heeded G.B. Shaw's admonition to Wilde:

> Wise kings wear shabby clothes, and leave the gold lace to the drum major.

Gary Schmidgall observes that Shaw had a "public posture of disdain for the frivolities of sartorial fashion: Oscar, of course, put those frivolities on a high alter," as did Milt.

And A.M.H. is the one-and-only person I have known well in my life who could rival Wilde for pure theatrics, showmanship, flourishes, in a word, *flair*. Is this not curious, to compare A.M. Harradence, Q.C., the Last of the Great Gunfighters, with Oscar Wilde, the greatest of the self-indulgent aesthetes of the late nineteenth century? There are many contrasts, of course, but striking similarities overall. It has everything to do with flair.

Social adulation was their great need, and it went to both of their brilliant heads. Thus, they both had the need to make a Dramatic Entrance and strike a Remarkable Pose. But A.M.H. had "honesty, sobriety and industry"; Oscar Wilde has never been accused of the last two virtues, and as to the first, at his famous trials, he did use the truth recklessly. Thus the comparison ends at these fundamental thresholds.

PART TWO
Milt and the Aesthetic Impulse

IT IS NOT ACCURATE to simply dismiss any aesthetic impulse in A.M.H. as non-existent. He kept his poetical sensibilities well hidden, it is true, but he was hardly a stranger to the beauty or the apt harmony of *le mot juste*; he was indeed a master of the dialect of his tribe, a communicator and persuader with few rivals in the forensic arena. As such, he appreciated and utilized the apposite quotation, and was not reticent about going beyond the soporific clichés of this or that legal or jurisprudential windbag to find the right historical or even literary allusion to a particular situation. In fact, Milt was capable of the most poignant prose as the occasion demanded, for example, when as a Justice of Appeal he was Calling young barristers to the Bar. There were times, indeed, when his oratory was both inspired and brilliant.

As I have observed, he might look at me in a quizzical manner if I lapsed into poetry, although he was fond of quoting any paean to flight or battle,[5] even if it be doggerel e.g., Kipling. In fact, Harradence was a devoted fan of the plodding Rudyard Kipling, fond of quoting Kipling's definition of "cold," i.e., "cold as Medicine Hat on a Christmas Day."

The ghost of Kipling always hovered about Milt's lectures and essays on the Art of Cross-examination, particularly *If.* Oscar Wilde, whom we have encountered already in these pages, always the most perceptive and sensitive of aesthetes, detested Kipling, "our first authority on the second rate, [who] has seen marvellous things through keyholes."

Milt was not critical of me; he did recognize much of what habituates the ordinary prose of one who has read a few good books and is not bound by professional jargon. Were I to rhyme off a list of references not for any cheap display of learning but to point up a dilemma or situation, Milt would be expressionless, then say, quietly, "Yaas. That's true." He was widely well-read, particularly in history and biography.

---

5. *High Flight* by Pilot Officer John Gillespie Magee. See Chapter 7, *poste.*

I know few lawyers who have troubled themselves with the reading of any decent literature or philosophy, let alone any understanding or appreciation of it, and I do not confine this critical observation to Canadian lawyers. In parts of the United States and Australia as well as this country, and in the United Kingdom, indeed, the language of the educated English-speaking person is nowhere spoken nor comprehended. Burke and Gibbon, Erskine, Macaulay, were not exceptionally erudite for their day: they simply expressed themselves in the manner expected of the average gentleperson of that era. Few read them today, save professional academics. I strongly suspect this is because the average product of our enlightened, non-challenging, frantically non-competitive "educational" curricula is unable to understand basic language and vocabularies. The vocabularies of such writers and speakers are not exceptional or difficult to the few well, classically, or self-educated citizens; they are like a foreign tongue to the greater percentage of the population. If you wish to destroy or dominate a culture, first destroy its language.

George Steiner observes that the tradition of 'cultured men' ran from antiquity to, roughly, the First World War:

> They will know by heart considerable segments of Scripture, of the liturgy, of epic and lyric verse. Macaulay's formidable accomplishments in this respect —even as a schoolboy he had committed to memory a fair measure of Latin and English poetry—were only a heightened instance of a general practise.

Now, Steiner mourns in the mournful company of a few of us,

> ...the most elementary allusions to Greek mythology, to the Old and the New Testament, to the classics, to ancient and to European History, have become hermetic.[6]

The principal explanation for the decline of the art of advocacy is the want of any ability in erudition or expression displayed by

---

6. "The Uncommon Reader", *No Passion Spent*, Yale University Press, New Haven and London, 1996.

most trial judges and the functionally illiterate lawyers who regularly appear before them. Vide, the expostulation of a late high ranking Justice of the Alberta Supreme Court (Trial Division) to Ned Cronin, a remarkably gifted barrister, just as Cronin began his peroration: "We don't need any forensic orators in this Court." No, I'm sure that he did not. And yet, even that learned jurisprude[7] would be a veritable Demosthenes compared to some of the less gifted who now populate the polyethylene woolsack.

It is not, therefore, in matters of expression and articulation that Milt was ever wanting; his sensibilities, particularly his ear, were highly developed, not surprisingly considering his excellent upbringing as a youth in Prince Albert, Saskatchewan, with its very positive influences. But I do not think he would consider that Wordsworth and Shakespeare were as indispensable to John Mortimer's *Rumpole* as the screenplay dialogue, mostly ranting, of *Patton* was to him. To Milt, theatre was everything, and if substance had to give way to form, well, something had to give in order to achieve the object, whether it be political or forensic.

In the disciplines of music, food, and potable wines and spirits, Milt displayed no spark of interest.

In matters of the palate, his taste ran to endlessly repetitive servings of bacon and eggs (the eggs "easy over," the bacon "crisp") or, for variety, a steak ("medium well") with fries. There was no disputation of any kind that could assuage Milt's need for the former, which he practically inhaled, the average sitting and consumption spanning three minutes max: the gorp and grease vanished into his maw and the plate wiped clean, including most of the pattern, as I would be starting my sandwich. Milt, to my knowledge—when on the road or immersed *incognito* in a case—had bacon and eggs for breakfast, for lunch, for dinner, as a midnight snack. As earlier observed, his cholesterol count at any given time must have been enormous, and no amount of whaling of the

7. See Mr. B. Levin in his article in The Spectator, 16 May, 1958, in reviewing *Lord Goddard: His Career and Cases by Grinshaw and Jones*: ". . . he (Lord Goddard) represents only too well the attitudes of most people in the country whose judiciary he heads. Perhaps every country gets the Lord Chief Justice it deserves." (Quoted in Graham Greene, Letters to the Press, 1945-1989, Penguin, London, 1991.)

heavy bag could provide an antidote. Jack Major, a dedicated long distance runner who has always presented the withered aspect of the Mummy in the film *The Mummy's Tomb*, always pooh-poohed my disdain of grease and meat gobbling, which reached—admittedly—a neurotic perihelion about 1978, when I was running marathons and averaging ten to twelve miles a day, eschewing meat and even fowl and sticking religiously to goat's milk, figs, and bland white fish. Most healthy people are profoundly boring, Major noted, and he advised that a good steak never killed anybody. This was an admonition from the oracle who used to run long distance in the days before it became fashionable. He was right. I returned to beef, lamb, kidney, liver, cigars, full-bodied burgundies, and single malt, all in good time.[8]

In vain, I lectured Milt that no one with tastebuds can eat beef "medium well," which in addition to being as tasteless as desiccated cardboard is also indicative of indecision and compromise. To grasp life, I counseled my friend, is to eat one's meat rare. He demurred: "Jesus Christ, you don't know where it's been, Cliff!" (With pork, that is true, which is why I avoid the society of politicians.) In his company, I once ordered steak tartare, my favourite. The callow waiter looked apprehensive: "It's raw beef." "I know that, you blithering idiot, that's why I ordered it." Now Milt looked apprehensive. I wolfed it down with a half-bottle of red plonk. Milt kept staring agitatedly at me, waiting for me to sprout fangs and a palmful of coarse hair.

Between 1968 and 1972 Bernice and I lived happily in Calgary on Twelfth Avenue, a major traffic artery to downtown and a truck route, in the heart of the unfashionable blue-collar worker Beltline. For $75 a month (cash), we occupied a rear downstairs suite in an old frame house, fully furnished after a fashion. In the

---

8. Major, more cadaverous than ever, now carefully chooses his food with an abstemiousness hinging on pottiness. His staple appears to be unadorned chicken breast on dry rubber bread. Pew. This can not all be blamed on Ottawa nor the Supreme Court. He always looks as if he is expiring from a terminal illness. Mrs. Helene Major, after anxious consultation with me, has applied to the War Crimes Tribunal to have Jack declared dead.

dead of winter, one had to break the ice on the toilet water. It is a compliment to Milt, and his partner John MacPherson, who were frequent visitors, that those humble surroundings, which suited us just fine, were not a matter of criticism or commentary. Milt would be perfectly comfortable and at home there.

Milt would come by wearing his "war-at-any-moment" phizzog. Bernice would always offer him something to eat. On one occasion, we were enjoying a particularly pungent searing curry for which she was famous. It was her own recipe, which counseled "cook until meat deteriorates." It could remove the lining of an unseasoned stomach in short order. Only *fundis* need apply: not even yoghurt quenched the internal flames. Milt ravenously devoured a heaping plateful, with Basmati rice (also an acquired taste), without letting up for one moment on the narrative of death and destruction that had prompted his visit. Surprised that he still sat upright, Bernice asked him if he would like another serving. "Yaas, please, marm," he responded, and knocked it back with the same dispatch and a flatness of affect that was truly remarkable. Ronald (now the Honourable Senator) Ghitter, Bernice's chess partner of the day, sampling the same batch, had imploded from heat and fumes, and we had to call the Fire Department. Milt was completely unaffected by the heat or the spices, and departed renewed. His was a constitution that was well suited to raw beef.

In music appreciation Milt was unequivocal: he could not stand any music. Experiencing my periodic angst of the unrequited concert performer, I once confided to Milt that I had been working for years, since the summer of 1961 in point of fact, on the third movement of Bach's *Piano Concerto in D Minor*, ever since as a child I had heard it performed by Sviataslov Richter. Milt looked at me, to borrow from Gwyn Thomas, as if he had just seen a mole for the first time. Nothing in his experience appeared to have oriented him to, or prepared him for, music. It was a dimension of human expression which to him was completely alien, as if from another universe. The possible exception was the military band; the rest was anathema. Like food, music simply did not register on his antennae.

One time, when he had dropped by our place, urgently requiring to engage my opinion of some burning issue, I had Mozart's sublime *Requiem Mass* on the turntable. Milt started to talk, then paused in obvious exasperation and apparent *physical* discomfort: "Could you turn off that noise?"

Never, over the years I have ridden in Milt's various Fishtail 8 driving machines, have I heard him play anything on the radio other than deliberate static, achieved by placing the dial between stations and cranking up the volume. That was necessary, he said, in order to prevent "them" listening to us. Many a trip was made in this acutely uncomfortable and foolish posture, with both of us yelling over the execrable noise. To my knowledge, he continues the practice.

In that vein, two senior RCMP officers approached Milt in his hotel room for legal advice arising out of an apparent service investigation. They were hardly in the room when he leaped to first the clock radio and then the television radio band, placing both in the loud 'static' mode. "Now," he said, "tell me what this is about. *They* can't hear us." As "they" were the clients, these precautions might have seemed excessive and probably even redundant, but one did not ever talk about such things to the great defender. The interview proceeded: Milt could not hear the clients; the clients could not hear him; "they" could not hear anybody.

As to the demon rum, in all the years I have known Milt I have never observed him to take more than a token tope. While he does not condemn others for imbibing, even to excess, he is as close to a teetotaller as they come and far too close for me. In that regard, he again emulates Diefenbaker, perhaps unconsciously. Dief advised Churchill that he was a teetotaller, "but not a prohibitionist." Milt never seemed to have the slightest interest in either brews, wines, or spirits, however excellent and readily available. I shared with the late Pat McCaffrey, Q.C., a lifelong devotion to the better standings and vintages of famous white Burgundies; Milt would have dismissed our reverence for, for example, a 1979 Chevalier Montrachet, as a dangerous addiction requiring medical crisis intervention.

I have noted that in Milt's current years in the age of wisdom, which invites reflection, he does on occasion have a glass of wine with dinner and will even indulge in a copita of sherry (one only) before luncheon. He favours the sweeter concoctions. I was cheeky enough to tell him that that would not do, and a true *aficionado* must drink something a lot drier, e.g., Tio Pepe. I told him, gravely, that he had to be careful of the public perception of persons who enjoy sweet libations or confections: Hitler loved chocolate and desserts. Milt responded, "Yaas. That's true."

Nor, one hastens to add, did Milt smoke. A lifelong fitness addict, he preached the absolute necessity to become and to remain "in shape" in order to meet the rigours and stresses of trial practice. One may remain confident that A.M.H. would not find the seductive curling blue smoke from an Egyptian oval, wafting from the libidinous lips of a painted hussy, to be sensual. Nor did he belong to the Bogart school of scene and female domination, requiring a dame to light his cigarette, she in turn to drape herself over him while she also lit up.

As I have stated elsewhere, it is now commonplace that the two phenomena most likely to ruin a man's career and aspirations (the third is unbridled aspiration) are booze and women, equally lethal, and, taken together, synergistically destructive. Milt seemed well aware of these truisms, and resolutely shunned both temptations. First, he eternally loved, and was always in love with, his wife. Second, I think he considered succumbing to the evils of drink a fatal weakness: the boozer was flawed, his or her brain cells irretrievably diminished with each dram. In vain might one remonstrate that he missed out on a lot of fun, that all of the authors featured in Sara Nickles' collection *Drinking, Smoking and Screwing*[9] were highly qualified for canonical status (i.e., the Western Canon of Drunks, Nicotine Addicts, and Fornicators), and that a large number of lawyers and writers were brilliant in direct proportion to their sinning. Milt was denunciatory, but he was firm. I am confident that he has not read Henry Miller, and that if he did he would not like Henry or his lifestyle at all.

If I ever needed proofs of the two perpetually warring sides of my personality, the fact that both Milt Harradence and Henry Miller continued to be my heroes speaks volumes.

---

9. My 55th birthday present from the always perceptive Dr. Sheilah Martin, Q.C.

Part Three
Folle à Grandeur

AS WITH MANY NEW PATRICIANS who shot to the top from relatively humble roots, Milt had certain *folle à grandeur*. Much of this sort of pretension is harmless and forgivable foppery, witness the Harradence heraldic shield gracing the family fireplace. Even at such foul venues as airport terminals, hucksters sell purported family crests mounted on wooden shields, which are one's personal announcement to the world that one is of noble ancestry. The fact is, if you provided the family name "Shitface," together with the requisite fee (all cards accepted) you can bet you would receive in due course a representation of arms doubtless granted the Shitface family by the College of Heraldry, to wit: two nerds rampant on a field jaune, surmounted by an egret or other great crapping bird, with a latin motto, "*in flagrente delicto*," or the like.[10]

The Harradence arms athwart his hearth are the outsize shield type, which in addition to the historic Harradence heraldic crest has swords or something bristling at each quarter, in order that Milt can give a good account of himself if cornered during a home invasion.

There were logical extensions of this preoccupation with historical continuity in Milt's other environs. He took great pride in the personally selected adornments of his chambers. The office itself was about the size of a small football field. At one end, remote and forbidding, was a huge table—*not* a desk—a table that could have been hewn from the primeval forest by the war axes of the Germanic tribes, c. 150 A.D., for a visiting Caesar. Behind this war room monument was an equally gargantuan high-backed swivel chair of tufted maroon leather. I once sat in it, my feet barely touching the ground, like #3 in *The Prisoner*. Under the table was taped a deadly firearm, probably a sawed-off shotgun

---

10. The so-called Evans' alleged arms are rather boring and probably bogus. My true escutcheon is that of landed gentry illegitimately descended from one of Richard III's bastards, and is a hangman's gallows and noose with, of course, a bar sinister together with the motto "S'blud!" My father has been a lifelong member of a society to vindicate Richard III.

loaded with 00 shot, aimed at a client chair opposite, which could be discharged by a movement of Milt's right knee, handily blowing off the balls of a perceived assailant, as required.

There was further, I remember, a large lamp with a red velvet shade and a matching one in black velvet. There were big client easy chairs of the Queen Anne type, coffee tables, and a Chesterfield, mostly red, but with—inexplicably—a tartan frond or border, no doubt the Harradence tartan (not, I hope, purchased at the Pearson International Airport). A library of imposing tomes decorated one wall, in case one wanted a racy legal read, particularly the Ontario Weekly notes to 1960, which A.M.H. had found in an attic and purchased from the estate of a dead solicitor. The contents were equally moribund and there was, I recall, little reference to criminal law. I always suspected one whole panel of books was a secret door to an escape passage, which would open with a "click" when activated by a button under the table. Of course, if one mistook the button that discharged the shotgun for that more benign button, complications might ensue. It would be disturbing to shoot the gonads off this or that visitor if all one wanted to do was to slip out the side door. This conjecture of mine was thankfully never put to the test.[11]

Dominating the wall behind the master's chair was a print with ornate gilt frame, a copy of a classic Ye Olde Englande scene depicting a brace of English gentlemen c. 1750 or so, in appropriate antique clobber with powdered wigs and frock coats, apparently debating some esoteric point of jurisprudence or philosophy before a roaring fire. Other aristocratic gentleman are in attendance. There is deployment of clay pipes and ale mugs, and one gets a warm feeling of conviviality, privilege, and proprietorship. I suppose it was some subliminal Georgian equivalent of Calgary's Ranchmen's Club, the sort of scene that Milt always aspired to and valued colleagues like (censored) and (censored) tried to convince one they were born to. I forgive Milt, but never them.

---

11. Robert A.M. Young of (then) Walsh Young, solicitors and trademark agents, had a secret button that closed his door. It did not open the door; it simply released a magnetic holder of the open door. Its utility always escaped me, but he was unabashedly delighted with this foolery, probably because he had the only one in the office and it denoted status.

Chapter Seven
"Order in the Theatre!"

Part One
"All the world's a stage, but most of us are only stagehands."

– *Charles Ross Campbell*

MUCH OF MILT'S WORLD was pure theatre. Things happened routinely in his law practice that never happened in forty years of boxing files to the poor dullards who moiled at the solicitor's end or the pompous pratts in the big firms who milked the cash cow clients on the civil litigation side. They indeed led lives of quiet desperation. Once in a while, a wedding or a funeral brightened an otherwise moribund existence. The men looked solemn and stuck on those Erewhon tears; their wives went to the millinery department and got another of those inverted flour pots that they stuck on their heads for such occasions. Otherwise, between golf games and luncheon at the Paunchmen's Club, they counted each day to retirement then counted each day to death. The days took forever to pass, but retirement and death came all too soon.

Harradence *was* different from all the rest, contradictions and all. With the obvious exceptions of a Bill Stilwell or a Jack Major, the Calgary legal community was a breeding ground for mediocrity and respectability, so dear to the lower rural middle-class mold. An adventure to the average professional contemporary would be a week in Las Vegas, a place specifically designed by God for testing nuclear devices. That or a golf tour in Florida would be enough excitement for a decade or so. Otherwise, in the post-war years preceding the early-eighties boom, Alberta remained a stultifying cow state: it produced no poets, no musicians, no composers, no writers (with some distinguished exceptions), no thespians—that is, of any world rank—and nothing that could be termed "art." Its denizens were mostly hard-working drabs or rural bumpkins. The Calgary Stampede and the Edmonton Agricultural Exhibition were popular places of mass worship. Public bars still had two entrances: "Men" and "Ladies and Escorts." Alberta exported Vodka but would not sell it in the province: it was too easy to rob an innocent's virtue with the doctored orange juice; this fact is reported by no less an authority than the Hon. J. C. Major. Calgary was a city peopled almost exclusively by proletarians and run by a few semi-plutocrats who wore funny hats, drilled for oil, and lived on acreages. Many achieved functional illiteracy. Inter-marriage within the self-styled dynasties of the local robber barons was common, as were their progeny who were packed off to Eastern boarding schools which celebrated their inferiority but took their parents' money. There are, of course, exceptions to these cruel generalities, but rare.

In such a milieu, where the locals were starved for entertainment of any kind, small wonder that Milt Harradence burst upon the scene like a stick of Alfred Nobel's best and rose to prominence like one of the more successful Von Braun rockets. He had not only the Right Stuff, but—more importantly for his calling—he had the sense of theatre of an Edward Marshall Hall. If Hall, K.C., intrigued worldly London and glorified the exceptional Bar of his day, it is not surprising that a virtual clone with his talents and timing could electrify the Urburghers of a burg like Calgary.

Here is but one account by an observant contemporary of the antics of Hall, K.C.[1]

> When I came to the Bar, Marshall Hall was nearing the end of his great career as an advocate. He was notoriously in ill-health and was allowed to address the court sitting instead of standing.... It was hardly possible for an advocate with such a brilliant sense of the theatre as he had not to make play with the properties which

1. C.P. Harvey, Q.C., *The Advocate's Devil*, London, Stevens and Sons, Ltd., 1958.

> infirmity had put into his hand. I remember an occasion when a civil case was being opened to a jury in the Royal Courts of Justice. I do not now recall what sort of case it was, nor who was opening it; but only that Marshall Hall was for the defendant and that he was not present when counsel for the plaintiff began his address to the jury. But just as the jury were beginning to get interested the door opened and Marshall Hall's clerk entered carrying his cushion and other odds and ends which he arranged as described by Marjoribanks. When counsel for the plaintiff was fairly into his stride again the door opened a second time and Marshall Hall entered, bowed to the Judge, sat down with great dignity and rearranged some of the objects on the desk before him. The jury were fascinated, wondering what he was going to do with them. However, he did nothing until counsel for the plaintiff had recaptured the thread of his discourse and had reached a point of some interest. It was then that Marshall Hall picked up what appeared to be a scentspray and squirted it three or four times up his nostrils.
>
> It is plain from Marjoriebanks' admirable Life that the art of the showman was so much a part of Marshall Hall's mercurial and enthusiastic nature that he could not resist the inclination to indulge it, where an advocate who accepted a more austere conception of his duty (as most of us do nowadays) would not have allowed himself such liberties; …

The definitive biography of Marshall Hall was written by Marjoriebanks, who chronicled the lives and times of a number of the great barristers of his day, as did Montgomery Hyde. In my early days at the Bar, these were required reading. Today, left-wing law professors do not teach law students about the great advocates; Che Guevara is more chi-chi. And irrelevant. And young lawyers today want to emulate some prominent U.S. trial lawyers who are said to have said, "I never defend a cause I do not personally believe in." Well, they, poor boobs, can never call themselves *barristers.* I have said often, truly, with respect to Milt or Major or Stilwell or myself: if we had not been criminal lawyers, we would have been mercenaries.

To recover from the bullshit of American practitioners of the art of advocacy, or, at least, such gentleman esquires having pretensions to such practice, let us examine again the uplifting words of the greatest advocate in British history, Thomas Erskine, in defence of Tom Paine:

> From the moment that any advocate can be permitted to say that he will or will not stand between the Crown and the subject arraigned in the court where he sits daily to practice, from that moment the liberties of England are at an end. If the advocate refuses to defend from what he may think of the charge or of the defence, he assumes the character of the Judge; nay, he assumes it before the hour of judgment, and in proportion to his rank and reputation puts the heavy influence of perhaps a mistaken opinion into the scale against the accused, in whose favour the benevolent principle of the English law makes all presumptions, and which commands the very Judge to be his counsel.

A.M.H. was a big fan of Erskine. The significance of the influence of that exceptional barrister of the past upon Milt cannot be overemphasized. It goes a long way toward explaining his love of legal wordsmithing and, more importantly, his fierce defence of the trained advocate's role to stand between the accused citizen and the might of the state and his/her duty to accept briefs for the defence of the basest and meanest of the realm.

Milt Harradence was the most dedicated family man I have known. He never, in all the years I knew him, ever looked sideways at a dame. And if I did, invariably accompanied by a leer, he would hiss furiously, "For Christ's sake! You don't know where she's been!"

So far as his projection of sexual allure to impressionable female third parties, which was innocent if instinctive, he had the male magic and magnetism of a cross between Kurosawa's *Yojimbo*[2] and Raymond Chandler's enigmatic gumshoe Philip Marlowe; on this last personality, Joyce Carol Oates notes: "This is a striking manly man whom woman adore, usually in direct proportion to his disdain . . . Marlowe is repeatedly suggested to be tall, dark, handsome; he is mistaken for a prizefighter…"[3]

A.M.H. was tall, dark, and handsome, and he was a prize-

---

2. Sergio Leone's *Fistful of Dollars* is a faithful rendition of this Japanese film classic.
3. Joyce Carol Oates, "The Simple Art of Murder," *New York Review of Books*, December 21, 1995.

fighter, in the ring in his youth, and in the courtroom for the most important years of his adult life.

Chandler's Marlowe was the ultimate "hard-boiled mystery detective" of the body of admirable pot-boilers identified by Oates as "the genre most indigenous to American literature." She speaks of the "powerful appeal" of this genre which "stems from an apparent simplicity that, in the hands of inspired practitioners, rises to a kind of classic purity."

Let me take her point, and by analogy make mine about Milt Harradence: his powerful personal appeal was 'generic' of his quintessential portrayal of another archetype well familiar to generations of North Americans, but a rarity in Canada. Milt was the "classic" (if that is the word, which I doubt) loner criminal defence lawyer, of the Perry Mason fiction genre[4] and the Clarence Darrow true-life version, both deeply embedded in the psyche of the western reader and television watcher. More significantly, all aspiring criminal lawyers in law school, whether they admit it or not, model their future projected selves upon one or the other of those glorious myths. Milt's portrayal of the tall and silent gunslinger barrister poseur was a genuine Canadian variant, because he factored in authentic echoes of the heroic Erskine and the flamboyant Marshall Hall, paradigms of the British barristers' star tradition. I say "portrayal" advisedly: Milt was also the greatest ham actor I have known.

Let us examine Chandler's romantic icon (Oates' term), "leaving aside for the moment the fact that, in real life, the private detective is the antithesis," at page 34:

> ...down these mean streets a man must go who is not himself mean, who is neither tarnished nor afraid. The detective . . . must be such a man. He is the hero, he is everything. He must be a complete man and a common man and yet an unusual man. He must be, to use a rather weathered phrase, a man of honour, by instinct, by inevitability, without thought of it, and certainly without say-

---

4. Of whom my father wrote me from London: "Why that incompetent District Attorney Hamilton Burger does not shoot himself over his persistent failures is beyond me!"

> ing it. He must be the best man in the world and a good enough man for any world . . . he will take no man's money dishonestly and no man's insolence without a due and dispassionate revenge. He is a lonely man and his pride is that you will treat him as a proud man or be very sorry you ever saw him.

Is that not A. Milton Harradence, Q.C., to the life? Continues Oates:

> . . .this bold proclamation, with its echoes of Hemingway, makes one thing clear: the detective is all that other men are not, the proper object of their envy, adulation and desire. He is the wish-fulfilment fantasy of the (male) reader of the genre . . .

(I find it an uneasy authentication that I read these words *after* I had written the second chapter of this memoir.)

Also like Marlowe, Milt, although scrupulously chaste, emitted a sexual potency that was cheerfully parodied by Terry Southern and Stanley Kubrick in their eerily apposite General Jack Ripper in *Dr. Strangelove*:

> Don't get me wrong, Group Captain. I like women. But they sense my power, the power of my vital bodily fluids. I like women, Mandrake, but I won't give them my essence.

As I note elsewhere, I doubt that Milt would find this passage as humorous as do I.

Man at the Top:
A.M. Harradence Q.C.
in his Library.
*(Calgary Herald
Newspaper)*

Mrs. Cecilia Agnes Harradence with her son
Sgt. Pilot A.M. Harradence, June 1942.

Left:
Middleweight Champion of Saskatchewan and Alberta Universities.
(Photo courtesy of Department of National Defence)

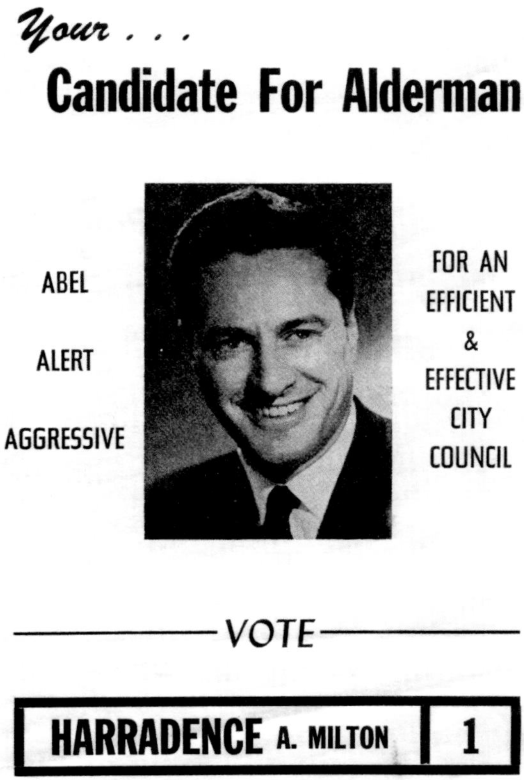

Your . . .

Candidate For Alderman

ABEL

ALERT

AGGRESSIVE

FOR AN EFFICIENT & EFFECTIVE CITY COUNCIL

VOTE

HARRADENCE A. MILTON	1

Left:

"Abel representation aggressively assured. Spelling less alert."

Below:

"The dumfounded residents must have thought they'd woken up in a loony bin. They had."

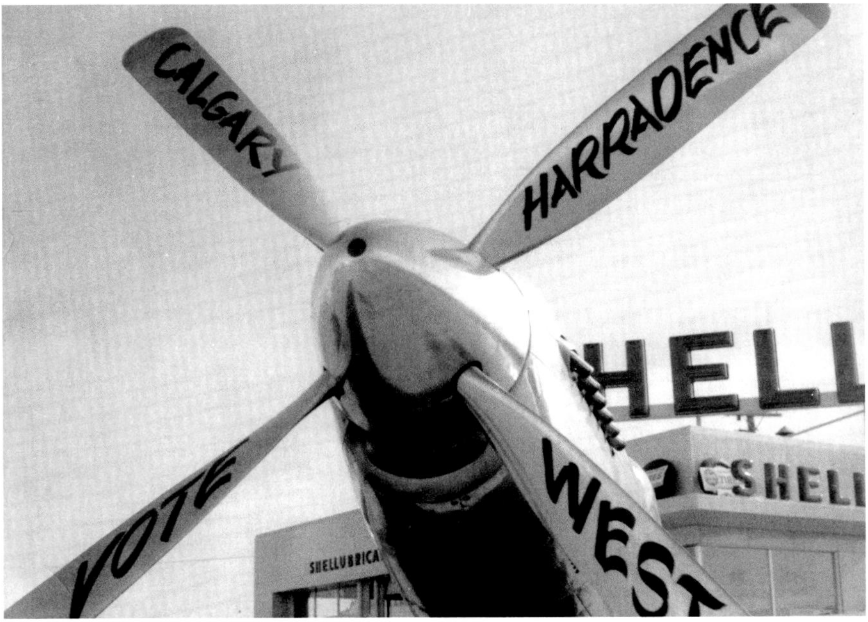

Thomas Innes cartoon in the *Calgary Herald*. *(Calgary Herald Newspaper)*

A.M.H. flying in formation with the RCAF Golden Hawks. *(Photo courtesy of Department of National Defence)*

Col. Milt Harradence, Confederate Air Force, with the fastest private airplane in North America. *(Photo courtesy of Department of National Defence)*

"… A group of middle-aged flying bikers called the Confederate Air Force…"

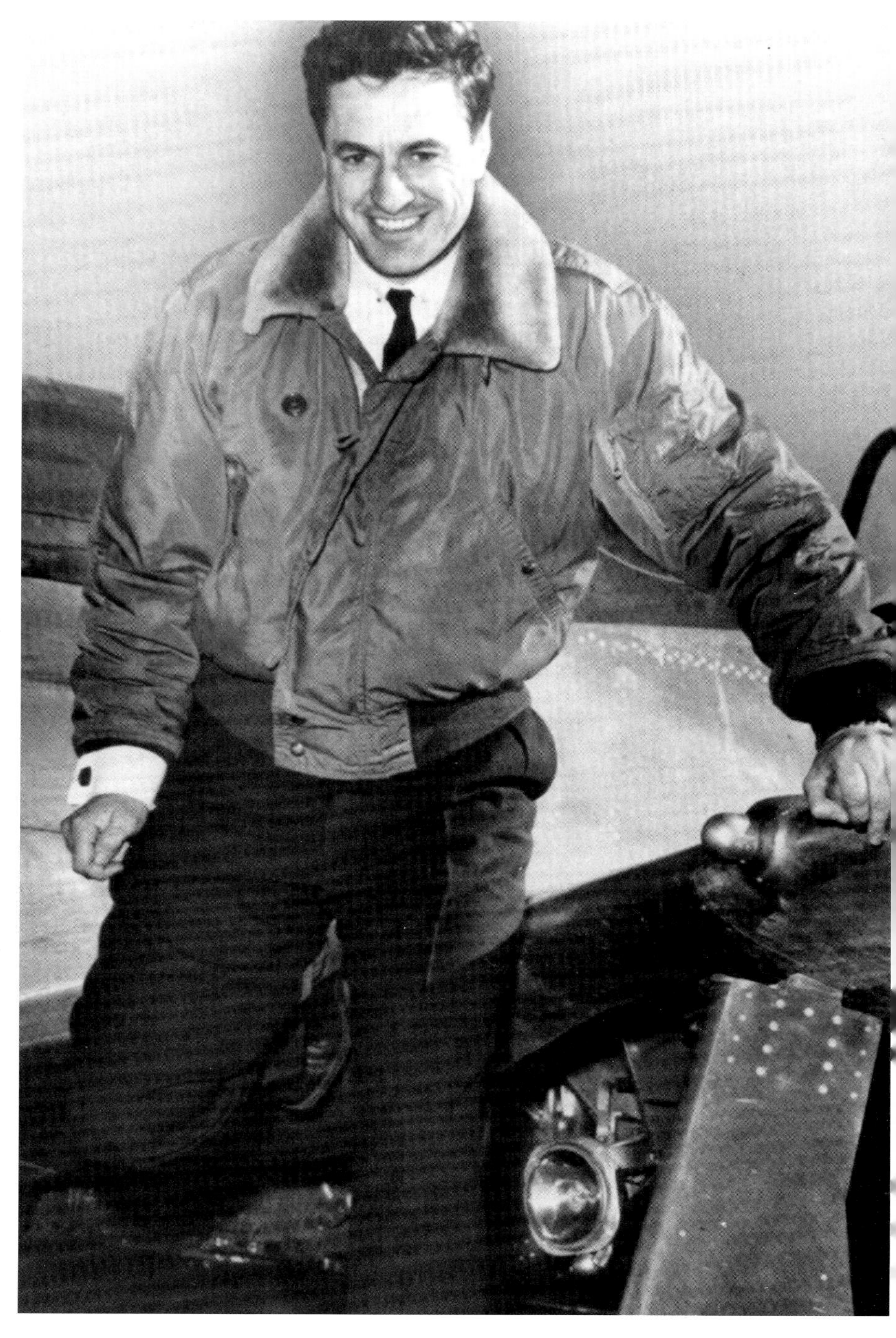

The dashing A.M.H.: "A cross between Cesar Romero and Tamerlane." *(Jim Knowler, the Calgary Herald Newspaper)*

RCAF Summer Camp: Flight Lieutenant Harradence, Wing Commander Cruikshank, and Flying Officer Greg Forsyth, following the successful strafing of an RCMP parade square.
(Montreal Gazette)

Jaws I and Jaws II.

Milt Harradence
with partner
John MacPherson.

Group Capt. Sir Douglas Bader an
friend and admirer Harradence.
(Norm Hendricks)

A.M.H. and the
Right Honourable
John Diefenbaker.

Della Street (Catherine Vanier)
and
Perry Mason (A.M.H.).

The Hon. Mr. Justice Harradence and the Hon. Chief Justice W.A. McGillivray, Chief Justice of Alberta, following Milt's swearing-in.
(The Report newsmagazine)

Mr. Justice Harradence with his secretary at the Court of Appeal for 13 years, Mrs. Joyce Simmons. "If it hadn't been for Mrs. Simmons, my tenure would have been addressed by both Houses of Parliament."

Mr. Justice Harradence swears in
His Worship Mayor Ralph Klein, October, 1980.
(Mathieson Photo Service)

Left:
The Harradence brothers,
Clyne Harradence, Q.C.,
and Milt Harradence, Q.C.
(Angus of Calgary)

Milt and Catherine Harradence with the author at the Retirement Dinner, 1996. *(Angus of Calgary)*

The retiring Justice, the Master of Ceremonies, and the Main Speaker Mr. Justice Major. *(Angus of Calgary)*

"The oldest pilot to slow-roll an F-18 at Mach 3 plus."

(4 Wing Photo Section, Cold Lake, Alberta)

Honourary Colonel, 416 Tactical Squadron of Air Command at Cold Lake, Alberta. *(Gold Photography)*

The Colonel inspecting a typical crate of World War II Vintage.

(416 Tactical Fighter Squadron)

Above:

Milt receiving a presentation on his retirement from Assistant Commissioner Don McDermid, Commanding Officer of RCMP K Division.

(Angus of Calgary)

Right:

The Honourable. A.M. Harradence, Doctor of the University of Calgary, Convocation April 1998.

(David Brown)

Milt and Catherine Harradence.

The Harradence Family: Catherine, Rod, Milt, Bruce, and Cathy, at home. *(Gold Photography)*

Part Two
Some Famous Examples of the Genre

IT TAKES A PARTICULAR FLAIR to extract large amounts of cash from persons of modest means in a faltering economy. Harradence, of course, was a master of the art. First, a warning: stories of Milt's allegedly extravagant retainers and charges are legion, most of them unsubstantiated. His brother, Clyne, takes great exception to the suggestion that Milt charged the huge fees associated by the public with high-profile criminal lawyers. In fact, quite often Milt got so engrossed in the case that he forgot all about getting any cash up front, and was frequently burned; other times, the retainer ran out long before the end of the case and Milt's energy devoted to the defence, but Milt carried on even when he was running on air. That being said, he made good money.

A case in point was the retainer of Harradence, Q.C., by two lads convicted of a serious crime and an appeal was in the offing. Milt was to be retained by the parents of the lads for the appeal, and he determined early that there was a perceived conflict. Therefore, he called in Bill Stilwell for the defence of one of the youths. Stilwell and Harradence met with the boys and their anxious parents in the palatial Harradence chambers. The lawyers listened to the stories of the boys. Milt looked grim, nodding throughout knowledgeably. It was clear that the audience was overawed by the solemnity of the barristers and the opulence of the surrounding. Then Milt said (which is surprising, considering that this was the first time he or Bill had heard the facts from the point of view of the two accused), "I've discussed this matter with my colleague, Stilwell. We are both of the view that there has been a clear miscarriage of justice." The parents nodded solemnly. The two young men looked relieved. Stilwell was, as always, poker faced. Then Milt said, "And now, it is necessary to discuss the financial arrangements."

Whereupon a great deal of money was placed on the table by the parents. The relieved parents and the two convicted felons were ushered out of the imposing surroundings by the solicitous

Harradence, Q.C., who assured them that no stone would be unturned in the pursuit of the appeals from conviction. He had barely closed the door when he turned to Stilwell and reportedly said, "Well, we've got the money." There was a pause while he grimaced. "Now we've got to think of something."

Sometimes it was necessary to bring in an entire committee of yes-men to graphically bring home to the clients the fact that an incredible number of person-hours were being expended upon their case. Milt thus dreamed up the round robin. On occasion, not only would he call in all of the juniors in his office to sit in on his interview with the clients and his analysis of their cause and prognosis for the defence, but he would even call me and perhaps his partner MacPherson to join the circle. It must be remembered that I never was employed by Milt nor worked at the same firm in any capacity with him, but we had such a close professional and personal relationship that I was not at all surprised when I would receive, usually in the early evening, a summons to "get down here." I usually got down there. I would enter Milt's chambers and take a seat with my contemporaries. Milt would then give a quick outline of the facts as related by the client (which usually bore little resemblance to what had really happened), then postulate an approach by the defence, often outrageous or hilarious at least to me, then jump up from his chair and go from junior to junior demanding "What do you think?" "What about you?" "And you?" It was sort of like a Monty Python send up of executive assistants meeting with the Texas oil millionaire turned film producer, and I could barely contain my mirth at these proceedings. However, I solemnly delivered a straight-faced commentary or suggestion or enthusiastic endorsement of the proposal. The clients were always overwhelmed by this show of masterful solidarity.

As already noted, Milt's superb sense of the dramatic impelled strange late night telephone calls. One such went as follows:

"Hello?"

"Can you talk?"

"Yes."

"Listen carefully. A man named Jaworski will be calling you tomorrow. He'll be arriving at your chambers. It's the trouble with that Goddamn jurat. You'll know what to do."

Click.

I did not know what to do. I never knew what to do. I had not the slightest idea what Milt was talking about. I did not dare ask my leader, "What jurat, who's Jaworski?" Thank God, Jaworski never called and never showed up.

There are many stories of Milt on his feet in court, many of them inspiring, some of them quite funny. Here are two of my favourites in the latter category:

Milt appeared before His Worship Magistrate Verne Read, an old hand, defending a kid for shoplifting. When the evidence was finished and Milt was summing up for an acquittal, he said, "And if this young man is acquitted, your Worship, he wants to go to law school."

Quoth Judge Read, "Do they enrol thieves?"

In the then Supreme Court (Trial Division), Milt pleaded a puker guilty to possession of the dread cannabis for the purpose of trafficking. The courts used to jug them pretty regularly in those days. Milt was in front of Mr. Justice Hugh John McDonald, and Brian Stevenson (now Assistant Chief Judge) was prosecuting. After detailing the young man's antecedents, Milt made the following submission:

> Now, quite frankly, sir, I'm not suggesting that this young man should not have some form of punishment and I mean severe punishment. I would suggest, however, that the ends of justice could be met with a large fine. And I mean a substantial fine. And further I understand that if you saw fit to fine this young man, the fine would be paid by the parents, relatives and friends of this young man.

The well of the court was indeed filled with supportive family and friends of the accused.

Mr. Justice McDonald thought about this, then turned to prosecutor Stevenson and asked, "Do you think a fine would be a deterrent?"

Brian Stevenson responded at once: "It will be a deterrent, to the parents, relatives and friends of the accused."

Milt's rapid-fire cross-examinations on the issue of identification, particularly where witnesses simply had a fleeting look of an accused person at the material time, were able tradecraft and frequently imitated by more junior members of the Bar. Juniors must always bear in mind, however, that they should never try to do what they have seen a more experienced barrister achieve, because they will fall flat. You have to develop your own style and stay with it. The only person who could cross-examine like Milt Harradence was Milt Harradence. Further, senior counsel often take liberties that no junior would be permitted. They can do it because they have the years, the experience, and the agility, and most trial judges are not only loathe but afraid to interrupt them. So many a junior gets a nasty surprise when he or she tries to pull off the same thing.

With respect to identification issues, Milt was renowned for peppering the witness with short sharp questions demanding a yes or no answer with little time in between for the witness to think carefully about his or her responses. This was particularly effective with civilians, for example, customers in the bank, who were present at the time of a robbery. Before the days of hidden ID cameras in banks, witness identification was crucial to a conviction. Noting the success of his technique, I attempted the same thing, but made the mistake of trying it on a seasoned police officer who happened while off-duty to wander into a bank when exactly that situation occurred:

Mr. Evans: *How tall was he?*
The witness: *About five-ten.*
Mr. Evans: *Did he have a moustache?*
The witness: *No.*
Mr. Evans: *Was he wearing a hat?*
The witness: *What kind of a hat?*
Mr. Evans: *I'll ask the questions here, witness.*
The witness: *Well, Mr. Evans, if you can tell me what kind of a hat he was wearing, I can tell you whether he was wearing it or not.*
Mr. Evans: *Moving on quickly.*

Every so often in Calgary some loser kidnaps somebody rich

or somebody nerdlike but who has rich relatives. If some benign villain kidnapped one of my relatives, I would pay the kidnapper to keep the victim. The usual reaction to the demand accompanied by menaces of the person snatcher, however, is met with inexplicable anteing up of large sums in small bills, with the cops fuming because the silly family never had the good sense to call them first. Moreover, certainly in these climes, in keeping with the mean standards of the general population, the kidnappers are invariably inept.

Three of such rocket scientists conspired to abduct the scion of a Calgary cognoscenti and hold him for a king's ransom. The victim was easily snatched while babysitting, or going to the 7-Eleven for a Slurpee, or something, and placed handily in the trunk of the kidnappers' car. This time the family, importuned by the usual threatening telephone calls with instructions where to drop the loot, made the right call and got the cops in from the outset. It was not too long before the police had a line on the three clots whose dreams of a South American sanctuary bathed in the afterglow of a million bucks were soon alchemized by swift police action into eight-by-eight cells with psychopaths for roommates. In the course of the investigation, the villain who held the loot, well knowing that it was but a matter of hours, if that, before the heavy step of Constable Boot was heard coming down the hall followed by the midnight knock, had the prudence to retain Milton Harradence for what was left of his defence, which turned out to be an early guilty plea in front of a Judge who was not likely to be scandalized by a fairly run-of-the-mill body snatch without injuries. It appeared that the client had retained in his possession a suitcase containing the requisite ransom in cash, which he had the presence of mind to commandeer as his companions took it on the lam in different directions. The first smart thing he did was to phone Milt.

Harradence ended up with the suitcase of cash in the trunk of his car at about 3 *a.m.*, on his way to the police station to turn it over to the police, followed by his client, in exchange for a deal, the classic "negotiated plea."

He stopped to gas up the MiltMobile. The young gas jockey filling the vast tank at the rear of the limousine was all agog at the number one news story of the evening, the kidnapping. He exclaimed, "Imagine having your hands on that kind of money!" Said Milt, "Well, sonny, it's closer than you think!"

Pat Peacock, Q.C., later President of the Canadian Bar Association but otherwise a good fellow, recalls a case where he was acting on the civil end for alleged defalcators, and Milt was retained for the criminal defence. Peacock was heading along the sidewalk to his office when suddenly Milt's block-long Cadillac came alongside and the electric window snicked down. Milt's voice said, imperiously, "Get in!" One did not question Milt in these circumstances. Peacock got in the car. Milt drove on without a word, and negotiated the entrance to his underground parking in his office building. Suddenly, he braked. "Get out!" he ordered. Peacock, somewhat unnerved by this strange encounter, tried to get out, but the door was blocked by a cement stanchion. "I can't," he said. "Why not?" demanded Milt. Peacock pointed to the pillar. Without a word, Milt drove forward three feet. "Now get out." Peacock got out. No explanation was ever offered for this encounter. Presumably, Milt had decided that it was unwise to discuss any aspect of the case when "they" might be listening.

An even more intriguing cloak-and-dagger episode was inflicted upon leading Ontario counsel, Earl Cherniak, Q.C., who is generally renowned throughout North American as Canada's "King of Torts" and whose career is itself worthy of a book. I advert once again to the eclectic nature of Milt's practice, which, although primarily criminal, still turned up some strange cases in other areas. In one such case, a bitter family dispute over testimonial capacity and the proof of a will in solemn form had spilled into the courts. No one is really clear as to who was acting for whom, but make no mistake that not only the deceased but a number of his surviving relatives now warring over the spoils of the deceased's demise were seriously rich people. Cherniak was acting for one faction; the venue was Calgary. The solicitors for the Calgary-based faction of the family retained Harradence, who in turn retained as his co-counsel William Stilwell. The battle lines had not yet been solidified, and negotiations were tentatively being pursued. To that end, Cherniak arranged to attend at Calgary and contacted Harradence, who indicated that he would meet him at the airport. Cherniak arrived late at night. The weather was chilly. He has a vivid recollection of his first glimpse of the great barrister and his laconic sidekick, both looking like death and dressed like undertakers, all in black. Stilwell is as tall as Milt, and they must have looked like a couple of genuine heavies out of New York. The only thing said in the entire encounter, by Milt as he was approached by Cherniak, "Harradence." The closest approximation would be Dirty Harry saying, "Make my day." Stilwell said not a word. The two of them turned and Cherniak, retrieving his overnight bag, followed. He was led to a block-long black Cadillac which appeared to be of bulletproof construction. Harradence got in the driver's seat, Stilwell got in the front passenger seat, and Cherniak, with some trepidation, got in the back. His nervousness was not mollified by noting what appeared to be a large calibre-repeating rifle under the dash, handy to the driver, in a breakaway sleeve. They drove downtown without a word being said. Cherniak was dropped at his hotel.

Milt had put the application down before a Judge "who could approach the matter objectively." At the end of the day, Cherniak said to both Milt and Stilwell: "You two guys are criminal lawyers, and I know you never cracked a book on this case."

One of my genuinely theatrical tangles with Milt was when the two of us were flown at the expense of the CBC to Toronto, in order to take part in a simulated courtroom dramatization of the trial of a passenger in a small plane on a charge of "endangering the safety of an aircraft." The CBC had done a few of these in a series that featured actual legal practitioners performing before the cameras in front of an actual Judge with actors as the witnesses before a studio jury of citizens, who then went out, deliberated, and delivered a verdict. The whole thing was encapsulated into an hour national program. This was a lot of fun, not least because we were before an able Alberta High Court Judge, "Red" Cavanagh, who himself had been a prominent member of the defence Bar in a long and distinguished practice before he went to the Bench. Milt was at his absolute dramatic best. At one point, as he was cross-examining the Crown witness who was detailing how Milt's allegedly intoxicated client had been throwing a briefcase around in the plane during flight, I groaned audibly. Milt paused, turned slightly, and asked, "Are you in pain?" The jury loved it. Then, in his peroration, he eloquently recited his favourite poem, *High Flight* by Pilot Officer J.G. Magee: "Oh, I have slipped the surly bonds of earth/And danced the skies on laughter-silvered wings ...," which had nothing to do with anything, but the jury was transfixed. In order to counter this, I had to remind the jury, "How would you feel if you were one of those passengers, trying to mind your own business, and some lunatic is throwing his briefcase about, drunk, in a small plane?" Well, this old ploy won the day, but it was obvious that Mr. Justice Cavanagh, also an old World War II pilot, was buying none of the Crown's case and summed up heavily for the defence. Apparently, no old hand pilot was going to be put off by some drunk in the back and the plane was never unsafe.

Considering Milt's penchant for drama, both within and without the court, I never thought it was probable that anything I ever did would cause him to comment adversely. In the early eighties, for no reason other than cussedness, I grew my hair very long and wore it in a ponytail. At the same time, I had signed a performer contract with the local CBC television to do confrontational interviews with this or that celeb which were aired after the evening news. The CBC brass demurred at the length of my hair, a scrap ensued, and I emerged the winner as there was nothing in the contract precluding my being hirsute. This was the subject of a noteworthy column by the ex-mayor of Calgary, Rod Sykes, which is included as an appendix to this narrative because it also speaks highly of Milt. In any event, in due course, and with the trial of Abacus Generallissimo Ken Rogers looming before a Bay Street jury in Toronto, I decided to dump the ponytail. I thought that this should not go unremarked, however, for posterity, and when my TV program producer got wind of the imminent shearing of the Evans tresses, arrangements were made to have a film crew attend at Astoria Hair Dressing Salon, where Kathy, who had been trimming the Evans hair and beard for many years, cut off the ponytail, and it was filmed in slow motion as it drifted to the floor of the salon. This in turn was aired to the evening's news viewers. The phone rang:

"Cliff, this time you've gone too far!"

"You're just jealous because you never thought of it."

Pause. "Yaas. That's true."

I have mentioned the courtroom antics of Marshall Hall, K.C. Harradence was a master of this sort of technique, and went one further. At an appropriately telling point in a major criminal proceeding with all eyes upon the star Crown witness and ears attuned to every utterance of that witness in examination-in-chief by the Crown, and with that examination arriving at the crucial point of the expected evidence while Milt glowered at the defence table, a signal must have been emitted from that location. Indeed, at that certain crucial point there entered into the courtroom a very, very tall, mysterious lady in dark glasses, wearing a very short dress and a huge black hat and spike heels; she would be six foot five easily and walked in as if she held the first mortgage on the courtroom. And everything stopped: the star witness hesitated, the Crown paused in mid-question, the Judge stared, the audience was riveted upon the mysterious vamp, who was carrying a plain brown envelope and who walked ever so slowly to the Bar, through the gate, and over to the defence table. She handed the envelope to Milt, who half rose, and muttered something. Then she turned and walked ever so slowly out of the courtroom. Meanwhile, the prosecutor had managed to continue the examination of his witness and had managed to start the witness's engine again. But for ten to fifteen minutes, nobody heard a word that the witness said, particularly as Milt elaborately opened the envelope and removed what appeared to be important papers, frowned urgently, half rose as if to make a submission to the court, then subsided with dreadful countenance. Talk about theatre!

The accomplished actress in this farce was the formidable Ms. Catherine Van Gaalen (now Vanier). At well over six foot five inches in high heels, a cascade of iridescent blonde hair, shapely legs *etcetera*, with the intellect of Pascal and the sense of humour of Monty Python, here was no shrinking violetta. The personal secretary/executive assistant to the Great Man—spoken of in hushed, reverent whispers about Harradence, Waite and Company as "The Duchess"—was herself a consummate public performer. She loved theatre as did her boss, and like him she was oblivious to danger, criticism, and public opinion. Indeed, she was immune. If one were to combine Madam Mao, Mata Hari, and Rita Hayworth, here was the blueprint.

My wife, Bernice, and I have always been among Ms. Van Gaalen's admirers. Bernice first encountered Catherine the Great on an elevator at the Palliser Hotel. It was the occasion of the wedding of Milt's son, Rod Harradence. We got on at the parking level, joined by the chilly personages of an Appeal Court Judge and his missus, who both nodded with jurisprudential reserve. (The august jurisprude had not practiced on "the criminal side," except as an ad hoc drug prosecutor in the early days when marijuana traffickers were shot, and he was deeply suspicious of all criminal lawyers.)

It was a busy time, being a large wedding, and the elevator had to stop at every level. On the next floor, John MacPherson, Q.C., entered, fabled as "Mini Milt," brash, cocky, disdainful and full of fun. On the next level, again, the elevator doors parted, and there stood Ms. Van Gaalen, gorgeously gowned with her trademark huge hat. The denizens of the elevator shrank back to give her passage. The door started to close but instantly recoiled as she gave it the heel of her hand. She could snap your spine like a toothpick.

Seeing us, she beamed, then scanned the rest of the passengers with a sneer.

"Well," said Johnny Mac, making conversation to no one in particular, "looks like a good crowd for a wedding!"

At once, Ms. Van Gaalen took him by both lapels and without apparent effort lifted him off his feet. He hung there, legs dangling. "What would you know, you stupid little shit!?" she snarled, then dropped him like a sack of sand.

The Judge and his wife were open-mouthed in horror.

Bernice guffawed and grabbed Catherine by the arm. "We've got to sit together!"

"Of course," rejoined Ms. Van Gaalen. We did.

Catherine Van Gaalen had worked for some years for William Stilwell. When Bill renounced the world and rode into the sunset in the general direction of Dapp, Alberta, she was offered the job with Milt. He was clearly the leader of the Criminal Bar; his exploits and mannerisms were already legends. He needed an executive assistant who shared his dynamism and desire to wow the proles, but who had a solid practical ability. It was all very well for Milt to rocket off to the defence of this or that hopeless cause in his latest fighter plane, but someone had to collect the dough and keep the shop running smoothly, with time out to participate in the theatrical extravaganzas that only A.M.H. could dream up. Ms. Van Gaalen was perfect for the part, with one stipulation by the master: "You'd better do something about the length of those skirts."

Naturally, Johnny Mac and I assumed that, although the comely Ms. Van Gaalen affected microlength skirts with little left to the imagination, Milt thought they should be shorter. He disabused our raillery in no uncertain terms: "You little bastards! I told her to look more modest. Jesus Christ!" We exchanged meaning looks. Ms. Van Gaalen thought this over for a while, then capitulated with grace, but not before she, too, expressed herself in like terms: "Dammit, Milt, I'm not an old bag yet." Milt growled, "You've got no choice."

This rule of deportment was relaxed for dramatic court entrances only, *supra*.

Ms. Van Gaalen went to work. She was extremely able and superefficient. Milt became uncharacteristically organized. She had her own office, at the entrance to his eagle's nest, and no one got past his portals without first depositing the balance of the retainer into her hands. Ms. Van Gaalen usually set the terms of hire of Harradence, Q.C. Indeed, I recall her barking into the telephone at some supplicant tardy in his remuneration that "it's no use giving me that B.S., Mr. Arbuthnot. Either you get five thousand bucks in here, cash or money order, or you never even get to speak to Mr. Harradence. Never. What's that? I am hanging up now." And she hung up on him. The money came in.

She, like Milt, dressed in striking outfits. In winter, she paraded about Calgary in a full-length mink coat with matching chapeau and muff. It is more than mere rumour that Catherine, too, was armed and dangerous, in order to back Milt if there was gunplay. The mink muff (or her black leather briefcase with gold fittings) concealed her weapon of choice, a Buntline Special loaded with dumdum ammunition. There is no question in my mind that Ms. Van Gaalen would blow out the half-baked brains of any creep without compunction. When Milt went to the Bench, the CIA should have recruited her for sophisticated fifth-column operations behind cold war lines. No gambling man would have put his money on the Commies.

It was a sight and an event to behold Milton Harradence, Q.C., stern of visage, and Ms. Catherine Van Gaalen, cool as a hired gun, entering the Trader's dining room of the Four Seasons Hotel at lunch time. There was not a diner in the place who did not stare in slack-mouthed admiration at this dynamic duo. This, too, was classic theatre and both played their respective parts of Perry Mason and Della Street to the hilt. Of course, between the aperitif and the appetizer, Milt was seen to be talking rapidly and Ms. Van Gaalen was seen to make some quick notes on the Irish linen napkin, whereupon she rose and stalked majestically from the room. Obviously, she had to place an important call. All waited in anticipation until she reappeared, swept the room with her disdainful gaze, then paced off the entire length of the packed dining room to their corner table with the carriage and detached hauteur of a world class model deigning to show off the latest from this or that famous designer at the Paris spring fashion show. "Ooooh" and "Ahhhh."

Milt would present his lion-like phizzog, as Mrs. Peel whispered the latest intelligence to John Steed, then he straightened, looked about him quickly, and said, "Yaas. That's true," or "We've got no choice."

Sometimes it was Milt who left the dining room and marched with frowning purpose to the phone area. The fact is, in either case, whichever one of them did "the walk" probably just went to the washroom. As Milt was later to say, with an uncharacteristic chuckle, "C.D., if only the public knew!"

Well, the public never knew. In Calgary, Alberta, in the sixties and seventies, it was possible to fool all of the people all of the time. If Milt had to live in the post-Second World War era he really was in the right place at the right time for him. The only other suitable venue with a similar incredulity index right off the scale would have been Hollywood.

So how much of A.M.H. was myth, anyway? Did he really believe that third parties were listening to his every utterance, that we were being shadowed by G-men, that the phone calls he did not get were the ones to fear, that licensed gunmen from Murder Inc. lurked at every corner, that Communist agents were sabotaging his aircraft, that conspiracies compounded daily against him and our small band of brothers-at-law?

The always perceptive Morley Callaghan, a great Canadian writer, observes: "For the sake of the peace of their own souls most men live by pretending to believe in something they secretly know isn't true. It seems to be a dreadful necessity. It keeps life going on … . it is true some men are much better at pretending than others. It's a built-in gift. The game for them takes on a reality that shapes their whole lives."[5]

This rationale is further elucidated by Lord Francis Bacon in his essay, *Of Truth:*

> Doth any man doubt that if there were taken out of men's minds vain opinions, flattering hopes, false valuations, imaginings as one would, and the like, but it would leave the minds of a number of men poor shrunken things, full of melancholy and indisposition, and unpleasing to themselves?

Which may explain why A.M.H., encountering Major by chance at the Executive Flight Centre at the airport, without any greeting or preamble, simply sat down beside Major and announced:

> I'll just have to hold both portfolios, Premier and Attorney General. I've got no choice.

---

5. Callaghan, Morley. *That Summer in Paris*, Stoddart Publishing Co. Ltd., Toronto, 1992.

CHAPTER EIGHT

Security of the Person

THE IMPACT of the invention of the gun upon the history of mankind is now a cliché, and its romantic rubric in association with the taming of the west, however erroneous, is the stuff of Grade B fiction *ad nauseum*. In fact, the west was made a great deal wilder by the introduction of repeating firearms, usually wielded by morons who were little above the stray curs fighting and fornicating in front of the General Store or the National Hotel of this or that hopeless backwater. With rare exceptions, no one of any consequence went west; anyone with any marbles at all was trying to get the hell out of there, i.e., east. The far side of the moon would have been a viable alternative. The greatest fear of the average circumspect citizen was of being randomly plugged by the likes of Billy The Kid, "Doc" Holliday, the Youngers, or others of their ilk.

Notwithstanding these irrefutable facts, the mob's association of manliness with the deadly deployment of firearms has persisted. Thus are we today afflicted with militant militias asserting this or that Amendment and their God-given right to bear arms, and, concomitantly, to blow away with impunity others who do not share their pathologies. This "mentality" (well, it is the opposite, surely, of a mental process) has infected Canada, particularly Western Canada. Recent efforts in the late nineties by the Minister of Justice for Canada to tighten up the wanton carelessness of citizens in the handling of firearms and ammunition and to establish a registration system therefor, however innocuous and unenforceable, has met with tumultuous irrational bellows and demurrers from otherwise sober men and women, supported by a variety of specious arguments. Much of this immaturity may be properly blamed upon (1) historically inaccurate western movies and (2) television, which proliferates (1).

In the 1960s in these parts, shootists were still revered. A relatively large cross-section of the population, mostly males who had served in and survived the last world war, were not troubled by the proliferation of increasingly sophisticated firearms at large in North America. Hunters had not yet been condemned by the sanctimonious "greens" who now plague us without surcease, the pendulum having swung so far left it has got stuck. I am obliged to say that one can appreciate to some extent the point of the anti-gun group: a Kalishnikov in the hands of an ethnic cleanser, with the ethnic cleansee on the receiving end, is a recent example of the uncivilized in possession of the too sophisticated.

The politicians and authorities, nevertheless, had prudently embargoed some invitations to chaos: sawed-off models, rapid-firing automatics and/or combat weapons, and handguns of all design and calibres were not to be carried or transported without permit by the man in the street. The events that led A.M. Harradence, first, to seek such a permit and, second, to secure it are now analyzed.

The fashionable wave of restricted firearms possession legislation would not have had a fan—or an adherent—in Harradence, Q.C. Milt felt strongly that it was necessary and desirable for all able-bodied men to be armed to the teeth, and *cap-à-pie,* and to be ready to repair for drill to the village green on the immediate public posting of Temporary Orders on the Outbreak of Hostilities. The rationale is found in the aphorism of Two Gun Pedro, made famous by Judge Leo Collins: "I have the pistolas; I am the boss!"

To that end, Milt prevailed upon the Solicitor General of the day, Roy Fahrenheit (see Chapter 3), to issue to him a special permit granting him license to carry concealed upon his person a deadly handgun, being a restricted and a prohibited and an offensive weapon, barrelled, "from which any shot, bullet or other projectile can be discharged and that is capable of causing serious injury or death to a person, including any frame or receiver of such a barrelled weapon and anything that can be adapted for use as a firearm," but not including an "antique firearm" manufactured before 1898 and not designed to use rim-fire or centre-fire ammunition. Thus, my 1854 Navy Colt is exempted, but it can only stop a balloon at five paces in any event. These were the days before F.A.C.s ("firearms acquisition certificate") and other pernicious restraints upon the freedom of the individual so common in the late twentieth century, but Milt still had to jump through a few hoops to gain the coveted dispensation.

An unpleasant citizen of those United States, with an extensive criminal record for violence and on the lam in Canada, had been detained by the authorities to assist them with their inquiries, and bail was denied. Milt was retained. In fact, the bum never paid him one cent, but Milt went to his usual inordinate lengths above and beyond the call of duty to try to overturn the initial Detention Order and gain sweet liberty for his client. His valiant efforts were rebuffed by the Court. In due course, the client was extradited, which in those days meant that the R.C.M.P. drove the guy down to the border, having tipped off their pals in Montana, and shoved the miscreant across the barbed wire into the waiting arms of the U.S. authorities. This did not sit well with Milt's erstwhile client, who subsequently caused to be mailed to Milt a series of defamatory letters *inter alia* threatening death or grievous bodily harm in escalating prose. Milt was initially miffed because all he had ever tried to do was his best for this creep, but as the barrage of blood-curdling threats intensified, Milt began to look over his shoulder and to frequent dark alleys less cavalierly. He applied to the Solicitor General of Alberta for a permit to carry a handgun for self-protection. This was nixed at various lower bureaucratic levels, but an appeal to the Minister gained a sympathetic ear. Roy Fahrenheit had served as a Captain in the British Army in Palestine, and himself had received serious death threats from some very nasty persons indeed, and he was certainly wary of blood oaths and empathetic to similar threatees.[1] In the result, Harradence got his permit.

His first pistol was a lethal Walther,[2] subsequently upgraded to a 9 mm. Browning high-power automatic that took a clip of twelve rounds, each of which made a small hole going in, and the place where it came out was so large that you could stick your head in and wiggle your ears and not get blood in them. The threats from the particular villain subsided in due course, but Milt's trepidation at an untimely demise at the hands of this or that disaffected client or even a pissed off cross-examinee increased. His tailor was instructed to construct a special reinforced pocket in each of his bespoke suits (themselves probably bullet proof) to house his deadly weapon when it was not seeing gore.

A Browning 9 mm. automatic is not a pistol you take along to a family picnic. Well, Milt *might*. It is a gun for people who hunt people or who themselves are being hunted by other people.

In addition, Milt had a loaded shotgun handy under the dashboard of his Fishtail 8, which motor vehicle also featured a taxi driver's all angles rearview mirror, causing Rod McLennan, Q.C., a leader of the Bar and a sometime passenger in the Harradence Miltmobile, to observe: "Paranoia increases your peripheral vision."

I remember when I had shown off to Milt my newly purchased black Jeep with eight cylinders, two half-turns, and a sonic boom (C.D. Evans Professional Corporation's official automobile for business). Milt appreciated the military aspect of the thing, but counseled, "Nothing a mounted AK-47 wouldn't enhance, m'boy!"

Milt was always under arms. Jack Major often gave him a ragging, and on one occasion said to Milt (in the presence of third parties) that he was too soft-hearted to shoot anyone, and even if he successfully drew his then Walther pistola from the tailored pistol pocket of his suit, he would probably shoot himself in the

1. For a ripping yarn, read *Winged Dagger* by Capt. (Ret'd) Roy Farran, DSO.
2. No relation to Johann Gottfried Walther (b.1684, Weimar), organist and composer and a relation of J.S. Bach.

foot in any event. Harradence was not amused. Once again, he caused to question Major's "loyalty."

Grudgingly agreeing that Major might have a point in the second part of his criticism, however, Milt adopted an ingenious but useless calf holster which was attached above his half-Wellington boot with something like a sock suspender. I have related the famous incident when he was rushing to a Benchers' meeting when the pistol, secured in the holster on his calf, gave way as he was racing up the mezzanine steps from the lobby of the Palliser Hotel to the second-floor meeting room.

The block-long white Cadillac with a carbine mounted under the dash was another logical step, but Milt also decided that he had to make his home bulletproof. I had come around to visit, and was met at the door by a shaken Catherine who said, "Thank heavens you're here! Will you please stop him."

"What's going on?"

All one could hear was "Boom, boom!"

I went out to the back garden and Milt was standing there with a golf club. I thought the worst had happened, that is, that Chief Justice McGillivray had actually got Milt to play golf; he had been trying for years, but Milt had properly resisted. He was taking incredibly vigorous swipes with the golf club at the window glass mounted on the ground level. He would pound away at one, hence the "boom, boom," and then move to the next window. Catherine was standing there with her hands over her ears. What Milt had done was to order the installation of Lexon glass to replace the ordinary windows, and he was testing its resistance to bullets, bombs, and other terrorist hardware.

My comment was a good line (not mine), "Milt, just because you're paranoid doesn't mean they're not out to get you." Now Milt questioned *my* loyalty.

Milt was interviewed on national television by Patrick Watson on his talk show. Watson asked him, "Why do you have bulletproof glass in your house and why do you carry a firearm? Is it the telephone calls that you get?" And Milt responded, in the manner of the Sphinx, "It's the telephone calls I *don't* get, Mr. Watson." Both Watson and the audience went "oooh, ahhh."

Further, in pursuit of protection, Milt had always encumbered his telephones at home and at the office with coils of tape-recording paraphernalia, the tape recorder being triggered by the telephone ringing or by his placing a call. I remonstrated with him that ex-President Richard Nixon had regretted a similar system, but I could have predicted Milt's response: "We've got no choice." I learned early on never to discuss the details of a case, whether past, present, or future, on the telephone with Milt. "If they're not listening to me, they're listening to *you*!" he hissed, admonishing me to confine my remarks to the weather and the making of appointments to meet. These latter arrangements always took a variety of imaginative turns, for example, behind the Cathedral at six a.m. and wearing a green carnation, that sort of thing.

Indeed, it was not unusual to receive an urgent telephone call from Milt at two or three *a.m.* He would rattle out the following types of orders in a hoarse whisper:

"Can't talk now. You know my car. Drive down to the Westin, head east on Third Avenue, in the block before the hotel, I'll be parked. If I flash my lights once, stop. If I flash them twice, keep moving."

I fell for this only once, and sure enough the headlights of the Fishtail 8 flashed twice. So I drove home. Naturally, the next morning, Milt feigned complete ignorance of the proposed assignation. I presumed the double flashing headlights signified a blown cover. I suppose I should have been happy that I did not have my balls shot off by person or persons unknown.

I do not wish to suggest that I was the only person in those years who received urgent imperative telephone summonses. Jack Major was sitting down to dinner at home one night, when the phone rang and, of course, Milt needed him to "get over here right away." Major inquired, "Is it that important, or can it wait 'til tomorrow?" Milt growled, "I said right away." So, Major had to drive all the way over to Milt's house, where he was greeted by a grim-faced colleague, who put his finger to his lips and quickly led Jack downstairs to Milt's basement bunker, which so far as I recall had walls with the thickness of the Maginot Line. That at least was the *enceinte* or outer wall, and because Milt could not get city approval for a moat and a drawbridge, let alone machicolations, there was an inner donjon which rivalled that at Loches and the keep at Rochester. Thus, when the outer works fell, Milt and his garrison could retire to the keep, which was the focal point of the basement. There were no doubt various booby traps for the intruder not steeped in tradecraft.[3] Into that hermetically sealed sanctuary Major was led, and particularly to a table on which there was a large box. Nothing was said. Milt opened up the box, and proceeded to remove a white canvass arrangement which looked like a cross between a boiler suit and an astronaut's asteroid shield, covered with white canvass with slits for the forearms and the lower legs. He motioned to Major to heft it; Major did so, noting that the whole thing weighed about fifty or sixty pounds. "You're going to have to get one of these," said Milt, "and we're gonna have to start wearing them." Where? What to? Why? Major nodded, trying to look as if he were clued in, and said, "Anything else?" Milt shook his head. Major left.

"Conspiracy," quoth the late Jessica Mitford, "is the Prosecutors' useful tool." Its use dates from Edward II, the not-so-distinguished heir of Edward (Longshanks) I. Milt thought so, too, but one would reasonably expect that once one had been elevated to the rarefied atmosphere of the Court of Appeal, the highest court in Alberta, one would no longer have to be concerned that one was being listened to by anyone. Milt had been on the court only a few weeks when he called me urgently to meet him, "Not in my Chambers," but at the statue of the two businessmen on the 8th Avenue Mall. I did so, and we proceeded down the middle of the mall surrounded by the usual noontime crowd of bank clerks with brown paper bag lunches, shop girls, drug dealers, runaway juvenile delinquents, derelicts, and assorted proletarians, all talking at the tops of their voices while street buskers and various beggars and lunatics vied verbally for attention. "What's going on on the street?" growled Milt. This was essentially an innocent ques-

3. I said to Milt that I thought all these fortifications were a bit much, to which he responded, with a meaning look, "Tintagel was taken from within!"

tion which should not, without more, cause a peace officer to enter upon a criminal investigation. Why, I asked him, were we walking down the middle of a crowded street in order to have a private innocuous conversation?

"Because they can't get us here with the parabolic mikes!" was his explanation.

"Milt," I said to him, "you are one of Her Majesty's Justices of Appeal. What makes you think that anybody, especially any police officer or spy master, thinks that you have anything important to say, anyway, about anything?"

Milt looked askance at me, and then said something he has said to me a number of times: "Sometimes, Evans, you're not funny."

On another similar occasion, it was also not funny. Again, we were stalking in a conspiratorial fashion down the middle of the mall, discussing policing in Alberta in the most general terms, when I said, "I hear there may be some support for re-establishing the Alberta Provincial Police . . . ." Milt went straight into orbit and I thought he was having a *grand mal*. "Jesus Christ! Don't *say* that, don't *breathe* that, don't even *think* of that! They'll get us for high treason!" Why, I wondered, then as now.

It was always a treat to accompany A.M.H. on a commercial aircraft flight. Just prior to going through the local gestapo, the desultory security guards with their probing instruments and calculated rudeness, Milt would advise their Corporal or shift supervisor that he wished to see the "Commander of the aircraft." If this request was not taken seriously, Milt quickly made his credentials known, and demanded assistance and cooperation. In due course, a civilian pilot would appear. Milt would snap to attention. "Are you the Commanding Officer of this aircraft, Sir?" The pilot would nod, looking about him furtively. Milt would then produce his pistol, butt first, together with the permit therefor, and advise the Captain that he was entrusting this firearm to his possession until they landed at the destination. The ragtag goosesteppers were duly impressed, as were any fellow passengers who gazed upon the solemn diplomatic transaction with awe. Milt certainly knew a thing or two about theatre.

The preoccupation of Harradence, Q.C., with security and privacy, and his deep-seated and sincere belief that he was being listened to at all material times carried over indeed to his years on the Bench. He no doubt had good reason to be cautious in his days in private practice, considering the high-profile nature of his daily strivings and the notoriety of certainly some of his equally high-profile clients, many of whom no doubt were at the top of the shit lists of various police agencies. The fact that Milt acted for years for municipal police officers and R.C.M.P. officers when they got in trouble with the law arising out of their performance of their duties, and the fact that they held him almost universally in the highest esteem and awe, did not assuage his trepidation either as lawyer or judge. Accordingly, he continued to be guarded in conversation on the telephone and to pack his loaded pistol upon his person at all times. On more than one occasion when he was in practice, I answered a summons to his hotel room, if we were engaged on an out of town adventure, and would note the pistol in readiness on the bedside table even though he was about to retire for the night.

Matters came to a head on the Court of Appeal in the following verified circumstances. Chief Justice McGillivray was presiding over a sentencing panel with Kerans, J.A., and Harradence, J.A. A prisoner convicted of a violent crime was conducting his own sentence appeal before the panel, choosing not to be represented by counsel. After listening patiently to the appellant's earnest harangue, the Chief Justice speaking for the Court dismissed the sentence appeal from the Bench. At that point, obviously disaffected, the prisoner stepped quickly out of the prisoner's dock and took a couple of paces toward the upraised Bench, finger pointing and shaking as he cried, "Let me tell you guys something . . .!" At this point, the belligerent was grasped by the security guards and hustled unceremoniously out of the courtroom into the prisoner's cage. The Court quickly retired, but they had barely reached the retiring room behind the courtroom when Milt pulled back his gown and pointed to the butt of his Browning sticking out of the specially fashioned pocket of his court trousers, and said to both of his horrified colleagues, "One more step and I would have dropped him!"

He meant it.

Chief Justice McGillivray, it is reported, subsequently haunted by the possible unwelcome headline, "Court of Appeal Judge Shoots Unarmed Prisoner," directed Mr. Justice Harradence (and any other Judges who were inclined to arm themselves) not to take his pistol into the courtroom. However, knowing that Milt would be chagrined that he could not take his guns to town when all he had sought to do was defend his colleagues, the Chief let him down gently by appointing him *persona architecta designata* to liaise with the Department of Public Works who were designing new "security arrangements" for Justices of Appeal in their courtroom. This followed a couple of well-publicized incidents in Canada, one in which a prisoner had held his own counsel hostage (to the delight of the police, no doubt) and another where a disaffected litigant blasted away several persons in the courtroom and barely missed the presiding Judge who had to duck down behind the Bench. Based upon his vast experience with fortifications, acknowledged by the Chief Justice and his colleagues, Milt was to design appropriate fortified positions in the event that presiding Justices came under attack. Fortification being a military art, Milt was the ideal choice to blueprint this construction. He entered into this project with his customary zeal and designed a most unique system. Regrettably, his highly imaginative plans that went beyond merely entrenched positions of safety, e.g., cleared fields of fire, obstacles such as explosive mines, barbed-wire entanglements, felled trees, and anti-tank ditches, were surplusage. But the proposed permanent fortifications themselves were ingenious, and consisted of the following:

In the event that the three Judges perceived an attack, any one of them could press a large red button; immediately, a steel shield shot up in front of the Bench, while at the same time the three Judges' seats dropped eight feet into a steel-reinforced cement well. As the insurgents or terrorists approached the Registrar's desk below the Bench (the Registrar no doubt being dead by this time), the floor opened up and they all fell through a trap door into a pit.

The only problem with this arrangement was that most of the

old boys on the Bench had dickey tickers or high blood pressure or related problems of the aged and infirm, and the probability was that, the first time such a system was deployed, any of the Judges who fell eight feet (except for Milt, who was always "in shape") would probably die when they hit the bottom, or before, of fright or the impact.

Therefore, reluctantly, the plans were scrapped.

Again, Milt was chagrined. "What do these people know!" was all he could say, as he stared out the window disconsolately, listening for the Call of the Wild.

It has to be acknowledged that Milt's design for the ultimate shielding of his fellow Court of Appeal Judges from a deadly assault, whether by sociopath or terrorist, rivalled the ambitious and expensive plans of de Cessart for the naval fortification of Cherbourg, enthusiastically endorsed by Louis XVI. On the other hand, one is also put in mind of Uncle Toby's obsession with the fortifications at the Seige of Namur and his attempted reconstruction of the defences at the gate of St. Nicolas and the demi-bastion of St. Roch, detailed with great good humour in the Rev. Sterne's Tristram Shandy. Well, having heard the true story, take your pick. One can always hope that a Court of Appeal Judge, somewhere, sometime, like the unfortunate Uncle Toby, might be shot in the groin. One does not wish them to be dead, but one does wish them to have a nasty experience once in a while.

No discussion of security of the person is complete without due respect paid, in our context, to Man's Best Friend. Milt was one of the best friends Major and I ever had, but neither of us could compete in his manly affections with his successive German Shepherd bodyguards, Kurt 1, Kurt 2, and Troy. (When Kurt 1 went to the Big Kennel in the Sky, I pronounced: "*Mistah Kurt, he daid.*" Milt gave me that look of his.)

My favourite dog was Police Dog Demon, who retired after serving several years with distinction in the Calgary Police Service, with multiple battle scars and divers arrests to his credit. He was mostly black and presented as a cross between a timber wolf and a Tasmanian Devil. I recall running across an internal police continuation report which read: "Police Dog Demon became excited." Translation: "Police Dog Demon went bananas and removed important parts of the suspect's anatomy."

A highlight of the famous prosecution of Jack Ruby in Dallas, defended by Melvin Belli, was the jury selection. Allegedly, Belli's co-counsel, a local, steeped no doubt in the quaint argot and arcane lore of the jurisdiction, persisted in asking every potential juror, "Do you like dawgs?" adding, gratuitously, "My client likes dawgs."[4]

Harradence liked dawgs. He particularly liked dawgs that looked impressive. He always harboured the kind of a dawg you would take to a knife fight, that is, of the species *Canidae*, with powerful jaws and teeth adapted to seizing and crushing. Thus, when I opined as how I might get a dawg, he said, "It's got to be a Shepherd." Well, I said, it could also be a Scottish Deerhound, a Rhodesian Ridgeback, a Bull Mastiff, a Norwegian Buhund, a Komandor, perhaps a giant Schnauzer. No. "It's got to be a Shepherd. You've got no choice." That, as Steve McQueen said in Tom Horn, appeared to be his last word on the matter. Personally, I am leery of the breed that assisted the Axis prisoner-of-war guards at Stalag 17. Fraenkel and Manvell, in *Adolf Hitler: The Man and the Myth*, report, "Hitler had his own Alsatian, called Blondi. *'Leaders should be seen with big dogs,'* he said." Oh, dear.

I consulted the *Encyclopedia Britannica:* "The dog figures prominently in many tales of courage and selfless devotion in the service of man, of steadfastness and perseverance, of attentiveness and seeming concern for his master." It was the "seeming" that put me off, i.e., they only kill their masters, not to mention "because the close social relationship between dogs and man appears to many to be similar to the human parent-child relationship, dogs have been used to test various theories of child training."

That was enough!

I detest all children, mine or anyone else's. I have none to my knowledge but have the reformed libertine's fear of the urgent piping voice from a crowd of strangers directed my way, "Daddy,

---

4. An interesting variation on the one question of the Soviet prosecutor at Nuremberg: "Do you now admit you are a fascist beast?"

daddy!" I am sure I would shoot first and ask questions later. Inexplicably—certainly to me—Milt demonstrated the greatest interest in and affection for children. Whenever he sees a kid in arms or a toddler in three-cornered pants, A.M.H. gives his avuncular kindly Uncle Milton growl, "There's a soldier! Whadda ya say, tiger?" Dear me. (I belong to the Evelyn Waugh/Philip Larkin school of child-hating: they are horrid, peevish, miniature adults; they should always be spoken to in an adult manner. One should pay absolutely no attention to their views or their tantrums. They should be transported at the age of eighteen years and force-fed Shakespeare, Cervantes, Dante, Proust, and Joyce. The stupid ones should be terminated with extreme prejudice.)

Milt would be no fan of W.C. Fields, who has always stood high in my esteem for his candid "Anyone who hates kids and dogs can't be all bad."

We shall spend no more time on children or on dogs. The only reason that I would carry a firearm would be, as occasion demanded, to exterminate barking dogs or noisy children, a common enough pastime in some Latin American police states. Milt's demonstrated high regard for both species is confirmatory of what at bottom I have always suspected: he is an old softy.

Chapter Nine
A.M.H. and the Fourth Estate

A Public Life, one hour of insight into a public figure's life and career. Once someone becomes a public figure, their life is no longer their own. So why not make it yours? Watch *A Public Life,* Fridays at 9:00 PM Saturdays at 7:00 PM.[1]

Esse est percipi (to be is to be photographed).

– *Utopia of a Tired Man by Jorge Luis Borges*

IMMORTALITY is not what it's cracked up to be. That explains why Sylvia Beach tried so diligently to protect James Joyce. People who achieve fame give their lives over to strangers, and from then on their existence is solely what others say and write and read about them. Says Gore Vidal in *Palimpsest* (Penguin Books, New York, 1995): " ...*what others want you to be you are going to be, despite all evidence to the contrary.*" Farewell to a private life. Farewell to life.

Having said that, so what! Harradence craved fame, perhaps even immortality. And who can blame him? Even I—over a prolonged stage, lasting about fifteen years, a lengthy mid-life crisis—wanted the same. I cannot imagine *now* what motivated me *then*, but... no one can. It's all very well with hindsight to puff that standing outside the mob is a private matter not requiring recognition or public distinction for doing so; at the time, in all probability, one wished at the least to be adulated as "different." Oh, grovel!

Journalists come in for more than their fair share of media bashing by all sorts of informed commentators, including of course, their own. Nobody bashes a journalist like another journalist. Thus, as a newspaper writer for several years, I frequently

1. A CPAC advertisement, 1996. "CPAC is funded by Canada's cable companies.

targeted the press, for a variety of real and perceived villainies: caprice, sensationalism, crass commercialism, gross invasion of privacy, defamation, banality, stupidity, etc., etc. Stupidity is probably the worst sin.

Journalist trouncers have much support at the highest philosophical and practical levels:

Graham Greene wrote to the *Sunday Times,* January 18, 1981:

> A petty reason perhaps why novelists more and more try to keep a distance from journalists is that novelists are trying to write the truth and journalists are trying to write fiction.[2]

Conor Cruise O'Brien elaborates:

> But when they [journalists] write for publication, they write with another part of their mind: one which is attuned to the elaboration of decorous fictions as reassuring substitutes for disreputable realities (I am speaking about most of the coverage and comment; there are honourable exceptions).
>
> … an alarmingly high proportion of communications, on the eve of the millennium, are suffering from some sort of cognitive degeneration, unless we assume that they are consciously lying, which I don't believe to be the case. However that may be, the picture of the world that we live in that we are receiving—through television, radio and the press—is a curious mixture of fact and fiction. The facts, mostly in the form of pictures, are very often horrifying. The fiction comes into the commentary and interpretation, heavily charged with wishful fantasy, unwarranted reassurance, and intimations of quick fixes.[3]

Graham Greene, again ditto, speaking to "the common disease of journalists of dramatizing at the cost of truth."

Perhaps the worst sin of modern journalists is the glorification of the mundane. They "give us accurate and prosaic details of the

---

2. "Yours, Etc." *Letters to the Press, 1945–1989;* London, Penguin Books.
3. O'Brien, Conor Cruise, *On the Eve of the Millennium,* Anansi, Ontario, 1994. Copyright 1994 C.C.O'Brien and the CBC. For a balanced comment on the rise of the mass media and One Penny Dreadfuls see John Carey's *The Intellectuals and the Masses,* Faber and Faber, London, 1992 (I come down on the side of the intellectuals).

doings of people of absolutely no interest whatsoever." (Oscar Wilde)

The place of journalism in the social spectrum is agreeably captured by John Lanchester in his novel *The Debt to Pleasure:*

> "Your precipitate social decline cannot fail to alarm your well-wishers," I told my brother, "You started as a painter, then you became a sculptor, now you're basically a sort of gardener. What next, Barry? Street cleaner? Lavatory attendant? Journalism?"

Finally, George Steiner identifies the narcissistic malaise of modern journalism:

> We 'undergo' much of reality, sharply filtered and pre-sensed, through the instant diagnostic sociology of the mass media. No previous society has mirrored itself with such profuse fascination.

All that said, none of us practising at the Criminal Bar in the sixties and seventies was at all adverse to the dramatization of bilge.

Harradence, Q.C., readily appreciated the dividends he might reap over "the intense competition between mass-circulation newspapers specializing in the emotional stimulation of the barely literate."[4]

Milt played all members of the Fourth Estate, from the most preposterous booze-riddled, jumped-up "veteran" to the most wet-behind-the-ears cub, like speakeasy pianolas. That is, aswamp in turgid open-mouthed admiration and stuttering adulation, they played any tune that the master set them to sing. Milt was provocative, controversial, charming, daring, accusing, always newsworthy—and he could *always* be counted upon for an eminently quotable quote, tomorrow's headline. That some of his outbursts bore little resemblance to the true state of affairs is a matter of total irrelevance. For example, that which was soporifically boring Milt could tart up into the Titantic Inquiry. He could often evoke empathy if not sympathy for some vicious thug with

4. O'Brien, Conor Cruise, *ibid.*

a hopeless cause simply by muttering darkly about government plots. And so on.

"The only way to treat the press is like a barrel of live and very poisonous snakes." Thus spake my learned junior, David Stilwell, with a singularly apposite comment; he added, dismissively, "I'm damned if I'm going to answer questions from grade nine dropouts."

A somewhat more cynical spin (if possible) was placed upon this disdain by David's father, and A.M.H.'s close associate, Bill Stilwell, whose famous aphorism is "I've lost many a case, but I've never lost a member of the press." He was referring more to his friend Harradence, Q.C., than to himself, actually expressing admiration for the adroit manner in which Milt manipulated the manipulators.

Case in point: Milt was one of the first Canadian lawyers ever to make use of the press conference. Naturally, the Law Society governors of the day frowned on such gross vulgarities, partly because no self-respecting journalist would write two words on any of them. And mainly because they never thought of it. Milt drew the media like a magnet. They circled around his *bon mots* like sharks, but ate out of his hand like tame dolphins (see Chapter 1, *supra*). Milt had learned the value of the press conference and the punch impact of the scrum on the courthouse steps from the likes of Race Horse Haynes, Melvin Belli, and the irrepressible Gerry Spence.

The bottom line is, Milt Harradence had a most satisfactory relationship with the press of his practice days, a continuing interchange, dialogue, and mutual admiration society that was equally rewarding to both parties. Milt had a craving for publicity; the Fourth Estate wanted to sell newspapers or TV advertising. This is a sure-fire formula that is tried and true throughout all of the areas of the world where a so-called "free press" is omnipresent. In short, like cannibals, they fed on each other.

Lest one is inclined to turn up one's sensitive nose and throw up one's cookies at the sorts of shenanigans and inanities that proliferate to every obscure corner of the globe that can be infiltrated by the ingenuity and brass of an ambitious reporter or the electronic probe of the goggle box, back off. Yes, many journalists are insensitive and impudent to a degree that only a hundred and fifty years ago would have seen them hang without trial; invasion of privacy is routine, distortion and misquotation rampant, profound ignorance a virtue, and a non-discriminating public has no frontiers to its credulity. "In centuries before ours the public nailed the ears of journalists to the pump. That was quite hideous. In this century journalists have nailed their own ears to the keyhole. That is much worse … ," said Wilde. That's all true. And it is a state of affairs eminently desirable to the struggling and established criminal lawyer alike, who would not have it any other way. The former want to make it and the latter, having made it, want to keep it. Hence the appropriate aphorism of Bill Stilwell.

So we shall waste no more time on the multifarious outrages perpetrated (and perpetuated) by the Fourth Estate. As the late raconteur and genuine character A. Webster MacDonald, Sr., said, "It doesn't matter what they say about me as long as they spell my name right," a more sophisticated variation of the old commonplace, "any publicity is good publicity."

I have found this invariably to be true. My wife and I both over the years enjoyed a close association with the print and television media: we were both weekly columnists for CBC radio, which to its credit loosed upon the Calgary a.m. drive-to-work public what producer Peter Loucks called "my two Frankenstein monsters"; Bernice also wrote food columns for magazines and was regional editor for a respectable national restaurant guide; the CBC audience called her "the voice you hate once a week." I went from CBC to CHQR, back to CBC, then to CBC Television, with weekly (sometimes daily) "uninformed commentary," which consisted of beating up on Bambi. I wrote weekly columns for (first) the *North Hill News*; Roy Farran was the publisher and the only person who had the balls to publish my stuff. I then wrote for the old *Albertan* (later the *Sun*), finally the *Calgary Herald.* These commentaries pissed off everybody and his dog, and gained me undeserved fame, which ameliorated my law practice immeasurably. These continuous contacts with the denizens of the Fourth Estate introduced us to many journalists who were admirable professionals and many others who were certifiable assholes or, worse, ignoramuses.

All had journalistic infallibility in common. Quoth Mr. Graham Greene:

> The infallibility of the journalistic is not, like the infallibility of the Pope, limited by conditions. A journalist is never wrong.[5]

You will not find many criminal lawyers knocking journalists; you definitely will not find Milt Harradence knocking journalists, either. They needed all the help they could get, but we needed all the help we could get. It all worked out well. Case in point is the "Barbeque in the Badlands" case, featuring Harradence, Stilwell, and Stevenson (*infra*).

From a crime reporter's point of view, "Barbeque in the Badlands" was Alberta's answer to H.L. Mencken's priceless "Gore in the Carribees." Relates Judge Stevenson, in part:

> The *Calgary Herald*, which at that time was published in the afternoon, had a deadline for stories for that day's edition of 11:00 a.m. Their reporter covering the preliminary was Gerry Deagle. As you know, the first item generally in a media story about a murder is the 'cause of death'. Because of Milt's strenuous cross-examination, that had not quite been established as yet. It was 10:45 a.m. Bill Stilwell looked behind and Gerry Deagle was waving at us and pointing to his watch. Bill tugged at Milt's coat and reminded him of the Herald deadline. Now all we were getting out of this case—besides our deep and abiding commitment to see that our clients each received a fair trial—was prominence in the media. Milt turned back to the pathologist, agreed with his conclusion about the cause of death, and closed with 'I have no further questions'. Gerry Deagle filed his story, the cause of death was established (smoke and fire) and we all made the front page of Monday afternoon's edition.

I have observed that Milt's diatribes often stimulated unintended hilarity in their recipients, particularly if they were Ber-

---

5. Greene, Graham, *ibid.*, letter to *The Spectator*, May 30, 1958.

nice or myself. Another memorable press encounter engineered by Milt followed the revelation of a "secret" memorandum circulating in the Federal Department of Justice having to do with the elimination of the preliminary inquiry in indictable criminal causes. The arguments pro and con the preliminary inquiry are debated *ad nauseum* and are of little interest to the public. The proposed elimination of the preliminary (and its replacement by Crown disclosure) is a *bête noir* that has been around for years in this or that menacing form. In fact, the February 1994 solution, by amendments to the Criminal Code, was more summary conviction hybrid offences, but increased penalties. What the Feds cannot do directly, they can be trusted to do through the rear door, like a stab in the back. For example, one's only appeal after a summary conviction is to the Court of Queen's Bench (one Judge), whose members are mostly incompetent to sit in appeal on more experienced Provincial Judges. Thereafter, one may go to the Court of Appeal only in point of law, thus increasing work for the Court of Queen's Bench and decreasing it for the Court of Appeal, who, in contrast to the schedule of a busy trial lawyer, have never been accused of overwork.

Anyway, Milt got wind of this memo—probably because it was a revelation that had been common knowledge for months—and called an immediate press conference at his chambers, Versailles west. Summonsed imperiously were several of the Criminal Bar *cognoscenti*, including A. Webster MacDonald, Jr., then President of the Criminal Bar, and Dick Armitage, then head of Legal Aid. Milt had arranged for everyone to sit behind his massive table and, of course, had tipped off his intimates in the electronic media. Cameras and mike booms bristled everywhere. Milt orchestrated the whole thing, barking orders like General Patton at the Bulge. It was rather like a troupe scene from a Gilbert and Sullivan operetta, with all the chorus dressed like criminal lawyers.

Milt got us all arrayed behind the desk looking stern and/or outraged, while he denounced the duplicity of the Federali:

> "Conceived in conspiracy and disseminated in secrecy and

shame...!"[6]

He got that far, when A. Web, Jr., lost control and burst into spontaneous laughter. This, regrettably, was caught on prime time, and rather put a damper on Milt's declaration of war. Milt was pissed off at Webby, but I too—managing to be off camera—had also guffawed loudly.

Milt and the press had a good mutual run. They exploited him and thought they were clever; he exploited them and was a good deal cleverer. Moreover, he was as courteous to them as he was to everyone. He effortlessly put them at their ease, and, in adopting his artful conspiratorial tones in his communications with them—accompanied by the usual A.M.H. tradecraft passwords, disguises, and subterfuges to confound the enemy, that is, the other side—most reporters, impressed by the theatre, naturally concluded that the master was making them, his privileged few, privy to certain hitherto unrevealed and recondite secrets of the Universe. Milt was hands on with the press and they knew it. They knew they could trust him.

6. That is actually what Milt said.

CHAPTER TEN
Politics

How easily you become for the moment a little part of your own tremendous notion of Napoleon.

– F. Kafka, Diary, 1911

THERE IS an important preface to be made to this chapter (as well as to some of the other observations of Milt in this book) because inevitably there are oversensitive souls who are bound to take umbrage at this or that revelation about our subject, voluntarily on his behalf. There are always such do-gooders and moral uplifters about, best ignored. They will characterize this account as a backhand with a slapstick, which emphatically it is not.

The fact is, Milt Harradence was a very shrewd judge of human character, or more accurately, human weaknesses and vanities. He was acutely skilled at individual and mob suasion. I point out that he had a few flaws himself, as do we all, and many will be correct in self-righteously identifying my several character infirmities, not to mention personality disorders, to which I plead guilty, and be damned to all of you. One of Milt's favourite phrases *entre nous* was, "if only the public knew!" and we always had a good belly laugh. He well knew what combination of snorts and exhortations could rouse a rabble, what permutations of sentimental and emotionally affecting pap could sway a dim-witted judge or a typical jury of *National Enquirer* readers, and he made full and effective use of them, the while enjoying a good guffaw with his mates at the expense of the peasantry. Many of his peers, gravely swallowing Milt's more obvious outrages and quackeries, may be relegated to these lower ranks. If they or any of them should now purport to cry "foul!" on his behalf, he would not thank them any more than an absolute monarch thanks a churl for fetching his crown. Some people are born to be adulated, and I have pointed out that Milt was one of these. To suggest that the sophisticated devices and theatrics he utilized so effectively to maintain the awe and envy—and the respect—of the common herd were as deadly serious as the befogged mob itself would be preposterous. Milt never took himself as seriously as did most of his followers.

PART ONE

Social Credit: Milt's Part in its Downfall

THERE IS SO MUCH about Milt that is heroic. Demonstrations of his raw courage against tremendous odds played daily in the Courts and in the air—and in the political trenches.

I also entertain no doubt whatever, reasonable or otherwise, that the second greatest disappointment in my friend's career was his inability to secure political office. He was a natural-born leader, and he wanted so much to lead; he was denied that despite years of effort and personal expense by the caprice and lack of imagination of a dull electorate.

Harradence's political career would fill its own book. In his growing-up years in Saskatchewan, he was heavily influenced by the career and the charisma of the great John George Diefenbaker, a prairie son who went from his pre-eminent position as that province's celebrated criminal trial lawyer to national prominence in 1957 as the leader of the Conservative Party of Canada and then Prime Minister of Canada by a landslide the following year. All schools know (at least, they used to know) the story, and Dief the Chief was storybook material. Milt, I am confident, modelled himself upon this heroic, blustering warrior. I do not think this was subliminal mimesis: Milt wanted to be a second Diefenbaker. If the circumstances had been different, if the configuration of planets had been in apogee rather than perigee, if the pyramidic scrolls had foretold the what-nots flying their flippidy-flappidy, if... if... if....

It was not to be.

One reason, and the principal reason for this thwarting of Milt's perfervid ambition, was one Honourable Ernest C. Manning, father of Preston the Reformer, leader of the Alberta Social Credit Party and Premier of Alberta for thirty-six years. It was Milt's singular misfortune to aspire to public office when Manning still held the hammerlock on the province, particularly the rural peasantry in its outer reaches and backwaters, who were the fundamental source of his iron grip. The churls and hinds who populated the remote hinterland of the province in the fifties and sixties still believed that if one put a horse hair in a bottle it would grow into a snake, that the cosmos was manufactured in six days with the seventh day off, and that Holy Writ was drawn in fire by the finger of Bible Bill Aberhart. Moreover, Manning was an excellent administrator, and his scrupulous honesty remains legendary. The more sophisticated cityfolk huddled behind their walls and plotted, wincing when a dung fork gleamed in the sun; they, as Milt, yearned for enlightened government with an urban edge or for any other government than Social Credit.

Timing, as they say, is everything. This writer attempts no analysis of the rise of Social Credit in Alberta. This boring subject has pre-occupied many a soporific tome, and is analogous to "A History of the Primates." Suffice it to say that a heritage of God fearment coupled with paranoid distrust about any thing or entity east of the Manitoba border had conditioned Albertans to the government of God. I consider Manning's moral zeal as close to that of Oliver Cromwell as any politician I have analyzed. I happen to admire Cromwell, but I am glad I avoided his sword. Bob Scammell, a lone Liberal in the right wing stronghold of Red Deer and the central snowbelt, summed up the entire Socred genealogy in 1956 as follows: "Alburdah begat Social Credit; Social Credit begat Aberhart; Aberhart begat Manning; and Manning begat the Promised Land." In the result, Alberta remained a creature that had not made it through evolution.

Judge E.L. Collins relates a vivid story of driving during that era on an Alberta highway and casually flipping on the radio, which must have been preset at a high volume, and the speaker blared "Anti-Christ!" He had caught the climactic expostulation of Ernest Manning's radio program, *Back to the Bible Hour.* The shock caused a thoroughly unnerved Leo to swerve wildly. He notes, "God alone kept me on the road."

It is a funny (peculiar) thing is this eventful life: one scales the heights of one's Calling and achieves the awe and respect of one's peers, superiors, and of the great unwashed, but one instead yearns, inexplicably, for an unrequited desire that is mystifying to those around us. This misplaced sense of loss, of failure, eats into us for the balance of our lives. One can understand why grown men, caught in its throes, sell their souls to the Devil. There are three things that bring you down in this profession: booze, women, and overweening ambition. In all the years I knew Milt he seldom if ever had a drink of anything stronger than tea. He was, moreover, a devoted husband and family man; I think Milt's home was the principal source of his strength. He was also too honourable to consider the option of soul-selling, yet I knew in his heart of hearts the frustration of his great dream to hold high public office was always galling in the extreme. Even when he sat on the Court of Appeal, if destiny had called persistently for him to lead the mass, he would have jumped to answer. Greatness, he felt, had eluded him. It was not to be thrust upon him.

Power, of course, is what politics is all about, including gender politics. (We shall stay off that latter topic: it is tedious, too much of the moment, and politically unwise. I promise to revisit it, in no uncertain terms, on another occasion. Suffice it to say, for our purposes, that being already damned, I declare that I do not give a flying fuck for the iron-faced females' brigade, nor for their male handmaidens and the wimps who attend them.)

It was axiomatic that an Alberta Socred would always vote for a Federal Conservative. In this, Milt and other like-minded and stout-hearted companions saw opportunity. If one could scratch a Socred and find a Tory, why not scratch deeper—beneath the cowpie veneer—and find a true *Provincial* Tory? The difficulty was that rather than oppose Social Credit from the far left or, worse, the wishy-washy Liberal left (which in Alberta have always been hopeless enterprises), Alberta Conservatives sought to oppose Ernest Manning on his own ground, the rationale to sway the city voter presumably based on the fact that the Tories had better tailors.

Milt become the leader of the Conservative Party of Alberta at a time when its fortunes were at a low ebb: the immediate retiring leader was the uninspiring but decent Cam (Mr. Justice) Kirby, and the one faithful plodder in the legislature was the late Ernest Watkins, Q.C., a gentleman barrister in all things instant, terribly English with dried tea leaves on his teeth and a Union Jack on his forehead. He and Kirby wore blue blazers and baggy grey bags and Olde Schoole ties. For they were jolly good fellows, and so say all of us. That was also, alas, Milt's burden: he, too, was thoroughly decent, believing in fair play and the Queensberry Rules, neither of which work well in politics. I believe that the true vileness of politics and politicians only became clear to Milt when his idol, Dief the Chief, whose autocratic leadership fomented rebellion, was felled by his own officers, the troops loudly deserting: a perceptive journalist of the day lamented stricken Diefenbaker "wandering the halls like King Lear, while inside the children divided the kingdom." It was only then, in my belief, that Milt realized the true impact of Russell Baker's famous aphorism: "[T]he dirty work at political conventions is always done in the early hours of the morning, around 4 *a.m.*: hangmen and politicians work best when the human spirit is at its lowest ebb."

Manning, as I say, was straight, but barnyard smart, and he made short work of the Calgary Kid, mainly by completely ignoring him. It is not a chore to ignore a challenger whose entire caucus could congregate in an AGT booth. The Tories' plan was to get Milt into the legislature, where, on his feet and in the full oratorical flight of an Edward Carson, M.P. or Burke[1] or Macauley, he would clear the Temple of the funny money mavens and sweep the Tories to power! (Cheers, alarums, swell prizes.)

A nice plan, but how to attract the attention of a public jaded

1. Perhaps not Edmund Burke. He earned the nickname "Dinnerbell" because every time he rose to speak in Parliament, the other members made for the dining lounge.

by oil revenues and the thoroughly sound administration of the Social Credit paternalistic party? Given that the Alberta Tory think tank was neither large nor gifted, one remains stunned by the most bizarre proposition ever promulgated by a right wing opposition party in the entire history of this country. That it happened is in hindsight ascribed to an elaborate joke that backfired, and may just be the most plausible explanation for what did happen. The story is that a well-known committed conservative in the traditional sense, of acerbic wit, allegedly suggested to Milt that the Tories, if elected, should nationalize the oil industry. Think of it: the aspirants to political power in the most archly red-necked province of them all, ruled for years by a red-neck government, proposed to turn over to the socialist hordes the usufructs, cens, rentres, and profits of the oil barons who built the province. It is—it was—unthinkable. But Milt solemnly announced this as a viable consideration for Albertans: "Not necessarily nationalized oil; but nationalized oil if necessary," or some such hilarious inanity. It was a gaffe of monumental proportions: the perpetrator insists that the original proposal was a joke, nothing more. From then on, on a "take us seriously" scale of one to ten, the Alberta Conservatives ranked a minus ninety-three.

More disasters followed.

If one could not take Alberta by an appeal to economic disaster, a different tack was indicated: personal charisma would have to carry the revolution. Like Dief, Milt wanted to wrest control of the right wing west from the ruling power clique. Kenneth Whyte[2] noted that "prairie political types" assaulting the national scene in the early twentieth century years "favoured a populist and crusading style of politics: big fixes, radical solutions, grand visions." J.F. Conway defines 'populism': "[It] has an essence that can be discerned quite readily. It must in some way be 'of the people', an organically rooted political expression of popular yearnings for positive change and improvement."[3] The disciples gravitated

---

2. *Saturday Night*, October 1995 edition, "How Odd Was Dief?" by editor Kenneth Whyte, page 20.

3. "*The Folksy Fascism of the Reform Party*," the *Literary Review of Canada*, June 1996, Vol. 5, No. 6.

toward "strong charismatic leaders inspired by the popular will, cooperative leadership—anything but a traditional party hierarchy." The irony for Milt, a patrician who yearned to be a populist, was that, at the provincial level, the first option is exactly how Aberhart and Social Credit came to, and held, power. Ernest Manning's honesty was impeccable, but his grip was Cromwellian. His imperial government was perhaps modelled on that of the Emperor Augustus Caesar: "[A]n absolute Monarchy disguised by the forms of a commonwealth."[4] He did not tolerate fools in positions of power any more than Milt would have if given the chance to head a government, and held the principal portfolios himself, including Attorney General. One could snipe at the sidelines that Manning was not a lawyer, but to what avail? The fact is, Social Credit was, as administrations go, an acceptable government, bearing in mind H.L. Mencken's admonition that "a government, at bottom, is nothing more than a gang of men, and as a practical matter most of them are inferior men. Its business, in civilized countries, seldom attracts the service of really superior individuals: its eminentissimos are commonly non-entities who gain all their authority by belonging to it, and are of small importance otherwise.... Government is actually the worst failure of civilized man. There has never been a really good one, and even those that are most tolerable are arbitrary, cruel, grasping and unintelligent. Indeed, it would not be far wrong to describe the best as the common enemy of all decent citizens."[5] The Alberta Socreds were probably the best of a bad bunch.

Milt was pushing on an open door, against an iron autocrat who also had the charismatic aura of a Bible-belt preacher so appealing to rural Albertans, the "sweating and persecuted husbandmen perennially guarding the horned cattle on the hill" (H.L.M. again). The attitude of Manning to the upstart challenger Milton is well illustrated by a contemporary cartoon by the *Calgary Herald's* talented Tom Innes which depicts Ernest Manning in pilgrim preacher attire languidly lounging against the saloon

4. Gibbon's *Decline and Fall of the Roman Empire*, Vol. I, Everyman's Library.
5. H.L. Mencken's *Notebooks*, Minority Report, New York, Alfred A. Knopf, 1967.

bar, armed with what appears to be an 1820 long-barrelled horse pistol, haughtily contemplating brash two-gun gunfighter Milt at the swinging doors, with the caption "Go fer your gun, Marshall—this town ain't big enough fer both of us." This cartoon now adorns Milt's office wall. (Photo section).

Milt, like Diefenbaker, was well established in his criminal law practice, already with a fearsome reputation, and much admired by the cityfolk. Further, he was a veteran who had volunteered during the war. His opponent (as the incumbent of Calgary West or some such boundary) was a backbencher and an Optometrist in and for the Province of Alberta named Fleming, also a vet, who is not otherwise noted by posterity despite his contribution to the commonwealth.

The election was called, and all hands repaired to the hustings. M.L.A. Fleming's sole prodigious effort toward re-election was to park his old Chevy Tudor at the bottom of the Elbow Drive hill that swept down to the Elbow River on its way downtown, sit on the hood in his dark brown Socred trilby hat and dark brown Socred overcoat (on which were pinned his service medals) and dark brown-rimmed Socred sedate specs, and wave from time to time to bored commuters. Nobody honked nor, apparently, noticed nor, obviously, gave a damn.

To counter this electrifying high-profile campaign, Jack Major suggested to Milt that, in keeping with his Campaign of Charismatic Leadership, he should do a tour of the constituency on foot with, preferably, an attendant band or at least an appreciative, noisy entourage. This dramatic exposure appealed to Milt, who always loved theatre and theatrics. But why not go one step further, Milt thought: Let's "shake these complacent bastards up," by parading through the staid Britannia suburbs in a military fashion, reminding the lower middle-class that here was a flesh-and-blood ex-serviceman, fighting criminal lawyer, and natural-born leader! Major added fatal gasoline to the burning fires of Milt's enthusiasm, by suggesting—purely as a joke, he also insists—that Milt should get a real crowd grabber, like, for example, why not mount Milt's private fighter aircraft on a flatbed truck and have it wheeled behind the parade? Why not indeed! Well, there were probably about ten good reasons why not, and a hundred more in hindsight.

Milt was elated. "Jesus Christ! That's it! We've got the bastards! *We've got no choice!*" Major ran for cover.

The denizens of the snotty suburb duly awoke one Saturday morning to loudspeakers blaring *The Thin Red Line, Soldiers of the Queen, The Royal Life Guards Regimental March, inter alia*, from a sound truck preceded by the candidate for office, obviously as mad as a hatter, marching briskly in flyer's leather helmet, goggles, and flowing white scarf. Bringing up the rear was a flatbed truck on which reposed The Fighter Plane. Dumbfounded residents must have thought they woke up in a loony bin. They had.

Milt did not shake them up all that much, garnering a few paltry votes to Fleming's landslide victory. Politics is a hard game.

"History and events are against you," I comforted my friend, "Look at Churchill: he was a leader for war . . . like you. As soon as he won the peace, those ungrateful swine—the electorate—threw him out."

"Jesus," cried A.M.H., "that's true! The bastards!"

"Look on the bright side," I counselled, "right now, they've got the government they deserve. One day, they'll be sorry."

"That's true."

As it turned out, it was not true: the Alberta electorate was not sorry, and never again gave a good Goddamn for Milt or for his valiant if misguided efforts, because E. Peter Lougheed and the Organization Men came along, swept Milt aside, grasped Power, and the rest, as they say.... This new lot cast themselves as "*Progressive* Conservatives," causing J.F. Conway to remonstrate that the opportunistic word "progressive," when cobbled onto "conservative," is a "cumbersome oxymoronic adjective." According to my old law partner, Dwayne Rowe, "progressive" is a "weasel word," that is, it sucks the life out of the words it is purporting to modify.

In 1967, Peter Lougheed won six seats for his Progressive Conservatives; in 1971, the Alberta Progressive Conservative Party formed a new government and Social Credit was consigned to the Tyrrell Museum of Palaeontology at Drumheller as just another dinosaur that had become extinct. The carefully crafted alliterative slogan of Lougheed's Tories "This Time, a Choice for a Change," plus the cunning hot-cold combination of blue and orange colours (incidentally, the colours of Apartheid South Africa) won the day. The triumphant Tories even put their vulgar colours on the provincial license plates, for Gawd's sake, in a calculated continuing subliminal brainwash of the great unwashed. A farmer on the eastern outskirts of Calgary painted his *house* blue and orange; either he was colour blind or the West was Won.

The Opening of the Legislature was particularly galling for Milt. This intense man, who had the same "deep hunger for public affirmation"[6] that afflicted his idol, John Diefenbaker, was humiliated when it became clear that he was omitted from the invitation list for the formal ceremony and, more significantly, the subsequent garden party. To me, such occasions are essentially a hogsty of snorting trough-mongers and slick bottom-feeders and happily avoided; to Milt, who had to be seen and recognized, to be thus kissed off was devastating: "After all my Goddamn work, out there in the wilderness. Where were *they* when we were in the trenches? The bastards!" Jack Major thought as I did, and gave his invitation to Milt. Milt took it and went. To understand this, and his complexity of yearning and thirst for stardom, is to understand why Milt, travelling with me from Costa Rica via Guatemala City to Toronto, abruptly switched his reservations at Guatemala Airport and jetted off to Beverly Hills, California. "Why are you going to stay over at the Beverly Wilshire Hotel?" I queried him. He merely stared at me: "you've got to be *seen*!"

"Seen? By *whom*?"

Not, apparently, by the dull Alberta electorate. Affronted by his rebuff at their hands, and the field now heavily occupied by his more sophisticated Tory successors, the frustrated aspirant turned his attention and admirable energy to more radical politics.

---

6. Whyte at page 21.

PART TWO
Taking Alberta Out

ONE OF THE PRAIRIE GRASSROOTS "movements" that never would die was the spectre of Western Separatism. It was an alien nation syndrome, a neurotic inferiority complex spawned by deep paranoiac prairie mistrust of Ottawa, its institutions, the "eastern" business-industrial elite, the French language, national politicians generally, and the "eastern" press. It did not help much when General Charles de Gaulle, President of France and fairweather ingrate to the English and Canadians who saved his selfish country, arrived at Quebec City in a warship as the guest of the Quebec Government, and proclaimed "Vive Le Quebec Libre!" from the steps of Montreal City Hall. Many a Westerner shared the sentiments of the Jackal about that time.

It had always been a fact, up to the nineties, that there were in Alberta about ten separatists with a million dollars each, and in Quebec about a million separatists with ten cents each. These factors have always historically cancelled each other out in a sort of Charles Atlas "dynamic tension," leaving the oblivious Feds to get on with the job of Canadian mis-government and, a process at which they particularly excelled, running up the deficit. Prime Minister Pierre Trudeau fuddled while Western Canada burned.

When Trudeau took to giving his critics the finger and shrugged off the complaints of Saskatchewan farmers with his callous "Why should I sell your wheat?" and particularly with the early rumbling of what later became the hated National Energy Program, separatism in Alberta got a shot in the arm and Milt heard the Call of the Wild. The left was not going anywhere in Alberta except into the toilet. Right-wing splinters thrust up everywhere, impaling the more retiring asses of the provincial Tories: the Western Canada Concept, the Western National Alliance (WNA), the political arm of the Independent Alberta Association; plus assorted offshoots and hybrids, their organization and membership generally a shambles. (None of these entities met with the approval of the madly nationalistic Dominion of Canada Party, whose membership could meet in a phone booth at

Drumheller, which issued a bull in the seventies: "Anyone advocating separatism is a traitor and should be tried for treason." What they probably meant was the Francophone traitorship, but they inadvertently tarred the western breakaway crowd.)

In or around the central Alberta snowbelt, locus of the farmers' and cattle dealers' trading empires and home to such institutions as the Agricultural College (a.k.a. the Alberta School of Swine Husbandry) and this or that Bible College of the Church of the Thirteenth Apostle, an avowed western separatist was thrust into public office in a hotly contested provincial by-election. There was consternation in general, and alarums resounded as far east as the nation's capital.

This was fertile ground for the Milt, who now found himself so disaffected with conventional conservative politics and policies. If he could not be the first separatist elected to the Legislature, he might be the first one elected to Parliament. "We've got no choice! We're taking Alberta out!" he proclaimed.

All I said was, "What do you mean 'we'?" I feared for the future, not of the province or the country—I mean, for *my* future. Why on earth Milt always assumed that I shared similar or any sentiments for politics in general or Western Separatism in particular is beyond me. As for politicians, my favourite characterization of them was that of e.e. cummings, "[A] politician is an ass/upon which everyone has sat except a man." And here was my best friend Milt, riding in on a herd of mixed metaphors, assuming that I was his lieutenant in Cloud Cuckoo Land! I demurred, but in vain: this *was* Don Quixote and the reluctant Sancho Panza to the life. I did not want to tilt with Milt.

Yet, I reflected upon his unstinting generosity and kindness. Once Milt was your friend, he was a friend for life, unto very death, loyal, decent, supportive. One meets few of that kidney in this imperfect world, where flatterers, opportunists, arrivistes, and gross vulgarians insinuate their way into one's life with hidden agendas and the basest motives. Milt's friendship was pure and unselfish: he really asked nothing of me save friendship in return, and, for all my transgressions, he never once judged me. "A friend is not a person who is taken in by sham/a friend is one who knows your faults, and doesn't give a damn." That was Milt. His presence, pre-eminence at the Bar, experience, ability, and manner, all commanded respect, but that was volunteered to him by all who knew him well, friend or foe. For his part, he went out of his way from early days, when I was nothing to him and a nobody in the profession, to help, encourage, even step in without remuneration to assist me in a case; he made a point of referring much criminal work to me, a junior. He was the person who, more than anyone else, started me in practice and kept me going through those difficult early years. I owe him more than I could ever describe. All his help and encouragement was freely bestowed without any string or caveat. And I was not the only one he started off, watched over, and tangibly assisted in their careers. He was always there for his friends. How could I *not* be his squire? Mark you, I had to pule about it on occasion.

"If I live to be a hundred," I moaned to Major, "I'll never understand why Milt glommed on to me."

"Better he gloms on to you than on to me," was Major's sharp retort, and he smiled the cruel smile he reserved for peremptory dismissals.

Apparently, Milt had tried to enlist Major to the separatist cause, with predictably no success, Major being a lifelong Provincial and Federal Tory, well-connected with the backroom boffins, and rumoured to be the largest individual donor to party coffers over an impressive time span. Neither Milt nor apparently Diefenbaker ever did appreciate the suasion or the clout of the smoke-filled back room, nor the aforementioned aphorism of Russell Baker. Major did, always.

Major rejected Milt's alarming and nonsensical aspirations for a western state ("all the lines run north and south, for Christ's sake; we'll use Inuvik as a seaport") in no uncertain terms. Milt reported to me, darkly, with the frowning countenance of Coriolanus, "Sometimes I wonder about Major's loyalty."

Milt's fascination with firearms, their killing power, and his yearning for the spontaneous rise of an armed peasantry behind a Wagnerian leader of Blut und Iron was something I watched carefully. Wat Tyler, Guillaume Cale, and Tudor Vladimir Esch came to sticky ends. In vain did one remind Milt that even the revolutionary sailors of the Battleship *Ptomkin* tossed their red flag overboard when things got dodgy. At this, Milt fixed me with his thousand-yard stare: "Did John Hampton pay ship money? Did he?" Moreover, I always had the gut apprehension that Milt, caught in a time warp and genuinely misinterpreting History and The Times, might have actually bombed St. Catherines Street.

That is not unkind. Milt was a Man of Action; he detested *inaction*; he was off the blocks at the shot and catapulted himself into Death or Glory. There was little reflection on the actual state of affairs. An example: in the early seventies, things hotted up in Rhodesia with the rebel Prime Minister Ian Smith actively battling terrorists or freedom fighters, take your pick. My wife was born in Mufilira, Zambia (then Northern Rhodesia) and had lived for years in Rhodesia. Even though there were 250,000 whites in Rhodesia, Milt naturally assumed that she would know the Prime Minister. The occasion was a party at the home of the ever hospitable Webster and Sheila MacDonald. As usual, Milt was brooding in the corner with his back to the wall, alert for an attack, when he spied Bernice and me and vigorously signalled us over. He said to Bernice, "Do you know Ian Smith?" Of course, she knew him, that is, she knew he was the Prime Minister of Rhodesia. So she nodded. "Get on the phone to him right now," said Milt, "and see if he wants me to get over there with the Sabre." He added, grimly, "We've got to make a stand."

What *kind* of a stand, who *for*, *why*? These questions never seemed to present themselves to Milt. Bernice stifled her usual derisive laughter and wisely filed the request in file thirteen. The fact that Milt never followed up on this bizarre direction does not necessarily lead to the inference that he was not serious. At the time, he would have been dead serious. And had Bernice got on, say, a pay phone and, like Group Captain Mandrake in Dr. Strangelove, borrowed enough coins to make a trunk call to the Prime Minister of Rhodesia, and had Ian Smith said, "Get over here," Milt would have gone at once.

Milt's expansive and expansionist sentiments were of the sort harboured deeply by the likes of Cecil Rhodes, Saladin, and the

Emperor Severus (c. 193 A.D.).[7] He was always one hundred years or so out of time, bless the man. Had White Rhodesia called Milt to arms, he and the F86 would have been gone on the next day, to give his all for a colonial elitist regime in its death throes, to lay down napalm over the Forces of Terrorism, farewell to wife, children, home, hearth, law practice, the full catastrophe! Unfortunately for Milt, the western democracies lined up with Mugabe's lot, and that was the end of that.

I felt obliged to remonstrate with my friend when he started to tremble at the prospect of unrestricted civil warfare in Alberta. One must be, and at the least I was, ever mindful of the lessons of history, impeccably articulated as always by Gibbon in his overview of the decline and fall of Rome: "Of all our passions and appetites, the love of power is of the most imperious and unsociable nature, since the pride of one man requires the submission of the multitude. In the tumult of civil discord, the laws of society lose their force, and their place is seldom supplied by those of humanity." I therefore addressed Milt: "Remember Arthur Koestler. What if the means becomes the end, and Darkness comes over the earth?"

"Arthur who?" was all he said, as he turned from me, already preoccupied—nay, hypnotized—by the stamp of marching feet, the snapping of battle colours in the wind as the rebellious peasant host begins to march, and the thunder of the drums. "Rejoice, we conquer!"

Well, not quite.

Later, I called Milt at his office and asked for "Il Duce." He was not amused.

I believe that Milt was genuinely sincere in his political convictions, which is a big mistake for a number of reasons more fully articulated by others. "Convictions," said Nietzsche, "are prisons."

---

7. Gibbon at 110, Vol. I: ". . . marching on foot, and in complete armour, at the head of his columns, he insinuated himself into the confidence and affection of his troops, pressed their diligence, revived their spirits, animated their hopes, and was well satisfied to share the hardships of the meanest soldier, whilst he kept in view the infinite superiority of [his] reward."

Wilde's Lord Illingworth advises:

> One should never take sides in anything . . . taking sides is the beginning of sincerity, and earnestness follows shortly afterwards, and the human being becomes a bore.

This sentiment is echoed by Gwendolen, the daughter of that tremendous old crone Lady Bracknell:

> In matters of grave importance, style, not sincerity, is the vital thing.

When Brian Stevenson made a jest about Milt in his Sabre Jet strafing St. Catherines Street, everyone laughed but Milt. His favourite recurring rejoinder to the reminder that easterners had helped Alberta out during the Great Depression was a snarling, "Yeh, they sent a few crates of dried fish, so fucking what!" The east, i.e., anything east of the Manitoba border (and *it* was suspect), was not a subject on which A.M.H. was rational; bilingualism and biculturalism were number one on his hit list. When the Gendarmerie Royale du Canada commenced a dragnet for a group of inane and psychotic western vigilantes who made nocturnal forays to shoot up bilingual signs in Banff National Park with cheap pump-action shotguns, Milt let it be known that, if they were apprehended, the best defence was at hand, gratis. "That'll shake 'em up!"[8] he warned, with menacing tones, "'em" presumably being the Federali and their western liberal pansy handmaidens and commie fellow travellers.

Separatists in Canada, despite the efforts of the Dominion of Canada Party, are given a great deal more leeway than elsewhere. Consider the mild attempt in 1994 by the 'pre-nationalist nation,' the Lazi of Turkey, to put out a journal partially written in Lazuri; the editor was arrested after the first edition and charged with "separatism" by the Turks. The forbidding prospect of a Turkish penitentiary would deter many a Canadian farmer, who would ditch his pitchfork and head for the hills if he had one whiff of Oliver Stone's

8. That A.M.H. patented phrase has occurred and will re-occur in this narrative, as will "We've got no choice!, "That's true!" and "It was a calculated risk."

Midnight Express. A.M.H. *did* correctly read a few nut cases "of the people." The trouble was, outside the rural strongholds, very few yearned to actually march under arms upon Ottawa.

The alarm I experienced at being dragooned into Milt's privileged circle of advisors was exacerbated from time to time by weird imperious nocturnal telephone calls. In the late winter, about March of 1974, the loyal and long-suffering Mrs. Catherine Harradence—long suffering in the sense that the Harradence family fortunes were forever hostage to political whimsy—successfully abducted Milt to the Hawaiian Islands for, of all things, a holiday and a rest. He was horrified by Hawaii, both the hedonistic lifestyle and the remote location, as indeed was I in 1957 when I went there with the Navy and, viewing Honolulu and its occupants, resolved never to return. If the President of France insists on nuking Pacific archipelagos, he can start with the Hawaiian group.

Milt hated holidays, whether near or far, witness his out and out *evasion* of the family cottage at Gull Lake and the carefree low-key lifestyle that went with that territory. The late William McGillivray, the most revered and human of any Alberta Chief Justice, recalled Milt's occasional dutiful reluctant forays to the lake venue. The visits were always brief. The McGillivrays were lakeside neighbours of the Harradences for years. Catherine and the children delighted in sojourning there for the summer, in exile, while Milt insisted on pursuing his current manifest destiny in the sweltering city. The Chief Justice well remembered a typical recurring lakefront scene: Bill, who was beloved of all children of all ages, would be frolicking in the shallow sand bars playing ball with a number of kids, when he spied, moving in stately, diffident fashion down the beach, his acutely uncomfortable neighbour, Harradence, fastidiously dressed as always in a tailored suit with all matching accessories with the single concession to beach anarchy of an ascot in substitution of the habitual fashionable silk tie. Bill would wave wildly and loudly remonstrate with Milt to come into the water; Milt would stop, stare at the wet and chaotic scene in some horror, little devils yelling, "Bill, Bill, throw the ball! Bill, to me, Bill!", then would abruptly turn on his heel and as abruptly flee to Gotham.

"I can't stand the Goddamn place," he would confide to me. It was only years—decades—later that Milt, in an acute reversal brought upon him by advancing age and a nostalgia for the never known, took the greatest interest and pride in Catherine's compilation into book form of a history of those lost summers. Surprised by this sudden attack of wistfulness, I cited T.S. Eliot's 'Burnt Norton' to Milt:

> Footfalls echo in the memory
> Down the passage which we did not take
> Towards the door we never opened
> Into the rose garden.

Milt, whom I believe to be deeply suspicious of all poets except Pilot Officer Magee and Rudyard Kipling, gave me a strange look. There are times, I am sure, when I revert to literary or historical reference, that Milt thinks it is I who is crazy.

So here was Milt phoning me from the wilds of Waikiki, that "Godawful place," at of course three o'clock *a.m.* "What time did you say it was there?" "Three *a.m.*" "Christ, I can't figure out the Goddamn hours difference." "I thought you had one of those wacko pilot's Oysters, or something, with the time and temperature of Mesopotamia..."

"Never mind that. What's going on on the street?"

"Nothing. It's three *a.m.* Pimps and prostitutes is all, I suppose."

"Look, I've got to get out of this Goddamn place. Now listen to me, Cliff. We're taking Alberta out! Spend no more than two thousand dollars on advance publicity."

"What on earth are you talking about?"

"Call Zane This and George That—they'll know what to do. This is Big!"

Click.

I certainly did *not* know what to do. Whose money? Publicity for what? To whom? I did not know any person named Zane This or George That, if those indeed were remotely real persons. What was I to do, look them up in the phone book? And in any event they, if contacted, probably would not know what to do either.

So I did nothing. I did talk to Major. He advised inaction and that I should try to get Milt sidetracked on a point of law.

Two days later, Milt called again at an ungodly hour: "Meet my plane tomorrow, from Vancouver on flight 1104. Give me a full report."

I did not go to the airport but hid at home with the phone off the hook.

Major was right. By the time Milt hit Canada, he had forgotten his telephone calls.

There were others.

Harradence's notoriety for leading the alienated hordes out of the wilderness and into a one-party paradise had spread to the very borders of British Columbia. An invitation to Milt, delivered no doubt by Hand of Officer "for your eyes only," was proffered by the prestigious Empire Club of Vancouver to address them upon the current recurring prairie phenomenon. Milt accepted at once, blind to the fact that Vancouver vied with Southern California for the title of "largest open air insane asylum in North America."[9]

The morning after his address, at six *a.m.* Calgary time, the telephone jarred me awake.

"Have you seen the *Sun*?"

Pause. Collection of thoughts. Eyes suddenly bulging at the prospect of vulnerability to importunation. I experience a vivid, riveting flash of Milt and me marching in matching leather helmets through Britannia, followed by a motorized B52 bomber, which suddenly runs amuck, over us and a few innocent spectators.

"It's dark here."

"The *Vancouver Sun*."

"This is Calgary. Why would I see a newspaper—or anything from the coast, now, here, at this hour? Why?"

"Get it and call me back."

Click.

---

9. For the world, Ireland has the title hands down.

I lapsed into the arms of Morpheus. Later, at the office, another urgent phone call from Milt:

"We're taking Alberta out."

"I've heard that line before."

"We're on the way, I tell you. Cliff, you should have heard the crowd! You should see the report!"

"I'm glad I didn't. Both."

"Cliff, this may be our window of opportunity."

"It's Chris."

"It's what? Crisp? I said this may be . . . "

"Milt, my name is Chris. How many times do I have to tell you that?"

"Tell me what, Cliff?"

"My name. My real name!"

"Cliff, what's that got to do with taking Alberta out?"

"Merv, everything."

"Who?"

"Merv, you're not ready to Rule if you can't remember your Attorney General's name."

"I'm appointing you my campaign manager."

"You've done that before. I want a new title and new responsibilities. How about Right Guide?"

(Pause.) "Pardon me?"

"Okay. Marker?"

"Cliff . . . "

"Acting Lance Corporal without pay?"

(Pause.) "Sometimes, Cliff, you're not funny."

Click.

Some days later, an urgent, top-secret meeting is called by Milt at his Chambers. Present are William (Bill) Stilwell, Zane This, George That, myself, a mesmerized media type we shall call X, and Larry Ross, then Milt's junior who was not quick enough to duck outside. Larry spends most of the time uncomfortably staring alternately at the floor and then the door. Milt is in full flight, and this is quite a sight to marvel upon. He has the exuberance and machismo of Burt Lancaster in *The Crimson Pirate* ("gather 'round, lads and lasses!"), but the jaw in the phizzog is locked into that "my God, war at any moment!" pose, and an air of gravitas theatrically contains the exuberance of the Moment.

"Gentlemen, I have invited X here because he is, as you of my inner circle know, one of the journalists I respect and trust."

X simpers like a mawkish bride being toasted by the "family friend" at a country wedding at the Millarville race track hall c. 1952.

"Gentlemen, we are taking Alberta out. I owe it to the people of this province. Comments?"

Stilwell (removing the ever-present toothpick, with a barely concealed smirk): "Milt, you've got no choice."

"Yaas, that's true."

I manage a coughing fit. Larry Ross looks desperate.

Bill rises, replaces the toothpick, shoots his immaculate linen cuffs as he unwinds to his full six-foot-three inches of lean, nasty rawhide barely disguised in his Gordon Edie pinstripe, removes the toothpick, and addresses Milt: "Still and all, Milt, what about the wife and kids? Have you thought of the sacrifice this will be for your family?" He replaces the toothpick and sits down.

I relax, somewhat. Bill is a genius, and he's at least hit the pause button.

Milt sags momentarily, like a cornered animal taking a dum-dum bullet, as the force of this revelation registers on the inner conscience chords. There is silence. Larry Ross stares longingly at the door.

At last, Milt responds. He leaps up. "Bill, you're right. What about Catherine? She's put up with so much, over the years. Such is vaunting ambition. And *what* about the kids?"

He paces in obvious agitation, duty to family, hearth, and home warring visibly with duty to the public.

"What could it be like for the kids? The father they hardly know. Playing with their little friends in the schoolyard. All of a sudden a golden jet streaks overhead! The other children exclaim, 'That's Milt! That's Milt Harradence!' Their own father, perhaps a stranger."

"And Catherine, out in the backyard, hanging up the washing, or whatever women do, when suddenly, that golden jet, streaking across the sky . . ." His voice drops, "Yes, Bill, you're right, by God!

What about Catherine and the family?"

A pause. Everyone looks at the floor now, hoping the danger has passed. Suddenly, Milt dismisses his scruples and his domestic obligations with an impatient wave of his hand:

"Oh, what do *women* know!"

Fears that Quebec might actually pull—at least, in A.M.H.'s time—were highly overrated. But for the "Harradence factor," that is the rise, either *there* or *here*, of a populist swashbuckler of a leader who would, first, inspire and, second, mobilize the forces of rabid jingoism, crying "havoc!" and sweeping all before.

The latest cyclical resurgence in Alberta separatism inspired Milt and a couple of his far rightist henchmen to foment revolutionary activity, most notably a rally at High River, thirty miles south of Calgary, then a hundred years behind the rest of the world, and at that time a hotbed of anti-Federal sentiment (although falling short of the paranoia in the remote Montana hinterland, where wild-eyed militia zealots armed to the teeth with an extraordinary assortment of anti-personnel devices loaded with Double-O ammo, parade in support of their God-given and constitutional rights to terrorize their fellow citizens.)

Milt and his cohorts were never seriously intending to vandalize a public building; although they and many of their fellow citizens were grievously offended by the hideously expensive Petro-Can twin tower Socialist edifice, erected in Calgary at taxpayers' sufferance, which they contemptuously labelled "Red Square."

At High River, the largest separatist rally ever held in Western Canada was staged in a packed hall in support of a fledgling—and shortlived—separatist group. A.M.H. was the featured speaker, to an audience of two thousand or so farmers and ranchers, gun enthusiasts, wackos, and assorted psychopaths. As Allan Bennett observed, "revolutions always attract the wrong people." Adds H.L. Mencken, "popular revolutions are invariably marked by gross excesses." And J. G. Farrell in *The Singapore Grip* cautioned: "The only trouble with a revolution is that it seldom improves things and very often makes them worse." In any event, High River, Alberta is an unlikely "Tiananmen Square." But it was fertile ground for the sowing of the separatist's seed, and Milt, who had, but for being too kind and too honest, the makings of a first-rate demagogue, seized the moment.[10]

As an orator, Milt could be absolutely spellbinding, and he was then at the height of his power. His sense of the dramatic, his natural flair, his impressive bearing, his wicked and original jibes and his superb timing, all were rhetorical winners.

Rhetorical excess, however, sometimes intruded when enthusiasm was permitted to overrule restraint. Such explosions of outraged roar and bellow were deadly serious to Milt, and unwittingly hilarious to some of the rest of us, notably Mrs. Bernice Evans.

Milt laboured mightily upon his keynote address scheduled for the High River rally. He unleashed his withering fulminations upon the remote poobahs and overpaid mandarins of the hated Ottawa in pejoratives calculated to bring the rural rabble to its feet as one man, hurling their fists and manure forks in the air in defiance. Alliteration was much—too much—in evidence. Excited with the draft product, Milt telephoned my residence for an opinion from me. I was out, and Bernice took the call. Flushed with confidence, Milt generously soliticited her views.

When he reached "snivelling, sniggering sycophants, secretly securing their sinecures at the sordid trough of swinish patronage ....," Bernice burst into explosive laughter.

Milt was taken aback. "What's so funny?"

"It is funny, Milt. It's absolutely marvellous."

"Yaas. Well, where can I find Cliff?"

Milt caught up with me at the office, but not before Bernice had filled me in, gasping with hilarity. "He's not serious, is he?"

"Was Spiro Agnew serious?"

"Oh, dear. I may have offended him."

Milt advised me later, in quizzical tones, that my wife had laughed at the most serious part of his speech. "Why do you think she did that? Is there something wrong with her?"

Nothing that a good dose of Milk of Megalomania won't cure,

---

10. See H.L.M.: "Demagogue: one who preaches doctrines he knows to be untrue to men he knows to be idiots."

I thought, casting about me for a plausible explanation. I said, "Well, you know she's from Rhodesia, Milt."

"Of course! That explains it."

Of course, that explained nothing. Milt was a sensitive but impulsive soul, given to charging with the Light Brigade unscathed into inconvenient cannon, but he could be mortally wounded by friendly fire. I requested Bernice not to invigilate any more of the master's poetical excesses. Regrettably, at a later press conference featuring a similar eruption from Milt (detailed in Chapter 9), I broke our rule of voluntary restraint and myself burst into uncontrollable laughter just off camera. Milt was right vexed and probably expressed dark reservations to Major about *my* loyalty.

As it turned out, albeit a negligible historical blip, the High River speech was a huge success. An appropriate comparison to those heady times may be drawn with the undisciplined and hero-worshipping crowds who flocked to observe the first aerial ascents (and often fiery and abrupt *descents*) by Montgolfier balloon, c. 1783-4: "As a spectacle it was unpredictable; its crowds were incoherent, spontaneous and viscerally aroused. Yet they were neither a mob nor a random aggregate. The sense that they were witnessing a liberating event—an augury of a free-floating future—gave them a hint of temporary fellowship in the open air..."[11] The learned author of that excerpt may not agree that the comparison is apt, but he must concede one fact: both spectacles featured hot air as the principal catalyst.

In or about the spring of 1977, at a time when Milt was attracting a great share of ink throughout Alberta with people breathlessly recounting his exploits at the Laycraft Inquiry, Milt's first cousin, Jack Horner, M.P., crossed the floor in the House of Commons, from the dinosaur wing of the opposition Tories, to the government, the Liberals. He had been wooed by the Prime Minister, Pierre Trudeau, who needed an Alberta minister, but had not one Liberal member from our province. Horner was vulnerable

11. Schama, Simon, *Citizens: A Chronicle of the French Revolution*, Knopf, New York, 1989.

because he was smarting from the assassination of John Diefenbaker, being—along with Milt, Eldon Woolliams, M.P. (Alberta's own Senator Foghorn), and others—one of the so-called "Diefenbaker loyalists." The bloodletting in the Tory camp had left a number of unhealed and festering wounds. Horner, therefore, stomped across the floor, escorted by the Prime Minister, and was forthwith elevated to the Federal Cabinet. Milt's brother, Clyne Harradence, was a lifelong Liberal, more large L than small L, I suspect: he hovered always near the top echelons of power for many years. Indeed, he became the national President of the Liberal Party when it was still in the ascendancy. But there was nothing "Liberal" about Milt, capital or small L. The best definition I ever heard of a Liberal was that of my father: "the man who opened the gates for the Trojan Horse was a Liberal."

Milt was almost desperate to become elected to public office, and to the amazement of a number of his close associates, he made the astounding announcement that he was thinking of following cousin Jack and switching to the Liberals. This was plausible, I suppose, in the framework of the political spectrum considering that cousin Jack was several places to the right of Attila the Hun. He wielded a great deal of power as a Federal Minister of the Crown from Alberta, and Milt saw doors opening that theretofore had been very much closed.

However, this was a delusion, a grand delusion, but nevertheless hopeless. During the Laycraft Inquiry (see Chapter 1 and the Appendices), Milt drove Jack Smith, Q.C., counsel for the Government of Alberta, and me (counsel for a former Deputy Attorney General) to the airport in his block-long white Cadillac, the Fishtail 8. On the way he gave us all the reasons why he should become a Liberal and run for public office federally, and we gave him all the reasons why he should not do either. At that time, I gave him my father's definition of a Liberal, and Jack Smith noted that a Liberal is a guy who leaves the room before the fight starts. That was enough for Milt.

"That's true."

Harradence was formidably endowed with leadership qualities. Given the right circumstances and the required political vacuum, he would naturally have succeeded in this arena. He inspired people, and one could imagine him leading fiercely loyal troops into the cannon's very mouth. But this was not to be: politics is above all capricious and mendacious, and success in it is too dependent upon the whim of the mob and the fiats of backroom rogues. He was well out of it. Macchiavelli was not Milt's prince. But you could never convince him of this. He remained forever frustrated.

Did A.M.H. suffer from egotism or insecurity? "The two often go together, of course," writes Murray Sayle of General Douglas MacArthur,[12] "... MacArthur was a performance artist, permanently on stage, and in character as a faultless hero... [but]... when the script went wrong, he was lost...." (See also my comments on Oliver Cromwell, another great military commandant, *poste*, Chapter 16.)

Milt had both overabundant common sense and perception, plus a keen sixth sense, in the combat conditions of the courtroom. No one has ever suggested that he successfully applied those same attributes in the political arena.

The western flare-up of separatism died down again, as abruptly as it started, a typical Canadian brush fire. But the Prime Minister was a student of history; no doubt he too read Gibbon: "Although the wounds of civil war appeared completely healed, its mortal poison still lurked in the vitals of the constitution." There was that chain smoking wild-eyed man, Levesque, in Quebec; and Harradence in Alberta, also a danger if he became unhinged and unleashed.

The latter thorn in Trudeau's side turned out to be easier to assuage than the former. Trudeau took counsel with his Western wizers and resolved the "western problem" by appointing A. Milton Harradence, Q.C., to the Court of Appeal of Alberta in early 1979. The Minister of Justice, the Hon. Mark Lalonde, a mortal enemy of A.M.H., not only strongly demurred but was quoted with authority as saying: "Harradence will be appointed to the court over my dead body." Trudeau, well apprehending the danger of a western insurrection to the fledgling Canadian constitution

12. *London Review of Books*, edition of February 6, 1997.

which was about to be repatriated, overruled his hatchet-faced Attorney General, whose life M. Trudeau apparently did not prize as highly as did M. Lalonde. Milt was annointed and appointed. The following is a verbatim account of the telephone call of the Right Hon. John Diefenbaker to Milt following the passage of the Order in Council:

> Milton, just heard the news of your appointment. I'm delighted. Delighted. You'll be an ornament on the Court. You'll make a magnificent contribution to the jurisprudence of the province. But Milton, what particularly pleases me is that the Minister of Justice said your appointment would be over his dead body. Milton, at the moment, I'm going through the obituaries.

The Calgary Bar had a dinner to honour Milt on his Appointment. Dwayne Rowe and I co-wrote and performed a tribute to Milt on the stage of the Palliser Hotel Ballroom, entitled "A View from the Bridge over the River Kwai Too far from Toko-ri." In the skit, *inter alia*, Rowe and I borrowed from the film *Alexander the Great*, featuring Richard Burton. There is an early scene of a discussion between Alexander's teacher, Aristotle, and the young prince. Aristotle says to Alexander that he must choose between a short life of glory and a long life of obscurity. Richard Burton screws up his pock marks and croaks, "I choose glory!" We staged Aristotle having a similar conversation with Milt but the dialogue changed slightly:

Aristotle: You must choose between a short life of glory and a long life of obscurity.
Milt: I choose glory!
Aristotle:But you've chosen the Court of Appeal.
Milt: Shit! I chose obscurity.

Chapter Eleven
Cops and Prosecutors

Part One
A.M.H. and the Police

HARRADENCE at one and the same time was the most formidable enemy and the greatest friend that the police ever had. Milt had a memorable line about the RCMP: "The RCMP are a truly great police force, but don't be fooled by the Musical Ride!"[1] During his regime as leader of the Criminal Bar, even the most battle-scarred police veterans of the courtroom approached an impending A.M.H. cross-examination with trepidation. Invariably stern and pressing, with his visage of thunder, he bore down upon inconsistency, irresolution, or intransigence with informed and relentless persistence. He might feint and jab, feeling out the prey, but the roundhouse right was almost inevitable. God help the waffling, prevaricating, or sloppy cop!

The experienced police officers would caution the rookies: "Watch out for this guy. He's good!" Some of the more bumptious youngsters scoffed at this good advice, confident that they—peace officers of Her Majesty the Queen—were more than a match for any sleaze-bag defence mouthpiece. The impertinent grins were quickly wiped off their callow pans, replaced by the whey-faced look of desperation. The old hands, smirking in the wings, watched the whiz-kids squirm.

---

1. A famous Norris cartoon of the sixties depicted two typical U.S. tourists in a crowd at the P.N.E., as the R.C.M.P. Musical Ride thunders by. The man says to his wife: "No wonder this country is so backward. The cops still carry spears!"

"Did you make notes of the interview, Constable?"

"No, but I remember well ..."

"Did you make notes, Constable?"

"No ... sir."

"Isn't it a practice of the members of the Calgary Police Service to make notes of all important details in an ongoing investigation?"

"Yes, well ... I do have notes."

"Isn't that the policy, Constable?"

"Yes, sir."

"But this incident is not in your notes."

"No, sir."

"Not in your notes at all, Constable"

"No, sir."

"May I see your notebook."

A reluctant proffering. An awful silence. Harradence scans the notes with a downturned mouth, then nods to himself knowingly.

"Constable, this entire investigation is recorded by you in exactly seven lines."

"Uh, yes, sir."

"Was the fact of the interview with my client an important fact?"

"Yes, sir."

"That is not in your notes."

"No."

"What about the Staff Sergeant's comment to the accused, was that important?"

"Yes ... sir."

"That is not in your notes, either."

"No, sir."

And so on, *quod demonstrandum.*

Exit, stage left, the demolished witness.

Over the years, of course, the apprehension of the cops in anticipation of a Harradence style of incisive and stylish cross-examination, always worse in the courtroom than the daunting thought of it, evolved to respect and then out-and-out admiration. So, naturally, when a policeman got in trouble he turned to the best; he wanted Milt Harradence to defend him. Milt would go anywhere in Canada, often without fee, to defend a police officer in trouble with the law. Many of his clients over the years were members of the RCMP and the Calgary Police Service, as well as other police forces. There can be no greater tribute to a criminal defence lawyer than this: that the police turn to him for help when they find themselves in legal difficulty. And it is a boon to the rest of one's practice, of course, because the public knows that the lawyer police officers go to has got to be at the top of his profession.

Further, many of Milt's referrals of clients came from the police, directly or indirectly. It was not unusual for experienced investigators to arrest and caution an accused; then, when the arrestee said he wanted to speak to a lawyer, they would immediately tell him to call the Great Defender. If the prospective client was hesitant, fearing ambush, he was encouraged by the referee:

"Of course he's good. He's our lawyer." And he would be given a telephone and Milt's number.

It was ex-Mayor (turned columnist) Rodney B. Sykes who, in a column *inter alia* paying tribute to his old friend and champion, A.M. Harradence, coined the phrase "If you're guilty/just call Milty." (That column, which appeared in the *Calgary Sun* newspaper, is an appendix to this book.)

Harradence was sincere in his frequent expressions of gratitude, as a lawyer and as a citizen, to the police forces in Canada.

Those of us who have some experience of the street, and of the tough (and sometimes unhappy) lot of the police, readily subscribe to the realities of policing since the era of the founding Peelers.[2] Where a peace officer finds himself accused of serious discipline infraction or public crime, there are three categories of defendant: in the vast majority of cases, the cop has not done anything wrong or even inappropriate; then there are a few who may properly be categorized as "a good cop gone wrong" i.e., who made a mistake; finally, there are a tiny minority of "bad cops." No one gets rid of a bad cop faster or more ruthlessly than his own

2. Not to be confused with the favourite entertainment of RCMP drug undercover operators.

fellows, because police are professionals. They are proud of their heritage and proud of their calling, which is service, service above all, and given at considerable personal sacrifice. Human beings being ingrates, few members of the public ever take the time to thank a police officer. Of all the public servants, it is the police who daily put their lives at risk in dangerous and exhausting work, for long hours and for little reward.

The abuse that the average police officer, male and female, is subjected to on a daily basis is staggering. That they generally react with remarkable restraint and exemplary equanimity and professionalism is a tribute to their training, their traditions, their experience, their tolerance, their common sense, and, sometimes, their leadership. Understandably, the odd copper gets a bit hot under the collar in times of intense stress or in the teeth of extremely provocative physical or verbal abuse. So, from time to time, however regrettably, when the limits of all human endurance have been reached or surpassed, the occasional dirtbag gets manhandled. No peace officer has to stand still to get hit. All peace officers have the positive duty to control persons disturbing the peace or breaching the peace, and to control their prisoners. Said Lord Goddard, "[A] peace officer may kill his prisoner if he has to." I agree.[3]

Empowering authorities, e.g., police commissions for municipalities, parliament for the RCMP, recognize that there are a lot of very nasty people in the world, and have therefore authorized peace officers, while in the execution of their duties, to deploy in their discretion a variety of anti-personnel devices, to wit: fists and feet, arrest control techniques, police dog Demon, pepper spray, batons, service firearms, including sidearms and shotguns (the latter in the police vehicle in a breakaway holster under the dash). As soon as a police officer actually resorts to such devices, or any of them, chances are good that some paper pusher or desk jockey somewhere higher in the chain of command will consider that the force was excessive and cause an investigation to be com-

3. I once quoted this passage in the Alberta Court of Appeal, which was met by shock and headwagging by two of the less streetwise appointees. Why do they put people like that on the Court?

menced of the police officer's conduct, be he or she ever so innocent.

The Criminal Code has, to this point, recognized that police officers must use force on occasion—even if their superiors have not—and that in certain circumstances the use of force by peace officers is a justification that provides a defence, in law, to an allegation of assault. That is, justified force, made out to the requisite standards, is a full answer and defence to a charge of assault, provided it is not in point of fact "excessive." Unfortunately, what is "excessive" force is a question of fact for judges or service or "civilian oversight" tribunals whose "street smarts," with some exceptions, of course, could use some development.

With Milt defending them, his police clients had a fighting chance at least. His services were almost exclusively in demand by police officers who ran afoul of the law, i.e., on the complaint containing the usual mendacities or absurd accusations, not a few of them from known thugs. To this it may be added that most police officers, accused of public crime, want their counsel to pull out all of the same stops utilized on behalf of the crooks, and then some.

In the days before our current Culture of Complaint, a complaint against a peace officer was relatively rare. Most were from the usual snivellers and whiners, and ended up in file thirteen. Some, regrettably, had to be proceeded with. Milt was always there for the member.

The Calgary Police Service was *smaller* then, of course, and management closer to the rank and file. Following an internal investigation, which the complainant inadvertently survived, the Chief Constable of the day advised counsel A.M.H. for the accused constable, "Milt, I guess we're gonna' have to proceed against our guy. Can't you do something, like, can you get one a them there *Kerkoraris*?" A *Kerkorari* plus a *Prohibition* was exactly what Milt got, serving it on the Chief Constable in the nick of time:

A.M.H: *Chief Constable, I regret that I have obtained a Court Order to shut down this inquiry.*
The Chief: *Jeez, Milt, I thought you'd never get here.*

Milt was and is clearly a great admirer of Dirty Harry and all of his lesser imitators. Every cop was entitled to at least one puke-thumping.

The law was to some extent obliging of this philosophy, and remains so, although a number of potty judgments have abridged its efficacy, and there are strident calls for its repeal or amendment by the same bunch who brought us the decline and fall of the Canadian Armed Forces, more than equal rights for some, affirmative action programs, and other doomsday projects.

The duty of a peace officer is to maintain the Queen's peace and to enforce the law. A police officer, if he or she acts on reasonable grounds, is justified in using as much force as is necessary for the purpose of doing what he or she is authorized or required by law to do. "Reasonableness" at the time, or with hindsight, does not enter into the measure of the force utilized. (Dim judges can never get this through their heads.) The requirement of "reasonable grounds" is exclusive to the reason for the police officer acting in the first place and is usually met by the cop being in the execution of duty in his or her perception, plus subjective apprehension of a breach of the peace or the lawful execution of process or an arrest, or repelling an assault.

As to the force deployed, it is a subjective call in the mind of the police officer at the material time, not the idealistic, altruistic social engineering of Judge Muse, the armchair voyeur, a year or so later; further, in the split seconds required to react in the real world, most often a noisy party or a seedy bar or a street confrontation with a drunk or the attempted detention of an intoxicated driver, the police officer does not have to "measure with nicety" the necessary force used. The police officer is nevertheless criminally liable for any "excessive" force, considering the circumstances.

A case in point is *R. v. C.*, the accused a twenty-plus-year veteran convicted by a Provincial Judge for busting the metatarsal escarpment of a troublemaker after other methods of suasion to discontinue his antisocial antics had failed. The arrestee, suffering from unrequited love, attending uninvited at his girlfriend's family residence about three *a.m.*, crept about the place surreptitiously (which is the reason her parents called the police in the first place, to which call the accused and his partner responded), then carried on noisily outside. This despite the replay of Burl Ives's hit record *Suzanne Regrets She's Unable to See You Again/She's Leaving for Europe This Sunday, She'll Be Busy Til Then.* The kid refused to take the hint, and the police officers asked him three times just to come with them and to quit the premises. The intention was to calm him down and drive him home. Fit and a sometime weight-lifter, the subject insisted on hanging onto the screen door handle. The cops then tried to pull him off, to no avail. Finally, Constable C. deployed his baton smartly to the thumb of the recalcitrant youth, who then let go. His testimony was that he was struck several times. The bone at the base of his thumb was broken. He also lied on an incidental matter, which gave the judge some pause in so finding; nevertheless, the judge accepted his evidence over that of the police officer. C. was convicted of assault causing bodily harm and, despite pleas to the effect that he was an untarnished veteran with an impeccable background, twenty-plus years on the force, and a grandfather and Christmas was coming up in a few days, the trial Judge (who is a dear old friend) on this occasion delivered himself of a politically correct judgment denouncing *inter alia* "goon squads" and utilizing other colourful phrases and socked poor C. away for thirty days. Ten minutes later, I was on the LRT with a blank Notice of Appeal, filling in the blanks, obliging Crown appellate counsel in tow. The judges were having some sort of Christmas party at the Court of Appeal, but one senior judge broke away to hear my bail application, requisitioning the judges' dining room for the purpose. It did not take long to convince the Court that there was an arguable appeal, and the Appeal Judge had Constable C. at liberty on his own recognizance with the words "welcome to Calgary, Judge X." (X had recently transferred to Calgary.) The clerks kept the office open long enough for us to get a certified copy of the bail order, and I was able to get Constable C. out the same night so that he could spend Christmas with his grandchildren.

The appeal came on for hearing before a Court of Laycraft, C.J.A., Belzil, J.A., and—there is a God—A.M. Harradence, J.A. Despite a spirited rebuttal by Crown counsel who had the accusatory emaciated aura of Cassius, the Court handily acquitted Constable C. In the course of argument, illustrative of Mr. Justice Harradence's appreciation of the essential elements of the "peace officer defence," Crown counsel addressed the Court:

Crown: *But the trial judge found that he struck the victim four or five times!*
Mr. Justice Harradence: *How many times do you have to hit them before they get the message!*

At that point, I got that nice warm feeling flowing over the Bench and knew that we were going to walk.

More practical heads prevailed in Milt's day in defence of police officers. A case in point is *R. v. M.*, a guilty plea by Harradence, Q.C., on behalf of a career police constable to a charge of assault causing bodily harm. The "victim," a horrid thug with a record for violence, had threatened M., who was arresting him and transporting him, with unspeakable violence to his wife and young child. The police officer had every reason to believe that this unsavoury person would carry out these threats. He subsequently arranged to interview the complainant, the latter then being in custody, M. posing as an investigating officer. Naturally, the complainant was placed in an interview room with M., and received a short, sharp sentence. There was no defence; the prisoner was in custody and entitled to the protection of the authorities, and no one was quick enough to look the other way. In the result, the Provincial Judge gave M. a suspended sentence, in view of the salient mitigating factors. The Crown appealed. The Appellate Division of the Supreme Court (as it then was) got the flavour of the thing without much trouble. Ominous storm clouds evoked by the citation by McDermid, J.A., of Lord Acton's duck-billed platitude, "Violence begets violent succession," cleared rather quickly with the setting aside of the suspended sentence and the substitution of a draconian hundred-dollar fine. Constable M., to my knowledge, remains on the police force.

In the same vein, *R. v. S.* stands out, a trial of a Detective on a charge of assault before then Magistrate Thurgood, Q.C., vigorously defended by Harradence, Q.C. I prosecuted, the theory of the

Crown being: a police pursuit involved a number of members chasing some vicious sociopath several blocks. The malefactor's driving was beyond criminal negligence. When he was finally cornered, he was detained by two of Calgary's finest, bent over, handcuffed, and frog-marched towards the squad car, when Detective S. arrived in a lather. He had monitored the proceedings on his radio, joined the pursuit, and arrived after the apprehension but not before his passion had cooled, whereupon he pulled a blackjack out of his back pocket (issue equipment) and smote the lout about the head and shoulders smartly, crying "You little bastard! You could have killed somebody!", both of which allegations were true. Anyway, fourteen police officers saw what happened, and I called one after the other in the case for the Crown, in a dreary procession of reluctant finger pointing at one of their own. After hearing a few of these witnesses, Milt hissed loudly at me, "Haven't you done enough!" I had, and Judge Thurgood had to find the detective guilty. He was fined a hundred dollars. It was the end of his career, and surely that was punishment enough in the circumstances.

I had a rather similar experience in the defence of a senior detective charged with assaulting a greaseball in the public courtroom, which anti-social correction in fact took place in front of Judge Edward Adolphe. A biker-type had just finished testifying for the accused, of the same ilk, and was leaving the stand when he recognized my client. My client, incidentally, had been light heavyweight champion of the Canadian Army. As the outlaw passed by my client, Court still in session, he made some gratuitous insulting remark to the detective. In turn, the police officer took the lout by his lapels and propelled him out of the courtroom. There was a brief verbal confrontation outside the courtroom, but discretion in the creep was the better part of valour, particularly when he noticed how tough my client was, and he backed off. Then he complained of assault. A very senior Edmonton Crown Prosecutor prosecuted the police officer for common assault before Judge Thurgood. It seemed a clear case of assault, but I put my client on the stand to explain why he suddenly reacted to a perceived threat in the courtroom and simply removed the disturber from the presence of the Court. Judge Thurgood wasn't buying any of that; however, his judgment was a masterpiece of innovation and recognition of the policeman's lot:

> Assault is defined as a touching of the person without consent. Here, there was a touching of the person's jacket. There was therefore in law no assault. I acquit the accused.

I whispered to the Crown, "Don't appeal and I'll buy the lunch." He didn't, and I did. We then conducted ourselves strictly in accordance with ethical guidelines adopted by Ontario Prosecutors: "A bribe is anything you cannot eat and drink in a day."

Well, those days are gone. And the granola gropers and the social engineers and the whey-faced academics all give their fervent Amens. They are aided and abetted in their goofy ideation by the new breed of Crown Prosecutor, for whom the successful railroad of an innocent cop is the equivalent of a carved notch on the old pistola, although they carve notches in their government issue briefcases. It's a brave new bloody world! Who, one asks, would be a police officer today? Some very dedicated and courageous men and women who sometimes probably wonder if they might be better off sweeping the streets rather than trying to keep them safe. And, tremble, tremble, who would be a peace officer in the future? In *A Clockwork Orange*, Anthony Burgess gave us a perceptive answer to the second question: crooks, ex-cons, and outcasts, because nobody else wants or is qualified for the gruesome job. Police officers in the next generation in the Brave New World will be recruited from the criminal classes. Taking the job might be a way to obtain early parole.

So, the next time any of the social engineers need a policeman, they can call a social worker. "With periods of immoral indiscipline ... (come) chaos and lunacy."

To which Milt Harradence and I say, "Amen!"

Harradence was made an Honourary Member of the RCMP "K" Division Officers' Mess, and an Honourary Member of both the Calgary Police Veterans' Association and the RCMP Veterans' Association, singular honours not to my knowledge ever accorded any other Alberta criminal defence lawyer to this day.

Part Two
A.M.H. and the Law Officers of the Crown

MILT HARRADENCE WAS GREATLY RESPECTED by the Crown Prosecutors and in turn returned their respect, courteous to a fault to even the most junior Crown counsel. I know this well, having been one who opposed him for five years. He was not only a close personal friend of many Crowns but their unswerving champion when they in turn needed counsel and advice. All criminal lawyers, whether Crown or defence, could always turn to Milt for assistance and counsel, which more often than not he gave freely.

During Milt's early days of practice, there was little qualitatively to distinguish Crown counsel from the cops, save a law degree, and nobody in those days really wanted to go to law school. Crowns were, for the most part, of the hard-boiled, red-faced variety; they wore porkpie hats, drip-dry shirts, and wide trousers like their bunko squad buddies. Although the prosecutorial service attracted some really first-class minds like William Stilwell, the late William Stainton, and Edward Adolphe, it also got more than its share of dweebs and goofs. Thus, in one municipality, for example, a perfervid Crown prosecutor roared around town in a white Mustang convertible rigged out with a special band police radio. (His father had been a police officer, and this Crown was a chip off the old blockhead.) Other horrible examples abound.

A quirk of the Edmonton prosecutors' office, which office harboured the largest nest of lifer Crowns in Alberta, was the proscription of law officer employees of the Attorney General of Alberta to follow their cases to the Trial Division or the Court of Appeal. For years, the august firm of Shortreed, Stainton and Enright were instructed in Supreme Court prosecutions, trial and Appellate, in the Edmonton Judicial District. This was resented by the rank and file prosecutors who did the initial work on the file, including having the conduct of the preliminary inquiry. Once there was a committal for trial, the aristocratic Jack Shortreed, Q.C., and his associates took the conduct of all prosecutions. He was as brilliant and relentless as was, reputedly, his late barrister father. He had the gunsight eyes of Jack Palance in *Shane*, and would uncoil himself in the same sinister manner, just before despatching some hopelessly brave but outmatched sod-buster. He was greatly respected but hardly a warm personality. He seldom deigned to make small talk with junior counsel. If, for example, in the robing room, one greeted him, "Good morning, Mr. Shortreed," he would look down his aquiline nose at one, as if to say, "If I wanted a weather report, I'd ask for it." (That is what the Captain of HMCS *Ontario* did say to me, c. 1957.) Shortreed's frequent appearances on behalf of Her Majesty before the Appellate Division of the Supreme Court (now the Alberta Court of Appeal) were always memorable: the old boys practically rose when he strode in. He would level an accusatory finger at the octogenarians on the Court: "That's not the law!" The persnickety judges of the day would quail visibly and say, "Oh, Mr. Shortreed, what is the law?" Shortreed would look at them disdainfully. "One moment, I'll get my commonplace book." Then he would tell them the law. Sometime later, Harradence actually obtained Jack Shortreed's "commonplace book." He paid him for it and proudly told me so. Why Shortreed wanted to get rid of it and why Milt wanted to buy it, I shall never know. Milt knew as much law as Jack Shortreed. I know it was very important to Milt to have the approval of giants like Shortreed and Edward Adolphe: he told me that he never did know where he stood with them, because these two great Leaders of the Criminal Bar in Alberta were both intensely private and unsentimental individuals and implacable foes of the defence, and shared no intimacies with anyone.

Not many young barristers in the fifties and sixties wanted to work for the Queen's shilling: the public prosecutor in Canada did not enjoy the cachet that glamourized the same job for his American cousin, the perfervid Assistant District Attorney, although the latter is to a great extent an ersatz Hollywood product. It was nevertheless notorious there that the path to a successful political career or a vault to the litigation department of a prestigious legal mill commenced with an appointment as a junior prosecutor in a large U.S. or State's Attorney's office. Crusading D.A.s had a high press profile, and their law officers also got a lot of ink. It was the exact opposite in Canada, probably because any serious money was only to be made by a professional in business or private practice; also, the Crown Prosecutor was expected to be a "Minister of Justice," in the term of the late Mr. Justice Rand. It is truly said, "the Crown never wins; the Crown never loses." Sounds quaint today, does it not? Like the police officer, the Crown Prosecutor laboured for long hours at low pay. It was only in the eighties that things got a bit better for Crown counsel, as the recession deepened and getting a job—any job—in the law was becoming increasingly difficult. Also, crime and punishment began to get more attractive in Canada. Young lawyers started to line up for prosecuting jobs. As man-made laws intruded more and more into the private lives of citizens—taxation, narcotics, wildlife, occupational health and safety, environment, imagining the Sovereign's death—prosecutorial departments, both Federal and Provincial, expanded exponentially. Further, and more significantly, the mindset of the Canadian prosecuting counsel was to change radically, from the objectivity of the "Minister of Justice," the "thirteenth juryman," to the more fashionable Victim's Advocate. Now, getting convictions was more important than presenting the facts. The whole thing has gone down the slippery slide.

The early eighties also ushered in the era of the aggressive Crown, and the Hon. A.M. Harradence, now on the Bench, was one of the first to pick up on it: "I don't like what's happening, Cliff." He spoke for many of us.

Inevitably, the Crown and the defence became polarized: Us versus Them, whichever side of the barricade one was on. The very worst product of this transitory period was the proliferation, in a sort of half-baked imitation of the hugely popular and successful American model, of the defence conspiracy theorist. The m.o. of this perfervid zealot is, there being no defence for his or her client, to put the complainant, the police, the prosecutor, and sometimes the Judge on trial. The only consensus this non-professional approach achieves is a pain in the ass for everybody, and the accused in jail for a lot longer than he or she deserves.

Chapter Twelve

Master of the Courtroom

At this point, the reader may be reminded that A.M. Harradence, Q.C., throughout his career dominated the courtroom as a master. I was reminded of this myself by Mr. Justice Major, who, as he perused successive drafts of the preceding chapters, was becoming noticeably more nervous. "There's not enough about Milt's cases," he complained.

There is something about Major's dry metallic twang emanating from that modern horror, voicemail, that is truly ominous. This plaint of "where's the beef?" bore overtones of the criticism that there was far too much levity in this work and not enough grave deliberation. All those hilarious happenings did happen, true, but "after all, this is meant to be a biography."

"It is not," I retorted to his voicemail, following the preamble: "This is Mr. Evans's mechanical secretary. I have fallen in love with Mr. Justice Major's mechanical secretary."

Just the thing to discombobulate Jack after a hard day of changing the law or tinkering with the Constitution, or whatever it is they do down there in Ottawa.

"This is not a biography of Milt," I said. "It is a book about me under the guise of being a book about him. It will tell the discerning reader far more about me than it will reveal about Milt. However, if you will stop puling, I'll lard in a few of the Great

Man's Forensic Triumphs. Other than that, the copy shall remain unchanged. *Post scriptum:* If you wish to dissociate yourself from this book, I will be greatly disappointed, but I will understand. Such a pre-emptive strike will in no way alleviate the defamations about you in the text."

At this point, the Supreme Court of Canada voicemail let out a dreadful whine—not unlike that of Lear on learning of the death of his youngest daughter[1]—which signaled the end of our negotiation.

The following excerpts are from a letter dated May 1, 1995, of the Hon. J.C. Major, Justice of the Supreme Court of Canada, to Marvin Bloos, Barrister, of the Edmonton Criminal Trial Lawyers' Association:

> I congratulate the Criminal Trial Lawyers' Association in their choice of Justice Harradence as the first person to be specifically recognized and honoured by the Association.
>
> Justice Harradence personified the ideal defence counsel. He was fearless in defence of his clients; that courage was combined with unusual drive, perception and intelligence. All these qualities were tempered by his rigid obedience to the ethics of the profession. As a Justice of the Court of Appeal he has not relaxed his vigilance in the recognition of human rights.
>
> My opinion and one shared by many is that Justice Harradence was the best cross-examiner we had seen. To stoop to a vernacular cliché, F. Lee Bailey could not carry his jock strap.
>
> I was always of the view that Alberta and maybe Canada was too small a stop to do credit to his remarkable talents.

This chapter is therefore dedicated to my friend's distinctive virtuosity as the Master of the Courtroom, and no single skill demonstrates so profoundly that mastery than the subject's ability as a cross-examiner.

His Honour Judge Irving Younger, Judge of the Supreme Court of New York City, much admired and quoted by Milt, opined that there were four requisites of the competent trial lawyer:

---

1. Sir Lawrence Olivier, endevouring to strike just the right balance for King Lear between sudden shock and intense pain,hit upon the sound of a fawn whose tongue is stuck to a frozen saltlick. As Milt would say, "Jesus *Christ*."

(1) Technical mastery;
(2) Assiduous preparation;
(3) Experience; and
(4) Talent.

In my own lectures on cross-examination, I have observed that (1) and (2) are available to all trial lawyers who are diligent; (3) may be acquired; (4) *the* prerequisite for greatness, is reserved for the very few virtuosi.

Harradence himself has done a good deal of lecturing on cross-examination. He said this in one memorable speech to the Canadian Bar in 1992:

> The third quality that goes to make a good cross-examiner is talent. Although it is unfashionable, anti-egalitarian, and elitist to speak this way these days, talent is also the rarest of the qualities that are necessary for a good cross-examiner. Either you have it or you do not. If you have it, it is because God gave it to you; if you do not have it, there is no way to acquire it. If you have the talent, you can acquire the technical mastery and develop the experience; you will be a Clarence Darrow. There are very few Clarence Darrows. I do not think I have ever met anyone who had that talent. Even without the talent, however, anyone can be a reasonably effective cross-examiner if he has technical mastery and experience.

Talent eludes the great majority of otherwise highly skilled barristers. Experience is a useful guide, and indeed indispensable to competent performance, but even years in courtroom combat cannot guarantee virtuosity. Only talent can do that, and so very few are blessed with this gift. What is truly frustrating to the merely able is that it appears to be effortless, the way Mozart or Bach knocking off a sublime trio or cantata in the hour before dinner is frustrating. At the end of the day, the majority of even extraordinary practitioners can only shake their heads in disappointment. All that damn work, study, even prayer, but to no avail: they still cannot do it the way Milt Harradence could do it, on his feet, without a note, shooting from the hip, breaking all the rules: *that* is virtuosity. A virtuoso knows no rules or makes his own.

Not that it is ever effortless. It simply *looks* effortless, as reduction of several issues to quintessence looks simple. One of the techniques of virtuosity as counsel is reduction, which also cannot be learned: you are either circumstantial or reductionist. Most lawyers have an incredibly difficult task cutting to the nuts of their case and their opponent's case, not to mention the vast majority of judges. The futile efforts of the former are hopeless; the "reasonings" of the latter are risible. Indeed, what made Jack Major both a great lawyer and a great judge was his uncanny ability as a reductionist. If only lawyers could ask themselves *before* the contest, "What is it we are *really* fighting about?" there would be a lot more criminal deals and civil settlements.

Milt Harradence had both the style and the technique, plus timing and that unerring instinct for the jugular and sense of theatre of which I have already spoken. Jack Major noted that Harradence's cross-examinations were, seemingly, "effortless." That in fact was Jack's term for it. Jack's favourite example was Milt's cross-examination of a hapless RCMP officer, testifying against his and Major's clients in a trial before Magistrate Graves in Canmore. The cops had routinely checked three hirsute youths in a psychedelic van on the highway near Canmore. They were found to be in possession of two kilos of marijuana which had been acquired in Vancouver. The case seemed hopeless, until Milt had a go at the poor cop on the issue of continuity of the exhibit, the dread cannabis, following which cross-examination the general impression was left in the Courtroom that the accused at the most should have been charged with carrying concealed sandwiches.

Subsequently, the RCMP officer approached Harradence, half in awe, half in resentment, and said: "You were reading my mind."

Milt liked to quote Judge Younger to young lawyers:

> No part of trial advocacy is easy, but cross-examination is almost impossibly difficult. The number of trial lawyers who are brilliant cross-examiners is probably fewer than ten in the country. Many trial lawyers can do a brilliant direct examination, a brilliant opening, or a brilliant summation: many others are brilliant in preparing a case. Cross-examination, however, is something spe-

> cial. It is subtle and difficult and complex beyond description. A reasonably effective cross-examiner must have a thorough mastery of the law of evidence and the law of procedure. He must also have a thorough mastery of that which is coming to be recognized as a separate and distinct body of law—the law of trial advocacy or trial techniques.

Milt was also fond of quoting Frances F. Wellman in *The Art of Cross-Examination.*[2]

> It requires the greatest ingenuity; a habit of logical thought; clearness of perception in general; infinite patience and self control; power to read men's minds intuitively, to judge their characters by their faces, to appreciate their motives; ability to act with force and precision; a masterful knowledge of the subject matter itself; an extreme caution; and above all, the instinct to discover the weak point in the witness under examination.

Harradence always said, you must *listen* to the answer. Case in point: *R. v. D.* The accused, an enthusiastic pilot of obscure airplanes, cracked up a Japanese Zero in Manitoba in 1974. It suffered a collapsed axle, resulting in a couple of charges under the *Aeronautics Act* including, *"As pilot in command, failing to report the accident within 48 hours."* Milt cross-examined the investigating police constable:

Q: *What time did you attend the accident?*
A: *The first time?*
Q: *Yes, the first time.*
A: [The witness gave a time].
Q: *And what time did you attend on the second occasion?*
A: [Witness gives a later time].
Q: *And that just gave* you *time to send a full report of the accident to the Department of Transport in Winnipeg?*
[The policeman's face fell and he looked at the Crown.]
Q: *He won't help you.*
A: Yes.

2. Copyright MacMillian Publishing Company 1936, Mrs. Ethel Wellman, 1964.

The relevant Act stated that if someone else sent in the requisite report, then the pilot in command did not have to. The accused was acquitted.

It is important to note here that Harradence practiced scrupulously in the tradition of the English Bar, that is, as a civilized mercenary, for hire to any client willing to pay the fee he commands. Private considerations or reservations on whether to undertake a brief are totally irrelevant. As I have noted, Milt was fond of quoting Thomas Erskine on that point. In particular, the more reprehensible the client and notoriously repugnant the cause, the greater the barrister's obligation to undertake that defence if his services are requested.

Thus, the pronunciamentoes of some adulated leading counsel south of the border were anathema to Milt and those of us who sought to maintain the best traditions of our profession. The protestations of some of these shining stars—that they would not undertake the defence of a client in whose cause they did not personally believe—are in my view unprofessional. At one time in this country, we would have found such assertions incompatible with the practice of advocacy.

I said "at one time." The scrupulosity that governed the barristers' traditional duty to vigorously defend the indefensible has been cast aside as cavalierly as his oath. I have commented elsewhere upon this undesirable development in law practice that I considered was a direct result of today's trial lawyers being held in thrall to egregious political correctness, and to the current trend to "marry your cause."

Milt was, as one would expect, the greatest practitioner of this duty to defend, without fear or favour and without compromise. As always, he led us by example. Never in all the years of our close association did I ever hear him suggest that he would refuse a brief from personal scruple. Every accused person was entitled to the most exhaustive defence available, and giving a mere one hundred percent to the cause was never enough.

In the courthouse coffeeshop one day, Milt was speaking encouragingly to a young law student who was contemplating a career at the criminal bar. However, she said, she did not think that she would be able to defend a man charged with sexual assault of a woman. "Then, ma'am," rejoined Harradence, witheringly, "you will enjoy probate practice." Of course, defending the basest and meanest of the realm requires a particular brand of courage. Few indeed have the fortitude of a Harradence. His brother, Clyne Harradence, Q.C., is also one of this rare breed and continues to this day to tread on sensitive toes and confront "delicate sensibilities." Clyne Harradence, speaking on the 1995 occasion of the institution of the A.M. Harradence Prize by the Edmonton Criminal Trial Lawyers' Association, had this to say:

> Milt excelled at cross-examination, but his approach to cross-examination is going out of style today. We're getting into a 'healing' and a 'caring' and a 'humanitarian' approach to witnesses—witnesses of the prosecution—who must be treated with kid gloves. You don't get the truth without putting some sort of concern in the mind of the witness: they must tell the truth. And if they don't tell the truth, they must know that they will be visited with consequences.

It is true that an adroit cross-examiner can often achieve more by ladling out honey and oozing charm, and no one was more the master of what W.V. Stilwell called "my transparent sincerity" with the appropriate witness, than Harradence, Q.C. However, the occasion more often requires bare-knuckled aggressive confrontation, and, as I have described elsewhere in this documentary, Milt had *la technique* down to virtuosity.

Harradence in his lectures always cautioned that cross-examination was a two-edged sword and would rhetorically ask his audience, "If cross-examination is that difficult and dangerous, why embark upon it at all?" He would then provide his two answers to that question:

> First, it may be (and frequently is in criminal matters) the only defence that you have; and, secondly, as Professor Wigmore said:
>
> "The difference between getting the same facts from other witnesses and from cross-examination is the difference between slow-burning gun powder and quick-flashing dynamite. Each does its appointed work, but the one bursts along its marked line only, the other rends in all directions."

Some examples of the Harradence virtuosity are to be found in the Appendices to this work. There are dozens of other examples of A.M. Harradence at the top of his form. Madame Justice Carole Conrad, at her elevation to the Alberta Court of Appeal, reminisced at her swearing in:

> I will also be joining on the Bench someone I used to watch in awe as an articling student. Namely, Mr. Justice Harradence. I want counsel to know that as a result of Mr. Justice Harradence, I am able to read a transcript and understand the written word is not always representative of exactly how the trial unfolded. Bill Gill, my principal, and Milt Harradence were counsel on the famous bookie trial in the late sixties. To this day, I recall Milt Harradence asking a question in a totally intimidating fashion and before the witness could gather his wits, he said: "Your silence is my answer." He then sat down and said, "It'll read well."

Of course, there is a great deal more to the many facets of effective advocacy than courtroom pyrotechnics, including the timely and carefully negotiated guilty plea which was also one of Milt's specialties. A.M. Harradence and his opposite number in Edmonton, John W. "Buzz" McClung, were the superlative Alberta practitioners of that art.

Speaking of courtroom pyrotechnics, it would be appropriate to close off this chapter by recounting another notorious example of Milt's sense of theatre. The conduct of the defence in the famous case of the *Barbeque in the Badlands* was undertaken by Milt Harradence, Bill Stilwell, and Brian Stevenson:

A guest of H.M.Q. of the "skinner" sub-species was allegedly set afire by three other inmates, subsequently charged jointly with culpable homicide; several other serving prisoners—of the "ratfink" sub-species—gave Queen's Evidence in exchange for early release.

At the preliminary inquiry in Drumheller, Harradence, Q.C., leading for the defence, set up his own tape recorder in the courtroom to record the evidence of the witnesses.

The preliminary inquiry proceeded, as reported by co-counsel Stevenson:

Each time an inmate took the stand, Harradence would make a big production of taking his microphone and pointing it at the witness. My cross went roughly as follows:

Q: *I understand that the deceased was serving a sentence for an incest conviction? Right?*
A: *Yes.*
Q: *And I further understand that in prison terminology such a convict is known as a "skinner." Right?*
A: *Right.*
Q: *And where does a skinner stand in the prison's social order?*
A: *Pretty low.*
Q: *Tell me, witness, in prison language, what's a 'fink'?*
A: *It's an inmate who rats on his fellow inmates.*
Q: *And where does a fink stand in the prison social order-above or below a skinner?*
A: *Below.*
Q: *And isn't that what you are? A fink?*

Anyway, Milt's recording program finally got to the Crown Prosecutor. In exasperation at its intimidating effect on the witnesses, particularly the inmates, he finally asked the presiding magistrate, "Your Worship, is all this recording equipment really necessary?"

To which the other co-counsel Bill Stilwell rose and responded, "We submit it is, Your Worship. We want to make sure we get everything down accurately. After all, some of these witnesses may not live until the trial."

The inmate on the stand at the time of this exchange had to be directed by the magistrate to answer counsel's questions from then on.

Chapter Thirteen
Costa Rica

Part One
Costa Rica — The Movie

JUST AS THE SACRIFICIAL carving knife descended in its first elaborate cut, the telephone rang. We looked at each other, let it ring a couple more times, and Bernice answered it.

"Merry Christmas, Milt."

A pause. "How did you know it was me?"

"Who else would phone just as we're sitting to Christmas dinner?"

She handed me the receiver and said, "*There never was such a goose.*"

"Can't talk. Have you seen the paper?"

"What paper? There is no paper. It's Xmas. You know, that time of year when Santa comes down your chimney without a warrant in Form 9 of the Criminal Code."

"*Yesterday's* paper."

"Sorry. I used it to wrap Bernice's Christmas presents."

"The balloon's gone up. Call me back."

There was nothing for it but to retrieve the scrunched public prints from the Xmas detritus. And there it was, on the front page of the business section, in bold face: "RCMP search extends to South America."

"Can we eat now?"

We did, then I called Milt. I tried the office first, of course. To my surprise, he was at home.

"Meet me at the airport tomorrow at 2:30 *p.m.*, no later," he commanded, "Catherine will have the tickets. Say nothing to anyone."

"Where are we going?"

Click!

Some things fell into place, as the electric light bulb over my noggin blinked on. About a week before, Milt had summoned me peremptorily to his elaborate chambers in Bow Valley Square 1. The four sky-scraper project was still a-building with several undeveloped areas.

As soon as I was seated, out of the line of fire of the blunderbuss mounted at testicle level beneath his huge table, Milt dialed a phone number with frowning concentration, then: "George, don't talk, listen. Call me back in ten minutes. I repeat, ten minutes. You know the number."

He hung up, rose, motioned me to follow, and we marched out the escape door of his office and down the back hall to a service elevator. I was by now used to a lot of cloak-and-dagger stuff with Milt, but was never sure whether to look appropriately grim or to burst into hysterical laughter at our actions that always presented as a cross-pollination of the Hardy Boys and Abbott and Costello.

We took the service elevator to the mezzanine level. There was no development whatsoever on this level, except, incongruously, three pay phones, which had been installed side by side in literally the middle of the large empty space. Milt marched up to them, stopped, looked warily about him, alert to sudden danger. At this point, like a wraith out of Kafka, a short, swarthy man in a trench coat—of course—approached from nowhere and made for one of the phone booths.

"They're *taken!*"

Taken aback, the man turned to Milt. "What?"

"They're taken."

The man dithered for a moment, then shook his head and made off in bad cess, looking back over his shoulder malevolently.

"RCMP.," muttered Milt.

"He can't be more than five foot two."

"That's how they fool you!"

At that precise point, the pay phone in the centre booth rang. Milt grabbed it.

"Hello, George. Yaas. Yaas. Yaas. When? Alright. Call me as soon as you get there. Yaas. Now, George, out of an abundance of caution, we don't want to get into a conflict situation, I've prevailed upon C.D. Evans, Q.C., who is here with me now, in this phone booth, to act for Martha. Yaas. Right. Call me."

He hung up. Just as well, because it was a bit of tight squeeze in the phone booth. All he said to me at that time was, "We're in funds. The client is on the move, *if you know what I mean*." There was no further explanation.

Then the Christmas dinner phone call. The paper reported in breathless journalese that the former President and Chief Executive Officer of a mutual fund company and his secretary were being sought by the commercial fraud section of the Horsemen to assist them with their enquiries about an alleged shortfall in the trust capital. It was believed that the lady and gentleman, who did not return the cops' telephone calls and singing telegrams to his modest four-section ranch in Southern Alberta, were "travelling abroad," and thought to be making for the wilds of Patagonia. Naturally, the flatfeet always thought that fugitives were heading for the southern tip of South America, it being notorious as a windswept archipelago of self-exile for various fleet-footed rogues.

Thus on Boxing Day, a day of rest to everyone in the western world but Milt, I presented myself at the airport. We're talking the seventies here, when Calgary "International" Airport had one entrance, one level, one domestic and one international ticket counter. Catherine Van Gaalen was on guard duty on the front steps to the entrance doors. Without a word, she took my hastily packed bag. Not knowing where we were going, I had thrown in anything. Bernice pressed her good Canon camera on me. "Take some photos." "What of?" "Whatever it is when you get there."

"Passport," snapped Catherine. "I'll check you in, kid. Milt's inside." She headed for the international counter and I headed for Milt, who could be picked out of a dense crowd in seconds: the Leonine head, the intense glare, the boxer's shoulders, the impeccable tailoring.

He was scanning the crowd. "I don't like the look of this." Of *what?* These things were never explained.

Catherine returned. At six foot five inches in high-heels, with her striking sheet of long blond hair and the full-length mink, she was not exactly invisible either. One would not have to be an unusually gifted cop to put a tail on these two.

"These are yours, kid. Don't lose them." She handed me a wad of airline tickets. "Milt says you're not to look at them til you're at thirty thousand feet."

As we negotiated the officious security checkpoint, an RCMP. officer of the airport (boneyard) detail species waved happily to Milt and winked: "Have a good trip south, boys."

"Jesus Christ! They're on to us."

When Milt was satisfied we were at thirty thousand feet plus, he broke radio silence: "We're on our way to Costa Rica, my boy. This is big."

"Costa Rica?"

"Yaas," he chortled, "no extradition treaty with Canada, the last time I checked."

Our routing on Air Canada was Calgary to San Francisco (overnight switch to Pan Am) to Los Angeles to Guatemala City (switch to Lacsa) to San José.

We arrived at San Francisco in time for dinner. We checked in at the Mark Hopkins, not the most retiring address if one is trying to be inconspicuous, then at Bernice's instruction made for Jack's Restaurant at 615 Sacramento. Jack's is very plain indeed. It does not advertise. Ties are obligatory. The waiters are all ninety years old, in long white aprons, and tell you cryptically what and what not to eat and drink. They brook no argument. "What's the attraction of this Goddamn place?" sniffed Milt, whose culinary tastes we have explored and who favoured the Calgary steak house sort of plastic plush ambience over the Spartan practicality and understatement of Jack's. "Good food, decently cooked. No pretensions. Efficient, knowledgeable, and unobtrusive service." He gave me that troubled, quizzical look.

Halfway through an excellent repast of sand dabs, the local fish indigenous to the Bay, washed down by me with a bottle of

Chablis, while Milt sipped suspiciously at his one modest glass, wary of a Mickey Finn, Milt suddenly smote his noble brow: "Jesus *Christ!* I almost forgot. I've got to get some white shoes."

"Some what?"

"White shoes. To go with my new tropical suit from Bergwall. Sharkskin. I've got to have white shoes. I can't wear black shoes. I'll look like an *asshole.*"

"Milt, its about 11:00 *p.m.* Where do you think . . . ?"

At 11:30, quitting Jack's, in a scene reminiscent of Le Carré, Milt commandeered a taxi. "Take us to a shoe store."

"A shoe store?"

"That's what I said. Drive."

Only in San Francisco could a taxi driver find an open shoe store at midnight. After an interminable trip—I was certain we passed over the Golden Gate two or three times on the outward bound leg—we arrived at a strip mall of discount houses and an open shoe store. A more hideous collection of footwear I have not imagined, but as Milt had always had a weakness for outrageous half Wellingtons, he plunged happily into the racks of winkle pickers, spiv strides, lurid tu-tone saddle shoes, wing-tips, for all I know Sisman Scampers, the full catastrophe. The clerk came up with several pairs of white shoes: suede, plastic, patent leather, even a sedate almost subdued lace-up model (naval officers for the use of, one pair each), which was the best of a bad bunch. Milt was fatally attracted to a soft-leather-loafer model with—horror!—shiny gold clips athwart the uppers. "What do you think, Cliff?"

"Well, if you want to be ambivalent, say between a fag and a pimp… "

"That's enough of that, you little bastard. They'll do."

Four hours of sleep and a dash for the airport, we were en route via Pan Am first class to Guatemala City. Milt was wearing the black silk, and I the bankers' blue pin, a right couple of toffs. Pan Am was, pardon the pun, flying high in those days, and it was customary on long hauls in a 747 for the swells in the expensive seats to be served "luncheon" in the dome, which was set up with linen table cloths and silver service like a Cunard dining salon. We were seated by the Chief Steward at a table with a couple who looked like they had survived the *Titanic* with someone else's life belts and money belts. They were certainly that vintage, and one could readily imagine them conning their way around the unwary wealthy passengers (second class, of course). Mr. had a long, mournful, whisky-soaked face that had survived obvious repeated vicissitudes; Mrs.' overwrought hair, rouged cheeks, and huge red mouth were awesome, turkey wattles hanging at her lower jaw; more flashy, vulgar bracelets and necklaces and rings than Cleopatra. It is these types of obvious frauds who so impress the members of the Calgary exclusive club *glitterati.*

"You gennelmen are obviously successful, I can tell by your clothes. You can always tell a gennelmen, I told Harry." Milt preened. Harry actually looked like a diseased, discarded dog. He said nothing at all through the whole ordeal. "I'm taking Harry for a nice long rest. You can't *believe* what the IRS have done to him. They've stolen a fortune from us, a fortune." Not half the fortune she and Harry stole, I thought. These vicious old creeps had badges of fraud all over them: trashy jewelry displays, trendy tailoring, Harry's lizard-skin shoes and garish Rolex; as I recall, Mrs. even had those rhinestone eyeglasses one laughed at in the Far Side cartoons, except hers were probably diamonds, likely looted off some mark's corpse.

Afterward, Milt observed: "You see, my boy. It's as I've always said. People judge you by your clothes. You see how that nice old couple reacted? And you can bet they've been around and are well connected."

"Seriously?"

Milt's sixth sense recovered. He smiled. "On the other hand, my boy, check for your fingers and then for your wallet."

We put down at Guatemala City. Milt was hesitant to disembark. "Wasn't there an earthquake in this god-forsaken place? I'm not getting off."

He did, because we had to implement counter-tailing methodology. At Guatemala City, therefore, we changed to Lacsa Air, the Costa Rican national airline. 'First Class' meant seats towards the front, one's knees under one's chin, the plane packed, heavy body odour and cigarette smoke pervasive. Why, when a later Pan Am jet went to San José? "Because they will think we're on our way to Panama, my boy, on the plane we just got off. They won't imagine we'd be on this tub."

They being the Horsemen, shadowing us to the lower reaches of Tierra del Fuego.

My suitcase failed to materialize at San José. San José, pop. 750,000 (then), in a temperate valley, was not the worst Central American venue to be stuck in with a wool suit, one white shirt, one pair of black socks. But still.

The clients were there to welcome us, effusively. The first thing I noted about Milt's client, Mr. G, were his eyeglasses, as thick as beer-bottle bottoms, and the new wedding ring on his hand, and the matching one on the hand of my client, signifying his timely marriage to the new Mrs. G. "The poor man is about totally blind," bemoaned Milt, "and the Musical Ride after him! The bastards!"

We were driven in their Land Rover to the Gran Hotel, San José. Mr. G negotiated the twisting, rutted road quite well for a blind man. The Gran Hotel was an edifice of decayed elegance that once hosted the likes of the Great Carouso and Sarah Bernhardt. It had Doric colonnades and a soaring lobby something like the Sistine Chapel, the obligatory wide staircase to the mezzanine, and for all I know, flying buttresses. The mezzanine level housed the Gran Ballroom, where old fugitive Nazis steered their stolid wives like wheelbarrows around the highly polished floor to the strains of Lily Marlene or Blue Angel, c. 1946, *et seq.* [1]

Milt was mightily impressed. "This will do."

All in all, the place was little distinguished from Calgary's 'venerable' cattleman's and railroad man's venue, the Palliser, before its Olympic facelift: high-ceilinged rooms with transoms over the doors, capacious crappers in the bathroom that went "Varrrooommm!" when flushed. "See," I said to Milt, demonstrating the one in his room, "just like the American Standard: flushed with pride." Milt again gave me that look which he reserved for the occasions when he thought I was rather too strange.

It was quite late at night, thus we adjourned to the following

---

1. I owe this image to John Mortimer, Q.C.

morning. We were to meet the clients at 9:00 *a.m.* in the lobby, and I shall never forget standing there with the clients when Milt made a theatrical descent of the sweeping staircase from the mezzanine floor, replete with a dazzling white suit, a black shirt, a white tie, and—of course—the famous San Francisco white shoes. It was sort of a reverse gig to the spangled number, *I'll Build a Stairway to Paradise*, made famous in the Hollywood musical, *An American in Paris.*

Milt had insisted that we get a "secure" place to brief with the clients, and in the result, after negotiations between Milt, Mr. G, and the hotel manager, we took over the entire Gran Hotel Ballroom. This was about a two-story job with a huge chandelier in the centre, the size of a large football field. Flunkeys placed a card table and four tin chairs immediately under the chandelier in the very middle of the ballroom floor. As it was the epicentre, Milt was convinced that "They can't get us here with the parabolic mikes" This incongruous setting caused me the greatest hilarity, which I could barely contain.

On that second day, my suitcase materialized and I had to go out to the airport to reclaim it. It appeared all in order, and had been passed through Customs, and I was somewhat surprised I was not obliged to pay a certain amount of "dash" to bail it out. That was before I got back to the hotel, unlocked the suitcase, and found that everything was meticulously in order with the exception of Bernice's expensive camera, which was gone. A lesson in cross-border courtesies.

We split up for individual briefings with our respective clients, and ended our attendance upon them with a motor excursion to view the walled lair of the fugitive, Vesco, urgently wanted by certain police forces in the United States and Switzerland to assist them with *their* inquiries. This huge layout was completely surrounded by a high concrete wall, barbed wire on top, and at the gates there were elaborate TV cameras watching the persons approaching them. Milt was again mightily impressed, and said so: "That's the sort of set-up I need at home." In view of his omnipresent preoccupation with security of the person, I would not have been surprised had he had just such a fence put up around his vulnerable residence.

One other incident on this first trip to Costa Rica with my mentor stands out in my mind: Milt had contacted a former acquaintance who had been prominent in business and social circles in Alberta prior to his moving down to that clime. This gentleman turned up at our hotel with a great fat fellow entrepreneur who he introduced as an expatriate American and the president of the Consolidated or Amalgamated Banana Company, or something like that. Presumably, this chap was a local bigwig and had vast holdings in the Costa Rican hinterland. There was a rather desultory visit. The room was very warm, and the transom over the door was open. The visitors went to take their leave after this social courtesy, and as Milt was showing them to the door of our sitting room, his friend remarked that there was a new dictator in Panama, which apparently had been a matter of some discussion in those precincts. Milt started, looked grim, turned to me, and said, "Well, while we're down here, we'd better check him out." That is what he said. The guests departed, and as Milt shut the door, we could hear through the open transom the banana baron addressing Milt's acquaintance: "Gee, that guy is really something! I'm impressed!"

This *was* bizarre. How exactly did Milt propose to "check out" the new dictator of Panama, or for that matter *any* Southern hemisphere comic Costa-Gavras cardboard general in highly polished jackboots with a ridiculous hat dripping with fried egg, sporting the Grand Order of Paulonia (third class) on his breast? I presumed we would get there and get off the plane, to be met by a concerned delegation with plenipotentiary powers:

"Hi, I'm Milton Harradence … the criminal lawyer from Canada … I'm here to check out your military dictator!"

"Come right in, Mr. Harradence. We've heard of you. How can we help? Are you any relation to Mervin Belli?"

"Melvin."

"Pardon?"

"Melvin. His name's Melvin. My name's Milton."

"Okay, Merv. Mervin."

"Milton!"

"His name's Milton?"

AMH (aside, to CD, whom he still calls Cliff): *"Cliff, can't these idiots understand plain English? Who's in charge here? Jesus Christ!"* Cliff (singing): *"Her name was McGill/but she called herself Lil/and everyone knew her as Nancy…* "

And so on.

The time came to return to Canada. Milt fretted disconsolately at the airport over two burning issues: (1) we were being followed, there was no doubt about that, and what to do about it; (2) how he could possibly get it across to the waitress in the aerodrome cafeteria that he wanted bacon and eggs. Milt's predilections for paranoia and for bacon and eggs (the order is irrelevant) have been discussed, *infra*. As he brooded over the fancy moves to be made to drop the tail, he remonstrated with the waitress: "Huevos, easy over, Marm … (to me) … for Christ's sake, don't they understand plain *English?*"

"No, Milt, this is a Spanish-speaking country."

"Don't these people know anything? Now, Marm …" This went on. Eventually, by a miracle, Milt got his bacon and eggs, which he promptly inhaled, notwithstanding the Huevos Rancheros he had equally inhaled about an hour earlier at the hotel. We piled onto the Lacsa flagship, some propeller-driven job that looked like it needed pedalling to get it off the runway. Milt strapped in, and as the instructions to passengers commenced *en Espagñole*, his reaction was exactly the same as when Air Canada did its bilingual admonitions: "Shut-up, for Christ's sake, shut-up, for Christ's sake…!" There were times when my fearless Leader demonstrated a low threshold of tolerance for other cultures. Anyway, the crate got off the ground and in due course staggered onto the Guatemala City runway, bounced a couple of times, and came to rest.

Milt was up and out of the plane like his pants were on fire. "Follow me." After a great deal of negotiation, he was able to exchange his flight to Miami, which was our scheduled route, to a ticket for him on Pan Am to Los Angeles. Then he was on a pay phone, again screaming at the Spanish-speaking operator, "Get me the Beverly Wilshire! The Beverly Wilshire! The hotel! In Los Angeles! Don't you understand …?" To me, "What do you have to *do* with these people?" Then, to the phone, "Harradence. *Harradence!*" To me, "She called me Harrandence! Jesus Christ!"

"Milt, this *is* a Spanish-speaking country."

"I heard you the first time, Cliff." He went back to harangue the operator.

Exhausted, he retreated from the telephone. "Well, I think I got through."

I took the opportunity to ask him why all this cloak-and-dagger stuff was necessary. He gave me a withering look. "You've got the originals. I've got the copies. Do you want me to draw you a picture?"

They called Milt's flight. I said to him, "It's a Goddamn shame. I'm going to duck out of Miami and get a trunk run to New Orleans if I can. You should get hold of Catherine and I'll call Bernice and we can all spend New Year's Eve in the French Quarter."

"No time for that," growled Milton.

"So why are you going to stay at the Beverly Wilshire anyway?"

He just looked at me. "You've got to be *seen*."

Milt's flight was called, and his trench-coated lone gunfighter figure headed for the ramp. Halfway along the ramp, he turned and smiled at me. "Happy New Year, m'boy. Now that bastard won't know *who* to follow."

I had time to get hold of Bernice in Calgary to see if she could line up a hotel—any hotel—in New Orleans, and I would check with her from Miami when I was negotiating tickets to New Orleans. I managed to get there, all right, and she was able to get down from Calgary and we got some broom closet in some run-down joint in the French Quarter, but it all worked out fine and I regretted that Milt and Catherine could not join us. However, as Milt would say, "You can never be too careful. Watch out for these people. Keep your guard up."

No doubt this comforted him as he dined in severe isolation in the Beverly Wilshire dining room on New Year's Eve.

PART TWO
Costa Rica — The Sequel

APRIL IS THE CRUELLEST MONTH, particularly as it is the usual harbinger of the Easter bunny not to mention lurid one-dimensional medieval representations of the Crucifixion. It was thus a fitting month to revisit the Central American fugitives with my swashbuckling Leader.

Milt followed the previous *modus operandi*, that is, the surreptitious nocturnal phone call: "Don't talk. You know where I am. Get on a pay phone and call me back." Whereupon, I fell back asleep. Ringggg! "Cliff . . ."

I staggered up and out and through a late snowstorm to a pay phone, and called Milt at his office on his 'secured' line. He barked embarkation orders into the mouthpiece. I had a few hours before I had to meet him at the airport. This time, at least, I knew where we were going, but it would be no use packing more casual attire because Milt always required us to be dressed like Los Angeles high flyers.

We had to take further instructions from the clients. After our return from the first adventure, we had consultations with the investigating officers as well as a poobah in the Provincial Securities agency, and we now had a reasonable picture of the regulatory and investigating authorities' theory. A special prosecutor was about to be assigned to the case. My mentor was, he said, "in funds," with tickets. I was to be there with my passport.

It wasn't until I got to the airport that Milt advised that this time we were going by way of Toronto and Miami.

The incident at the Toronto airport hotel is indelibly etched in my memory. We had left Calgary on an evening flight and were therefore checking in at about 1:00 *a.m.* Milt was hunched over the details of registration with frowning purpose as I surveyed the capacious lobby. The hotel was a high-rise hotel for transient high-flyers of business aspect and had a cocktail bar on its ground floor that did a lively and steady trade into the early hours, inviting weary travellers with flashing neon sign. This evening was obviously no exception. Two of the most gorgeous vamps I have ever seen entered the lobby through the front doors looking like they enjoyed life at the high end, dressed "to the nines" replete with fun furs and flashy cocktail dresses. These were decidedly not feminist suffragettes, but most assuredly ladies of public life. Eye contact was established, and they flashed brilliant expensive pearlies in our direction as they glided into the lounge.

"This," I said to Milt, "may be our lucky night." Milt had not missed the brief action nor my reaction. His face contorted into that wrathful Old Testament countenance I well knew, as he growled: "Stay away from that stuff! You don't know where they've been!"

That was it. Milt marched me to our lodgings, which were about three floors up and at the end of a hall: his room was the last on the left and mine right at the end. We bade good-night, and I waited for what I considered to be a decent interval, klunking around and putting on the gogglebox for sound, before surreptitiously opening my door with the intention of at least vicarious drooling and a drink. As I tiptoed carefully past Milt's door, it was suddenly opened, and Milt was standing there, fixing me with an accusatory piercing eye: "Where are you going?"

"Uhhh, to get some... toothpaste."

"Wait here." I did. Milt disappeared momentarily, then returned with a tube of toothpaste.

"Use mine."

I retreated, chastened, to my room.

The next morning early, we flew to Miami. We had a four-hour stop-over before switching to a Pan-Am flight to Guatemala City, and Milt was resolved that we should lunch at the Fontainbleu, a venerable Miami edifice and a choice hangout for the Rich and Famous. "Why are we going to this particular dry-docked Cunard Liner?"

"You've got to be *seen.*"

We piled into a cab, and braved the imposing facade, marble foyer, Persian rugs, snotty waiters, and liverish clientele of the great hotel. The repast was excellent, although Milt, requiring to remain on the alert for tailing gumshoes or double agents and other persons of the stalking fraternity, eschewed the superior Burgundy, leaving me no choice but to drink the whole bottle. It was at this point that Milt discovered he had lost his wallet, and the Maitre d' had to accept payment from his now drunken junior.

With scarce time now to make the flight, we performed a frantic assault upon an American Express office and secured my leader a new card. Then a mad dash to the airport.

Upon the way, Milt expanded upon the conspiracy theory he mentioned over the house terrine. As we were leaving the Miami Airport and passing the luggage carousal, we ran smack into Jim Coutts, then a powerful *eminence grise* of the Prime Minister's office. Milt was actually startled, then later perturbed. We both knew Coutts, me from university days, and Milt from Coutts' brief sojourn in Calgary some years before. Coutts being a notorious Liberal and Milt a prominent Tory, they had little in common. Coutts was considered to be very close to Prime Minister Trudeau and highly influential in the dank corridors of power in the nation's capital. An idly cordial exchange yielded Coutts' admission, obviously in jest, that he was in Florida to visit Disneyworld, and where were we going? accompanied by the Smile of the Tiger. "That we can't say," snarled Milt, and we made off, Milt in haste.

Now, en route to Central America, Milt was chewing, fretting actually, over the sinister meaning of this Encounter in Miami.

"You don't think he is *really* going to Disneyworld, do you?"

"Milton, why would one go to Disneyworld if one already worked there?"

"Yaas. That's true." Pause. "Then what was Coutts *doing* there? He must have been on our plane. I never saw him. Did you?"

"No."

Pause. "You don't think the RCMP. . . .?"

"What? The RCMP. what? Sent the Prime Minister's principal secretary to spy on us, for this case?"

"This case, my boy, ain't exactly Mickey Mouse, if you get my meaning."

I didn't, and told him so.

"Still …," Milt sighed. "Goddamnit, you never know it with the Horsemen!" He lapsed into silence, a twitching jaw betraying his suspicion that things were going all the way to the Top.

This theory remained untested.

We were greeted at the San José Aerodrome by the clients. As I recall, it was Good Friday. They were anxious, and pleased to see us. They had been on the run and on the defensive now for over a year. The fugitive cerebellum is subjected to massive attacks of paranoia, and the "circle the wagons" mentality is soon in evidence. Notorious in the public prints—of both Canada and Costa Rica—was a daring expedition of recent date in which the Mounties had literally commandeered an entire DC-9 aircraft, flown it down to Costa Rica, persuaded the local Chief of Police to invite a fugitive businessman around to the substation for a chat about "minor passport formalities," burst out of the closet, seized their prey, and whisked him back to Canada. In those days, there was no *Charter of Rights*, and once hauled into a Canadian Court of competent criminal jurisdiction (which may be an oxymoron), the hapless kidnappee folded and copped out to five years of penal servitude. Thus did Mr. and Mrs. G fearsomely anticipate the chilling swish of muffled boots upon the back stairs, followed by the heart-stopping nocturnal knock. "What was that?" "The wind, only the wind." In such precipitous circumstances, when one lives but day to day, the imagination plays fearful tricks.

To make matters worse, they reported, in subdued tones, it's "Gringo hassling time" again. "Gringo hassling"—the summary importunation and even detention on specious grounds of temporarily resident North Americans—flared up from time to time, and this was one of those times. The cops in this Central American democracy do not carry guns: they carry screwdrivers. The principal sanction against the transgressing citizen is a summary removal of his motor vehicle license plates, leaving him and it stranded. I guess if the cop felt threatened, he could put out an eye or two at the same time. It was equally notorious abroad in Costa Rica that most visitors on temporary residence permits, who were not tourists by any stretch—like Mr. and Mrs. G, our clients—were people who were in their relatively hospitable country for their health.

"Health?" I queried my Senior.

"Yaas," he rejoined meaningfully. "It's not healthy for them to be in Canada."

That is, they had (in the timeless words of Quigley, JQB) "taken it on the Arthur Duffy" and were now "on the lam," flight no doubt spurred by the sure suspicion or even knowledge that the police authorities required their presence at the precinct for a heart-to-heart chat. Any one who has viewed *The Lavender Hill Mob* or has followed the fortunes of Ronald Biggs knows that the coppers do not give up on fleeing expatriates that easily. Indeed, the Gs had moved so much, even within Costa Rica, that their curtains matched the sidewalk. They were now thoroughly spooked. Milt was their saviour.

This time they had arranged to put us up at the Excelcior Hotel, a decaying clapboard and stucco joint that had seen better days, and Milt said so. The clients explained that the Gran Hotel was full up with a convention of banana planters. I suspect that the Stomp of the Banana Boys was a convenient pretext, and the more pressing reason was that the clients' pocket book was getting a bit stretched and they were not anxious to again incur two days rental on the Gran Hotel's Gran Ballroom.

The clients withdrew, to meet us again the next morning. As we checked in and deposited our passports with the archetypal perfunctory functionary at the desk, Milt tensed. Something was up. As an urchin struggled toward the dubious elevator with my suitcase and Milt's two steamer trunks, Milt took my arm hurriedly and steered me after him with imperative urgency, muttering, "Say nothing." A double door curtained with hanging beads separated the seedy reception area from the elevator hall, and as soon as we were through it, Milt put his finger to his lips, his eyes narrow and alert to imminent attack. The bellboy had staggered to the one noisy elevator. Milt thrust his hand into his pocket, pulled out a fistful of the local funny money, which currency enjoyed the same buoyant reputation with foreign economies as the dirham and the baht, selected a large red note with a faded picture of some swarthy revolutionary, and gave it to the kid while motioning him to take the bags and go. Go! The youth's eyes bulged out at the size—and probably the worth—of the bank note; he cried,

"Caramba!" Milt, meanwhile, signalled me frantically to "stay put"" (I had seen such gestures in late-night flicks on the goggle-box, notably *Delta Force*), as he leaned to a breach in the beaded curtain and squinted at the reception area.

The reception area consisted of a plywood counter with cracked vermiculite top, a low table out front strewn with old newspapers, a pole lamp, and a couple of rickety easy chairs, all the stuff looking as if it came from the bargain basement of a discount house. It was not unlike the last motel I stayed at in the far north. When we had arrived, Milt had noticed immediately a moustachioed man reading an English-language newspaper, lounging in one of the chairs smoking a cheroot. Now, spying on the scene, he hissed, "The guy with the paper. He's talking to the clerk. Now he's looking at something. A registration card. Jesus Christ!"

"Follow me!" he whispered. Impressed with his famous sixth sense, and trying to act as if I was alive to the urgency of the moment, I fell in behind him and we marched, single file, boldly through the lobby, past the desk and its two conversationalists, and out into the street. Milt wheeled right and I continued behind, almost in lock-step. It must have been ninety-five degrees fahrenheit plus, even in the dark of evening, and I began to sweat profusely in my Bergwall-bespoke grey pinstripe. We proceeded in this hilarious manner for about a block, when suddenly Milt dived into the blank maw of a narrow alley, roughly pulling me in beside him. The stench was overpowering, probably decaying bodies, I imagined. What evils lurked in this desperate place, I wondered fearfully, as Milt slowly put his head round the corner of the brick building and did a recce. "Alright," he said, "it's clear."

We walked back to the hotel, Milt taking pains to keep us in the shadows of overhanging hibiscus hedges or bougainvillea bushes, or, as Milt growled, "Whatever the hell these Goddamn *weeds* are." I cautioned him to be vigilant, as these dense growths "could harbor deadly night-flying snakes. I read somewhere that you have thirty seconds to cut off your bitten part with a machete, or you're dead. J.G. Farrell said so in *The Singapore Grip*." J.G. Farrell said no such thing, but I loved Milt's reaction. "Jesus Christ!"

exclaimed Milt, "who'd *live* in a place like this?"

The next morning, mildly jet-lagged, I was up and out for a run to the local soccer field and back to the hotel. It was indeed "Gringo hassling" time. I was stopped by a grim-faced policeman. I had taken the precaution of taping my passport to my upper arm. He examined it, with insolent punctilio, then warned me, ominously, "Señor, put on your pantalons." I learned then that men did not display bare legs in public places. I slunk back to the hotel through back alleys, which did not look as sinister by day. Not a dead body to be seen.

Milt was again resplendent in his white suit. We had breakfast in the run-down café with its simple desultory waiter, the same kid who had handled our baggage. Milt was sure, being steeped in anticipatory tradecraft, that our luggage had been examined by the police as we slept. I thought it most unlikely, but as I had lost my wife's camera on the first trip, I made sure this time that I had nothing worth losing anyway. Milt was scratching at his left forearm, and finally he doffed his jacket and rolled up his sleeve, to reveal a line of raised red marks obviously left by some biting varmint. I laughed. "Oh, yeh?" said Milt. "Go look in the mirror, wise guy." I did so, into the yellowed and cracked café glass, and saw a sinister meandering line of little angry welts crossing from my right temple, over my nose, to my left cheek. I had been in both north and southern Africa with Bernice on extended trips, so this was no big deal. "Probably bed bugs," I told Milt. "Tonight, what we do is, you turn off the light, when I holler 'now,' you switch it on while I yank back the top sheet. You'll see the little buggers scatter." Milt glared at me. "Don't even think of it, Cliff. We're getting out of here. Christ, we've got a foreign disease!"

We met with the clients, lunched separately with our respective charges for the giving of the fullest independent advice, and briefed for the better part of the day. Milt advised that the accommodation was substandard, and the clients promised to move us the next day. Also, Milt had hinted, it might be a good idea to move "for security reasons." The clients nodded solemnly. They knew.

The clients, always accommodating, arranged to move us to a

high-rise apartment which came with, *inter alia* (a Latinism I learned at the feet of Berger, JA, who would declaim it in his best hortatory fashion), a swimming pool. I did not consider it to have the charm of the Excelcior—nor the other endearing features—however, I did convince Milt to return to the Excelcior with me for dinner, as, quite by chance, I had discovered in the basement an excellent restaurant run by an alumnus of the Fontainbleu. To Milt's horror, I dined superlatively on rabbit and a bottle of Aloxe Corton, while he hunched over his steak medium well and glared about him at possible eavesdroppers or fifth columnists.

The next day, the banana barons having dispersed, each to his fiefdom, the clients were prevailed upon to obtain a modest meeting room at the Gran Hotel. Milt and I returned to the venue of his star staircase turn. It was Easter Sunday and the place was like the tomb. At lunch, matters being concluded, the clients departed and Milt and I found ourselves the only customers in the Gran Hotel coffee shop, with one scruffy serving lad on duty, moping in the corner and batting fruitlessly at flies with his dirty dish towel. It was terribly hot. I was dying for a cold libation, and summoned the lad and asked for a beer. "No, Señor, eet is eempossible. Ees Easter. No booze, Señor." I stroked him with one of those strange local bills, he smiled, and disappeared. Milt looked disconsolate. "I wouldn't do that if I were you, Cliff."

The waiter returned with a large china teapot and two cups, both cracked. Those were placed with ceremony before us. Milt demurred, as I helped myself to the ice cold beer from the teapot.

At this time, the entire population of San José was in church, this being a manifestly God-fearing nation, sorely afflicted with family duty, community responsibility, and the Catholic Church. We could hear them from the packed cathedral down the street, belting out the Spanish equivalent of "Gladly, the cross-eyed bear." A more benign and peaceful place could not be imagined, yet in this deserted café Milt squirmed, alert to ambush at any moment. Suddenly, he leaned forward across the rickety table and fixed me with a riveting look: "We run into any trouble in this place, we'll fight our way out back to back!"

Trouble was not the least interested in presenting itself. The next morning we found ourselves heading back for Miami, then homeward. This time, Milt forebore to change planes. Perhaps it had finally occurred to him that most of the male population of Central America had moustaches and that many of them read English newspapers. That being said, he never relaxed his eternal vigilance.

EPILOGUE TO CHAPTER THIRTEEN

IT IS A REMARKABLE event in itself, in the course of this substantial criminal litigation, that the clients voluntarily returned to Alberta at their own expense to face trial.

"Jesus Christ," exclaimed Milt, on being apprised of this latest intelligence, "Do I have to paint them a fucking *picture?*"

"Well," I said, "it's probably the night-flying snakes."

"Of course," said Milt, grimly, adding, "both the serpent kind and the human kind. *They had no choice.*"

What ensued was even more remarkable:

Mr. and Mrs. G faced a number of charges alleging fraud and related activities. It was always a mystery to me that Mrs. G, who presented as a putative star Crown witness, found herself to be an accused person, but that is perhaps because, during the course of the investigation, she became Mrs. G and not compellable as a witness against her new husband. I thought it was capricious of the cops to charge her when the evidence was too thin to spread on a piece of melba toast. The authorities did proceed in a civilized manner, that is, the clients were not arrested when they arrived at the Calgary Airport, and when we appeared with them to speak to consensual judicial interim release, both Milt and I initially elected for a preliminary inquiry. A preliminary inquiry is often a necessary dress rehearsal for the Crown, but it has a number of advantages for the defence, particularly where, as here, we didn't want to take a chance with some draconian Provincial Judge being unexpectedly seized with the matter. As it happened, when we turned up for the preliminary inquiry, the Crown moved to withdraw the separate Informations and replace them with one

Information with joint charges against both accused, for ease of proceeding. Eureka, or, more appropriately, Caramba! The Judge who was presiding for the preliminary hearing happened to be the one Provincial Judge that we would have elected for trial. The lists were blind, and so one took one's chances. And here he was, and the question was, how could we seize this Judge of the matter so that he would be the one to hear the case?

The Crown withdrew the old charges and presented the new charges and Milt was quick to note that we then, as a matter of law, had to elect mode of trial on the new Information. So, we did so: "trial by magistrate." The poor old Crown prosecutor just about fainted, but Milt was quick to advise the Court that if this took the Crown unexpectedly, as they were simply ready for a preliminary inquiry, then there was no objection to a reasonable adjournment for a few days before the trial proceeded, but would the Court please make an Order excluding witnesses. The Judge obligingly made that Order, and—by God—he was now *seized* with the matter.

So, the trial came on for hearing before a Judge whom we were confident might scrutinize the Crown's evidence more critically than some of his fellows. Further, as earlier noted, trial by magistrate in a major fraud litigation is a risky business for the Crown, because frequently where the defence elects a preliminary inquiry, committal for trial is effortless, based on the test, "where there's smoke there's smoke," and the prosecution can then plug the holes before the matter comes on for trial in the High Court. So we had two advantages, and we pressed them. By this time, it should be noted that Mr. G was walking with a white cane and was referred to by Milt as "the blind man," and my client was eight months pregnant, and was referred to by me as "this pregnant lady." This irked the Crown considerably, as did the progress of the Crown's case, which started to go into the toilet early on.

In the result, when the Crown closed its case, my address to the Court was brief, to the effect that I had been in the Courtroom for about four weeks and had the distinct impression that I had wandered into the wrong Courtroom, because there wasn't any evidence that I heard implicating my client in anything. The Judge agreed, and the Crown was non-suited with respect to Mrs. G. Milt elected not to call evidence, and the Court reserved, heard argument, and in due course acquitted Mr. G of all charges.

Unfortunately, there was an obverse side to the alleged transactions which had taken place in the Judicial District of British Columbia, seizing their Courts with jurisdiction, and in due course the B.C. Crown proceeded against Mr. G and a prominent citizen of that jurisdiction on a number of charges arising out of the impugned transactions. Allan MacEachern, Q.C., now the Chief Justice of British Columbia, acted for the co-defendant. This time, a jury of twelve intervened, both accused were convicted after a lengthy and exhausting trial, and each sentenced to three years in the pen. This sentence was imposed notwithstanding that, by that time, Mr. G was not only groping with the white cane but was being pulled around in a wheel chair by a seeing eye dog, Mrs. G handing him carrots and clutching baby G in full view of the jury. Who could be dry-eyed? On the other hand, as Oscar Wilde observed, "*One would have to have a heart of stone not to burst out laughing at the death of Little Nell.*" Exit, Mr. G, as a guest of Her Majesty the Queen.

It was, indeed, the conduct of the British Columbia end of this taxing case that so exhausted Milt, setting him up and setting the stage for his succumbing to the blandishments of the Prime Minister and accepting his appointment to the Alberta Court of Appeal.

Chapter Fourteen

Weird Scenes

NO SURVEY of the life and times of the Great Barrister would be complete without at least references *en passant* to what can mischievously be described as bizarre episodes: 1. Alderman Harradence; 2. Chairman of the Calgary Convention Centre Authority and the debacle of *R v. Klein*; 3. The Riot in Cell Block 16; 4. The Great Cash Robbery and one-million-dollar-plus insurance recovery saga.

The first two matters deal with Milt's inexplicable viral attacks of catatonic civic service. Why a senior barrister of his eminence and ability, his prodigious energies, and intense attention already sorely tried by the rigours and demands of his law practice would still choose to saddle himself with these painfully dull and pedestrian chores is a great mystery. Moreover, to one accustomed to moving comfortably in the most exclusive circles of the Cowtown *culturati*, the daily shock of obligatory social intercourse with dullards and, worse, civic boosters much his inferiors in station and intellect must have been an egregious experience. Nevertheless, he volunteered to serve in these ignominious posts with good heart and performed his stultifying duties honourably if erratically.

1. Alderman Harradence

We have in this narrative earlier remarked upon the Harradence lust for elected office. His longings for political prominence and immortality were not to be assuaged in the provincial or federal arenas, arenas indeed in which the principal denizens were hyenas and jackals. The good-hearted, ever-idealistic Milt was defeated in that milieu or, rather, sordid stew, by persons who were less principled then he: the "winners"—that is, the prevailing gang of thugs—subscribing to the dictum of Macchiavelli, who promulgated in *The Prince* that persons in positions of power who "cling to moral principles such as those prohibiting dishonesty, breaches of faith, and the killing of innocents invariably end up defeated by adversaries who lack such scruples."

One may reasonably conclude that Milt's early entry into the utter banality of city politics was seen by him to be a cruelly necessary stepping-stone to the provincial or federal venues. The proximate explanation for his seeking the office was the prodding of a senior lawyer, whom Milt greatly admired, for Milt to carry the banner of some entity called The United Citizens Association. Many a terminally boring MLA or MP got his or her political leg-up by dogged service in the civic trenches. Thrust continually in the public eye, like an unwanted stye or infection, by the intrusive media, when they are not thrusting themselves in their endless round of self-abasement, their names become—as with tinpot dictators and advertised commodities—household words. Voter ID—that is, name recognition—is the all important factor in democratic poll balloting, as Ralph Nader no doubt reminds Al Gore, c. 2000. The writer's theory is that any notorious serial killer, side by side on the ballot with any mere selfless public servant, has a better chance of securing public office by popular vote than the decent fellow, which simply proves the insightful theories of H. L. Mencken and e.e. cummings (see *infra*).

Alderman Harradence was elected to public office in the 1957 Calgary Civic Election. Touting name cards have been found among his personal papers, together with campaign photographs, the hawk-like phizzog set solemnly in frowning visage mode. The campaign itself does not lend itself to comment, civic election tussles being beyond or beneath satire. Conjure up any civic politician and one is put in mind *instanter* of the Monty Python candidates for the Silly Party, or the contenders for the post of Minister of Silly

Walks. (The internationally renowned forensic pathologist, Dr. John Butt, could do a hilarious imitation of one particularly aghast Alderman fulminating about dead bodies in his bailiwick.)

One gathers that Milt's incumbency was a dismal two-year term of trial for the young crusader, who quickly found his reformist zeal hijacked by snivelling and whining citizens demanding the installation of this cross-walk or that traffic light, more frequent garbage collection, zoning squabbles to be defused, property tax pules to be addressed, and grave-faced attention to their opposition to a halfway house in their neighbourhood for unwed mothers or paroled child molesters or homeless vagabonds or other botched. The factioneering of fellow Aldermen and low-grade lobbying by seedy businessmen, the mindless boosterism, the dreary and endless Council meetings, the soporific committees and sub-committees, the hideous round of social appearances and ribbon cuttings, all took their toll of his higher sensibility.

There was a marked difference of political philosophy between the UCA and the labour aldermen. AMH got into several public confrontations with a bald opponent on Council he called "Curly." Following one such occasion, in the bathroom, the media had to intervene to prevent a fist fight.

No other memorable event of this epoch presents itself to Milt. Indeed, on reflection and looking back on his aldermanic term, Harradence has very little independent memory of that period of time.

2. The Calgary Convention Centre Authority

Civic boosters are a humourless lot. So the hilarity of Woody Allen's Idiots Convention in *Love and Death* with its "Welcome Idiots!" sign hung up on the Vladivostok Convention Centre would be lost on them. Scratch a conventioneer and you will find an idiot, the one scratch card game where you win every time.

Calgary, long suffering under its self-imposed typecasting yoke of the annual Exhibition and Stoopede, in truth longed to be a centre whose core attractions did not depend upon an inexhaustible supply of hay and horse manure. The more yokels in a gaining economic centre become prosperous, the more they approach middle class respectability, and the more they yearn therefore for the trappings of the seemingly sophisticated and cultured denizens of more established burgs. The Calgary *uber-burghers* longed to break the grip of the pervasive cowboy culture that continued to mesmerize the local yokelry, and to drag Calgary—kicking and screaming, as they say—into the 20th Century. To this, there was much opposition. In one of my columns of my short-lived tenure as a columnist for the *Calgary Herald*, in July 1982, I bemoaned the tyranny of the simian majority and blamed the Calgary Stampede as the major culprit in the unbalanced demographics that allowed the village idiots of the city to outnumber its landed gentry. I stated, *inter alia*:

> The Stoopede has the scientific faculty of taking the yahoo saturation point to the Nth power, thus, as the population of Calgary approaches infinity, the percentile of cretins, goons, wildly staring lunatics, small town baton twirlers, brutes of various descriptions, and low-grade morons approaches infinity plus one.

I sought redress of this "*plethora of mindless boosting and Babbitry*" (what I got, needless to say, was a barrage of hysterical denunciations from concerned civic boosters, plus indictments from mental health workers castigating my colloquial usage of "cretin" and "moron," however accurate).

But the pretenders to *culture*, as in The Arts, in preference to the roar of the tortured animals and the smell of the crowd, were gaining in strength and in political clout. *How ya gonna keep 'em / down on da farm / afta dey seen Pareee!* Indeed. Thus, as the city grew in population, area, infrastructure, affluence, and commercial influence, its superb natural setting and affordable "lifestyle" and honest administration and reasonable taxation and cheap gas and electricity attracted a species of migrant superior to the motley rabble of remittance men, sod-busters, dirt farmers, sheep herders, cattle baronets, fugitives from justice or oppressive regimes, bogus carpet baggers, flim-flam men, snake oil salesmen, bootleggers, burned-out trappers, and down-at-heel opportunists who had originally set down roots in the old town. New blood and new money and old oil were the catalysts for an unprecedented growth explosion, and the demands for cultural initiatives, innovations, developments and community "improvements" that went with it: witness the Philistines' Philharmonic, the Public Library, the University, the Glenbow Museum, the theatre ("*one does so enjoy Calgary during the Season*"), cocktail lounges, suburbs, golf and recreation clubs, community organizations, shopping centres, new hotels, restaurants, radio stations, supermarkets, bingo halls, VLT machines, random violence, and culpable homicides. Calgary, grown more opulent, flexing its new-found prosperity and its brashness and boldness, its Spruce Meadows and Saddledome, its future venue for the 1988 Winter Olympics already a glint in its citizens' eyes—Calgary, or at least a few of its prominent and richer denizens—wanted *recognition*. That is, a place in the late 20th Century sun, not national but international cachet and acclaim. This would take more than pancake breakfasts, more for that matter than the Hays Breakfast, downtown square dancing and the Science of the Chuckwagon. The cowtown *cognoscenti* grew restless, expansive, and expansionist: the *thymos* at work.

Therefore, Calgary had to have a Convention Centre. Other, bigger cities had convention centres. Smaller cities had convention centres. Edmonton had a convention centre. Without a convention centre, how could there be any attraction for, well, conventions, for example the Rotary Convention, political leadership conventions, the Shriners' Convention, music festivals, a gathering of the Clan, of drilling mud salesmen, of widget manufacturers: jolly rotters with moolah. A convention centre would be a Good Thing for the City, its entrepreneurs, business folk, promoters, hucksters, shopkeepers, persons in trade, hoteliers, what have you. For with conventions come conventioneers, on spending sprees because "on expenses." Their purpose: to appoint or elect their wizers and poobahs for the coming term; to tune up or tune into the latest and the best, the current and choice, the politically correct, in widgets or travel combos or breast implants or business dodges of their trades and callings, to gawk at the locals and the new environs, to Have A Good Time—translation: get drunk and be somebody, however briefly, and maybe get a stray wink wink nudge nudge, Jeez.

The Calgary Convention Centre Authority was duly organized

and incorporated. Its mandate: to advertise and promote Calgary as a convention centre *par excellence;* to provide the meeting and recreational facilities requisite to such hysterical foregatherings; to assist in the organization of the guest convention; in sum, to gain glory and loot for the municipality and those who dwelt within her boundaries. "Welcome, Idiots!" indeed.

Quaere, quoth the alert reader: what has all this utter bilge got to do with the great Milt Harradence? Why would one of Canada's most successful and busy premier criminal lawyers get involved in an executive—nay, chief executive—capacity with a flack palace by the booboisie, of the booboisie, for the booboisie? Of a dull day, check out the vanity wall of the Calgary Convention Centre and you will encounter a photogravure gallery of some of the more uplifting personalities of the Alberta *Boosterati.* To one's astonishment, there is the phizzog, *nobilmente,* one ear and one nose, of A.M. Harradence, Q.C. (as he then was), Chairman of the Calgary Convention Centre Authority in 1975.

The casual viewer's amazement can be captured by the illustrators of contemporary comic book characters of the seventies and eighties, eyes popping, mouths agape, blown up by Andy Warhol into their fifteen micro-seconds of fame: "Wha . . .!" "how th' . . .?" "Holy . . .!"

This is how it happened:

In 1975, the Mayor of Calgary was a brilliant and colourful maverick, cadaverous in appearance and commanding by nature and inclination, named Rodney B. Sykes, who, as Frank R. Dabbs reports, "*dominated civic politics from 1969 to 1977.*" His Worship Mayor Sykes deserves his own book: he was formidably articulate, highly intelligent, intellectually superior to most life forms, intolerant of fools and toadies, and he said exactly what he thought, often to his detriment, but he didn't give a damn. He was seldom if ever bested in debate, and most frequently those dullards who were foolish enough to challenge him verbally were summarily dispatched and removed in body bags. (The only public debate featuring Sykes that ended in a loss by audience acclaim was his famous debate at the University of Calgary against the equally brilliant orator Bernice Evans, who teamed up with another student to defeat Sykes and his partner, the pious prelate and Alderman Father Green. Sykes won the rematch.) Sykes had his enemies, many of them, but he seemed always to revel in controversy and delighted in scorning and putting down his detractors, most of whom were not worthy of his steel. He could be as charming as a career diplomat one moment and as vicious as a viper the next. He was an absolute master in defusing one political crisis by deliberately inducing another. Heads and reputations rolled. His greatest assets were his keen inquiring intelligence and his well-developed sense of humour.

Rod Sykes on balance approved of me, which speaks volumes for his discernment and acumen. He was also a devoted fan of Milt Harradence (for a microcosm of our little universe, see Appendix from the March 10th, 1983, edition of the *Calgary Sun*). I remember one cordial street exchange with him with particular vividness: I ran into Mayor Rodney as I was exiting the Calgary Police Building, which was across from the old City Hall. I was then a Crown Prosecutor but also had a controversial opinion column in the then (now defunct) *Albertan* newspaper, ill-received by most good Ur-Burgers and paunchy wholesalers of the Rotary and Paunchmens' Club species.

Said Sykes: "I've been reading some of your columns, and sometimes I wonder how you keep your job."
Said Evans: "I've been reading some of your public statements, and sometimes I wonder how you keep your job."

We parted like two amiable ambassadors.

In 1975 during the Reign of Sykes I, a furore erupted—probably media-inspired—over the awarding of the contracts for the construction of the Convention Centre facility. As with all such humdrum city scandals, this was the usual tempest in a pisspot. Rodney, seeking allies in strategic places as always—for that is the essence of politics—and determined to imbue the fledgling Authority with gravity and legitimacy, prevailed upon his much admired acquaintance, A.M. Harradence, Q.C., to assume the mantle of the Chair. Milton did so, grimly, as usual out of his strong misdirected sense of public duty. The allegations of impropriety were all the expected nonsense and the principal event in the whole debacle was the alleged bugging of a January 20th, 1975 in-camera meeting of the Authority by an informer or mole. In fact, A.M.H. was not even at that particular meeting. The media attacked with relentless boredom, at one point fulminating: "the Convention Authority refused to appear before the media when summonsed." Indeed. Alarums.

At that time, Alberta's beloved rubber-faced, loquacious Ralph Klein—in due course of events to become not only Mayor of Calgary for two terms but later the Premier of Alberta for three terms (and, at 2001, counting)—was plying his early life as a crusading television reporter with a specialty in City Hall issues.

Harradence was convinced the alleged bugging was an artless rumour, that is, until Ralph Klein broadcast the fact of the surreptitiously taped meeting in a controversial documentary on the Convention Centre aired on CFCN-TV. Egad! Prior to that revelation, Chairman Harradence, queried by importunate media as to why the bugging had not been reported to the press, responded dismissively: "The City Police have more to do than launch an investigation into rumours concocted by the media." Then he had to eat his words but at a suitable remove from the action.

Klein having revealed on prime time the fact of the Authority meeting being bugged, the cops had no choice but to investigate. In the result, the intrepid news reporter was charged for allegedly breaching the Protection of Privacy Act, it being illegal even to reveal the existence of an unlawfully intercepted private communication. The defence mounted by the eminent barrister C. D. O'Brien, Q.C. was Freedom of the Press, an amorphous and shapeless right at best, or something equally esoteric. To the immense relief of everyone concerned—particularly Chairman Harradence—reporter Klein was discharged after the preliminary inquiry by his Honour Judge Thurgood, there being "no evidence" upon which a jury, properly instructed in the law, unless insane, might return a verdict of guilt.

In October, 1980, Ralph Klein was elected Mayor of Calgary and took office on October 27. The day after Mayor Klein was sworn in as Calgary's 32nd Chief Magistrate, Sheila Pratt reported in the October 28th, 1980, edition of the *Calgary Herald* Mayor Klein's coining the term "ultimate irony" to describe his Oath of Office administered by none other than (by then) the Honourable Mr. Justice A.M. Harradence.

"'Harradence and I are friends and we laugh over it now,' says Klein over martinis and a club sandwich in a downtown hotel. 'But that's when I really grew up as a reporter. There was a lot of pressure during that story.' The Convention Centre documentary was one of Klein's bolder journalist ventures.... "

In his admirable biography of Premier Ralph Klein (Greystone Books, Vancouver, 1995), veteran reporter and writer Frank Dabbs commented perceptively on the close relationship that had developed between the veteran criminal lawyer and the seasoned news reporter.

> Ralph Klein was sworn in as Calgary's 32nd Chief Magistrate on October 27th, 1980. The ceremony took place in the windowless flag-lined council chamber with Mr. Justice Asa Milton Harradence presiding. Colleen, wearing a stylish, almost brash broad-brimmed hat, held Theresa's hand as Klein took the oath and began an eight year apprenticeship in power.
>
> Milt Harradence was a reassuring presence for the thirty-seven year old novice mayor. As a criminal defence lawyer, Harradence had a simple rule of thumb for his relationship with journalists: 'lose a case, but never lose a reporter.' Consequently, the Judge had the trust of most, including Klein. He was a quiet mentor to many, including Klein. Although Harradence's status as on the bench now precluded Mayor Klein from seeking much in the way of direct counsel, no one missed the weight the Judge added to the occasion, weight that Ralph badly needed.
>
> It was Harradence's capacity to communicate, to convince an audience, that indelibly impressed the new Mayor. Klein's speaking style was, and is, usually the hyperbolic prose of his United Appeal press releases and letters, ranging from the florid to the colloquial but always stilted and cumbersome. Although Klein never matched Harradence's gift for spoken language, consciously or unconsciously he cloned his public style: wry humor, terse dismissal of opponents and an intense eye-to-eye contact that charmed the wary and reassured his true believers. Klein mastered

> the Judge's clarity, dramatic timing and conviction. To the extent that Harradence copied John Diefenbaker, when Klein speaks, the old ghost stirs.

(The diminutive Dabbs once took a friendly poke at Harradence in his newspaper days, to which Milt quipped, "a little Dabbs'll do ya.")

Incidentally, a judicial inquiry into the Convention Centre brouhaha was eventually instituted under the Hon. Mr. Justice Steer of the Court of Queen's Bench, which in due course, after evidence and submissions, exonerated everybody except the hapless mole.

3. The Riot in Cell Block 16 The Harradence Commission

The 1973 Harradence Commission of Inquiry into unrest at the Provincial Correctional Institution at Spy Hill was one of the outstanding theatrical productions of Milt's career. It also featured a cast of principals and hangers-on right out of Damon Runyon. There wasn't exactly a riot in cell block 16. Spy Hill Gaol had always been a low-security sort of place that hosted mainly petty thieves, drunk drivers, bottom-rank dope dealers, barroom hooligans, and arrestees on Warrants of Committal for failure to pay assorted and accumulated traffic tickets. The more desperate criminals were appropriately clapped in irons at the maximum security penitentiary in Edmonton, or the pen at Bowden, Alberta, the latter charm school strategically located across Highway #2 from the RCMP Police Dog Academy.

The Spy Hill guests were housed in not unpleasant facilities, given three squares and one phone call a day, and empowered to play basketball or watch TeeVee and other entertainments. It was not the worst time a minor felon could draw. Why some of the snivelers and whiners in the place were complaining in the first instance is not fully understood, but complaints there were, over a period of time, culminating in vague threats by inmates of reprisals and strikes and the like. The allegations were essentially of guards chastising inmates with prejudice. Naturally, the scumbags and bottom feeders of the media got hold of all this and blew it into gigantic proportions, with the result that the average citizen hovered quaking in or under his or her bed by night, waiting for hordes of crazed escaped prisoners to lay waste to all that they held dear. So, predictably, the Provincial Government set up a Commission of Inquiry. The Honourable Commissioner? A.M. Harradence, Q.C.

This was Milt's great moment as a senior criminal lawyer (and loyal old Tory), and he rose to the occasion in all his trench-coated magnificence.

The issues to be aired before the Hon. Commissioner were somewhat narrow, that is, the current relationship between the prisoners and their guards, instances of alleged harassment (physical and verbal), and recommendations for reforms, if any. The estimates of counsel were for six to eight days of evidence at most. In fact, the Inquiry expanded to eight months, and became the Royal Commission into the Care and Feeding of Provincial Gaols and their denizens.

The venue was sited at the Southern Alberta Institute of Technology in Calgary. J. Patrick Peacock, Q.C., was appointed Counsel to the Commission. Some usual suspects of the Criminal Bar found themselves acting for various parties: Web MacDonald, Jr., and Lorne Scott acted for the inmates; William Stilwell represented the Correctional Officers. Art "Butch" Roberts, former Chief Inspector in the Calgary Police Service, was appointed Investigator to the Commission, and he and Pat Peacock visited the jail and interviewed numbers of inmates and correctional officers, several of whom were subpoenaed to the Commission as witnesses.

In particular, the Commissioner was ever alert to the right of the public to be fully informed of the proceedings and thus a great deal of opportunity, not to mention license, was extended to the members of the Fourth Estate who covered the event from every angle. They did not experience too much trouble gaining access to an audience with the Commissioner and his Counsel, which generated sensational headlines. Indeed, the press were in attendance at the sittings of the Inquiry in droves and there were front and centre headlines for about half a year.

Pat Peacock's recollections are representative of the inadvertent hilarity that was generated by the deliberations of this solemn forum. He recalls in particular the matter of the Warden of Spy Hill being called to testify at the hearings. The Warden of the day was absolutely one of nature's gentlemen in every way, and greatly respected by the public and counsel. Commission Counsel Pat Peacock met with Commissioner Harradence in his anteroom prior to the commencement of the day's hearing. Said Harradence: "We have big problems." He showed Peacock the newspaper. Peacock observed, "Well, there is nothing about us." Exclaimed Milt, "*That's our problem.* We are on page three!"

The hearings convened. Halfway through the Warden's evidence he mentioned that he was speaking to the Deputy Solicitor General. He was immediately interrupted by the Commissioner: "You had a discussion with the Deputy Minister?" "Yes, sir." "Did your discussion involve these proceedings?" "Yes, sir." Harradence reeled back. "I'm adjourning this inquiry. Counsel are to investigate whether there has been tampering with this witness."

The press went ballistic, with appropriate lurid headlines, reports, and commentaries.

Peacock and Roberts repaired immediately to Edmonton. They sought an audience with the Solicitor General but received no access. Instead, they met with the Deputy Minister, who was asked by Investigator Roberts, "Did you have a conversation with the Warden about the inquiry?" Responded the Deputy, "Yes. I asked the Warden if he had any indication of when I might be called as a witness. He said 'no'." That was all there was to the conversation. They went back to the Inquiry and it reconvened.

Intoned the Commissioner: "I have satisfied myself beyond all doubt there was no such impropriety as with tampering or influence." The Inquiry therefore proceeded, but the public interest was duly satisfied.

The questionable intelligence that there might be some kind of riot or insurrection by the inmates unless there was response, intervention, and payoff to their demands prompted the Commissioner to attend at the jail to meet with the prisoners in their enclave, the headquarters at the material time being the prison gymnasium. With breathless and panting media at his heels, speculation rampant, and expectations of homicide or mayhem or both high, Commissioner Harradence strode into the den of disaffected prisoners, grim-faced, resplendent as always in trench coat with military epaulettes, and had a palaver. This was all done with great dramatic moment, appropriate theatrical pauses, and the best of the Harradence panache.

After the brief meeting, where Milt "spoke to them man to man," he responded to the shrill shrieks of the battalion of reporters shoving mikes in his face: "Didn't you think you were in danger?" "What if they had jumped you?" And so on.

Milt struck a pose and flashed a narrow-eyed grimace so artful that Cecil B. deMille would have been proud of him. He growled: "It was a calculated risk." He turned on his heel, and marched away. Ohhhh and ahhhh!

Milt with his usual timing and instinct had managed to breathe life into what was surely one of the most tedious clichés of moviedom. But the audience was wowed. On reflection, it may have been calculated, but there was little or no risk: as noted, Spy Hill lockup then was a hoosegow for petty and low-level criminals, not particularly desperados. Anyway, it was as always great theatre, and only Milt could have pulled it off.

Oh, yes. The findings and recommendations of the Commission? Christ, who knows!

4. THE GREAT CASH ROBBERY CAPER

Just as I was getting started in this dismal trade, Milt Harradence was retained by a firm of insurance adjusters to assist in the recovery of an awesome sum of stolen cash, which, after a harrowing and convoluted series of events, resulted in almost full recovery. The following is Milt's own account of these extraordinary events in 1965:

> On February 11th, 1965 a Vancouver company was robbed by four men of $1,200,000.00. The bills, en route to Ottawa where they were to be destroyed, had each been punched with 3 half inch

holes. When these holes were punched the bills were not flush with each other. As a result, by the skillful use of a razor and scotch tape, bills were created from the mutilated money. These were then successfully passed to Eastern Canada, but were detected in Edmonton by a shopkeeper on April 17, 1965 when two men attempted to pass them in his shop. The police were called and the two arrested. $12,548 of the mutilated money was found in their hotel room. On April 19, 1965 a Vancouver city police officer committed suicide after shooting his wife and six children. He and other members of the Vancouver City Police had been under investigation in connection with the robbery. The two men arrested in Edmonton, one of whom was a former Vancouver police officer, were released on bail and later moved to Calgary.

The Federal Government held the Vancouver company liable for the entire loss of $1,200,000. A well-known Toronto firm of Adjusters was engaged to deal with the matter. When the two accused men moved to Calgary the adjusting firm's top man arrived in the city. He retained me to assist in the recovery of the balance of the mutilated money.

The adjuster was a man of striking appearance, extremely able and with a wealth of experience in the industry. I promptly dubbed him "The Man from Black Hawk". The head of the Vancouver City Police Homicide and Robbery Section also arrived in the city. He was a no-nonsense Police Officer with a formidable physical presence dedicated to the arrest of the robbers and the recovery of the money. He was ultimately successful in both endeavours.

I was present at several interesting conferences with both visitors. The Calgary City Police and the Royal Canadian Mounted Police were alerted and kept informed.

Around the middle of June 1965 matters reached the stage where it became necessary for me to fly to London, England. As I was engaged in a trial at that time, I obtained consent of counsel for the Crown to attend on the presiding Justice that night and to advise him that the Crown did not oppose an adjournment of the trial. I presented the facts to a startled Justice who promptly granted the adjournment.

To provide maximum flexibility I had the operational funds in Calgary converted into specie and placed in the only vault in the city not governed by a time-lock. The company agreed to provide personnel to facilitate the removal of the bills at any hour of the day or night. After obtaining the adjournment I contacted the company and had the funds reconverted into a company draft payable to me. That required recounting of the money and, as it was a large amount, it took some considerable time.

I left the next morning for London, England via Toronto. I was met at the airport by the "Man from Black Hawk" and taken to his Principals and advised them that the amount of the operational funds must be increased by 20 percent and deposited in my name in a Canadian Bank in London without restriction. Not surprisingly I was immediately asked what had become of the operational funds in Calgary. I informed them that those funds had been converted into a draft payment to me. I produced the draft and inquired if anyone had a pen. The alacrity with which several of those instruments were thrust at me was truly amazing. The Principals advised me of the name and address of the Canadian Bank where the operational funds would be deposited and that the funds would be in place on my arrival in London.

My first stop in London was at the bank for I was concerned that if there was collusion at any stage in the deposit transaction someone impersonating me could withdraw the funds, as my arrival in London was after the bank opened. I identified myself satisfactorily and advised the banking officer that the funds would be withdrawn either by draft or in specie. I asked to have sufficient funds on hand in either English, Canadian, or American bank notes. He confirmed that he would have those bank notes on hand.

I then set up operational headquarters in the Savoy. Later, at the Savoy, I received a telephone call that necessitated the dispersal of a small portion of the Operational Funds. The funds were to be picked up at the Savoy the next morning. That morning I entered the dining-room for breakfast. I had just been seated when I was approached by a Bellboy who asked "Do you have a package for me, Sir?" I handed him the package containing the money and told him that I would require a receipt for the package. He was back shortly with the receipt signed in the name of the master-mind of England's "Great Train Robbery."

Later I was contacted by the English Settlor (Adjuster) who gave me the name and address of the firm of Solicitors who he had retained, assuring me that they were one of the top firms in the city. He also said that a Senior Executive of the "Man from Black Hawk" principals had requested an interview with me at their Head office. The office was most impressive, Oriental rugs with ankle-deep pile, classic art work in the reception area and in the hallways. There was an all-pervading silence with uniformed orderlies gliding noiselessly about. One of whom took me to the executive's office which was equally impressive. Our conversation was formal and brief and our respective positions clearly outlined and understood. He concluded by saying, "Mr. Harradence, while there is a great deal of money involved, the most important thing is our reputation." I replied, "There is only one thing more important, Sir." "What is that?" he inquired. I replied, "My reputation."

I then attended a meeting at the firm of Solicitors retained by the London adjuster. I was ushered into their conference room where several members of the firm were seated around a large conference table. The head of the firm was easily identified by his demeanor and presence. He asked me to outline the situation. During that outline his eyes never left mine. Part of the way through the outline one timid soul queried, "Oh, do we want to be involved in something like this?" He replied, without even a glance at the questioner, "Yes, I think we do."

Events moved along rapidly but at a critical juncture I was informed by the head of the firm that he had been alerted that certain steps were being taken which we both agreed would place the entire operation in jeopardy. I was also concerned that if these steps were taken my personal safety would definitely be at risk. So far there had been eight deaths related to the robbery and I had no burning desire to be the ninth. We agreed that before these steps were taken we would obtain the advice of Senior Counsel. He stated that to do so on short notice was quite impossible but he would try. I was left with the impression that he felt that he would have had a better chance of contacting the Pope by dialing him direct.

However he was back shortly with an expression of amazement and wonderment on his face. He had accomplished the impossible. Eminent Senior Counsel was on the phone and wished to speak to me. Eminent Counsel put several pointed and relevant questions to me which I firmly and positively answered. I shall never forget his final comment. "What you are doing is most unusual but I see nothing wrong with it." He conveyed that conclusion to the head of the firm. The steps were not taken and the original operational plan carried on smoothly.

I had a gut-feeling that the mutilated money was still in the Vancouver area and I was sure that I would soon have its exact location. Once that location was revealed it was imperative that it be recovered at the earliest possible moment.

With the advantage of the time differential in mind, I phoned the "Man from Black Hawk" in Toronto and told him that I was confident that I would soon have the location of the mutilated money and it was my feeling that it was still in the Vancouver area. I advised him to leave on the earliest Air Canada flight to Vancouver via Calgary. I gambled that by the time he reached Calgary I would have the exact location which I would communicate to my law partner in Calgary, who would then meet him at the airport during his stop-over. He agreed and told me that he would be staying at the Hotel Vancouver. A code was agreed upon by which we could positively identify each other on subsequent telephone conversations.

My gut-feeling that the mutilated money was still in the Vancouver area was correct. The money was at a Victoria, B.C. address. I phoned my partner, gave him the address and asked him to meet the "Man from Black Hawk" at the airport and advise him of the address. There was no need to impress him that that address was to be revealed to no one else. He left immediately for the airport, located the "Man from Black Hawk" and later confirmed that the message had been delivered.

It was now just a matter of waiting. The head of the London firm of solicitors asked me if I had plans for the week-end. I replied "No." He then invited me to spend the weekend with him at his country home. I was delighted to accept. We were driven to his magnificent residence on the outskirts of London in his chauffeured Jaguar limousine. I was escorted to a sumptuous great suite and then was taken to Dinner at his club with him and his charming wife. Upon our return to their home he placed a telephone in the suite with a request that no matter what time the call from Canada came though he was to be advised.

I had left word at the Savoy that any calls to me were to be forwarded to his residence number. Regretfully no call came through that evening and I felt that I should return to London to locate the "Man from Black Hawk". I was chauffeured back to the Savoy.

I was able to contact him at the Hotel Vancouver and confirmed by our code that it was he. He told me he had, on his arrival in Vancouver, gone to Vancouver Police Headquarters and accompanied senior officers to the Victoria address where $1,185,165 of the mutilated money had been found and was now at Vancouver Police Headquarters. He had not phoned earlier as the Ferry schedule between Vancouver and Victoria was in a complete shambles.

He had just gotten into Vancouver and was trying to catch up on his sleep. I promptly phoned the H.F. telling him we had been completely successful and it was in order to release the operational funds in his trust account and that I would be in his office Monday to finalize matters. He was delighted and said "Even though it was Saturday he would ring up a certain Solicitor in London. It would make his week-end for him."

On checking out of the Savoy Hotel I produced my American Express card for payment. The clerk, acting as though the card was contaminated, pushed the card back to me with his pen, saying in a haughty manner, "The Savoy, Sir, does not accept plastic." I replied, "Then you'll have to take my cheque." The clerk then even more haughtily asked, "Do you have a reference, Sir?" I referred him to the bank official with whom the operational funds had been deposited. He went into his office obviously to confirm the reference and shortly returned with an embarrassed and sheepish expression saying, "I wish my banker would say that about me. We'll gladly take your cheque, Sir."

On my return to Toronto the "Man from Black Hawk" and I were treated like conquering heroes by his principals. I was invited to speak at the weekly luncheon of the Toronto Adjusters. I was then paraded through each section of the principals' head office by the manager after he had taken me to lunch at his club. He introduced me to each section as "the famous Mr. Harradence." All went well until he introduced me to the C.E.O. of the principals' English head office, who was visiting. Unfortunately he and I took an instant dislike to each other which neither of us made any attempt to conceal by our manner or verbal exchange.

However the prompt payment of my account was a clear recognition of, and gratitude for, the service performed and the result obtained.

CHAPTER FIFTEEN
The Court of Least Appeal

What could be expected of men who never consulted experience in any of their reasonings?

– *David Hume*

JANUARY 1979. The telephone by the bed, as usual, rang at an ungodly early hour. I knew who it was, so I rolled over, picked the handset out of the cradle, and replaced it. Then I went back to sleep.

It rang again, insistently.

"C.D., I've been struck off the Roll."

I said, fighting somnolence, "What?"

"I've been struck off the Roll."

I said, "Milt, they can't strike you off the Roll without a hearing. We've got them. We can appeal."

"No", said Milt, "I think this is final. C.D., I have been appointed to the Court of Appeal."

And thus did Milt mount the woolsack and ascend to the outer ether.

What—after almost forty years in practice—is my overview of the Bench? (1) I don't like intellectually dishonest people, and a surprising number of Judges deserve that criticism;[1] (2) I don't like self-congratulatory asses who are snotty and "judgy" and rude to young lawyers and lord it over 'inferior' tribunals; (3) I don't

---

1. What's the test? H.L. Mencken defines intellectual honesty: "A taste for cold facts and the talent for grappling with them." Franz Kafka, who brought us *The Trial*, had "inflexible intellectual honesty," which, together with his "psychopathic sensitivity finally broke down his health." (Schocken Classics note to Franz Kafka: Diaries).

like cocktail party networkers from the intellectual ranks of drone solicitors or failed politicians who pull off appointment plums in payment for years of bag man or suckhole activity over experienced candidates better qualified. Other than that, to borrow from Paul Fussel, I have no strong feelings one way or another. There are, as always, honourable exceptions.

Whenever a Court of Appeal panel shuffles sonorously into the courtroom, I imagine I can hear the strains of the opening bars of Elgar's *Symphony No. 1*, scored for double basses and brass flourishes *fortissimo* and *nobilmente*, so great is their Lordships' collective dignity. One can well understand why they feel, as did Elgar, that at the conclusion of their deliberations, "the rest is silence."

One must update these observations to embrace current developments, that is, the epidemic elevations of female persons to the higher courts.[2] I have observed elsewhere that the strident and shrill Feminist lobby took over this profession in the down and dirty manner of a longshoreman cleaning out a waterfront saloon. On an elementary level, this victory—and it was a clear victory—has been wholly admirable: the conspiratorial ambitions of many a male fascist bigot have gone down in flames as women appropriated their previously unassailable prerogatives and ascended *en masse* to their places on the courts. Some of them are truly exceptional jurists; regrettably, with respect to some others of that lot, their life experience, "street smarts," and legal acumen and experience vary within the parameters of woeful to marginal. (I am obliged by S.15 to add that these remarks apply equally to the males of the species *jurisprude.*)

For my humble part, I have always had to suppress hysterical laughter as the Tribunal severely lines up, whether male or female, all half-glasses and baggy pantaloons and those ridiculous imitation court coats bought at a robemaker's penny sale. The only personage who ever dressed properly for the Court of Appeal was me. I had my court coat made by Ede and Ravenscroft, which was intended deliberately to teach the Lords of Appeal a lesson in

2. The Alberta Court of Appeal is known to the Criminal Bar as the "All Girls' Band."

dress and deportment. But no, they still purchase those seedy barristers' vests with an extra row of buttons stitched along imaginary lapels, which they think makes them look judicial. They are in the result unwittingly humorous.

It is rare for any denizen of such courts, male or female, to have advertent humour at all, save for the heavy-handed sort of jest made invariably at the expense of some poor young counsel who has neither the wit nor the venom to answer back and put them in their places.

Collegiality is a current buzz word popular with social-engineering judiciary whose collective consciousnesses have been raised. Collegiality is premised in the fiction that ten or twelve lawyers, ranging in intellectual quotient from brilliant to not usually gifted, with completely diversified backgrounds and levels of attainment varying from legal factory senior scrivener to Kiwanis apple clown, who—with rare exceptions—cannot tolerate each other's company, would not in any circumstances practice law in partnership with each other, nor invite each other to their homes, can achieve consensus upon issues affecting the lives, the liberty, and the bank accounts of the populace.

I feel particularly sorry for those judges with talent having to muck in with those without. The prospect of having to take one's meals in such dreary company is sobering. It is truly said, "a convoy is as fast as its slowest ship."

A.M. Harradence had rare talent. It is to my mind a great pity that he forsook the Bar—which was the showcase for his talent—for the obscurity of the Alberta Court of Appeal. Or, as I have always styled it, the Court of Least Appeal, because it is the least appealing of all of the courts.

The phone call from the Justice Minister's flunkey was the catalyst, but the seeds had been sown. Milt readily abandoned the independence of the criminal practitioner, the robber baron's last redoubt. And for what?

March 1979. In a courtroom crammed to the gunwales with family, friends, acquaintances, admirers, politicians, Important People, lawyers, and others, before a Bench of overpoweringly sonorous omnipotence including the Chief Justice of Alberta and all of the Court of Appeal, the Chief Justice of British Columbia, the retired Chief Justice of Alberta, the retired Chief Justice of the Trial Division of the Supreme Court, High Judges, Middle Judges, Low Judges, *ad nauseum*, Asa Milton Harradence was sworn in as One of Her Majesty's Justices of the Court of Appeal of Alberta. The usual flattering addresses were proffered by the usual suspects in the usual obsequious and effusive homilies, including the writer who was given special leave by Chief Justice McGillivray to pay tribute to Milt on behalf of the Criminal Bar. I well recall him coming into the court with the entourage on that day, fierce and proud, with that "my God, war at any moment" expression on his face that he had cultivated for decades, and I will never forget Jack Major (as he then was) leaning over to me and saying, "Evans, would you ever have known that Milt had not been sitting on this court for twenty years?"

A reception followed at the upscale penthouse of the venerable Palliser Hotel. John MacPherson, Q.C., Milt's partner of some twenty years, was less than enamored with Milt's decision to go to the Bench, and greeted Milt in the reception line as follows: "Now your cheque's the same colour as the janitor's."

In my respectful view—and I am confident the late John MacPherson would agree with me—Milt should never have become a judge. I have a couple of theories as to why he succumbed to the blandishments of the offerors who wielded the gift of the Sovereign in the appointment process, and why he ascended with such alacrity to the woolsack and donned irrevocably the judicial ermine. They are both viable.

My friend was always at his happiest on his feet in the courtroom—any courtroom, anywhere—battling it out with a witness or a thick judge and putting his elastic-sided half-Wellington boots to a snotty crown prosecutor. (On one occasion, as Milt was demolishing my star witness, I printed a rough sign and held it up to him from the Crown counsel table: "Your boots are on backwards." Milt stopped in mid-question, the stabbing finger retreated slightly as, to my delight, he looked down at his feet, impeccable in spitshine sabots. "You son of a bitch," he hissed. "What was that?" from astute Judge John Harvie, who missed nothing. I rose quickly: "An exchange of information between counsel, your Honour." The judge frowned. The trial continued.) It was inexplicable to me that my mentor should even think of an Appointment. Note the capital A. At a certain point in nearly every moiling lawyer's career, usually at the twenty-year-or-so mark, he or she begins to hanker for a slower pace and the concomitant prestige of a judgeship. That is, at a certain point in every marginally successful but middle-class mentality lawyer's career. Those of us who were born to be the princes of this profession accept our rank and the toil it requires to maintain that position. But the flotsam, and the mediocrities, that vast majority of practitioners, after fifteen to twenty years of boxing files and suffering insults to their intelligence from the Bench, yearn in their guts to join the insulters.

I do not understand this. Why should one wish to join a group of persons for whom, individually and collectively with some exceptions, one has contempt? Why would one go from being a Leader at the Bar to a mere hey-you to the Chief Justice's secretary, one more blob in a gaggle of blanks, all preoccupied with their pensions, their prostates (in the male case of course, of course) and their seniority?

If one has stubbornly refused to take part in the obscene self-abasement that accompanies the application for Judicial preferment, and one has achieved some modest eminence, it is not long before the local judicial appointments poobahs are importuning one with that *soto voce* between-you-and-I-and-the-Minister query, "Isn't it time you were thinking of an Appointment?" The Appointment is with a capital A (as I have noted) and the entire word is highlighted in bilious, easy-to-read yellow.

Today all the wrong people seek judgeships for all the wrong reasons. And they are appointed by the wrong people for other wrong reasons. Those are facts. Again, there are exceptions.

A.M. Harradence was and is an honourable exception. He did not seek an appointment. It sought him, but in circumstances—as I have explained in the earlier chapter on politics—that provoke analysis.

I must remark at this point that the elevation of a practicing barrister from the street to the Court of Appeal (even in Alberta) is a rare event, and today it is reserved to an exceptional few, like Harradence. Although it was the norm in early years, many appointments being blatantly political, today's egalitarian lip service requires most High Court Judges to go through the ranks as if in the Continental system. Only the best now go direct from practice to the Appellate level. A.M. Harradence was one of the very best.

Even that might not have been enough. First, I do not think that Milt wanted it: he was at the absolute height of his career, and he loved to do what he loved best, he loved combat. Second, he had made a very big splash as an Alberta separatist enthusiast: this absurd movement had enjoyed a resurgence in Alberta in the late 1970s. An avowed separatist had actually been elected to the Legislature of Alberta. A prairie legislature is a nothing place, particularly to the mandarinate of Ottawa which is the Centre of the Universe, but this particular event caused concern in the Prime Minister's office. Milt, moreover, due to his inflammatory public pronouncements falling just short of a call to join him in strafing Quebec City with live ammo, was perceived—and actually feared—to be the natural leader of the Revolt of the Western Masses, the first president of an independent and totally loopy right-wing Alberta, expanded upon in Chapter 10. Action this day.

As noted in Chapter 10 it is my theory that A.M. Harradence was approached by an emissary of the Feds with plenipotentiary powers, and the carrot of the Court of Least Appeal was dangled before his eyes.

One of Milt's failings was a respect for that Body—he was a very respectful person, in point of fact. But he still demurred. Fate intervened, in the body of a former client who had every reason to be grateful to the great barrister (and to his private investigator, Peter Tarrant) for his acquittal, who had the temerity at that exact time to tax Milt's account for services rendered. Amazingly, he did not tax the fee, which I gather was commensurate with the services rendered, but the out-of-pocket disbursements. Who'da ever thunk! and at that same time, Milt was just coming off an attack of the cultural bends from defending an eight-month jury trial, with co-counsel Allan MacEachern, Q.C., in Vancouver. He was exhausted. He had been dogged by the flu that had hung on for weeks. And here was this ingrate whining to a clerk in a clapboard courthouse in some backwater about Milt's bill; Milt is sitting there suffering this shower of shit, and the phone rings and it is Ottawa calling.

The mouthpiece tells Milt that the Powers want to appoint him, now, to the Alberta Court of Appeal. Milt is taken completely by surprise. He looks at the disaffected client, eyes full of rejection of his efforts, his professional work! He looks at the clerk gravely totting up his reasonable disbursements, probably with a blunt pencil on brown wrapping paper. The clerk probably makes in one year about one tenth of Milt's fee for this defence. "Thank you, that flunkey," says barrister Harradence, "the answer is Yes."

And Milt is now a *Judge.* The clerk falls to his knees. The ex-client runs out the door. Milt quits the clapboard courthouse and the practice of law.

The Prime Minister is happy with all of this: a palpable threat to Canadian unity (translation: Liberal party dominance) has been finessed, without bloodshed. Months later, this word comes to Milt and he is one mad mother. More on this, *poste.*

Before we move on to the second theory of Milt's elevation, it is important to remind the reader that Harradence throughout his career, although invariably treating all judges and courts with the greatest courtesy and respect, harboured strong private views critical of these institutions. I well remember appearing with him before the Court of Appeal when it was constituted by unsmiling, patrician eminences who had high opinions of themselves and low opinions of every lawyer who appeared before them, and even lower opinions of litigants. It was a tragic case of a young lad with absolutely no anti-social background calmly walking into his school with a rifle and dispatching the kindly janitor. The lad was clearly insane—as we used to call the defence in those days—but was convicted at trial after the Hon. H.W. Riley, a great Judge, wrestled publicly with the demons of demonstrable mental aberration brought about by the voluntary ingestion of some toxic hallucinogen. He found the accused guilty, and there was an appeal, but in the interim the prisoner had been again remanded to psychiatric observation as unfit to instruct counsel due to the terrible ravages of his LSD flashbacks. Milt had adjourned the appeal with my consent as Crown counsel. I distinctly remember that Milt confided to me in the barristers' robing room that his client had described the three judges on the Court as "three little green men from another planet." "All in all," Milt summed up, "not a bad description."

Milt's firm, as earlier observed in this history, had bifurcated on his elevation. Johnny Mac had spun off with Terry Semenuk and Alain Hepner, three very able criminal barristers, to form MacPherson and Company. As noted, I fell heir to a number of former or almost clients of the great man, some of them referred to me indeed by MacPherson and Associates. Mac was very well established in his own fiefdom as the King of the Impaireds, averaging three to four trials a day at multi-dollars a crack with a built-in summary conviction appeal, and he actually discouraged the heavier cases. To take on an attempted murder would for him result in an appalling loss of income.

Harradence, coming up on his first-year anniversary on the Bench, was obviously having second thoughts about whether he should have taken the "Goddamn appointment" in the first place. A combination of circumstances conspired to cause a rising disquietude within the new Justice of Appeal: he found some of his fellows indeed dour, dull, and dispiriting, the three Ds. He was uninspired. There was no longer a war, no danger, no do or die. As I had reminded him, he was no longer a target for government plots; there was no surreptitious surveillance; there was no excitement in his life. I would have to tell him: "Milt, I've got news for you—you're a judge. *Nobody* is listening to you. Trust me." This disturbed Milt greatly.

My concerns that Mr. Justice Harradence was being co-opted by the pillars of the Court was alleviated to some extent at a dinner at the Edmonton Centre Club on an occasion when he was sitting with the Court at Edmonton and I happened to be up there doing a case. He obviously wanted to unburden himself, and I listened patiently to a two-hour diatribe about "those bastards" plotting to appoint him so that he could not take Alberta out of Confederation, and so on and so on. The hated National Energy Program was about to be implemented and Milt was furious. Moreover, he had got wind of my theory—a theory held also by Jack Major, who could attest to its veracity better than I—of the political reasons for his appointment to the Bench. I had to do some fast verbal footwork. Fortuitously the implementation of the Criminals' Code, the *Charter of Rights*, was about to become the reality. I lectured Milt with great solemnity, to the effect that, given the backgrounds and mindsets of his petrified colleagues, the only judge on the highest court of Alberta capable of turning the dream of the Charter into concrete relief for the villains of the world was him. I told him that it was his *destiny* to write the defining and leading *Charter* judgments for his generation of Appellate judges.

"You mean . . . ? He began.

"You've got no choice!" I said. That was an end to the matter.

Subsequently, I checked with Major and entreated him to reinforce this notion in Milt's cerebellum. I then called Mrs. Catherine Harradence and determined that, indeed, Milt had been casting about with threats of resignation. This upset her to a considerable extent, because, for the first time in a number of years, Milt was actually spending some time with his family. I reassured her that he now had determined that he had a higher destiny and would have to remain on the Court.

Once Milt was safely reconciled to his noble fate, I had to rag him a bit. "Well, look on the bright side," I said to my friend the Judge, "J.G. Farrell said that in order to be respectable you do have to know what society approves of, and what better place to have a daily lesson on the subjects of societal approval than society's chief approver-or disapprover—the Court of Least Appeal!"

"You little bastard," was his only response.

Not too long after Milt was appointed to the Court, he was assigned from time to time to preside with his brethren at the Northwest Territories Court of Appeal sittings at Yellowknife. The N.W.T. C.A. was the Alberta Court of Appeal wearing different silly hats. Some of its judges loved to go North: Sam Lieberman was a devoted angler; Bill Stevenson had practiced there, conducting challenging cases in remote, frozen wastes, bunking down on the local schoolhouse floor after flying in on a Twin Otter with the Court party led by a pious Judge Sissons or Bill's pistol-packing former law partner, Mr. Justice William Morrow; Buzz McClung was interested in the history of the North and, anyway, Buzz loved the law wherever it might be found, even at the frontier.[4]

Milt hated everything about any place north of 60, including the trip. For one thing, there was not a decent tailor to be found. For another, there was "that Goddamn *raven!*"

Milt was up North for a sitting and preparing his elaborate toilette prior to joining his companions for breakfast. The Court was ensconsed at a Yellowknife hotel which, prior to its renovation, and for that matter, subsequent to its renovation, was not the Taj Mahal. Hearing a rustling at his window, he raised the blind (one of those old-fashioned types on rollers) and looked straight into the eyeballs of a malevolent, gigantic raven. Even the cool gunfighter was startled, and probably jumped about a yard. "Get out of here," he snarled, but the beast stood its ground, defiantly, staring him down in the manner of Wild Bill Hickock about to throw down on a barroom belligerent. Milt duly reported this disquieting experience to his fellows, which caused them a great deal of mirth. Ravens are a very common sight about northern townsites: they are apparently oblivious to the harsh weather conditions and are admirable scavengers, and grow to great proportions. They are not an endearing creature at the best of times, and their frantic hopping and raucous crowing can get on one's nerves. The event would not have been remarkable, save for its repetition. Some months later, again conscripted to northern duty, Milt was staying this time at another Yellowknife hotel. Again, prior to joining his fellow judges at breakfast, he suffered exactly the same experience. Milt was absolutely convinced that it was the same raven, no doubt part of the larger conspiracy against his

4 For example, Buzz forwarded to me Dean Emeritus Wilbur Bowker's magnum opus, Murder in the Shushwap, a marvelous legal history. In 1997, Buzz published his own superb history, *Law West of the Bay*, dedicated to Dean Bowker, Q.C.

life that had been fomenting for lo these many years, and he communicated his conclusions darkly to his compatriots. They were as singularly unsympathetic as on the first occasion. Milt did not let up on his conviction, and thereafter spent much of his time on northern circuits looking furtively over his shoulder, bracing for an attack from behind which, as he understood from Alfred Hitchcock movies, might not be that unusual. Thus the raven continued to haunt Milt.

I suspect that somewhere in his subconscious lurked a dim memory of Edgar Allen Poe's dismal poem, probably boxed into his head as an impressionable schoolboy by some harridan of an English teacher. Whatever the source, his disquietude and foreboding were real and intensified exponentially as he approached Yellowknife via Outrage Airlines, for sittings of the court.

The one occasion that I accompanied him up to those remote precincts remains forever plugged into *my* subconscious, and still surfaces in the post-nightmare stirrings before dawn after a restless sleep, wherein "repose is tabooed by anxiety." I say at once that I am confident that Milt was not a willing party to these outrageous snubs, at least not in any sense that his participation was either conscious or voluntary.

I journeyed to Yellowknife to argue a murder appeal. The Appeal Court sat there a couple of times a year at that time, and in order to "show the flag" to the local yokels it was a tradition during the sittings of the Court that it hosted a cocktail party for the local Bar, visiting firemen, and other minor dignitaries, officials, and politicians. This soiree was, of course, by invitation only, held in the posh suite of the only seven-story building in the small northern city.

I had travelled to Yellowknife on the same plane as Mr. Justice Harradence, in fact, we sat together. As he was presiding with his colleagues, needless to say we did not discuss the case, but he knew why I was going of course.

Yellowknife had at that time a small, communal airport of the type one still encounters in the more remote reaches, for example, Tierra del Fuego. With the arrival of the commercial flight of the day, the place had packed with arriving and departing passengers, friends and relatives, bags and bundles. As Milt and I were waiting for our luggage, a balding eminence loomed out of the crowd, sporting a blue blazer with the regimental crest of Her Majesty's Royal Ox Cart Drivers, an ascot, a pipe, and an insufferable air. He greeted Milt warmly and announced, "I have the Mercedes at the curb." Have you noticed, some people drive cars, and others drive "the Mercedes"? In any event, Milt took pains to introduce me to this fop, who gave me the old limp wrist handshake and the fishy stare when he realized that I was a minion. Apparently, he was a relatively new arrival as a Judge in the North, and my brief encounter with him on this occasion verified the stories I had heard about him from court veterans.

Our bags arrived, and this personage then exhorted my friend Milt to go with him, while pointedly ignoring me. Milt gave a half-hearted shrug, took his bag, and departed with his colleague. I was left standing there with my face hanging out. Luckily, I was able to grab a ride in the back of Legal Aid boss Doug Miller's half-ton, he seeing some relatives off and spotting my plight.

Milt had suggested I join him for dinner in the dining room at the Explorer Hotel, and I did so. We had just finished the main course when yet another judicial eminence presented himself at our table, and *he* exhorted Milt to go with him at once to the aforesaid Bench and Bar party. Again, Milt introduced me. I got another limp wrist. Then I was left sitting there alone, Milt again reluctantly departing.

I was hardly surprised at the N.W.T. scenario I have described, and on a scale of one to ten, this was at most a two. It is simply another proof of the gap that inevitably widens between old friends when one of them goes to the Bench.

It is worthy of restatement that relatively insignificant events such as this indelibly stamp our lives, but my life prior to and subsequent to these events has had numerous similar, recurring episodes, redolent with sour *déjà vu*. No rationalization is needed. One obvious thing, such inhospitable behaviour of my friend's colleagues in this instance simply illustrates what we all know and what I have earlier expanded upon: criminal defence lawyers are generally considered by other lawyers and particularly by the

Bench to be rogues hardly removed from the lowlifes they defend; for the other, equally obvious, from the time that my dear and redoubtable wife and I became one impregnable unit, we deliberately conducted our lives with obvious disdain for the hypocrisy, small-minded provincialism, prissy conventions, suffocating social climbing, and the appalling ignorance of other lawyers and their domestic companions. We were outspoken, critical, and arrogant. Our views, for a five- to six-year period, were inflicted upon the local populace via our respective CBC radio programs, causing great foment. We remain so, uncontrite, blind to compromise, a majority of two. As recently as late 1996, I was solemnly reminded of this questionable anti-social aberration by close law associates, considerable years my juniors, who were expressing collective concern that I, by my indiscreet public pronouncements, was becoming 'marginalized' (their term, thank God!) and would be thrust out of the legal community if I kept up this unacceptable behaviour. Heretics in their midst are not tolerated by socially acceptable citizens. Well, I shall deal with that in no uncertain terms in my own autobiography. For now, we return to Milt.

I must now elaborate upon the second theory referred to above for Milt's acceptance of this high judicial Office: there is a bunker mentality that overcomes even the most independent-minded appointee to the Bench. There were other *indicia* that Milt had succumbed, in some small measure, to this deadening of the sensibilities. How he could transmogrify and re-invent himself from fearless, outspoken, erratic, and romantic, if slightly loony, maverick to the staid gray-flannel facedom of an Appeal Court judge may have more to do with theatre than reality. The man Harradence could not change so, and no one who really knew him ever believed that he could or would. But Milt is an excellent actor; moreover, he was not without social ambitions; and he well knew that the only societal forgiveness a loner criminal defence counsel can achieve is tolerant *quasi*-acceptance by the larger legal community when he manages, over great odds, an appointment to a High Court. This suffocating clutch to polite society's compassionate bosom is by no means *grudging*; it is the whole-hearted fetid embrace of the remorseful convert by the Entity in Power, be it the Church, the State, or the Profession. He renounced the Revolution, and as its reward the legal community at last granted Milt Harradence Holy Communion, all past sins forgiven, redemption in the bag. Saved, despite his apostasy, but at what cost?

Which is why C.D. Evans will never want to be a judge.

If Asa Milton Harradence was now *accepted* by his former estranged peers, he also accepted them. Contrast a locker room discussion of the writer and the great barrister following a typically disastrous, demeaning, stick-in-your-craw appearance by both of us on behalf of two wretchedly doomed appellants before the (then) Appellate Division of the Supreme Court of Alberta with a discussion between us but a few months following his appointment to that same Court.

In the sanctum of the barristers' robing room, all discussions being a privileged occasion, we were discussing the perversity of the Court that day, that is, of the three blobs, and one in particular. As I recall, Milt's description of that eminent personage was, "An arrogant, unpleasant windbag." I concurred, abetting his judgment with one remark not as a caveat but as an amelioration, "And stupid. Other than that, I concur with my brother Harradence and have nothing to add."

Some short time after Milt's anointment and elevation, he engaged me upon the same subject person, having been sitting with that *eminentissimmo* the previous week, only this time he observed, "You know, old X is really a very nice man." An interesting recantation, nay, *revision*, I rejoined, "and inexplicable, considering our joint former objective assessment of that pompous twit."

"Now, my boy, these fellows when you get to know them are really not at all that bad."

"Jesus H. Christ on a f— *crutch!*"

"Now, Cliff, we can't be hard and fast in our judgments of people. It's … different … you know … from this side of the Bench."

"No, I don't know. And I don't want to know. I do know how your precious new brethren treat young lawyers, poor shit-scared kids with their knees knocking together, how they treat any criminal defence lawyer. That I do know."

"Look, Cliff, now you're making too much out of this. We'll talk about it, boy."

But there was nothing to talk about. Now I knew that we inhabited two completely different planets.

Things are never the same—even between old comrades who have fought shoulder to shoulder on the same side of the barricades—when one of them takes the judicial ermine. Judges wield power and enjoy usufructs and inordinate privileges; they are also cloistered, and rightly so. They have no further right to be a part of the practicing profession. But we do not wish to be a part of their world, either. ". . . *as Thomas Jefferson observed long ago, the moment the lust for public office enters a man's mind, there is a subtle corruption in his character.*" (H.L.M.)

I have always had a disdain for lawyers who try to be chummy with judges, who socialize with them and suck up to them. There is a line over which a true professional must not cross. The judiciary do not draw that line; it is drawn by the Leaders of the Bar. Well, by some of us.

Milt loved the dramatic historical reference. His Chief Justice from 1985, the Honourable J. H. Laycraft, was also a student of history. I opposed a Crown appeal before Laycraft, C.J.A., Prowse, and Harradence JJ.A. The issue was whether a citizen charged initially with second degree murder, then indicted on committal for trial for first degree, should lose his bail. In full stride, I blurted to the Court, "Bail has been a right of freemen since *Magna Carta*." Milt nodded, warmly approving. Laycraft, C.J.A., looked more than sceptical, a look I knew well. Later, Milt growled at me, "I think you went too far."

Years later, still mulling over my possible overzealous misstatement, I consulted Sir Ivor Jennings, and satisfied myself that my blurt was, inexplicably, accurate, reference Article 36 of King John's Charter of 1215. I wrote to Chief Justice Laycraft, now retired, and cited my authority *nunc pro tunc*. "See," I said to Milt, "I was right." "Lucky guess, you little bastard."

Milt also warned me in a friendly manner about my excessive

sarcasm in argument before the Court. "Well," said I, "you were sarcastic."

"Yaas. So I was."

"Milt, sometimes there is no nice way to tell the Court of Appeal that the trial judge is a nincompoop; you just have to say it."

"That's true. You've got no choice. Yaas."

A number of principles informed the judgments of Mr. Justice Harradence. These carried over from his days and experience in practice and were corroborated by the *Canadian Charter of Rights and Freedoms* which came into existence after his appointment. At their core was his resolute affirmation of the rule of law, the reverence for which he shared with the late J.V.H. Milvain, the impeccable and inspiring Trial Division Chief Justice before whom Harradence had appeared on so many occasions. We pause to observe these principles did not necessarily inform Milt's colleagues on the Appeal Court Bench, as most of them had neither his days nor his experience in their practices.

Keith Ewing and Conor Gearty, in the *London Review of Books*, edition of February 6, 1997, page 8,[5] spoke to the rule of law thus:

> The rule of law means different things to different people, but at its core it means that government must be conducted in accordance with the law, and must have legal authority for its actions.

To this must be added Milvain, C.J.'s oft-repeated assertion that civilized society (as we know it) could not exist without adherence to the rule of law, wherein he also expressed the necessity for a societal code of conduct. Milt, always the good citizen, greatly endorsed this, witness his reverence for appropriate marks of respect, common courtesies, the protection of Womenfolk and lawful authority. But what concerned barrister Harradence, in practice and on the Bench, was the zeal with which government agencies, particularly the investigating authorities, enforced the Criminal Code.

---

5. *"History of a Dog's Dinner"*; Ewing and Gearty on the Police Bill.

The governing principles of Mr. Justice Harradence's seminal judicial pronouncements were as follows:

1. There must be clear statutory or common-law authority for the infringement of a citizen's security, privacy, and liberty.
2. Even the basest and meanest of the realm is entitled to proof beyond reasonable doubt and the most vigorous defence; Milt always favoured quotable quotes from the great Thomas Erskine (see *infra*).
3. Mr. Justice Darling's admonition that a thousand suspicions do not add up to a finding of guilt, which A.M.H. was also fond of quoting. [Speaking for myself (to adopt the subjective punctilio of a fellow Bencher) a hundred suspicions added together is about enough to morally justify hanging the average thug. I know, I know, cynicism is as arid as dry grass. That's why I love it.]
4. Give a poor, beaten-down bastard a break if you can. Milt is not exactly a devoted reader of the great Russians, but he would embrace Dostoyevski's fervent precept: "Compassion is the chief and, perhaps, the only law of all human existence."

With these principles of guidance firmly in mind, Mr. Justice Harradence kept his more hawkish or callow colleagues on the straight and narrow. On a less formal basis, in the dreary day-to-day business of the Court, if A.M.H. sat on the criminal panel one can imagine with some delight his unequivocal admonitions to his fellows in the back room.[6] Court of Appeal Judges in particular always came to their coffee breaks, let alone their grave deliberations, with down-turned mouths. Milt's salty and forceful rhetoric must have jolted the complacency of his colleagues with the zap of a cattle prod effectively deployed. I am confident they found his views both educational and instructive. Upon Milt's retirement from the Bench, the loss of his necessary brake to the

---

6. Harradence is reliably reported to have expostulated in that venue to a recent female appointee to the Court, elevated from the ranks of academia, "Woman, that's not the law!" I suppose a complaint went forward to the Thought Police or to the Egg Marketing Board or something.

characteristic kneejerk censure of the Court dealt a mortal blow to the defence Bar of Alberta. "Denunciation" and "Deterrence" have always been the favourite convenience pegs of the majority. Dostoyevski's article of faith and love should stand to them as a devastating rebuke, not, alas, that they would have the slightest idea what he was talking about.

Many of Mr. Justice Harradence's judgments in criminal causes were significant. He was, of course, a subject of gossip and envy by some of his fellow jurisprudes at various levels of court. It is noteworthy that in four important appeal judgments in a row, he dissented strongly from the majority, but was upheld by the Supreme Court of Canada.

After the first three cases went in this fashion, some of his fellow judges began to get some sort of message filtering through the little gray cells, and a renewed respect for their still flamboyant colleague. Too many judges, in my experience, contra the *Magna Carta*, do not know the law nor are they minded to keep it well.

Vindication by the Supreme Court of Canada must have been a supreme victory, for the old warrior Milt had not had great successes as an advocate before the Supreme Court in Ottawa. In fact, his experiences before that nest of remote and chilly autocrats who peopled its Woolsack in the early sixties was discouraging, to say the least. I accompanied him once as his junior, and it was a horrible experience. This was an application for leave in a criminal matter, meritorious I say, and the Court was singularly unreceptive. I marveled as my Learned Senior crawled uphill on broken glass, to be summarily kissed off. Later, we walked the icy, wind-blown streets of the foreign capital, two alienated aliens, strangers in a weird land. "Let's get out of this Goddamn place," growled Milt. "Let's get back to Canada!"

Let us in turn wind up the disquieting subject of appeal courts with an amusing and much needed break from their standard soporific fare.

When Clyne Harradence, Q.C., sought an "occasional call" to the Alberta Bar for a particular case, the stage was set by his brother, Mr. Justice Harradence—before whom he was to be called—and by the writer, who was, with the connivance of Milt, to introduce Clyne to the Court. Unknown to Clyne, we went to a bit of trouble to ensure that the Court of Appeal hearing room set aside for the occasion would have an audience. These things ordinarily attract few observers.[7] For an "occasional Call" in Alberta, to do a single case, we always had a courtesy where one did not just send the money and get a piece of paper and a token, good for one hot dog at Coney Island. There was actually a hearing in front of a Judge. It was an honour to introduce Clyne before his brother Milt. Clyne was surprised when he arrived at the Court of Appeal at 4:00 o'clock on a Friday afternoon for a fairly routine application, really a family event, to find the courtroom had a substantial audience. In this case, the Court was populated by a number of articled students to both the Alberta Court of Appeal and the Court of Queen's Bench, plus some employees of the Registrar's Office, prominent among these Madam Registrar Jackie Ford herself. Clyne seemed somewhat mystified by the show of interest in what was expected to be a brief application.

"Order!" Mr. Justice Harradence entered the hushed upstanding Courtroom with his usual show of intense severity. What follows is pure theatre:

In the course of introducing Mr. Harradence, Q.C., for his Call to the Alberta Bar, I advised the Court of a discretionary bar to his Call that I thought I, as an officer of the Court, had to disclose. Milt's face turned to stone:

"What is that?"

I said, "Well, when he was a law student—and maybe it's mitigating to have this stated before his Call—dropping the dummy full of ketchup out of the low flying aircraft over the college football game may not have been the worst thing that happened."

Milt said, "There's more?"

A ripple ran through the attending audience as I advised the Court, as I had to, that Mr. Clyne Harradence, Q.C., had been

---

7. I arrived at my office one morning to be reminded that I had forgotten all about the introduction of the eminent Edward Greenspan, Q.C., of Toronto to the Alberta Bar for a particular case. Brian Waller, Q.C., was introducing Eddie to Chief Justice Kenneth Moore. I arrived late in blue jeans and a black leather jacket. As I entered the Court, the Chief Justice broke off Waller's submissions by asking me, in a loud voice, "Are you the accused?"

third-partied as a law student in a civil action and had failed to give a good and legal account of himself. I told the Court that Clyne Harradence and a relative of his had taken over the management of the campaign of a candidate for president of the Students' Union at the University of Saskatchewan. This had not been with the full accord of the young candidate, but they told him, "Let us handle this." I advised the Court that a mutual friend of Clyne's and his relative had arranged with a colleague in London to provide a written endorsement of the candidate by George Bernard Shaw. It appeared that Mr. Shaw had passed away previously but this "endorsement" duly arrived and the candidate, flattered by his volunteer advisors, brought this to the attention of the major newspaper circulating in Saskatoon, who fell hook, line, and sinker and—on the front page no less—published the endorsement and received first a phone call and then a Statement of Claim from the solicitors for the Estate of George Bernard Shaw. It did not help that Shaw was quoted as saying: "You'll never have a quiet world till you kick women out of politics."

Thus, Clyne Harradence was third-partied by the newspaper as was the other relative.

Milt said, "And do they appear today?"

I said, "My Lord, I understand that the solicitors for the Estate of George Bernard Shaw have been served with a Notice of these proceedings."

Milt said, "Madame Registrar, page in the hall."

Jackie Ford left the Courtroom purposefully and we heard her calling:

"The solicitors for the Estate of George Bernard Shaw! The solicitors for the Estate of George Bernard Shaw!"

Clyne was sitting there, his life passing before his eyes. The students enjoyed this show thoroughly. Madame Registrar returned:

"They do not answer, my Lord."

Milt said, "Very well, Mr. Evans, I have taken into account the mitigation you've offered and therefore Mr. Harradence, *dubitante*, welcome to the Bar of Alberta."

The transcript continues:
Clyne Harradence: "You two bastards."

Chapter Sixteen

The Year of Loss

Not there to bid my boy farewell,
When that within the coffin fell,
Fell—and flashed into the Red Sea,
Beneath a hard Arabian moon
And alien stars. To question, why
The sons before the fathers die,
Not mine! And I may meet him soon.

Alfred, Lord Tennyson,
on the death at sea of his second son, Lionel

GRIEF IS AN INTENSELY PERSONAL MATTER and outsiders should not intrude upon it. The most that one can or should do is to assure the bereaved that you care, then leave them to the healing of silence. The yammer of emoting acquaintances must surely be as traumatic as the loss itself.

Writing this chapter is for me a painful duty, as it is with trepidation that I presume to write about a dear friend's loss of his son, and later in that same year, the loss of a partner who was, in all things instant, his surrogate son. I shall confine myself to a few personal observations of my own knowledge, and then I ask the reader simply to pray for their quiet rest and the assuagement of this giant man's profound sorrow.

The observance of D-Day will always have a tragic significance for Milton and Catherine Harradence and their family. On June 6, 1986, a single-engine airplane with two occupants went down in a thunderstorm, crashing in the rugged and forbidding terrain of Kananaskis Country near Calgary. Three friends of the pilot and passenger, including Milt's eldest son, Rod Harradence, went in search of the first plane. Rod was himself a skilled pilot, although he was not the pilot on this occasion. Their single-engine Cessna in turn ran into the granite edifice of Mount Lougheed, and was demolished. There were no survivors of either crash.

An extensive air and ground search ensued, involving military planes and personnel as well as several volunteers, including Milt, daughter Catherine, and son Bruce.

Rod's crashed plane was located by ground searchers on June 9.

In a catastrophic twist of these vicious fates, as the air search continued for the unlocated first plane, a Twin Otter aircraft carrying three military officers and five volunteer spotters also crashed. All were killed.

The first lost plane was found on June 18. Both occupants were dead.

The total death toll: thirteen dead, including Milt's eldest son.

Rod Harradence was uncannily like his father: tall, muscular, handsome, that same toothsome grin; and charming and decent. He was all that sons should be and more. He had qualified as a pilot, which was a matter of justifiable pride to his high flying father, and at the time of his cruel death was flying commercially, recently married, his beloved young wife pregnant with their first child. What further felicitous circumstances could be the rationale for unleashing the destructive machinations of a heartless and witless nature can not be imagined. It is truly the good who die young, and one wonders sometimes if God does it on purpose. I am sure that Milt has had to ask himself that question on those countless occasions of helpless and sorrowful reflection on what was and what might have been. But for the Olympian fiats. But for.

In late July of that same year, Milt's *annus horribilis,* John MacPherson, Q.C., was obliterated in a one-car motor vehicle accident early one morning while driving to Calgary from his home at de Winton. Johnny Mac, whom I have referred to earlier in this narrative, was an early protégé of Milton's, having articled with him and practiced with him as his partner for over twenty years of the closest association. His death was also a sudden shock and capricious tragedy. He was brash, bright, combative, good company, and much his own man. He and I had parallel careers: we were only three months apart in age, and called to the Bar one year apart. I fought Mac in the courtroom as often, or perhaps more often in our junior years, than I met Milt. He was one hell of a lawyer, and enjoyed our nickname for him, "Mini Milt." His being taken so untimely was a great loss to the Criminal Bar and personally to Milt.

The combination of these two disasters in such close nexus was a double blow from which, I am convinced, my stricken friend never fully recovered.

After it was confirmed that Rod's plane had crashed with no survivors, Milt steeled himself to view the site. It was something he had to do, perhaps the necessity to confirm its awesome finality in his own mind. CFCN-TV had deployed a helicopter that had visited the wreckage. Milt asked to be taken there, and this flight was arranged by the station. Thus did the aging fighter pilot make his lonely and heartbroken pilgrimage to bid farewell to his pilot son.

I believe it was later that day that I went to see Milt at home. There was nothing one could say and nothing that one could do. The family was gathered bravely together, and I hugged each one in my turn. This hospitable home had welcomed me on many previous occasions, and even the pall of this unspeakable tragedy could not for one moment dull the characteristic warmth of the Harradence household.

The sympathetic presence of Tom Duckworth, Q.C., Milt's neighbour, legal contemporary, and close friend, added, if possible, a further poignancy to this sad convocation. Tom was a big, bluff, kindly man with a great heart. Short years before, a police constable had arrived unexpectedly at the Duckworths' residence. His duty was to advise Tom and Marguerite that their son, who had been travelling in South Africa after completing his university degree, had been killed there in a motorcycle accident. Details were sparse, their subsequent agonies excruciating. Such a blow. Thomas now comforted Milt in what for him must have been a harrowing excoriation of a mortal wound. The strength and fortitude that friends can be capable of in times of adversity has always caused me to marvel.

Later, the three of us walked in River Park, the verdant expanse of meadow overlooking the Elbow River that fronted their properties on 14A Street. After a while, Tom went home and Milt and I continued. We walked, I recall, for a couple of hours. Much of the time we were silent. At intervals, Milt spoke to me—and surely also to his inner self-about the things that were in his heart. All I could do was listen, and when it came time to part, I put my arms clumsily about him and I wept, that weeping of impotence and rage that accompanies our inability to express our sorrow and empathy, our ineptitude in providing any relief or comfort in such wretched misfortune.

Milt seldom spoke thereafter of his lost son to other than his family and closest friends. Oliver Cromwell—some of whose better attributes are found in A.M.H.—lost his eldest son, young Oliver, during the Civil War. Subsequently, his young nephew was killed in battle. He wrote to his sister's husband, Valentine Walton:

> Sir, God hath taken away your eldest son by a cannon-shot. It brake his leg. We were necessitated to have it cut off, whereof he died. Sir, you know my trials this way…

Says Dame C.V. Wedgwood:[1] "It is the only reference in all his letters to the death of young Oliver."

The automobile accident that claimed John MacPherson was also a freakish catastrophe. John had been separated from his wife but had earlier that night been visiting at the family domicile near de Winton, south of Calgary. The visit was happy and affectionate. Mac departed for Calgary at a late hour, driving north on a municipal road allowance in a friend's borrowed car. He was in good spirits. The road, with which he was well familiar, ended at a T intersection, marked by the usual checkerboard, and one went right or left on the intersecting highway. Inexplicably, the car missed the turn and barreled into the ditch. Mac was wearing his seatbelt. He apparently slipped to one side with the impact, and by a ghastly irony was choked to death by the seat restraint that should have saved his life.

News of his death struck the legal community like a juggernaught. Johnny Mac was one of those indestructible, irrepressible persons that one knew to be immortal. Suddenly, and brutally, he was gone.

Web MacDonald, Jr., and I were pallbearers. Prior to the funeral service, we hoisted a few to Mac's memory at the Royal Duke. Then it was the sad ceremonials in a crowded downtown church, eulogies and off-key singing of the usual hymns, homilies and professional mourners, Mac all alone in his wooden box. The Calgary Police Service mounted an Honour Guard and fired three sad salvoes over the departing coffin. We buried Mac at the Okotoks Cemetery. Dolores and the kids, shattered, clustered around the coffin, while one of the boys read a poem they had written for their dad. The prairie wind blew gently. Again, I experienced

1. Wedgwood, Dame C.V., *Oliver Cromwell*, Corgi Books, London, 1975.

angry impotence. It was all so senseless. And, with Jorge Luis Borges, *"I felt what we all feel when someone dies—the remorse, now pointless, for not having been kinder. We forget that we are all dead men conversing with dead men."*

After the funeral, I was dropped off by the hearse because I wanted to walk awhile by myself and write my own poem for Mac, which I did:

Warm sunny day at the end of summer
Gentle breezes playing 'round
Webby and I took Johnny Mac
And laid him gently in the ground,
The piper played *Amazing Grace*
The cops had an Honour Guard
I saw Milt's face at the burial place
Like us, he took it hard,
And later on I walked alone
Down Seventh Avenue
And I wondered, when we die this way
Why we live the way we do.

I was always going to see if John Martland could put this poem to music but, as with so many things in this life, I just never got around to it.

A year later, August 1987, I actually entered the verboten precincts of the Ranchmen's Club, to dine with Milt at his invitation. We drank the memory of Johnny Mac. We spoke of Mac and, of course, of his late son, Rod. We resolved to mark this sad anniversary yearly, the two of us.

As we parted on this solemn occasion, Milt said, "I thought they were meant to bury us."

That about summed it all up.

CHAPTER SEVENTEEN
Heroes

My son, from me learn valour and true constancy,
from others, success.

– *The Aeneid*

WRITERS WRITE because they want immortality; usually for themselves, not for their subjects.[1] Few have the mastery of the language, the intellectual rigour, or the originality to make the Canon. The likelihood of any work of mine ever making an objective list of aesthetic excellence and, if not gaining immortality then perhaps occasional resurrection, is obviously remote. However, one has the concern that future generations, if inadvertently exposed to this particular work, might be inclined to be less amused by Milt Harradence's eccentricities than alarmed. More to the point, it is inevitable that some contemporaries of his and mine will condemn this personal record as a cruel lampooning of or a diatribe against the friend I wish to make immortal. To them I say this: If, in recounting anecdotes and occurrences of our association, I have failed to emphasize the thorough decency of this man, his great ability, his commanding presence, his personal charm, and his abundant generosity, all making in sum a hero, then I rectify that now. At the same time, I emphasize J.C. Major's contention that without that eccentricity of which I have made much, Milt could not have been the person—or the lawyer—that he was.

All of us need heroes. Milt Harradence was and is one of my heroes; he was and is a hero of the legal profession. There will

1. Dr. Johnson said, "Only blockheads write, except for money."

never be another like him. Peter Tarrant is described in the *Calgary Herald* edition of October 13, 1996, as "a veteran Calgary private investigator who has worked for hundreds of lawyers, including Harradence, at more than sixty law firms in the world." Said Tarrant: "They broke the mold with Milt." Milt, in turn, had his heroes.

In the days before "role models" and "mentors," one had heroes. The terms "hero" or "heroine" are no longer in vogue to describe the giants of the profession who are revered, mainly because neither term is gender neutral, and also because it is not fashionable anymore to declaim Newton's oft-quoted aphorism, "If I have seen farther, it is by standing on the shoulders of giants."[2] Nowadays people take what they want from their betters without acknowledgment.

Today's insipid role model is a far cry from the hero of yesterday.

A classic hero of the legal profession is Oliver Wendell Holmes, United States Supreme Court Justice, noted principled dissenter, soldier, philosopher, statesman.

Closer to home we have, of course, Dean Emeritus W.F. Bowker, Q.C., whose quiet, exemplary heroism was captured by his colleague, Dean Trevor Anderson, in his tribute to Wilbur Bowker on the occasion of the latter's retirement:

> For the great influence exerted by the Dean was achieved without being designed, and by example, not precept or exhortation. Under him the school was governed not by decrees, proscriptions and discipline, but by expectation. Students and colleagues knew that the Dean himself lived by high personal and professional standards; his example made those standards valid for them; and they willingly undertook the obligation to try to live up to his expectations, and felt keenly the desire to avoid the injury he would feel if they were to fall short.
>
> Ultimately, a community, however soundly conceived its law,

---

2. Not Newton's, actually. See Robert K. Merton, *On the Shoulders of Giants*, Harcourt, Brace and World Inc., New York, 1965, wherein the author notes: "It is of some interest that Newton's aphorism is a standardized phrase which has found repeated expression from at least the twelfth century."

> must depend upon the ministers of the law and their ethical quality. Professional responsibility is not established by preaching homilies. The young will attach to such matters only such importance as they probably have in the actual life and work of the leaders of the profession whom they respect. Wilbur Bowker provided that example in his teaching, his scholarship, his treatment of students and colleagues, of complete integrity. It was clear to all that knew him that ethics were as essential to his life, or that of the profession, as oxygen is to existence.

Dean Bowker continues to inspire generations of law students, lawyers, and judges. A genuine saint, he is at the top of the heroic stanine.

There are also many heroes with clay feet, nonetheless deserving of the honourific. That is because the distinction between the hero and the role model is that the latter has no apparent fault; the former has several, but his disciples do not give a damn. They do not give a damn because it is the principal feature of heroes that they, being of heroic proportions, loom larger than life. The role model merely demonstrates to his or her imitators that even the mediocre can "succeed"; for example, it has been conclusively established that any half-wit with a good press flack can become president of the United States, or failing that, of the United Widget Corporation.

The hero represents *inter alia* the unattainable; the person we want to be, with all our hearts, but can never be. They just don't make heroes anymore, and the ones they did make were one of a kind.

Milt Harradence was and is a hero. *He bestrode his narrow world like a Colossus.* He had many imitators, but there was only one Milt. As with all heroes, he had many enemies; he was envied, resented, even vilified by the human blanks of his profession; as with many heroes also, his behaviour at times presented as bizarre. But no matter: his virtues eclipsed his faults.

The analogies I have drawn in this text—to Philip Marlowe, to General Patton, to the lonely mercenary gunslinger, to Seigfried—are apposite. No one who knows Milt could look upon him as an ordinary mortal. He was, in fact, an extraordinary human being.

And to those who did not know him but saw him from afar, or striding across the goggle box screen, or in full flight in the courtroom in this or that hopeless case, he was the stuff of legend. He lived the legend. Indeed, he believed much of the legend. That much of it, as with all legends, was pure bullshit, created with smoke and mirrors, is irrelevant. The point is, his method worked, and his admirers were left both extremely grateful for him and perennially awestricken by his derring-do swashbuckling. It is true, he was more Don Quixote than Batman—although he imitated Batman to the life, even to the Miltmobile and the flamboyant gear and gadgets. It is not an accident, mark, that Don Quixote remains perhaps the most enduring of the great flawed heroes of classic literature. His heart was immense, as was Milt's great heart. It is to be commended that such a heart—with its cause of right, truth, and justice—should too often rule the mind.

It seems therefore appropriate to set our stage with its major motif at the outset being Richard Strauss' *Thus Sprach Zarathustra,* and to end this account on equally heroic notes being the strains of the stately opening statement of the first movement of Elgar's First Symphony.

Milt's aspect presented as a fresh and open countenance when in repose, that is, when he was not posing, which itself denoted strength and steadfastness of character. I have always thought that a person's face mirrors his innermost private being, that an evil or untrustworthy person wears his inner cancer on his face. I am in good company in this observation, and it is better said by Oscar Wilde's Basil Hallward in *The Picture of Dorian Gray:*

> Sin is a thing that writes itself across a man's face. It cannot be concealed. If a wretched man has a vice, it shows itself in the lines of his mouth, the droop of his eyelids, the molding of his hand.

In his features, A.M. Harradence presented without sin. And, like all virtuoso cross-examiners, he well knew what Hallward was talking about as he searched for the signs of sin on the face of his latest challenging adverse witness.

Jack Major early on spotted Milt's genuine respect for genuine heroes. Group Captain Sir Douglas Bader was among the foremost in those privileged ranks. Milt told the *Calgary Herald*, "[H]is personality and vitality are something I shall never forget." We have already noted that Bader's life is manifestly the stuff of legend.

When Group Captain Bader visited Calgary a few years ago, Milt was front and centre in the welcoming party, but demurred to appear on the same stage with his hero because he had not served overseas. He did not consider himself worthy of the honour. That story more than any other except perhaps Milt's letter on behalf of the injured airman (see Chapter 3) illustrates precisely the *bona fide* high moral fibre of Harradence, his sense of propriety and place, and his profound deference to those who have achieved genuine distinction. Moreover, he recognized excellence and was quick to intuitively spot the phony and poseur.

Harradence, Q.C., made no secret of his adulation of the Right Honourable John George Diefenbaker, who was also a family friend from his youth in Prince Albert, Saskatchewan. Said Milt to the *Herald:* "As a boy, I came under his spell because we both lived in Prince Albert. He is the reason I decided on a career at the Bar. I had the privilege of watching him in action at the Court House . . . when he walked into a Courtroom, he completely dominated it, and when he rose to cross-examine, the atmosphere was electrified."

Dief the Chief was also considered by many to be one of the most eccentric leaders Canada has ever had. Mind you, next to the tippling John A. MacDonald, who according to the learned John Schmidt was once booted out of Parliament, or Mackenzie King who was given to consulting his mother through a crystal ball, Dief was just plain folks, particularly as he emanated from the Wilds of Saskabush, the venue that gave us Louis Riel *and* the Harradence Brothers, Milt and Clyne.

Milt and his brother were brought up in the stern and disciplined outer reaches of the northern Canadian Prairie and inculcated with the solid if dreary values of the day and the jurisdiction. Parallels to Frank and Jesse James of the Tennessee Hills are inescapable. Small wonder they fell under the spell of the Chief, who, as they grew up, was establishing his fearsome reputation at the Criminal Bar in Saskatchewan. Dief was a teetotaller, a visionary, a spell-binding orator, and he loved Canada—the Canada of the Red Ensign with no BS about the French Question and no tampering with the Crow Rate—so he had overwhelming appeal to A.M. Harradence.

Milt's other hero was the homicidal and egocentric General George Patton, immortalized by George C. Scott in a celluloid extravaganza that A.M.H. has viewed about as often as the late Howard Hughes watched *Ice Station Zebra* (and the writer *Dr. Strangelove*).

I have earlier noted that when Milt was in his fifties and at the height of his powers at the top of his profession, one was hard put to tell whether he was Milt playing Dief, playing Scott, playing Patton, playing Milt, and so on *ad infinitum.*

(I was always reticent about asking Milt who his favourite character was in my favourite movie, because I feared he would say, "General Jack Ripper," a megalomaniac of massive proportion.)

It is interesting that all of Milt's heroes—with the exception of Group Captain Bader—were by any contemporary standard completely nutty. Mind you, one has to remember that Milt came from a background in Western Canada where fluoridation was universally denounced as a Communist plot.[4] Those were simpler times.

One of Milt's conspicuous acts of courage in the face of false flattery was the salvo he fired at the University of Calgary while still at the Bar. Some of the Cowtown legal *cognoscenti* liked to hobnob with the academic *illuminati,* which was more social than sociological. Bernice and I went to only one gathering of "Town and Gown"; it was so soporific and so self-consciously mortifying that we wanted bags over our heads and escaped at the first opportunity. Sample conversation: engaged matron: "Was it your conscious decision not to have children?" Bernice Evans: "We are not in the habit of making decisions while unconscious."

---

3. The *Prince Albert Herald* newspaper published a poem respecting an elderly local man said to have died of fluoridation: *"And inscribed upon the wreath was/the old man lost his kidneys/so the kid could keep his teeth."*

Milt would have nothing to do with that sort of thing. In the mid-seventies A.M.H. (and other prominent legal lions) received a gilt-edged invitation from the University of Calgary to join something New and Exciting called—if one is ready for this—the Chancellor's Club. Oh dear. Milt's scathing response and rejection of the honour was a classic of his craft (Appendix).

Thus, in April 1998, I was amazed to receive an invitation to attend the Spring Convocation of the University of Calgary. I was amazed because it was sent at the behest of the Hon. A.M. Harradence, Q.C., former Justice of Appeal, who according to the announcement was to receive the University's honourary degree, "Doctor of the University of Calgary." He was also to deliver the Convocation Address to the assembled graduands, academics, friends, relations, and hangers-on.

A prior engagement in Toronto mercifully spared me the hilarious spectacle of various fops and flitches mincing down the aisles of the Jubilee Auditorium to the lilt of the Trumpet Voluntary, wearing multi-coloured pillows on their heads and outrageous billowing gowns, in strict order of precedence, followed by three to four tedious hours of "Honouris Canceloris this," and "Fac Deus noster that." I did write Milt a letter, reminding him of one of the late Judge Allan Cullen's great lines:

> A friend of mine is to be anointed a Doctor of the University of Calgary. He gets to put the letters D.U.C. after his name. It's a good thing he was not made a Fellow!

Many—including this writer—look to Harradence as their hero, among them champion boxer Willie deWit and Pat Graham, the executive director of the Seventh Step Society of Canada, an agency that assists offenders to rehabilitate through self-help.

Milt's interest in Willie was noted earlier. Willie became World Amateur Heavyweight Champion and Olympic Silver Medallist. Milt had boxed at the University of Saskatchewan and was the inter-varsity middleweight champion of the Universities of Saskatchewan and Alberta. Hugh Carson, boxing coach and trainer for a number of years, wrote in 1951 of a series of matches he had viewed: "Harradence was the best I saw." It is a sad coincidence that Willie deWit lost his father and brother in a plane crash shortly after Milt's loss of his eldest son. Milt became his mentor and close friend and a surrogate parent. It was on Milt's suggestion that Willie attended law school when he retired from professional boxing. DeWit told the *Herald*, "[H]e's the most honest person I've ever met."

For Paddy Graham, Milt was "my lawyer, my friend and kind of a role model ... there are a number of people who helped me change my thinking, my attitude and eventually my behavior, and Milt was certainly at the top of the list." Graham, said the *Herald*, "credits Harradence with playing a major part in getting him out of prison and keeping him out. They've known each other for forty years, and when Graham at age fifty graduated from University, Milt's son Rod received his degree at the same time. Harradence was there to congratulate them both."

There is yet another, distinct persona of A.M. Harradence that I have not heretofore developed. I have expressed earlier my admiration for Oliver Cromwell, Lord Protector of England, 1653 to 1658. Milt certainly had a number of the positive characteristics—and some of the negative ones—of Old Ironsides, a complex character who is known among other things for his celebrated admonition to a flattering Court painter to paint his portrait "warts and all." Certainly Milt had Old Ironsides' inner strength and deep moral convictions. Quoth he, "Trust in God and keep your powder dry!" Among those positive attributes are courage and idealism, powerful eloquence, immense confidence, the constitution of an ox, a formidable and unique personality, devotion to duty, and a conscientious family man.

Dame C.V. Wedgewood, in her admirable compendium of Cromwell, summarizes some of his more appealing attributes and some of his eccentricities: "... a deep respect for the law; ... the strong affections, the love of justice; ... he was a man capable of hewing a way out of the labyrinth; ... a clear and bold judgment; ... [he] was not the man to abandon the idea merely because its realization seemed impossible." She also observed: "*Outbursts of boisterous mirth and horseplay which seem out of key with his earnest nature.*" (For example, see Col. Ridgedrawers, Chapter 3).[5]

Sound familiar? The casual reader wonders at this parallel. There is no doubt in my mind that, had A.M. Harradence taken command of Ship of State, Alberta—either as elected leader and Premier, or by insurrection of the peasantry as usurper—he would have ruled with the iron fist of the Lord Protector of England. Milt never found democracy persuasive: autocracy was more his style; revolution as a means to power was justifiable by the end. Those who opine otherwise are naïve.

Even from the sinecure of the Court, Milt, like Oliver, decided to name his successor. His years on the Bench had convinced Milt of the necessity that there should always be former criminal defence lawyers on the Court of Appeal, their obligation, as noted, to straighten out the often bent reasoning of the former debenture mongers and fuzzy academics. Milt was delighted to have McClung and, for a time, Major as his judicial colleagues: they redressed the preponderant differential in favour of dubious convictions. Major, however, moved on and up to the Supreme Court of Canada, and Milt was beleaguered by his loss and by his then fast approaching supernumerary status, followed by obligatory retirement from the Court at age seventy-five. Therefore, I received a peremptory summons to his Chambers: "I can't talk on the phone."

I turned up at Milt's Chambers in my usual leather jacket and blue jeans and he was right vexed. "You can't come here like that." Yes, I could, and I told him so. This caused him great concern, because his plan of succession was that I should apply for the vacancy that would be created on the Court of Appeal by his pending retirement. That was all very interesting, I told him, but I did not want to be a judge. Milt told me I had to think about it, and I departed. A couple of days later, he arrived unannounced at my office and presented me with a plain brown envelope marked

---

4. Oliver Lawson-Dick, ed. of *Aubrey's Brief Lives* notes: "He [Henry Martin] was one of the King's judges and, when it came to Cromwell's turn to affix his name to the warrant for King Charles' execution, he wrote his signature hurriedly and then, in a burst of mirth, he smeared the ink of his pen across the face of Henry Martin, the secretary." (Mandarin, London, 1992).

"Confidential." He told me to open it, and I did so, noting that he had provided me with the standard blank application form by aspirants to high judicial office. "Sign it," he said.

"Sorry, Milt. I thought about it, but I don't want to be a judge, and that's that."

"You've got no choice."

"This time, I have. I decline, with thanks."

Major later told me that Milt had advised the Chief Justice that he had no intention of retiring until he was assured that an appropriate successor—that is, an experienced criminal lawyer—could take his place on the Court. Despite the protestations of his colleagues that appointments did not happen that way, Milt was adamant, and it was only kicking and screaming that he went into his supernumerary years before the final boarding process.

The poignancy of that process was exacerbated by the sad fact that, by the end of 1995, Milt was almost completely deaf. I expect the major contributing factor was the self-inflicted damage to his inner ear by his years of stunt flying in single-seater fighter planes. As his hearing got progressively worse, and the most advanced hearing aids proved less and less effective, elaborate amplification devices were set up in the courtroom so that the ailing Judge could hear argument. Milt soldiered on as always, and it is a tribute to his resources of humour that he was amused by my following observations to him: it is difficult to maintain the momentum of paranoia if one cannot hear the muffled, guttural threats whispered at one over the telephone at odd hours. On the other hand, not being able to hear and not knowing whether or not he was being threatened with death or receiving a computerized political message and barbecue invitation from the Reform Party, Milt's paranoia actually intensified.

Willie deWit got the worst of this, as he got together with his mentor at least once a week as the days ticked away towards unavoidable and inevitable retirement. I am happy to report that shortly after his retirement, Milt received a cochlea implant, which greatly improved his ability to hear one-on-one conversation provided there was minimal background noise.

In May 1995, the Edmonton Criminal Trial Lawyers Association honoured Mr. Justice Harradence at its spring banquet by the establishment of the A.M. Harradence Prize to be made annually. I had the honour to be the keynote speaker at this auspicious occasion, and my speech that night was the stalking horse for this book.

On October 16, 1996, the Alberta legal community and the Calgary community at large gathered 700 strong at the Palliser Hotel to honour the old warrior on his retirement. Brian Stevenson, Willie deWit and I put together a committee a number of months before, including Appeal Judges, Queen's Bench Judges, and members of the Criminal Bar. The evening was a smashing success, with Milt receiving tributes from a vast number of colleagues, friends, and acquaintances, presentations by the Royal Canadian Mounted Police and the Calgary Police Service, and tributes by Stevenson and Major with this writer as M.C. It was the largest legal dinner ever held in the history of the Province and a fitting send-off for my friend.

Included in the Appendices are significant tributes to Mr. Justice Harradence on the occasion of his retirement from the Bench: transcripts of the remarks of the Chief Justice of Canada, the Hon. John Sopinka of the Supreme Court of Canada, and the Hon. Chief Justice of British Columbia. I have also put in a letter from retired Chief Inspector Roberts of the Calgary Police Service; it confirms the great esteem in which A.M.H. was held by the police. Also of interest are the *Calgary Herald* stories written by Helen Dolik, which showcase a remarkable career.

It is a touching detail that all of Milt's secretaries over years attended the dinner: Virnetta Anderson, Bev Bromley, Joyce Simmons, and Catherine Vanier, together with Dorothy Klatt, who had been Milt's office manager for twenty years. Of Mrs. Simmons, his secretary in the Court of Appeal for thirteen years, Milt noted: "If it hadn't been for Mrs. Simmons, my tenure would have been addressed by both Houses of Parliament."

Milt continued to sit for a couple of months, April 1997 being the retirement month. I had assumed that he would sit up to that point, but it was on December 9, 1996 at about 10:00 a.m. that my office received an urgent call from Milt's colleague, Madam Justice

Carole Conrad, looking for me. Apparently, it was Milt's last sitting day in Calgary, and she had been advised of this just before she and Milt and Rene Foisy were to preside in Court of Appeal Chambers. It being fairly early in the morning for me, I was sitting up in bed reading the paper, drinking coffee, which civilized existence was shattered by the telephone call. I had to rush off to Court and was lucky, when I stopped briefly at the office, to encounter Milt's former investigator, now our investigator, Peter Tarrant, who, together with Earl Wilson, accompanied me to the Court of Appeal. I hurriedly got gowned. Chambers days were generally quite crowded with gowned counsel, as these were formal applications attendant upon extant appeals before a three-person court. I stalked directly into Court in the best manner of Milt's former secretary, Catherine Vanier (formerly Van Gaalen), as though I held a mortgage on the joint. It has always been a tradition of the Bar in England that the *Habeas Corpus* application requires the immediate attention of the Court, as it deals with the liberty of a possibly wrongfully imprisoned subject, and all other matters must stand down while the Court gives ear to even the most junior counsel with such an application. Apparently, as I entered the courtroom, Milt passed a note to the chairman of the Court, Mr. Justice Foisy, which said, "This looks like trouble!" The address I had to give was off the top of my head, but fortunately the Court had installed an automatic taping system and my words were not lost to posterity:

> My Lord, My Lady, My Lord, this is not a *habeas corpus* application, but I respectfully, My Lady and My Lord, claim a right of audience as I understand that today is the last sitting day of my great and good friend, Milt Harradence. And if I may proceed, I would ask leave to say a few words of tribute to the Honourable Mr. Justice Harradence. I thought I'd used them all up on October 16 — but I found some new ones!
>
> Now, My Lord, My Lady, my friend, I well remember about a month before February of 1979 I got one of your famous nocturnal telephone calls and it went as follows:
>
> "C.D., I've been struck off the roll."
>
> (I was of course fast asleep). I said, "What?" and you said,

"I've been struck off the roll."

I said, "Milt, they can't strike you off the roll without a hearing. We've got them. We can appeal."

"No", said Milt, "I think this is final. I am ascending to the outer ether and to the woolsack."

Well, Sir, that was some seventeen and a half years ago and a month later I received leave from the Honourable Chief Justice of Alberta to pay tribute to you on behalf of the criminal Bar at your swearing-in, and had the honour to do so. I recall you coming into the Court with the entourage on that day, Sir, fierce and proud, with that "by God, war at any moment" expression on your face, and I'll never forget Jack Major (as he then was) leaning over to me and saying, "Evans, would you ever have known that Milt had not been sitting on this Court for 20 years?"

Well, you've been sitting on the Court, Sir, for almost 20 years. I would like you to know, on a personal note, that you left the Northwest Territories Court of Appeal with a bang. I was speaking to their annual dinner last Saturday night, which was composed mostly of Milt Harradence stories which were of course very well received.

Now, My Lord, I speak I know for your colleagues (I hope), for all the members of the Bar, for all of us in this courtroom, for the legal community. Sir, you have been—in the prediction of the Right Honourable John Diefenbaker—you have been an ornament to the Bench. You have been a constant inspiration to the Bar. You are an example to all of us, My Lord, for maintaining our traditions. You have done great service to the Court, to the Bar and of course to your country. We all trust, My Lord, there will be no unseemly haste for you to go back to defending and that you will wait at least two weeks after your retirement in April before you put up the shingle.

And finally, in the words of T.S. Eliot, "Fare forward, traveller!" God bless you.

(I have included in the Appendices an edited transcript of the tributes of leaders of the Edmonton Criminal Bar on Milt's last sitting day in Edmonton, January 30, 1997.)

After Court, I waited for Milt in his private Chambers, accurately described by the *Calgary Herald* as "more museum than workplace: almost every square inch of the Judge's office wall is covered with photos, plaques, mementoes, awards, miniature flags and aeronautical memorabilia ..."

I figured that this would be a good time to tell him that I was writing this book. Because of his acute deafness, I was obliged to write in capitals on a pad. He frowned as he tried to decipher my printing, then said, "I cannot allow this to happen."

I knew that he would say that, and counted silently to ten. At six, he relented, "Mind you, if you're doing it..."

I duly informed Jack Major, who was starting to get nervous at the prospect of writing a foreword for, thus lending credibility to, a work that was more and more shaping up as a fictional satire. More case content was required, said Major. I decided to ignore his concerns, because I was as convinced that Major wanted his piece at the front of this tome as I was that Milt would kill anyone who tried to prevent its publication, warts and all. Then later I revisited Major's suggestions, and decided that perhaps the manuscript should be beefed up with more course content for foreign students.

Milt Harradence epitomized the best traditions of the Bar; he was their quintessential spokesman, and in my view, one of the last. The traditions I refer to I attempted to articulate in a no-holds-barred address to the student body of the U of C Faculty of Law in my Milvain Chair keynote speech. I owe a large debt to lawyers of the calibre of Harradence for their tutelage in these fundamental precepts of our profession, now, alas, rarely observed with scrupulosity.

That antique phrase "best traditions of the Bar" to me encapsulates all that is admirable about the practice of law and assists us to distinguish it as a unique profession. I tried to come up with a list—not exhaustive—of these best traditions, with which not everyone will agree as appropriate or accurate. It is my thesis that, as lawyers in a strong common law jurisdiction stagger into the sputtering years of the last decade and approach the Third Millennium, the best traditions of the Bar are not only being eroded but are being replaced by the worst traditions of the new Bar. These worst traditions include intolerance of dissent, humourlessness, political correctness, frantic inoffensiveness, fees as the bottom line, and winning at all costs.

The best traditions of the Bar include relations between barristers of unfailing courtesy, embracing duty as our great business with all private considerations giving way, the objectivity of the Crown, independence from pressure groups and received wisdom, the maintenance of traditional codes of dress and deportment, close professional relations between counsel and the Courts, and, perhaps most important, honour in all things.

As these best traditions have been superceded by unprofessional practices, advocacy has gone into decline. The calling of Milt Harradence and Jack Major and Bill Stillwell and Brian Stevenson and me has always been that of a persuader of the trier of fact. But today there are signs outside courtrooms, "No advocates wanted," and there is little employment for advocates at all, and little or no appreciation of advocacy. Indeed, in most courts, forensic or debating ability is actually discouraged and frowned upon as being somehow underhanded: it is unfair for the educated, intelligent, well-read barrister to use skills not available to the philistine, lazy, and incompetent dope on the other side. This is all part of the leveling process so prevalent in our society and in our profession. There is no need for our contemporaries to emulate Macauley or Erskine when functional illiteracy will win the day.

The reader may remark that it is not nice to be so critical and judgmental of my colleagues, present and past, many of whom have now shuffled off this mortal coil. Nonsense. I am perfectly well qualified to do so, being twice the barrister those old windbags were and these new poseurs are. How can you say this, the reader cries, in all humility? In all humility, I say, it is not that Milt or I were any good; it is simply that the others were so bad!

With that note on the most dramatic erosion of our best traditions, I come to the end of my tribute.

A.M. Harradence, Q.C., was—and still is—the quintessential barrister and continues to be an inspiration—and a hero—to all members of the Criminal Bar, senior and junior.

Said Francis Bacon:

> I hold every man a debtor to his profession, from the which as men do seek to receive countenance and profit, so ought they of duty to endeavour themselves by way of amends to be a help and an orna-

ment thereto.

Said Chief Justice Hughes, late of the United State Supreme Court:

> The highest reward that can come to a lawyer is the esteem of his professional brethren. That esteem is won in unique conditions and proceeds from an impartial judgment of professional rivals. It cannot be purchased. It cannot be artifically created. It cannot be gained by artifice or contrivance to attract public attention. It is not measured by pecuniary gains. It is an esteem which is born in sharp contests and thrives despite conflicting interests. It is an esteem commanded solely by integrity of character and by brains and skill in the honourable performance of professional duty. No subservient 'yes men' can win it. No mere manipulator or negotiator can secure it. It is essentially a tribute to a rugged independence of thought and intellectual honesty which shine forth amid the clouds of controversy. It is a tribute to exceptional power controlled by conscience and a sense of public duty—to a knightly bearing and valor in the hottest encounters. In a world of imperfect humans, the faults of human clay are always manifest. The special temptations and tests of lawyers are obvious enough. But, considering trial and error, success and defeat, the bar slowly makes its estimate and the memory of the careers which it approves are at once its most precious heritage and an important safeguard of the interests of society so largely in the keeping of the profession of the law in its manifold services.

Here is Harradence welcoming a new lawyer to the practice of our profession, at the young person's Call to the Bar:

> However, there are things that must not change. One is the great traditions of our profession. Amongst those are service and sacrifice in advancing a client's cause. Another is maintaining the independence and integrity of our profession. The great Thomas Erskine said in his celebrated defence of Thomas Paine in 1792:
>
> *"I will forever, at all hazards, assert the dignity, independence and integrity of the English Bar, without which impartial justice, the most valuable part of the English constitution, can have no existence."*

> It is essential that new members of the Bar who now, as officers of the Court, fall heir to these great traditions continue to honour them in the discharge of their duties to the client, to the state and to the court.
>
> You are embarking on a great adventure. I found my 28 years at the Bar a continuous and exhilarating challenge—an experience which witnessed all the extremes of human emotion and revealed both the degradation and the ethereal beauty encompassed by the human spirit. The demands are heavy and relentless. But there is no form of human endeavour that offers greater scope to seek fulfillment of one's own aspirations and at the same time to be of service to your fellow man.

Milt Harradence said that. And that, my colleagues and readers, is what we are all about. As always, it took Milt to articulate it for all of us.

Appendix

LIST OF APPENDIXES

The gruesome grin that calls a kill! You mean *Jaws*? No, just Milt.

"When Harradence starts a cross examination with that smile," said a woman news reporter at the Law Courts building last week, "then you know that what is about to follow will be too horrible to watch." For a long time, she said, the smile had seemed sinisterly familiar — the head bent forward, the eyes peering upward toward the hapless witness, the broad, toothy grin. Then one day she placed it. The shark in the movie *Jaws*. That was Milt Harradence all right, just as he was moving in for the kill. It was therefore altogether foreboding last Thursday when Calgary lawyer Asa Milton Harradence, Q.C., ranked by a national magazine as one of Canada's 10 best criminal lawyers and appearing before the Laycraft commission on behalf of three Edmonton police officers, rose to address himself to a particularly savory morsel. Here was no green constable or nerve-wracked detective on the stand before him. Here indeed was nothing less than an assistant commissioner of the Royal Canadian Mounted Police. He was D. J. Wardrop, chief of the Mounties in Manitoba.

The assistant commissioner was already in some trouble, however. He had read a bold statement into the record, answering the charges of Edmonton police officers that his Mounties had "bugged" their hotel room in Winnipeg. Now the assistant commissioner had a new charge of his own. The Edmonton policemen, he testified in a prepared statement, had actually "contacted the clerk on the hotel desk and ascertained that the room was not rented to (RCMP) Inspector Maduk, but in a fictitious name. From there they were able to secure the master key and an attempt was made to get into this room. They were unable to gain entrance and concluded that the night lock was on and the room occupied . . . Since allegations are evidently being freely made, perhaps it was time we stopped trying to allay groundless suspicions and got down to some unethical attitudes and reaction from members of that (Edmonton) force." But the trouble had already arisen when inquiry counsel Ron Berger made a quiet observation. A hotel master key would have been able to bypass a night lock. Why therefore hadn't the Edmonton detectives entered the room? The assistant commissioner had been somewhat stumped by that one. He now faced Mr. Harradence. The text of the cross examination follows:

Q **Mr. Harradence:** Assistant Commissioner, when you received the call from Assistant Commissioner Wright, you were informed that the deputy attorney general of Alberta was concerned?

A **Mr. Wardrop:** And I believe the attorney general as well.

Q So therefore this would not be a complaint from some minor citizen, was it?

A No.

A Yes, yes.

Q And that man of equal rank had been instructed or contacted by the deputy attorney general and the attorney general of Alberta?

A Yes.

Q And you made no notes?

A No.

MR. HARRADENCE AND MR. JAWS
The results are sometimes too horrible to watch.

Q And the complaint itself, if founded, would really involve a serious criminal offense, would it not?

A Exactly.

Q So really what we had was the attorney general in one of the provinces of this country complaining that a criminal offense may well have been committed by members of the Royal Canadian Mounted Police in connection with activities with the Edmonton City Police, is that correct?

A That could have been the case.

Q Not could be, it was, wasn't it?

A That was the basis of the complaint, yes.

Q Yes. Now then, that being so, you made no notes at that time?

A No.

Q Would you not agree with me that this would be a serious situation for the force if the allegations were true?

A Yes.

Q And they were coming from a man of equal rank, as far as you were concerned?

Q Treated it very casually?

A I treated it commensurate with the information that I had, if it's casually then it has to be casually.

Q Yes, I think you will agree it was treated pretty casually?

A It was pretty casual information the way it came to me.

Q Even though it came from an officer of equal rank and came from the attorney general of the province of Alberta?

A At that time I was advised that the attorney general had further information that he would not divulge, the only information was that Inspector Maduk was in the hallway of the same hotel.

Q If he had additional information would that not perhaps concern you?

A I wanted to know about this additional information before I started accusing my people.

Q Well now, why would you have to accuse them?

A Well —

Q Wouldn't you simply call them

in and interview them?
A I did call them in.

Q Why wouldn't you make notes, why didn't you make notes?
A I just didn't.

Q You just didn't, and that is your answer?
A That's my answer. I had it all in my mind as well.

Q Did you. Well then, let's just see what you did have in your mind. If I may read from your report: "This unsubstantiated suspicion continued to the point that they contacted the clerk of the hotel desk," where did you get that from?
A Inspector Maduk.

Q Are you sure?
A As far as I recall, yes.

Q You're not sure then?
A I would say it was Inspector Maduk.

Q Well now, Assistant Commissioner, it pains me to press you, but I must, I put it to you, sir, that you don't know that it was Inspector Maduk that gave you that information?
A I can't recall.

Q You can't recall?
A The exact words.

Q No, in fact you don't recall him saying that, do you, Assistant Commissioner?
A As I am of the opinion he told me this, yes, that's all I can say. I can't be any more definite than that.

Q No. Just an opinion?
A Yes.

Q That he said that?
A Yes.

Q No recollection, just an opinion?
A This is what I recall.

Q Do you recall it or is it an opinion?
A This is what I say, this is my opinion that he was the one who had told me.

Q Could have been someone else?
A Could have been Chief Buchanan.

Q I see, it could have been Chief Buchanan or it could have been Inspector Maduk, anyone else?
A No.

Q So at least we have narrowed it down to two. And where, if it was Chief Inspector Buchanan, did you find out where he got his information?
A He interviewed the special I people.

Q Who is that, Chief Buchanan?
A Chief Buchanan.

Q Interviewed who?
A The special I people, Staff Sergeant Gislason, Williams and Deering.

Q Well then, would they be the persons who contacted the hotel clerk, well somebody must have contacted the hotel clerk because, "the unsubstantiated suspicion continued to the point that they contacted the clerk"?
A The Edmonton City Police.

Q Pardon?
A The Edmonton City Police.

Q Where did you get that information?
A I've told you.

Q Either Buchanan or Maduk?
A Or Maduk.

Q And you say Buchanan contacted the special I section?
A Right.

Q Well now, would the special I section have contacted the clerk or do you know?
A I don't know.

Q You don't know. Now then, "from there they were able to secure the master key," now as my learned friend Mr. Berger said, you used the word master key, did you get that from Buchanan or Maduk?
A That would have come from Maduk.

Q Oh, you are sure of that?
A Yes.

Q Well then —
A But I'm not sure of the wording master key or duplicate key, I was of the opinion they obtained a key to the room, now the master key, that word could be erroneous.

Q Well now, you have used the word master key, and if you got the master key, Assistant Commissioner, you'd have to go to some length in a hotel to get that, wouldn't you?
A I would think so, yes.

Q Pardon?
A I would think so, yes.

Q I would think so, and yet you put that in without being sure?
A Yes.

Q So that would indicate conduct on the part of the Edmonton City Police for which you had no substantiation whatsoever, isn't that so?
A I couldn't substantiate it, no.

Q No, but yet you put it in your report?
A I was of the opinion that that is what had occurred and I reported it to the CO —

Q Opinion based on what?

THE RCMP'S WARDROP
A particularly savory morsel.

A On information that I had.

Q From who?
A Maduk.

Q Did Maduk tell you that they had got the master key?
A I was of the opinion, from conversation with him, that they had obtained a key and tried —

Q A key?
A A key.

Q And yet you put master key?
A As I told you I used the word master, and it could have been a duplicate key, a key.

Q Well now you've told me sir, used the word master, they'd have to go to some length to get it?
A Yes.

Q And therefore I suggest to you, sir, that you are imputing conduct on the part of the Edmonton City Police for which you had no substantiation whatsoever, isn't that so?
A Yes.

Q Pardon?
A Yes, I can't prove it, no.

Q And yet you allege it in a report?
A Yes.

Q I used the word earlier, speculation, would you say that's what this is?
A No, not speculation.

Q Well it's either speculation or fabrication?
A It's not speculation.

Q Well then it must be fabrication?
A No, it's what I was led to believe.

Q Pardon?
A It was what I was led to believe.

Q And yet you can't give me any reason for that belief. Now then sir, with respect to dates, you stated that Inspector Maduk first told you it was the 11th, and from that you got two days later a sweep was conducted, is that correct?
A Yes.

Q That would make it the 13th?
A Right.

Q And then you learned that there was in fact an error, as I said you took two days from the 11th to the 13th?
A Yes.

Q Why did you take two days?
A I explained already that Maduk was in the room two days, and I presumed that it was, he was in the 11th and the 12th, and I just, it was the day after the two days that he was there that the sweep was done, and I calculated it to be the 13th.

Q Well then if that's the case then the sweep, the corrected version of the sweep would be the 12th, has to be if you took two days?
A It was the 11th.

Q Well now Assistant Commissioner —
A He was there two days, 9th and the 10th, 9th and the 10th, and the 11th you see is the day the sweep was, and I just had the 11th as being the first day he was there, the 12th being the second day and the 13th the day of the sweep.

Q If you go one day back, and that's what you are doing, then the sweep had to be conducted on the 12th?
A No, the 11th, he was there the 9th and the 10th, those were the two days that would have been equivalent to the 11th and the 12th.

Q I'm afraid you've left me somewhere Assistant Commissioner, if you took him as being there on the 11th, and two days later it was the 13th —
A 11th and 12th.

Q But you said the sweep originally was conducted on the 13th?
A I calculated it to be the 13th.

Q Yes, and you did that by taking two days from the 11th?
A That's correct.

Q If you go back one day to the 10th you get the 12th, don't you?
A It's the 11th, he was there two days, the 9th and the 10th, okay, and the third day is the 11th, right?

Q Well Commissioner, I'm just trying to go on your evidence. When do you say the sweep was conducted, Commissioner?
A As far as I'm concerned now it was done on the 11th.

THE STERN HARRADENCE
Was it fabrication or speculation?

Q Now it's on the 11th?
A Yes.

Q We've really come back three days haven't we, the 13th, the 12th and now the 11th, but you really don't know when it was conducted?
A I wasn't there, no.

Q But you are relying on information?
A Pardon?

Q You are relying on information?
A Yes.

Q Who did you get that from?
A Chief Buchanan first.

Q Chief Buchanan?
A Brought it to my attention.

Q Did he tell you of the date it was done?
A No.

Q Pardon?
A No, the time they were in the hotel I don't recall.

Q So you were just making assumptions again, were you?
A Well —

Q Looks that way, well it's to be that way, an assump an assumption really made w would be made to clear your r wouldn't that be it?
A No.

Q What was the assumption n for then?
A It's the information that I had.

Q The information that you No notes were kept?
A No.

Q Now then, what dormant file do you know what those files that were referred to by Mr. Berg
A I presume he was talking a the Royal American files had been supplied.

Q A presumption again?
A Well, I don't know.

Q You're the commanding officer,
A I can't tell you what he talking about.

Q Now, sir, you are the command officer of that division.
A These are the files that . . .

Q You don't know what files is talking about?
A I don't know.

Q Yet these are the dormant f which apparently corrected dates and you don't know what f he is talking about?
A No, I'm not sure.

Q Pardon?
A I'm not sure of what files is referring to, no, but I presu they were the Royal Ameri Shows.

Q You presume again?
A Yes.

Q You're speculating again?
A Yes.

Q In fact, this whole report speculation?
A No.

Q Yes.
A I don't believe it is, but . . .

Mr. Harradence: I have nothing furth Mr. Commissioner.

A radio reporter observed th Assistant Commissioner Wardrop w visibly trembling when he left the b He departed immediately for Winnipeg

Milt Harradence

When he strides into a courtroom, Calgary's Milt Harradence goes to war. Be it murder, rape, a traffic offence, spitting on the sidewalk, he'll take anything that walks into his office — you can't be too choosy in a city with a low crime rate — and jump right into the middle of things, swinging, sometimes missing, often connecting, creating confusion, wearing everyone down till he's the only one left to pick up the spoils. At 53, he's a tall, handsome, commanding presence who can often win a case simply on the force of his overpowering personality. And it doesn't have to be in a courtroom. Defending three jail prisoners charged with killing another, he convinced the Crown prosecutor before the trial that there wasn't much of a case against his clients, even though a jailer had overheard them boasting about what they'd done. "I don't know how he did it," says a lawyer, "but the Crown settled for pleas of *manslaughter*. Only Harradence could have pulled it off."

As a youngster near Prince Albert, Sask., Harradence was impressed by criminal lawyer John Diefenbaker, who often used to drop in to the family farm to chat with his parents. Harradence carries on many of Dief's tricks of the trade. The furrowed brow, the accusing finger, the rolling phrases. A trifle hammy, perhaps, but no one ever said Harradence was a great orator. He often says awkward things in court. "If you're *men*," he once told a jury, "you'll acquit my client." But more often, he's got an instinctive feel for the right move. Unlike most lawyers, Harradence rarely takes a note in the courtroom. "Who needs notes?" he says. "Guys are so busy writing, they don't get the courtroom atmosphere. There's a lot they miss by not looking around."

Unlike well-prepared lawyers, Harradence often bounces into court with his defence still unclear in his mind. "He's open to anything," says a Crown. "And he usually come up with something. Very quick to seize on a chink in our case and start chip, chip, chipping away. Even if there *is* no chink, he'll blow some little thing up till it almost seems like it might be something." A superb cross-examiner, he's especially good at destroying the testimony of doctors. "Very fragile egos," says Harradence. "They're used to asking questions, not answering them." Especially good in fraud in which, like the Shadow, he can cloud men's minds so that they know not what is truth and tend to throw the whole thing out of court.

Harradence once threw an army court martial into pandemonium when he told his client, charged with striking a superior, among other offences, not to appear in uniform. Then at the trial, Harradence pointed out with great relish that, without his uniform, his client could not be positively identified as a member of the armed forces and therefore was not liable to any military discipline whatsoever. The court threatened to throw *Harradence* in the can but then, sheepish, settled for a guilty plea on a reduced charge.

Though law is not his strong point, criminal law is, as someone once said, five per cent law and 95 per cent psychology. Harradence has the psychology. He'll often take a case for little money because it promises good action. Not that it's always appreciated. He packs a Walther PPK pistol and, while he won't say why, you get the feeling that a few clients have promised to look him up after they get out. If they don't think they got their money's worth from Harradence, they're obviously consumers who will never be satisfied. "In every case," says Harradence, "you leave a little bit of yourself behind in the courtroom."

Parlee, Irving, Henning, Mustard & Rodney

Barristers and Solicitors

W. O. PARLEE, Q.C.
W. M. MUSTARD, Q.C.
C. H. KERR
M. D. MACDONALD
J. T. BYRNE
S. F. GODDARD
M. J. TRUSSLER
R. B. DAVISON
W. J. KENNY
C. E. CAMPBELL
H. L. IRVING, Q.C.
M. C. RODNEY
L. S. WITTEN
T. A. COCKRALL
E. L. BUNNELL
C. R. HENNING
H. D. MONTEMURRO
N. G. CAMERON
T. E. SPRATLIN
D. B. LOGAN
COUNSEL:
HON. S. B. SMITH, Q.C., LL.D.
W. J. M. HENNING, Q.C.
A. T. MURRAY
R. A. NEWTON
K. F. BAILEY
R. J. BUTLER
A. B. SULATYCKY
J. D. KARVELLAS
D. M. GUNDERSON
D. J. ADAMS

27TH FLOOR, ALBERTA TELEPHONE TOWER
EDMONTON, ALBERTA, CANADA T5J 2V3
TELEPHONE (AREA CODE 403) 425-0810
TELEX 037-3509

IN REPLY PLEASE REFER TO:
S. Bruce Smith

2nd September, 1975.

Mr. A. M. Harradence, Q.C.
Barrister and Solicitor
502 Texaco Building
600 - 6th Avenue S.W.
CALGARY, Alberta.

Dear Milt;

I am enclosing for your records another copy of the Canadian Magazine of July 19, 1975. I congratulate you upon the great complimentary article about you. I have no doubt that you have already copies of it but I thought you might like to have another one.

I must say that I thought you were much more entitled to be classed amongst the top ten Canadian lawyers than some of the people described in the article.

My best wishes.

Yours sincerely,

Bruce Smith

S. Bruce Smith

SBS/eg
encls.

A. M. HARRADENCE, Q.C.
SUITE 810, BOW VALLEY SQUARE 2
205-5TH AVENUE S.W., BOX 9024
CALGARY, ALBERTA, CANADA
T2P 2W4

September 9th, 1975

Parlee, Irving, Henning, Mustard & Rodney,
Barristers and Solicitors,
27 Floor, Alberba Telephone Tower,
EDMONTON, Albetta.

Attention: Honourable S. B. Smith,
Q.C., LL.D.

My Dear Chief Justice:

Thank you for your very kind letter of September 2nd, 1975 and the enclosure.

It must be most gratifying to be associated again with your old firm, and we of the Bar are delighted to welcome you on your return to private practice.

I am frequently in Edmonton and would be most pleased if you would do me the honour of having lunch with me on one of these occasions.

Yours faithfully,

A. M. HARRADENCE, Q.C.

AMH/cp

C. D. Evans

Saturday, August 3, 1974. The Albertan.

The unpleasantness at the Paunchman's Club

A GATHERING of notables attended at Bos Taurus' famed Paunchman's Club last Thursday evening for the annual general meeting, which was followed immediately by the traditional Fishfry and Purloo.

Pandemonium erupted at the business meeting when Mr. David Grandchester, a rather modern young man, rose on a point of information to inquire as to the progress of an adjourned reference moving for full club membership for women. The motion he referred to had been tabled for further study in 1926.

The chairman repeatedly called for order during the ensuing uproar, and several of the older members were observed to wake up.

* * *

During a lull in the melee, Mr. Grandchester persisted in badgering the chairman on the point. In a moving address delivered to the backs of his outraged colleagues, he declared: "Surely in this epoch of a general lowering of inequitable barriers between men — uhh, ahh, that is, people — female persons should share our privileges to ring for a glass of sherry, to read the Manchester Guardian weekly supplement and to help us eat up all that 10-year-old cheese in the dining room."

Mr. Grandchester was forcibly removed from the great hall and sequestered with several of the elders. Anguished screams emanating from the top floor of the club could be heard into the early morning hours.

His wife, who had chained herself to the elegant blue canopy stanchion, was shot from an upstairs window by an unidentified member bearing an elephant gun.

* * *

Mr. Gladstone Carpetbagge then solemnly reminded the members that the principal object of the Paunchman's Club was the unobstructed perpetuation of a species of smugly superior landed gentry, namely, themselves, and that the so called "reforms" of sycophants, such as Mr. Grandchester, were but the ominous warning signs of a dread malaise inflicting society — creeping egalitarianism. Moreover, he admonished, it was a malaise that threatened to destroy all that the members held so dear: patronage, position, property and power. To lusty rebel yells of "The Four Ps! The Four Ps!". Mr. Carpetbagge was borne thrice about the great hall upon the shoulders of four Captains of Industry.

Further condemnation of Mr. Grandchester came from Colonel Blimp. With upraised forefinger and a great deal of hyperventilation, he cautioned the meeting that unless the dangerous ideas of idiots like Mr. Grandchester were ruthlessly suppressed at the outset, there was always the possibility, however remote, that the public might find out that the landed gentry of Bos Taurus were only farmers who had made their money so long ago that their origins had been decently forgotten.

In hushed tones, the Very Reverend Pontificatus called upon those present to join with him in prayer to the Great Cattle Baron for help in these troubled times. He assured the members that there was abundant Holy Writ from which they could conclude with reasonable certainty that the Big Four rode side by side up yonder with the Trinity. Expressing himself unalterably opposed to the imposition of cruel and unusual punishment, he nevertheless stated that Mr. Grandchester and others of his ilk should be lashed to within an inch of their miserable lives.

* * *

Someone cried "Face the flag!" and as one man the membership rose and burst spontaneously into Pomp and Circumstance March Number One. On that uplifting note, the business portion of the annual meeting adjourned to hear the boring guest speaker.

Hon. Willie Wooley, failed BA (Oxon), notorious local fop and buffoon, addressed divers overstuffed members in overstuffed chairs on "The Judicial Image: An Overspeaking Judge Is No Well-tuned Cymbal."

He began his address:

"My Lords the Most Appealing Justices, My Lord the Chief Justice of the Court of Common Please and Thankyous, My Lords, Your Honor the Chief Judge, Your Honors, Your Worship the Chief Magistrate, Your Worships, Your Majesty the Mayor, Your Lunacy the Lord High Poobah, Your Piousness the Reverend Archbishop, Your Old School Tieship the President, Honorary members, distinguished guests (including myself), undistinguished guests, gentlemen, and others . . ."

* * *

At this juncture, Mr. Wooley forgot where he was in his speech, gulped a brandy, and collapsed from fright and fumes.

He received a standing ovation, an honorarium, and an honorary life membership.

By the end of the evening, the unpleasantness at the Paunchman's Club had been decently forgotten.

4 August 1966

Dear Milt

Sorry it took so long to get these pictures to you. We have been very busy and the airline strike has put us behind the eight-ball.

First - I'd like to say thanks again for joining us during our Armed Forces Day week-end. I hope you had a nice trip home. People are still talking about that man in the yellow Mustang.

Lefty Gardner finally made it back to pick-up his P-38 Lightning. He left yesterday for Texas.

I'm leaving for St Petersburg, Florida, August 18th. I'll fill you in on all the details in October at the CAF Air Show.

Say hello to Jim Knowler for me.

With warmest regards

Mel

MELVIN L. DUPAUL
Major, USAF

APPENDIX

DEPARTMENT OF THE AIR FORCE
HEADQUARTERS 2750TH AIR BASE WING (AFLC)
WRIGHT-PATTERSON AIR FORCE BASE OHIO 45433

16 February 1967

FEB 20 1967
CALGARY, ALBERTA

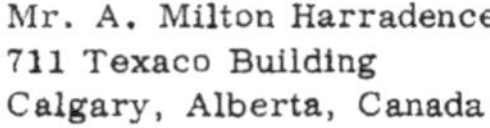

Mr. A. Milton Harradence
711 Texaco Building
Calgary, Alberta, Canada

Dear Mr. Harradence

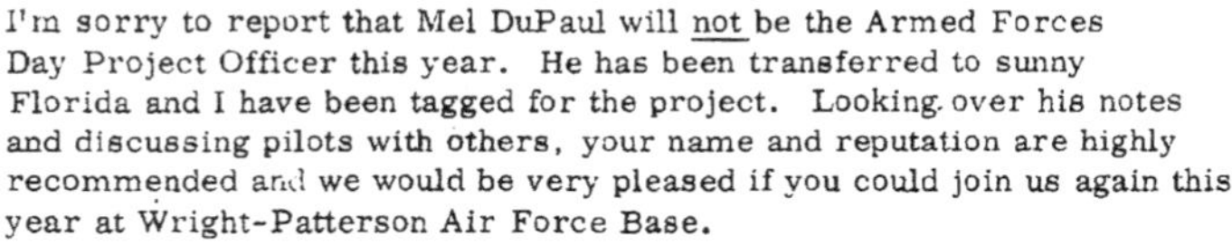

I'm sorry to report that Mel DuPaul will not be the Armed Forces Day Project Officer this year. He has been transferred to sunny Florida and I have been tagged for the project. Looking over his notes and discussing pilots with others, your name and reputation are highly recommended and we would be very pleased if you could join us again this year at Wright-Patterson Air Force Base.

Since we are also celebrating our (Wright-Patterson AFB) 50th anniversary, we hope to have a very interesting show. Your Confederate Colonels are planning on attending again this year and we are all looking forward to an enjoyable and memorable get together.

All of the arrangements will be approximately the same as last year. If there is any way I can be of service to make your trip a success, please write or call me at the following address:

Lt Colonel Harold H. Sperber
2750th Air Base Wing (EWO)
Wright-Patterson Air Force Base, Ohio 45433
(Office phone: Area Code 513, telephone 257-3521
or 257-3980)

With warmest regards.

Sincerely

HAROLD H. SPERBER
Lt Colonel, USAF
Armed Forces Day Project Officer

Aerobatic Display By '1st Canadian'

By JIM KNOWLER
[Herald Staff Writer]

DAYTON, Ohio — Calgary's Milt Harradence, handling his P-51 Mustang like a fighter ace, performed aerobatics during Armed Forces Open House at Wright-Patterson Air Force base near here at the weekend.

Flying in overcast but rainless skies Saturday, Mr. Harradence flew for about 30,000 spectators, and returned Sunday on a bright and sunny day for about 124,000 people, who crowded the mammoth base to watch almost six hours of air demonstrations.

The show attracted static exhibits from Canada, England and the U.S., but Mr. Harradence was the only foreign flyer to be invited to participate in the actual flying display. He is the first Canadian to fly in the show's long history.

The base lays claim to the title "birthplace of aviation," as the Wright brothers were raised in the area and flew their short but historic junkets from mid-Ohio farm fields.

Mr. Harradence, well-known in his Mustang to western Canadian aviation buffs, flew as part of the Confederate Air Force's 30 - minute demonstration of Second World War fighter aircraft.

A. M. Harradence

City Man To Fly In U.S.

A Calgary man has been invited to participate as the first Canadian flyer in Air Force Day Open House, at Wright-Patterson Air Force base at Dayton, Ohio.

A. M. Harradence will fly a P-51 Mustang in the show, the largest air demonstration in North America.

Mr. Harradence, once the owner of a P-51, is a member of the Confederate Air Force of Texas, and will fly an aircraft belonging to that organization. The Confederates will send a six-aircraft display.

200,000 EXPECTED

Major M. L. DuPaul, officer in charge of the USAF show, said the open house, a two-day show on May 21 and 22, will attract more than 200,000 people.

"We chose Mr. Harradence to put on his aerobatics display, because many of us have seen him, and know there is no one in the world who can fly the Mustang the way he does," he said.

Major DuPaul said never has a Canadian, military or civilian, flown in the show.

The air field at Dayton is used annually for the show and is the home of the Wright brothers, the recognized fathers of flying.

WIDE VARIETY

The show will include most of the major aerobatic fliers from the U.S., an army paratrooping display, a SAC bomber wing, static displays from the RAF, a one-hour fly-past, air refueling, ice-testing and seat ejection demonstrations, military and private ground exhibits, antique aircraft and car displays, and model aircraft.

Mr. Harradence will stage a 10 - minute flying display on each of the two days.

APPENDIX

THE HONOURABLE A. MILTON HARRADENCE
JUSTICE OF APPEAL

COURT OF APPEAL OF ALBERTA

COURT HOUSE
611-4TH STREET S. W.
CALGARY, ALBERTA
T2P 1T5

October 5, 1982

Lady Joan Bader
Withers Farm
Marlston, Hermitage
Newbury, Berks.
RG16 9UR
England

My Dear Joan:

It was with shock and sorrow that I learned of Douglas' passing. Shock because death is only visited upon mere mortals and I could never conceive of Douglas in that mould.

Sorrow for many reasons, some selfish in that I looked forward to his visits to Calgary with great anticipation.

When in his company I found his zest for life contagious. The courage and fortitude that he constantly displayed revealed a depth of spirit that enriched the lives of all of us fortunate enough to call him friend.

It was one of my proudest and happiest moments, when at the dinner given in his honour by the University of Calgary last November, Catherine and I were named as close friends of yours in the City of Calgary.

Sorrow also because the world is in desperate need of heroes and his leaving this earthly scene creates an aching void.

The example that he set by triumph over personal adversity, his inspirational leadership and magnificent courage in conflict, in peace his untiring and selfless dedication to instil hope and restore confidence to those physically afflicted have earned him a special place amongst England's great. In the words of Edward M. Stanton:

"Now he belongs to the ages."

Catherine and I grieve with you and extend our deepest sympathy. We hope in the near future your plans include a visit to Calgary and we look forward to seeing you at that time.

Sincerely,

Milton

P.S. Please forgive me for not writing this in my own hand but my writing for the most part is illegible.

The Calgary Sun, Thursday, March 10, 1983 11

Evans and the CBC

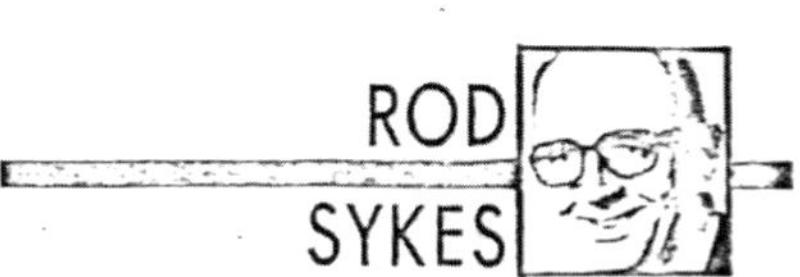

Have you noticed the new fashion in half-glasses? It produces those topless spectacles, and all sorts of people who wouldn't normally want to be considered a topless spectacle are buying them: Judges, lawyers, planners and all who want to look intellectual when they aren't really qualified. In fact, we have a whole new crop of half-glassed experts.

* * *

Herge has died in Brussels at the age of 75. For the sake of those who don't read comic-strip books, I should say that he was the most successful children's author of his time. His characters were Tintin, the innocent boy detective; Tintin's much more intelligent little dog, Milou; and his great friend, the rather dimwitted Englishman, Capitaine Haddock. There were over 50 million books printed in more than 30 languages, as well as a number of movies and records. I have most of the books and most of the records, and they're still fun.

What brought this to mind was one C.D. Evans, since the passing of Milt Harradence one of the city's most prominent criminal lawyers.

Harradence (long may he live) is not dead but he has passed away from the life that the rest of us live, since he became a Justice of the Court of Appeal. He was never one of your dull-as-ditchwater lawyers when he practiced. I well remember the slogan of my friends of the criminal classes: When you're guilty, call for Milty. His passing could have taken a good deal of the fun and the excitement of life, were it not for Evans, who now fills Milt's vacant elastic-sided boots.

While Evans is undoubtedly an excellent lawyer, particularly if your case looks hopeless, he is also quite bright in a lunatic way; and it was not until the other day, being interviewed by Evans on CBC, that Tintin came to my mind and I suddenly realized that Evans was Capitaine Haddock to the life. That was the great thing about Herge; his characters were absolutely believable. (Some people may think Evans is not, but they're wrong).

When interviewing, Evans lays a trap for the unsuspecting interviewee: He lets his face relax so that he looks witless. The party of the other part usually falls into the trap, whereupon Evans moves in for the kill, his face transformed by a lively expression of evil delight. By that time, it is too late for the hapless interviewee and the CBC sends for the disposal squad and plastic bags, and starts looking for another victim.

That is Capitaine Haddock to the life, the vacant expression followed by the sudden and unexpected action; but what is more to the point is that both Evans and Haddock look alike: Both are furry creatures, furry but by no means cuddly. Haddock's hair and his beard run together in wild confusion. Evans looks the same, like a Persian cat, you know — throw a bucket of water on it and nothing's left but a scrawny wretch, Haddock (or Evans) to the life.

I don't know when our interview will be broadcast, because we had a thoroughly lively and enjoyable chat but the CBC seems to be nervous about showing it. I've told them that if they tamper with it, I'll write a column about CBC censorship, and Evans will probably sue them. He's good at that. The trouble with the CBC, I think, is that when they get off familiar ground like abortion, aboriginal rights, women's liberation, perverts' rights, native land claims and acid rain, they're completely lost. They want to change the world but, because they're on the public payroll, they're trying to do it without anyone noticing.

That leads me to something very funny: I said that Evans was furry, long hair, beard and all arranged like the bottom of a neglected garden. Well, the CBC knew that when they signed him up to a contract for interviews, because how could you miss it? After the interviews started, however, they got swamped with complaints about this long-haired creature from outer space and, being the CBC, they started to worry.

Now when I say "swamped," you must read that the CBC way: It means more than three, all the same day. (When you have an audience the size of their's, your scale of measurement has to be adjusted.) Anyway, the CBC called Evans in for a heart-to-heart talk about his looks. That was a mistake. At first he thought it was breath, or perhaps the old Lifebuoy problem, because those would come to mind naturally when some nitwit clearly didn't want to say in plain English what it was he wanted to tell you; but finally Evans, who is skilled in the art of cross-examination, established that the CBC was upset about his face. That was no shock to him, because so was his mother, when first she saw him, and so was the law society some years later.

Evans pointed out that they had approached him to host the interview program, that they had made him do tests and that he hadn't worn his head in a bag, and that they had negotiated a contract for his services, which contract did not require him to alter his appearance or wear a mask to spare a CBC audience. They admitted all charges, and then planned their trump card with pride: "The corporation is prepared to pay to have your hair and beard trimmed." That was the offer. No wonder there's a deficit — now it's personal grooming at public expense. Where will it end?

The upshot is that, admitting no responsibility or liability, Evans now ties his hair back with a little rubber band just as schoolgirls do; although, speaking personally, I think schoolgirls suit the style better. The CBC does not supply the rubber bands, however. Honor is satisfied and the show goes on — but when are they going to broadcast the Evans-Sykes interview? What are they afraid of? I'll keep you posted. Meanwhile, watch for C.D. Evans — a good man behind all the hair and whiskers.

THE CHANCELLOR
THE UNIVERSITY OF CALGARY

December 6, 1976

Mr. A. M. Harradence, Q.C.
810 Bow Valley Square Two
205 - 5 Avenue S. W.
Box 9024
Calgary, Alberta T2P 2W4

Dear Milt:

Further to my letter of last July regarding the annual fund drive for the Chancellor's Club. Because you are a valued member of the Club, I did not want you to miss the opportunity of making your donation before the end of the year.

A minimum contribution of $100 (tax-deductible) per member each year is necessary in order that we may continue to operate the Club in the manner that has become the custom.

I appreciate your support and look forward to seeing you in February at our formal dinner for members and spouses.

Sincerely,

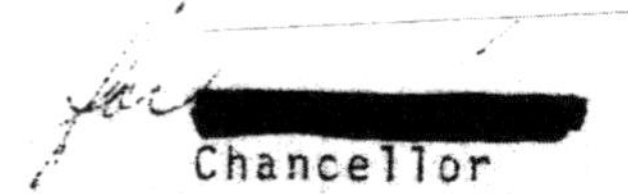

Chancellor

APPENDIX

A. M. HARRADENCE, Q.C.
SUITE 810, BOW VALLEY SQUARE 2
205-5TH AVENUE S.W., BOX 9024
CALGARY, ALBERTA, CANADA
T2P 2W4

PERSONAL AND CONFIDENTIAL

December 8th, 1976

The Chancellor's Club,
The University of Calgary,
2920 - 24 Avenue N.W.,
CALGARY, Alberta.
T2N 1N4

Attention: [redacted]
Chancellor

Dear [redacted]:

Thank you very much for your letter of last July and your letter dated December 6th, 1976.

With the passing of time, I find that I have less and less in common with the academic community and it would seem that the only contact I have with the community or representatives thereof, is when a donation is sought.

I feel that perhaps this would be as good an opportunity as any, to make it clear that under these circumstances it is perhaps in the best interest of both the community and myself to sever whatever tenuous relationship exists.

I would not close without wishing you and your Club every success in the future.

Yours sincerely,

A. M. Harradence

A. M. HARRADENCE, Q.C.

AMH/cp

A. R. Roberts
Security Consultants

Sept. 19.1996.
803-Piermont Place..
VICTORIA, B.C..
V8S 5J7.

THE HONOURABLE BRIAN STEVENSON
Assistant Chief Judge
The Provincial Court Building,
323-6 Ave. S.E.
Calgary, Alberta.
T2G 4V1

Dear Brian:

What a pleasant suprise to hear from you and especially to hear about the dinner for Milt. I have purposely held off on replying to you letter hoping that I may be able to attend but am sorry to say that I will not be able to for the following reasons.

I am presently recovering from a quadruple heart by-pass operation and have been advised by my doctor not to travel any distance away from home. Also during the last year I have had a fusion of the lower spine, a double hernia operation and just last week have come down with "Bells Palsey"

I was so hoping that I might be able to attend but I am afraid I just wont be able to make it. However I will be there inspirit and can well imagine some of the great stories that will ensue. As you are well aware Milt and I were friendly adversaries and I truly consider him a great friend.

I also received a letter from Susan De Demers, Secty. to Madame Justice Carole Conrad asking for a "brief remininisence" on some of the stories I remember about Milt. I am unable to get over to Vancouver Brian so I am going to take the liberty of enclosing my remarks in this letter to you as I know you will no doubt have some dandy stories to tell and you might just be able to mention a couple of my thoughts on the matter.

If I had but one word to describe Milt Harradence it would be "flamboyant". When I was first working homicide I can remember Milt in his satorical elegance addressing the court with that crooked smile of his and then glowering at the witness. Later during my career as Chief Inspector In Charge of the Detective Division I had on a number of occasions had to appear in court on a serious charge where Milt was the defence lawyer. As you may vbe aware Brian I had an avid interest in Interrogation Techniques and had a fair amount of succss

A. R. Roberts
Security Consultants

page 2.

One of my most vivid memory of Milt was during a murder case where Milt was appearing for the accused and I was giving evidence on a statement that I took from the accused . Milt asked me about the accused's behaviour prior to giving the statement. His demenour ? His emotional state? Was he crying? I truthfully answere yes he was sir and with that Milt in his own inimitable way asked, "And I suppose Chief Inspector you were crying too were you? And to that I answere "just a little sir"

During my time on the force I do not know a police officer that did no t admire , somewhat fear but most certainly respect His Lordship Milt HARRADENCE.

During the latter years on the force and also when I became Director o f Security for Ron Souther's group of companies I enjoyed the lecture cicuit .

I lectured to many a advanced training and intelligence course at Ottawa R.C.P. Police College, B.C. Police College, ReginaPolice College many police forces in the U.S.A. from Texas, New York, California, Arizona and last but now least the FBI training Accademy at Quantico, Virginia and on each and every one of them I would mention Milt HARRADENCE's performance and cross examination.

I personally admire Milt and consider him a friend and I only wish I was there to give him my regards wihich I hope you'll might do for me Brian. Thank you again for the invitation and I know it will be an outstanding success.

Yours Truly,

Art Roberts,
Ex-Chief Inpsector
Detective Division.

CHIEF JUSTICE OF B.C. ALLAN McEACHERN

CHIEF JUSTICE McEACHERN: Well, good evening, I am delighted to be joined in such distinguished company to offer a tribute to my old friend, Milt Harradence, and I bring greetings from all his friends in British Camelot where, as everyone knows, it only rains at night.

I have been given a pretty specific instruction from Madam Justice Conrad to keep it brief and she has given me a script that I will attempt to follow. I was first asked to say what I remember about Milt when he was young. Well, I didn't know Milt when he was young but I have heard lots of stories and I wonder if anyone remembers the time when Milt came to Calgary with the Saskatchewan football team and painted the Calgary campus green. I am told that was not well received in Calgary.

I was next asked to give my most vivid memory of Milt and I have to say that there are a number of possibilities. The first one is the very first time he came into my office he introduced himself, looked furtively around my office and said, "Has this place been swept?" I replied that it had not. He looked troubled and said, "Let's go for a walk," which we did. In the same thing, I was visiting him in Calgary one time and after working very late in his office he agreed to walk me back to my hotel. He was on my left and as we crossed the entrance to a lane on my right we heard a sound up the lane. I looked to my right to see what it was and when I looked back I was staring in the largest gun barrel that I had ever seen. And that's the kind of excitement that one experiences when associated with Milt.

I was next asked to give my favourite story about Milt. Well, there are many, but one that I would like to record if it hasn't already been used is a poem that I am told was written about Milt and it went like this:

"It was Judgment Day in the Court of Appeal
and all the judgments were read. Harradence
allowed a Crown appeal and everyone dropped
dead."

I also like Milt's description of a long trial that he and I shared somewhat unsuccessfully for our clients here in Vancouver. Milt described it to me later in these graphic terms. He said, "After the trial was over, our two clients went jail, the Prosecutor went to the hospital and we both went to the Bench."

I have been asked to say something about Milt that I will never forget and the thing that I remember about Milt from a general impression point of view is his incredible professionalism. Despite his well-known reputation as a high profile, immaculately dressed, well-instructed criminal lawyer with great style and poise, Milt was always a perfect professional in court. He dressed appropriately. He was respectful to the court. He treated witnesses fairly and he was in every respect a lawyer that any young person aspiring to a career at the Bar could well follow him as his example.

His style of cross-examination was always well-rehearsed, very careful. He would stand perfectly dressed, stare at the witness with a rather studied carelessness. He would begin with a few innocuous questions and then as he got to the heart of the matter, there would be a hardening somewhat in the attitude and he put questions to which he knew there was only one answer. Milt, in my view, was one of the great cross-examiners of all time and I always admired his remarkable style.

The next one that I have been asked to say is who could help but admire something about Milt. I have already mentioned that. What I admire about Milt was one I have already said and his magnificent presence in court. He was a counsel worthy of the reputation he earned and was, in my view, one of the top Canadian counsel of this or any other generation.

I was asked to say what was Milt's best advice. The best advice I ever heard Milt give was simply, "Don't call your client if you don't have to."

I was asked if I could describe Milt in one word and that's very easy to do. The one word to describe Milt is "class". Milt was a classy lawyer and a classy person and I am proud to have had him as a friend. Thank you.

CHIEF JUSTICE OF THE SUPREME COURT OF CANADA ANTONIO J. LAMER

CHIEF JUSTICE LAMER: Dear Justice Harradence, better known as Milt. As the Chief Justice of Canada, let me say that I am delighted to bring greetings. Congratulations and thanks on behalf of the Canadian judiciary for the tremendous mark you have made on the legal system during your years both as counsel and as a member of the judiciary. I know that your friends, your colleagues and the members of this court will miss you, although I must say that we here in Ottawa probably will welcome the diminution in the dissents that contributed to our statistics as regards appeals as of right.

Speaking personally, I am also very grateful for the fact that Canada's geography has prohibited you and I coming together as boxers as I did, as you, for a while engage in that sport which as you well know is somewhat less popular now than it used to be.

On behalf of the members of the Supreme Court of Canada, I know there will be a couple of them there, and of the Canadian judiciary, let me wish you a happy and prosperous retirement and congratulate you on all of your accomplishments. Bonne chance, bonne retraite, et au revoir.

ICE JOHN SOPINKA SUPREME COURT OF CANADA

ICE SOPINKA: I congratulate you, Milt, on years of outstanding service to the country, both as a leading counsel and as a judge in Appeal. I do, however, with a certain touch of sadness because we are losing a rugged individualist on the Bench who always had principle in mind and was his own man.

Both as counsel and a judge, you had the knack of getting to the heart of the matter immediately, whether it was the weakness of the case or the strength of the case. By way of illustration, I recall our first encounter when we had a case before the Canada Labour Relations Board here in Ottawa. We were both opposing certification of a union. I was acting for the company and you acted for a so-called independent union. The allegation against you was that your client and particularly the president of the so-called independent union was merely a puppet of the employer. Your first question to the president who you called as a witness was: "Sir, I understand that you were present during the crossing of the Yalu." That put to rest any doubt that your client was a puppet of anybody.

This same knack was carried into your judgments and while frequently in dissent, they certainly tended to keep the majority on their toes.

Milt, all the best on your retirement, we shall miss you.

JUSTICE MILT HARRADENCE

Calgary legal eagle soars to retirement

Dean Bicknell, Calgary Herald

HARRADENCE: Hundreds will honor him at Palliser Hotel dinner

HELEN DOLIK
Calgary Herald

A rookie lawyer stared at the rifle and the clip of live ammunition in the open ashtray of Milt Harradence's white Cadillac.

The gun's butt was on the floor and its barrel pointed up. He asked Harradence — rated one of the top 10 lawyers in Canada at the time and on his way to being named a judge — if it was an exhibit for a trial.

"No, son," Harradence told Noel O'Brien, now a prominent Calgary criminal lawyer. "There have been some threats on my life."

Asked to describe Justice Asa Milton Harradence, people use words such as: Maverick, integrity, forcefulness, champion, defender, horror — this from a person he cross-examined — and friend.

He's made a difference in many live[s] — from an angry, young con who took the straight and narrow, to a heavyweight Olympic boxer-turned-lawyer. His friends are police officers, lawyer[s], judges, the political and business elite and Alberta Premier Ralph Klein.

Close to 700 people are expected to pay tribute to Harradence at the state[ly] Palliser Hotel Wednesday at a black-tie, $60-plate dinner to celebrate his co[l]orful and distinguished career. It's believed to be the largest legal dinner in Alberta history.

The dinner sold out in less than a month so a second room with closed-circuit TV was added to handle the overflow. Harradence is due to retire next April when he turns 75.

See Harradence, Page A[5]

HARRADENCE . . . continued from Page A1

He's a man who belies his age. Harradence never takes the courthouse elevator. He climbs the stairs — two at a time.

O'Brien will be one of the 700 at the dinner. He was a young nobody when they met two decades ago, freshly minted from law school in Ontario and looking for a [illegible]red after 2½ days in a windowless office at a Calgary corporate law firm.

O'Brien phoned Harradence — a charismatic criminal-courtroom star, widely ranked the best in the West — at home on a July long weekend.

Meet me at the Owl's Nest for breakfast at the Westin, offered Harradence. They spent the day together, including a memorable ride in Harradence's signature Caddy — the Miltmobile, as one close friend affectionately called it.

Harradence hired him on the spot and O'Brien will always remember the legal legend took the time to mentor a wet-behind-the-ears lawyer.

> "He was like a two-gun bolt of lightning in a courtroom"
>
> **Lawyer Chris Evans**

Harradence is a former boxer, pilot, politician, lawyer, and since 1979, a respected judge at the Alberta Court of Appeal in Calgary.

"There are a lot of mimics but not anyone who has reached that particular plateau," says O'Brien.

He kept a gun under his desk, in his car and strapped to his ankle. Death threats occurred frequently enough that Harradence was one of the few Canadians granted a permit to carry a concealed, restricted weapon.

Even in the hushed lobby of the appeal court, his mini-biography on the wall notes his habit of carrying hidden sidearms "to the consternation of his colleagues and bemusement of the bar."

Harradence was a Calgary alderman and a former leader of the Alberta Tory party, but he's best known as the stylish, flamboyant lawyer who championed the un[illegible]g and roamed the skies in private fighter planes. He's defended accused cops, murderers and fugitives. Some cases he did for free.

"He was like a two-gun bolt of lightning in a courtroom," says lawyer Chris Evans, a close friend and the dinner's master of ceremonies. "You never knew where he was going to strike, and he was deadly."

Calgary's flying lawyer once landed a movie role in a war film, but it rained for 18 consecutive days on location in Spain. The weather cleared just as he had to leave for the courts of Calgary. He owned three aircraft: a Mustang, a Vampire and an F-86 Sabre.

Blessed with movie-idol good looks, Harradence favored French cuffs and suits. While other counsel slapped on jeans and T-shirts for weekend office work, casual dress for Harradence consisted of an ascot and dress pants.

As a practising lawyer, his office was opulent with floor-to-ceiling crushed velvet drapes, a red carpet and leather couch. One client, following Harradence into his office, removed his shoes before walking in.

There are reports of spectators cheering him in a Saskatchewan courtroom and carrying him out on their shoulders. He's an honorary colonel of the 416 Tactical Fighter Squadron in Cold Lake and the only judge who's an honorary member of the Calgary Police Veterans Association.

In the 1970s, he was asked by the province to look into charges of brutality by guards on prisoners at the Calgary Correctional Institute. The 1974 report of his one-man inquiry cleared the guards but attacked the prison system, saying government agencies were "abysmally ignorant of the fundamental facts of prison life."

"To call the Spy Hill Jail the Calgary Correctional Institute is akin to calling Attila the Hun a diplomat," the report said.

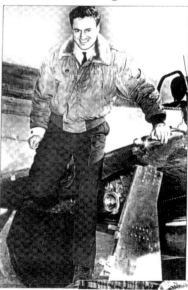

Judge has three loves – family, the law and flying

To a visitor, Milton Harradence's office at the Alberta Court of Appeal is more museum than workplace.

Almost every square inch of wall is covered with photos, plaques, mementos, awards, miniature flags and aeronautic memorabilia.

A table near his desk holds pictures of his three children, including son Rod, killed in plane crash in 1986. The office reflects the three loves of his life: Family, the law and flying. He's married to Catherine.

The person who most influenced him was former prime minister John Diefenbaker — a family friend.

"As a boy, I came under his spell because we both lived in Prince Albert," Harradence says. "He is the reason I decided on a career at the bar. I had the privilege of watching him in action at the courthouse in Prince Albert.

"When he walked into a courtroom, he completely dominated, and when he rose to cross-examine, the atmosphere was electrified."

The late Second World War ace Douglas [illegible] who lost two legs prior to the [illegible] inspired Harradence. His [illegible]onality and vitality are something I shall never forget."

Just as Harradence looked up to Diefenbaker, a number of lawyers view Harradence as their mentor. Former boxer and Olympic silver medalist Willie de Wit, now a lawyer at Evans Martin Wilson, springs to mind.

De Wit met Harradence in 1982, and the two kindled a friendship after a dressed-to-the-nines Harradence visited the sweaty gym to watch the well-known heavyweight boxer train. In his youth, Harradence boxed at the University of Saskatchewan, where he was the middleweight champion.

For de Wit, whose dad died in 1987, Harradence is part father figure, mentor and close friend. After de Wit retired from the ring in 1988, Harradence suggested he return to school. 'What about law school?' he asked de Wit.

De Wit respects Harradence's advice and wisdom, and values their discussions.

"He's the most honest person I've ever met," says de Wit.

Pat Graham, 67, executive director of the Seventh Step Society of Canada — an agency that assists offenders rehabilitate through self help — credits Harradence with playing a major part in getting him out of prison and keeping him out. They've known each other for 40 years, and when Graham, at age 50, graduated from university, one of Harradence's sons received his degree at the same time. Harradence was there to congratulate them both.

"He was my lawyer, my friend and kind of a role model," says Graham, his voice warm as he talks about Harradence.

"I always maintain there are a number of people who helped me change my thinking, my attitude and eventually my behavior, and Milt was certainly at the top of the list."

Graham used to go watch Harradence cross-examine witnesses — "he would just tear a person to bits."

Harradence rarely took notes of testimony. He kept his eyes on the witness. He was courteous to a fault, but deadly as a cobra. He owned this disarming smile — some described it as a wolfish grin, while others thought it closer to a shark — then whamo!

Peter Tarrant, a veteran Calgary private investigator who has worked for hundreds of lawyers, including Harradence, at more than 60 law firms in the world, says "they broke the mould with Milt."

Tarrant remembers Harradence dragging him across Chinook Centre into a jewelry store to meet a woman during the busy Christmas shopping season. He had bumped into Harradence at the mall.

"Madam," he said, with a theatrical flourish. "This is the man you want to thank. . . . Don't thank me, you have to thank my investigator."

She was the sister of a wrongly accused bus driver in a case 25 years ago. Harradence had represented the driver, the attempted sex assault charge had been dropped and she'd wanted to thank the lawyer all these years.

■■■

There were no boundaries to work and leisure for Harradence. Following a rare vacation to Hawaii, he drove straight to the office before unpacking at home.

He embraced the new technology of car phones. His law students wore beepers. Midnight and early morning calls were routine.

Calgary lawyer Brad Nemetz, who used to work with Harradence and now toils at Bennett Jones Verchere, recalls taking a mountain-climbing trip to British Columbia. Harradence wanted to know how to contact him.

Nemetz painstakenly explained that the only way he could possibly be reached was to phone the heli-ski lodge. The lodge could then radio the alpine hut and someone could be dispatched on foot across the glacier to find him.

"What's the number?" Harradence asked.

■■■

Harradence was appointed to the Court of Appeal in 1979, leaving behind a thriving practice and jangling phones.

"I think most counsel subconsciously anticipate spending the final year of their legal careers on the bench," says Harradence. "However, there is always great reluctance to leave the practice. As someone said: going to the bench is like going to heaven — but not yet!"

After 28 of years as a lawyer, Harradence felt it was time to move on. "What I miss most about leaving the practice is the fact that you are no longer a competitor but rather a referee — and the transition isn't easy."

Harradence is frequently asked what he'll do once he hangs up his judicial robes in April. "Put my feet up and watch the world go by," he says.

When asked if he had any regrets, he says just one. "That the demands of my practice cut heavily into time with my family. If I were to do it over again that's one change I'd make."

Milt and I have a common background in aviation but I did not appreciate his competence and skill as an advocate until I had the pleasure of having him appear before me as Counsel. It was at that time that I became aware of his dedication to the cause of justice and his devotion to the rights of an accused person. Let it be said, however, he never ignored the need to protect society from those who were guilty of criminal conduct and was not overly lenient in imposing sentences on those who did.

Sitting on a Panel with Milt was always stimulating, and at times, an exciting experience. I recall an occasion when we, as a result of Milt's persuasive advocacy, had reduced a sentence and Milt was giving one of his forceful lectures to the Appellant. Milt gave him that well know penetrating stare and said:

> "If I see you back here I'll bury you do deep that they'll have to pipe oxygen to you through a straw."

I am pleased to have the opportunity to record one instance of Milt's failure to live up to his reputation of being a leader in sartorial splendour. At one formal function, he admired the shoes I was wearing. He inquired about them and at great expense duplicated them. --Please note this footwear at our next formal function.

IN THE COURT OF APPEAL OF ALBERTA
EDMONTON CRIMINAL SITTINGS
HEARD JANUARY 30, 1997

IN THE MATTER OF THE LAST SITTINGS
OF THE HONOURABLE MR. JUSTICE A.M. HARRADENCE

THE COURT:
THE HONOURABLE MR. JUSTICE J.W. McCLUNG
THE HONOURABLE MR. JUSTICE A.M. HARRADENCE
THE HONOURABLE MR. JUSTICE R.L. BERGER

MR. JUSTICE MCCLUNG:
Good morning. I want to, on behalf of the Judges of the Alberta Court of Appeal, welcome all of you to this informal ceremony honouring our friend, Mr. Justice A. Milton Harradence of Calgary on the occasion of this his last Edmonton sittings.

At the outset I want to say that Mr. Justice Harradence, despite his Spartan stature and youthful countenance, will attain his seventy-fifth birthday in April. By that he is exposed to a declaration of "Statutory Senility" and he will be forced to leave this Court which he has served with energy and dedication for some eighteen years. Mr. Justice Harradence's judicial career, I think, can be summed up as the fullest extension of his lifelong passion for due process of law and the preservation of our fundamental liberties, and if it is possible to encapsulate the Harrandencian jurisprudence in one sentence, it would be that first uttered by Mr.l Justice Joseph Storey of the United States Supreme Court some 150 years ago and it is as follows:

"Sitting here, we are not at liberty to add one jot of power to the National Government beyond what the people have granted it by the Constitution."

Now I will call upon representatives of the Edmonton Bar to address His Lordship. First I will ask Mr. Jack Watson, Q.C., Appellate Counsel of the Provincial Department of Justice.

MR. WATSON:

I get a chance here today, I understand, to address three co-counsel on a case, but it will not form part of my remarks. These, of course, are remarks that I have prepared that are entitled Remarks On The Occasion of "Milt's Last Case".

It falls to me as the grizzled veteran of the Alberta appellate justice system to pay homage to one of the outstanding 'characters' of the Alberta legal community on the occasion of his last case. While put in mind of the John Mortimer story, "Rumpole's Last Case", I must immediately say that there is nothing to compare in the sense of physiognomy or physique between that fictional character and the subject of my remarks. Indeed, there is more to compare in physical structure between myself and Rumpole. I will say more of this anon.

There is a sadness, of course, with the retirement of any person of such signal attributes as The Honourable Mr. Justice A. M. Harradence of the Court of Appeal who was, incidentally, one of the very few judges ever appointed directly to the Court of Appeal. I must confess, though, that one of the things that troubles me some is that when I think about the fact that you are retiring from the Court of Appeal and I had criminal trial experience with you myself, I begin to hear footsteps. In the legal profession, one must always remember what Satchel Paige said about never looking behind you.

Nonetheless, I choose to look back somewhat. I must apologize in advance for lacking the wordsmithery skills of the panel President here. My remarks will be nothing in comparison to the well-deserved tributes given to you on November 2, 1996, in Calgary, when luminaries of all sorts turned out in your home base of Calgary to speak highly and humourously about you. There was an article in the Calgary Sun, and I pause to mention, yes, it was the Calgary Sun, not he Herald, which duly and compactly described the matter as "Justice Served". Despite our differences of opinion, you being a lawyer and Judge and me being a civil servant with a law degree, I harbour no doubt about your contribution to Justice in Alberta.

Let me say that it has been, I believe, my anointed task to strive mightily over the years to try my absolute best to draw back Judges of the Court of Appeal of Alberta from the brink of error on which they routinely teeter. With respect to yourself, I know that your strength of personality is such that you cannot be drawn anywhere.

This brings me back to that old hackneyed phrase well-applied to yourself about being the great dissenter. I was always happy that you were dissenting in cases of mine. It is when you wrote majority judgments that I was in trouble.

Let us not forget, though, how easily it comes to all of us to celebrate your long and distinguished service. Indeed, you have the ability to attract attention to yourself, not the least of which by the elegance of your dress, the dignity of your bearing and that sonourous voice of yours. It does not surprise me a bit that they should, last fall, have had a video cameraman and others interviewing staff in this building for the purpose of some sort of Lucasfilm or 20th Century Fox production about you. You were a natural for the movies. I am left to recall that it seems to me that either you, or your airplane, had a cameo role in a movie called The Battle of Britain some years back. It strikes me that if that is so, you probably were paid to union scale for that acting performance. No doubt that is the only time in your life when you ever had to work down to scale. Your sartorial choice, if anything, belies this. As a young prosecutor I was routinely told of the mystical power that you had over the Courts. You were a stemwinding speaker. I can recall one day watching you in action before Judge Lucien Maynard in Docket Court here in Edmonton, and your formidable address to him put Cicero to shame. There was not a dry eye in the house, except, perhaps for the learned Judge. His response was, "Thank you, Mr. Harradence. Bail Refused." This brings me to another story at which I will close my remarks and turn the podium over to my long time friends and colleagues Alex Pringle and Shelagh Creagh, in order to say a few words of their own. This last story concerns my inquiry of The Honourable Judge Perry Marshall as to whether he had any tales about you. He mentioned to me that it was his knowledge of you that you did bestride this narrow earth like a colossus, but that you would not set foot in Grande Cache. He used to preside out there all the time, but when on the verge of seeing you there, he would receive what he characterized as a somewhat last minute but immensely polite and courteous telephone call from you saying that it had been your firm desire to attend to that trial before him, but that regrettably you couldn't make it there from Bangkok. He said that this occurred on a number of occasions, as you transmitted and phoned cheerily from Glasgow, or Buenos Aires, or Singapore or Nairobi. He said that he felt he was also traveling the globe himself. At any rate, let me close my own comments by saying that I have always had great fun appearing in front of you and that I appreciate very much that you have always treated me with more respect than I deserve. You are a classic Albertan and we will miss you around here. On behalf o myself and my colleagues on the Crown side, I wish you all the best. I now call on Alex Pringle to balance my remarks from his side of the Bar.

MR. JUSTICE MCCLUNG:

Thank you, Mr. Watson. Mr. Pringle?

MR. PRINGLE:

My Lords, Mr. Justice Harradence, it is with great pleasure that I have been asked to give a few remarks on your behalf today. I couldn't make it down to Calgary for your reception down there as I was in Ottawa and I am very thankful for the opportunity to speak today. I know a lot of my colleagues at the Defence Bar wanted to be here this morning. There are some here, but, as you know, this happens to be a trial day and many of them are in trials at this very minute and I know several have expressed their regrets at not being able to come. My first encounter with you, Sir, was like many of the young lawyers in this city or younger lawyers in this city that are my age. We say younger when I am looking up at the Bench at this point in time, because as you know, My Lord, all three of the Justices that are sitting today are ex-criminal lawyers. As a younger lawyer my first encounter was word-of-mouth, which word would travel through word-of-mouth when you would come to town and some of use would come down to watch you, just to watch the very famous and renowned Milt Harradence defend a case and it was always a great learning experience and also an inspiration to come down and watch you defend a case, as you did it in a very passionate fashion, but also in an extremely ethical manner, and learned several lessons. I watched the Voss case, a good part of the Voss case that Mr. Watson has already alluded to. I have watched you defend other individuals here in Edmonton and I learned a great deal in those moments in the courtroom watching you. I could never duplicate it, because the one thing that I distinctly recall is how charismatic you were in the courtroom and how when you went into a courtroom your presence just dominated the room. Everybody's eyes were riveted upon you, because you were such a strong personality and you were so magnetic in the courtroom. I am not trying to embarrass you, sir, but it was definitely very very true and I saw some of the best cross-examinations I have ever seen in a courtroom in the twenty-five years I have been in courtrooms, just in those few times I came down to watch you, and they were memorable. I also in the arly part of my career after watching you a few times, I have had the occasion to be your agent in Edmonton from time-to-time and I can recall getting calls from you at off hours from telephone booths where you were seeking assistance with respect to cases in Edmonton and the thing that I remember is how devoted you were to your law practice. The law was never a job for you. It was a passion and when you see an older lawyer, and it is not that much of a difference between us, but when you see an older lawyer that has that degree of passion and interest in his job, even at the stage that you were in your career, it was a large inspiration that brought me very clearly to realize that I wanted to be a criminal lawyer and you had a great impact on that and I know you had an impact on several other members of the Bar here in Edmonton in that regard. I also learned another thing from you. When you came out of a law school and you had a civil libertarian bent, there was a tendency to think that the police were not to be trusted and the prosecutors were not to be trusted and that you had to be wary of them, but you taught me that you should respect the police, that you should treat the police and the prosecutors with dignity. I know that you often defended policemen when you were a defence lawyer and did it as a public service and you had a wide perspective of the system, which I think was a valuable thing to learn as a young lawyer. Many of us wondered why you would go to the Bench when you did. Your career was in full flight at that point in time. You were at the top of the profession and we certainly thought that you enjoyed your work, but as I have practiced criminal law I have come to realize that at a certain point you tend to think of changing your life to devote some time to public service and I am sure that that is what you decided at that point in time, is to devote part of your life to public service at great personal cost. I think probably you missed the practice of law and being in the private bar, but my view of it is that you probably did that a s public service and I think we certainly all appreciated it, because we also benefited from you as judge, in addition to the benefits that we received and the guidance we had received when you were a defence counsel. Your judicial career over the past eighteen years, as Mr. Watson said, is people think of the dissents, because the dissents in a lot of your cases have been extremely important. It might be said that you have a record, perhaps, for the number of dissents in this Court through the years, but I also would say you probably have a record for the number of dissents that have been upheld by the Supreme Court or have been followed by the Supreme Court of Canada and those decisions are very important. I can think of several of the decisions that are now landmark decisions of the Supreme Court of Canada where you were the dissent in this Court that really allowed the counsels that were representing those individuals the opportunity to get before the Supreme Court of Canada and, as you know, the Supreme Court in those decisions have followed, to a great extent, the reasons that you provided in dissent. Mr. Watson, he and I have argued several appeals before you and other members of your Court where you were sitting on the panel and when I talked to him earlier this week about you, he commented, one of the things that he always seems to have noted about you was your voice and I noticed he referred to it earlier and I have heard him describe your voice as basso profundo and that is one of his terms, he used it earlier this week, and certainly I believe that he though your voice was basso, but I don't think he always believed that it was profundo. I can tell you that I have had some very enjoyable experiences in this Court where I have been arguing cases and watching Mr. Watson and have heard, partway through the argument I have heard you say, "MR. WATSON" and then you would go on from there and ask him a question and then there would be a few more questions and I have seen Mr. Watson actually arguing the case vehemently at the start and then by the end of the case after you have questioned him and other members of the Court have started to take the stance that you have, I have seen him actually agree with your position at the end or at least on the way out of the courtroom he has said...

MR. JUSTICE MCCLUNG:

But as a lyric soprano.

MR. PRINGLE:

I think I would like to say a couple of words about your contribution as a judge. I think, Sir, that one of the things that you have always as a lawyer and as a judge, one of the things that has been extremely important to you is the fact that you feel the traditional criminal law values are extremely important to our judicial system and you always, I think, tried to respect those traditional criminal law values and I am talking the values that have been established in our system over centuries and I am talking about -re-Charter values, the true traditional criminal law, you always tried to respect it in an age, at least in recent years, where those values have been watered down, to a certain extent, by certain judicial decisions and I think your judgments have always recognized the importance that the criminal law has, not just to the individual accused, but as an instrument where society has proper balance between government and the individual and where individual values, all citizen's values and rights are respected. You have always had that perspective and I know that you have made a great contribution in maintaining those traditional criminal law values which are extremely important to our system. The second contribution that I would like to point out with respect to your judicial career is that I think that you were, as a judge, one of the leaders with respect to the development of the Charter, particularly in the criminal law area. Your judgments with respect to the Charter, many of which were ultimately accepted by the Supreme Court of Canada, if your cases went there, were sort of the pioneer judgments with respect to the Charter and I can think of one, a couple of examples just offhand. The Bridges case, which is the Canadian equivalent to the Miranda decision from the United States, the Greffe case dealing with unreasonable search and seizure and many others, and you have made a very significant contribution with respect to the development of the Charter in this country. My lord, I hope that I have not embarrassed you but my remarks are with the utmost sincerity. It has been a great pleasure to know you and it has been a great pleasure to work with you both as a lawyer and appear in front of you as a judge and I wish you the very best with respect to your retirement and I hope that you come back to Edmonton from time-to-time so that we can see you and maybe swap a few stories when you come back. Thank you.

MR. JUSTICE MCCLUNG:

Thanks very much, Mr. Pringle. I will now call upon Ms. Shelagh Creagh, one of Her Majesty's counsel representing the Federal Department of Justice.

MS. CREAGH:

Thank you very much for the opportunity to speak here today. I am deeply honored that you thought of me and invited me to come and speak. Unfortunately, you have put me in a conundrum that I find myself all too often falling in these days, and that is following Mr. Watson. You must realize this is a challenge, because Mr. Watson generally leaves so few words unsaid that it is always a challenge to figure out what to say when you speak after him. Let me begin by posing another conundrum for this Court to consider. What do you get if you cross say the legal acumen of a J. J. Robinette or Bill McGillivray, the courtroom style of an Arthur Martin, the wit of a Steven Leacock and throw in, just for fun, say the style of Giovanni Versace. You know, I have no idea what you get, but it is really close to but not quite Justice Harradence, because this mythical creature, while it captures a lot of what is you, Justice Harradence, misses something I think very important and that is the spirit and the enthusiasm that you have shown us over the years. Now, articulating how one would describe that spirit and enthusiasm, I think you can appreciate is a very difficult task, and I did some research. Principally, I spent a lot of time on the telephone with a rather seedy Q.C. in Calgary that I really won't mention any further, but it is clear to me that there are three real elements to that spirit and that enthusiasm and both my learned friends have touched on those earlier in their speech.

The first is your innate appreciation and your constant demonstration of a very amorphous concept that we refer to as "the best traditions of the Bar". Now, I could not today give you chapter, bible and verse precisely of what is encompassed by that phrase, but I know that in my dealings with you, both as a trial counsel and as an appellate judge, that that was very much always in the fore. Perhaps one can for the purpose of today say the two things that really come to mind with respect to those are the work ethic of the barrister and the spirit of service to the client and service to the law. The second element that I see in that is the element of courtesy. Now, you and I have had many battles over the years and I must say that I can recall one day in a courtroom in Calgary where one colleague of mine in the defence bar told me that he would go and buy me a toothbrush and, yes, he would stand bail for me if things got really bad and they did get really bad on that particular day, but both you and I, or particularly you, I suppose, more than me did see that case to the end and saw it I think properly to the end, but despite those kinds of run-ins, your courtesy never dimmed. I can recall many occasions walking down the streets in Calgary, either being there with my parents or in Edmonton and seeing you on the street and you always had a moment to stop and to chat and to talk about something, no matter what. Operation Dismantle, the Cruise missiles, anything in the world and it was always the most pleasant and personable conversation ever. I thank you for that. I thank you for your courtesy and I thank you for setting that example.

Lastly, and I think one of the most important aspects that you have demonstrated over the years, is the concept of mentoring and that is this, and I apologize if this does not come out as well or as polished as it should, but barristers learn early in life that the only other people who really understand you and can really support you are other barristers. Spouses try really hard and are very supportive, but they never really sometimes understand precisely what it is that is going on in a barrister's mind, what a barrister's life is like but other barristers, and from those persons one always draws support. One needs to find the mentoring, one needs to find the help and you very much demonstrated to us and showed us time and time again the importance of that consideration and the importance of that particular idea and you have made it clear over the years this is not a duty, this is not an obligation. This is just what we do to be barristers and I thank you for that, as well.

I took some time to think how I would try to encapsulate all of these ideas, that is that one must strive, one must do one's best to produce something like the law that is something that is of a use or a benefit to society and my colleagues have talked much of your decisions and your cases and I am not going to dwell any further on those. It came to me the other day that what I want to say is encapsulated by the motto of an institution to which I understand you also belonged in your life and to which you still have a great deal of loyalty and following and that is the Royal Canadian Airforce. Their motto, as I understand is "per ardua ad astra", loosely translated as "Through Bolts and Bars, We Reach the Stars", and I think that to me sums up the best traditions of the Bar that I have been labouring so long to explain to you this morning.

From my colleagues at the Department of Justice, My Lord Harradence, all the best to you in your coming years. Please do not be a stranger to Edmonton. Please come and see us again. I know we will all look forward to seeing you.

Thank you, My Lord.

MR. JUSTICE McCLUNG:

Thank you, Ms. Creagh. Well, as we all know, Mr. Justice Harradence has never allowed the prosecution to split its case, but today, Sir, you have the right of reply.

MR. JUSTICE HARRADENCE:

My Lord presiding, My Lord Berger, Ms Creagh, Mr. Watson, Mr. Pringle, Members of the Bar, Ladies and Gentlemen. May I first thank Ms. Creagh, Mr. Watson and Mr. Pringle for your very kind remarks. Those remarks and your attendance have made my last appearance as a sitting jurist in Edmonton an most memorable and a most happy one, but I think I must note that as there are members here, senior members from both the Defence and from the Crown office, that my retirement may well be viewed from different perspectives.

My Lord presiding in using the words "Statutory Senility", I first heard that back in 1969. It was on the occasion of Mr. Justice Porter of this Court on his last sittings. His Lordship was really not enamoured with the new legislation and had referred to it that as he encroached upon Statutory Senility, he did so with some trepidation.

His Lordship, Mr. Justice Porter, did not deliver himself of many judgments, but he did have a most remarkable turn of phrase and I can recall on one occasion I was in the courtroom and the Crown conceded the appeal. They did so on the basis that the counsel did not think he could support the finding by the learned trial Judge that the accused's voluntary statement was, in fact, so. There was some indication from the evidence that it may have been prompted by a generous application of the constable's flashlight to certain parts of the appellant's anatomy. When the appeal was allowed, Mr. Justice Porter turned to Crown consel, Mr. Justison, and said:

Mr. Justison, the compliments of the Court, and perhaps you might advise Constable O'Malley that a five cell flashlight is a source of illumination and not a negotiating instrument.

Members of the Bar, Ladies and Gentlemen, thank you once again for your attendance and thank you, again, Ms. Creagh, Mr. Watson and Mr. Pringle for those very generous and very kind remarks.

MR. JUSTICE McCLUNG:

This ceremony is now closed. We will retire.

Copyright and Photo Acknowledgements

COPYRIGHT ACKNOWLEDGEMENTS

The author and publisher wish to thank the authors and publishers listed below for permission to reprint copyright material:

The London Review of Books, London, U.K., for excerpts from Michael Howard's "Over the Top," Sir Frank Kermode's "Not Entitled: A Memoir," Shannon Borg's "During the War," Murray Sayle's "MacArthur," and Messrs. Ewing and Gearty "History of a Dog's Dinner."

Random House Inc. for excerpts from *A Distant Mirror* by Barbara Tuchman, New York, 1978.

The Edmonton Journal newspaper for excerpts from its 1977 news article on A.M. Harradence.

Stoddart Publishing Co. Ltd. for excerpts from *That Summer in Paris* by Morley Callaghan, Toronto, 1992.

Alfred A. Knopf Division of Random House Inc. for excerpts from *Citizens* by Simon Schama, New York, 1989.

David Higham Associates Limited for excerpts from *"Your's Etc." Letters to the Press* 1945-1989 by Graham Greene, London, 1991, ed. by C. Hawtree.

Yale University Press for excerpts from *No Passion Spent* by George Steiner, London, 1996.

Literary Review of Canada for excerpts from J.F. Conway's "The Folksy Fascism of the Reform Party" and Russel Barsh's "The Human Face of Justice," June 1996.

Random House, Inc. for excerpts from *Palimpsest* by Gore Vidal, New York, 1995.

Stoddart Publishing Co. Ltd. for excerpts from *On the Eve of the Millennium* by Connor C. O'Brien, Toronto, 1994.

McClelland and Stewart Ltd. the Canadian Publishers for excerpts from *The Debt to Pleasure* by John Lanchester, Toronto, 1996.

Kenneth Whyte for excerpts from "How Odd Was Dief?," *Saturday Night Magazine,* October 1995.

ITPS , Hampshire, U.K., for excerpts from *The Advocate's Devil,* by C.P. Harvey, London, 1958.

The New York Review of Books for excerpts from Joyce Carol Oates's "The Simple Art of Murder," ©December 1995, NYREV Inc.

Calgary Herald Newspaper for February 1979 article by S. Zwarun, 1980 article by S. Pratt, *Canadian Magazine* "Top Ten Canadian Lawyers, 1975," T. Innes Cartoon, Helen Dolik's article "Calgary Legal Eagle Soars to Retirement," 1996.

Alfred A. Knopf Division of Random House Inc. for excerpts from *Minority Report* by H.L. Mencken, New York.

Phoenix Press, London, for excerpts from *The Decline and Fall of the Roman Empire* by Edward Gibbon.

Frank Dabbs for excerpts from *Ralph Klein: A Maverick Life*, Greystone Books, Vancouver, 1995.

Scribner, a Division of Simon and Schuster, Inc. for excerpts from *The Art of Cross-Examination* by Francis Wellman, copyright ©1936 by MacMillan Publishing Co., copyright renewed ©1964 by Ethel Wellman.

Penguin Putnam Inc. for excerpts from *The Book of Sand* by Jorge Luis Borges, New York, 1980.

Faber and Faber Ltd. for excerpts from *Collected Poems by T. S. Eliot*, London.

The Calgary Sun Newspaper and Mr. R. Sykes for reprints of Rodney Sykes' column, and C.D. Evans' column. (Appendixes)

The Report Newsmagazine (formerly *Alberta Report*) for reprint of its June 13th, 1977 article, photograph of A.M. Harradence, and cross-examination excerpt.

David Higham Associates Limited for excerpts from *Smiley's People* by John Le Carré, Hodden and Stoughton, London, 1980.

Schocken Books, imprint of Knopf Division of Random House Inc. for excerpts from *The Diaries* by Franz Kafka, New York.

Care has been taken to trace the ownership of any copyright material, both text and photograph. Some sources, with reasonable inquiry, could not be traced.

PHOTOGRAPHIC ACKNOWLEDGEMENTS

The author and publisher wish to thank these photographers and companies for permission to reproduce copyright images created or held by them:

Mathieson Photo Service and Mathieson and Hewitt Photographers, Calgary, photograph of swearing-in of Mayor Klein and photograph of C.D. Evans.

4 Wing Photo Section, Cold Lake, Alberta, for photographs taken on the day of the C.F.-18 flight at Cold Lake, Alberta.

L/Col. J.D. Graham, Commanding Officer of 416 Tactical Fighter Squadron for photographs of A.M.H. in uniform while acting as Honorary Colonel.

Department of National Defence for photograph of A.M.H. flying in P51 Mustang in formation with Golden Hawks, 1963 and A.M.H. standing on wing of his sabre jet at Abbotsford, B.C. Air Show, 1967.

Gold Photography, Calgary, for colour prints of A.M. Harradence in legal robes and Air Force uniform, and photograph of Harradence family.

The Montreal Gazette for Wing Comm. Cruikshank, A.M.H. and F.O. G.R. Forsyth at St. Hubert, Quebec, July 1954.

Calgary Herald Newspaper for two file photographs of A.M.H. from article June 11, 1979 and by Jim Knowler, May 1966.

The Report Newsmagazine for 1979 photograph of Chief Justice W.A. MacGillivray and A.M.H.

Walter Petrigo, Calgary, for photograph in *Canadian Magazine* article, Appendix.

Philippe Landreville Inc. and the Supreme Court of Canada for photograph of the Hon. Mr. Justice Major ©Supreme Court of Canada.

Department of National Defence for boxing photograph of A.M.H. (photo courtesy of DND).

David Brown and the University of Calgary for photograph of A.M.H. as Honorary Doctor of Laws, May 1998.

Angus of Calgary for photographs taken at retirement dinner October 16, 1996.

William Bailey, Calgary, for photograph of A.M.H. on back cover.

(Norman Hendricks, Calgary, is credited for photograph of A.M.H. with Group Captain Sir Douglas Bader.)

Bibliography

BIBLIOGRAPHY

Schmidgall, Gary (1994), *The Stranger Wilde* (New York: E.P. Dutton).

Le Carré, John (1980), *Smiley's People* (London: Hodder and Stoughton).

Howard, Michael (1996), *Over The Top* (London: London Review of Books).

Kermode, Sir Frank, *Not Entitled: A Memoir* (London Review of Books, Reviewed by Michael Wood).

Borg, Shannon (1996), *During The War* (London Review of Books).

Sayle, Murray (1997), *MacArthur* (London Review of Books).

Ewing, Keith and Gearty, Conor (1997), *History of a Dog's Dinner* (London Review of Books).

Rice, Edward (1990), *Captain Sir Richard Burton* (New York: Chas Scribner's Sons, unit of Simon and Schuster).

Painter, Sidney (1995), *William Marshall* (Baltimore: The Johns Hopkins University Press).

Tuchman, Barbara (1978), *A Distant Mirror* (New York: Random House Inc.).

Rodgers, W.R. (1952), *Direction to a Rebel* (Little Treasury of Modern Poetry) (New York: Chas Scribner's Sons, unit of Simon and Schuster).

Hardy, Thomas (1952), *The Man He Killed* (Little Treasury of Modern Poetry) (New York, Chas Scribner's Sons, unit of Simon and Schuster).

Author Not Known (1977), Article in *The Edmonton Journal* newspaper (Edmonton).

Callaghan, Morley (1992), *That Summer in Paris* (Toronto: Stoddart Publishing Co. Ltd.).

Schama, Simon (1989), *Citizens* (New York: Alfred A. Knopf Inc., Division of Random House Inc.).

Greene, Graham (1991), *Yours, etc., Letters to The Press 1945 - 1989,* Ed. C. Hawtree (London: Penguin Books; ©David Higham Associates Limited).

Steiner, George (1996), *No Passion Spent* (London: Yale University Press).

Conway, J.F. (1996), T*he Folksy Fascism of the Reform Party* (Toronto: The Literary Review of Canada).

Barsh, Russel (1996), *The Human Face of Justice* (Toronto: The Literary Review of Canada).

Vidal, Gore (1995), *Palimpsest* (New York: Random House Inc.)

O'Brien, Conor Cruise (1994), *On The Eve of the Millenium* (Toronto: Stoddart Publishing Co. Ltd.).

Lanchester, John (1996), *The Debt to Pleasure* (Toronto: McClelland and Stewart Inc.).

Whyte, Kenneth (1995), "How Odd Was Dief?" (Toronto: *Saturday Night Magazine*).

Harvey, C.P. (1958), *The Advocate's Devil* (London: ITPS).

Oates, Joyce Carol (1995), *The Simple Art of Murder* (New York: The New York Review of Books; ©NYREV, Inc.).

Kafka, Franz, *Diaries* (New York: Schocken Books Inc., Division of Random House Inc.).

Innes, Tom, Political Cartoon of A.M. Harradence and E. Manning (Calgary: *Calgary Herald* Newspaper).

Zwarun, Suzanne (1979), Article on A.M. Harradence (Calgary: *Calgary Herald* Newspaper).

Pratt, Sheila (1980), Article on Mayor Ralph Klein (Calgary: *Calgary Herald* Newspaper).

Canadian Magazine Article, The Top Ten Canadian Lawyers, July 1975.

Dolik, Helen (1996), Calgary Legal Eagle Soars to Retirement (Calgary: *Calgary Herald* Newspaper).

Mencken, H.L., *Minority Report* (New York: Random House Inc.).

Gibbon, Edward, *The Decline and Fall of The Roman Empire* (New York: Everyman Library; Phoenix Press, London).

Wellman, Francis (1936), *The Art of Cross-Examination* (New York: MacMillan Publishing Co. ©1936, copyright renewed ©1964 by Ethel Wellman; Scribner: A Division of Simon and Schuster Inc.).

Wedgwood, Dame C. V. (1975), *Oliver Cromwell* (London: Transworld Publishers, Division of Random House Group Ltd.).

Borges, Jorge Luis (1980), *The Book of Sand,* trans. di Giovanni (New York: Penguin Putnam Inc.).

Lawson-Dick, Oliver (Editor) (1992), *Aubrey's Brief Lives* (London: Mandarin Paperbacks).

Dabbs, Frank (1995), *Ralph Klein — A Maverick Life* (Vancouver: Greystone Books).

Eliot, T.S., *Collected Poems* (London: Faber and Faber Ltd.).

Sykes, Rodney (1983), *Newspaper Column* (Calgary: *The Calgary Sun* newspaper).

Merton, Robert K. (1965), *On the Shoulders of Giants* (San Diego: Harcourt, Brace and World Inc.).

Bennett, A., Miller, J., Moore, D., Cook, P., (1962), *Beyond the Fringe* (Toronto: Capitol Records of Canada Ltd.).

Proust, Marcel (1913) *Swann's Way* (Vol. I: *In Search of Lost Time*) trans. Moncrieff and Kilmartin, revised by Enright (New York: Modern Library ©Random House Inc.).

Magee, Pilot Officer John Gillespie, *High Flight.*